TSB

Confessions of an Ex-Hooker (Aged 66 and a half)

a.k.a

DON'T STOP BELIEVIN'

Trevor Stott-Briggs

ISBN: 978-9948-23-454-8

ABOUT THE AUTHOR

Leaving a cold, wet and gloomy Lancashire, on 1 March 1976, he set out from the UK on a journey across Africa not realising that he would eventually work in 34 countries across a span of 45 years. Along the way he picked up a wife and somehow engineered four kids - all boys – as he only has one formula. Always competitive and loving cars, he was involved in karting, rallying, circuit racing and anything with engines and wheels. And when he wasn't racing, he was playing, organising, coaching or refereeing rugby. Eventually, he found himself in the UAE and in possession of a body that did not work too well after breaking his neck in a sporting accident. So, he thought it would be a good idea to write a book about it. But, unlike most authors, he has never lived in Chipping Norton or Surrey, but did once own a time share in a resort, on a tiny island called Boracay, in the Philippines.

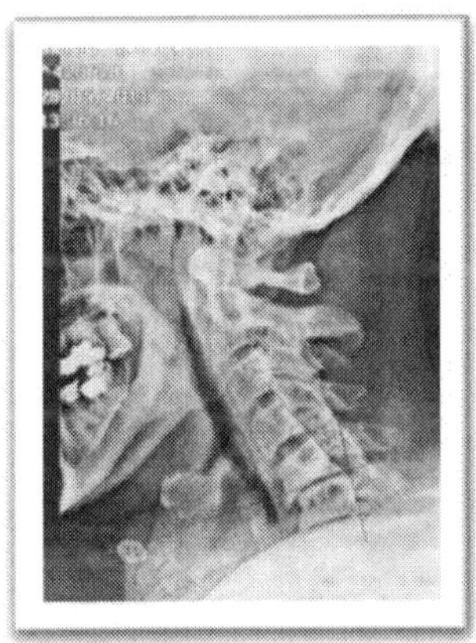

OTHER BOOKS (STILL TO BE) WRITTEN BY THE SAME AUTHOR . . .

TSB – Confessions of a Lancashire Lad (aged 26 and a half)
a.k.a
EE BY GUM!

TSB – Confessions of a Nondescript Nomad (aged 56 and a half)
a.k.a
RUCKIN' 'n ROLLIN' 'n RACING

TSB – Confessions of a Grumpy Old Man (aged 76 and a half)
a.k.a
KEEP ON KEEPIN' ON!

DEDICATION

I would like to dedicate this book to my wife Agnes and all my children, Elliott, James, Kyle and Colby. That's the lot – at least as far as I know . . . But really, I have to make a special "Thank You" to Agnes as she has had to put up with a great deal while I have taken this long road to recovery. So, thank you, my darling. Thank you soooooo much!

This book is full of songs, lyrics, YouTube videos, movie and TV clips etc. which have somehow passed through my mind as I have been writing it. Therefore, I shall start as I mean to go on, with a very funny clip of Peter Sellers reciting the lyrics of the Beatles song *A Hard Day's Night*, imitating Sir Laurence Olivier, one of the World's greatest Shakespearian actors, when he did the soliloquie in Richard III. It may be funny, but Agnes, I mean every word he says . . .

CUE YOUTUBE VIDEO: A HARD DAY'S NIGHT
PETER SELLERS

DON'T STOP BELIEVIN'

CONTENTS

	Acknowledgements	i
	Foreword - Forewarned is Forearmed	ii
	2011	
1	The Accident	1
2	Earlier that Day . . .	4
3	The Game	10
4	Situation Normal . . . (But Actually AFU)	17
5	Nightmare Ward	21
6	Thunder Road	25
7	Dr. Mohammed	29
8	Nurses, Bed Baths, Chocolate Cake & LBMs	37
9	Boys Will Be Boys	42
10	Ouch! That 'Kin Hurt	46
11	Things Start Stirring	50
12	How to Conquer the World	53
13	Just Too Busy Being Fabulous	59
14	You Have My Support . . .	65
15	Glee on the Gogglebox	70
16	Nostalgia Isn't What it Used to Be	74
17	Well, Goodness Gracious Me	80
18	How to Choose a Nurse	87
19	Radio Ga-Ga	91
20	When the Going Gets Tough . . .	97
21	Would You Like Some Kimchi With Those X-Rays, Sir	104
22	I Didn't Know Whether to Laugh or Cry	107
23	Die Another Day	114
24	In Your Dreams!	117
25	The Cast Away	120
26	Rocky Mountain Exorcism	124
27	Transformers – The Truth is Out There	131
28	While You're Down There	141
29	Kenny & Accalia and the Rock 'n Roll Kid	145

30 Here We Go Round the Mulberry Bush 150
31 Cloud Nine – Hammad and Joyz 158
32 Macca, The Boss and Me 162
33 Xmas 2011 – Jingle What? Jingle Where? 169

2012

34 Glitz, Glamour, Garages, Grunge & Greggy's Gimmick 177
35 Fun, Fun, Fun 185
36 Reiki and High Spirits 193
37 Grumpy Eileen. 198
38 From Rock of Ages to Seven Dwarfs 202
39 I Only Have One Penis . . . 208
40 The Fastest Invalid Carriage in the World 218
41 On the First Day of Xmas . . . I Wanna be a Rock Star 230

2013

42 When I'm 64 241
43 Blitzkrieg 245
44 Dem Bones, Dem Bones, Dem Dry Bones 253

2014

45 Happy Bidet 261
46 We're All Going on a Summer Holiday 265
47 Motivation is a Four-Letter Word 273
48 Ayurveda – Hot Oil and Oatmeal 279
49 I Still Only Have One Penis . . . 287
50 Spring Break 296
51 TINSTAAC 302
52 Lightning Strikes Twice at the Y.M.C.A. 305
53 Biking on the Dark Side of the Moon 309
54 A Knight's Tale 314
55 Trains & Boats & Planes (Part 1) a.k.a. Bomber Briggs Tours 319
56 Trains & Boats & Planes (Part 2) a.k.a. Juke Box Jury 329
57 Strictly Come Dancing – a.k.a. The Eagles Have Landed 343

2015

58 How Many Fingers am I Holding Up? 353
59 A-Tishoo! A-Tishoo! We All Fall Down 365
60 Don't Stop Believin' 374

ACKNOWLEDGMENTS

As they say at the Oscars and the Golden Globes – "I wanna thank . . . blah, blah blah . . ." followed by a list of everyone that breathed anywhere near their movie, right down to the guy that delivered the pizza. Well, I used to laugh at that but now I sort of know how they feel. My recovery, rehabilitation, physiotherapy, work, play, writing this book, life, the universe and everything has involved so many people that there are just too many to mention. Many of you are featured in the pages of this book, but if I missed you its only because the pages would stretch to infinity and beyond with everyone's name in it. But I thank you ALL for helping me – day by day – to get back on my feet.

I must make a particular mention of all the thousands of people who post videos on YouTube and write reams of info on Wikipedia. Thank you for all the material and knowledge that has helped me to try and capture some of the memories, feelings and emotions that I have had over the last six years.

And I would especially like to thank Neal Schon, Steve Perry and Jonathan Cain of Journey for writing *Don't Stop Believin'* and allowing me to feature it in this book as it has been the cornerstone of my recovery.

But also, I do wanna thank the pizza delivery guy for all the pizzas that fuelled my brain to get everything that happened down on paper . . .

DON'T STOP BELIEVIN'

FOREWORD - FOREWARNED IS FOREARMED

As Forrest Gump famously commented, "Laife is laike a bax of chocolaates. You nevver knaw what you're gonna get".

Well, that is certainly true for me. Here I am, in April 2017, writing a Foreword to a book. What do you write in a Foreword? I am not really sure as I have never even written a book before! But, from the moment I arrived in the hospital after my accident, I knew that I wanted to write down all the things that happened to me as I went through the recovery, operation, and rehabilitation phases.

My sporting accident happened at the Sharjah Wanderers Rugby Football Club 10-a-side Tournament in Sharjah, United Arab Emirates in February 2011. As a result of breaking my neck – or rather, having it broken for me - I went, instantly, from being a very fit, active and mobile sixty-two-year-old rugby player, referee, runner, and fitness enthusiast to being a quadriplegic - a "disabled person" who was paralysed below the waist and with upper limb spasticity that meant I could not even feed myself. However, even though I did not fully appreciate the extent of the damage to my body, right from the beginning I vowed that I would I would walk, and even run again – whatever that took.

None of the doctors would give a prognosis as to how well I would recover, or how long it would take for me to recover. The reason for this – as I found out from many physiotherapists over the next five years – was that the potential for recovery for someone with my kind of injury was actually very slim. In fact, most would have said that I would not be able to walk again. But somewhere deep down in my brain I never accepted that and was determined not to spend the rest of my life as a "disabled person" in a wheelchair. Even now I prefer to call myself "Temporarily Unable" rather than "Disabled".

This book has been written in short "sound bite" chapters covering all sorts of personal experiences throughout my rehabilitation. The intent is, as far as possible, to make them interesting and to view the sometimes terrible experiences through a positive lens and an amusing perspective. One thing is certain; this book is not meant to be morbid or miserable!

Music, movies and cars have played a big part in my life and in my recovery. For months during my recovery, I was in a body that would not move. Miraculously, my mind began to move in ways my body could not. It worked overtime, compensating for the inactivity of my limbs. It was as if my memory blossomed and opened like a combination of a children's pop-up book and a music box.

Consequently, I have included the titles and many references to songs, lyrics, movies, and cars in the chapters so that you, the reader, can share an additional mental image or musical memory that either prompted or was evoked by the story. I am hoping these will add mood, colour and depth to the stories in the same way a soundtrack gives additional emotion to the story unfolding in a movie!

Many of you will already have them swimming around in your heads. But if you don't, you can listen on YouTube by clicking on the link if you are reading the E Book or scan the QR Code with a code reader app, such as NeoReader, on your smart cell phone if you are reading a hard copy. It's a free download if you don't already have it.

There are also lots of irreverent quotations and sayings, modified words, neologisms, paraprosdokians and fractals and, hopefully, these also add to the flavour of the book.

So thank you to all those contributors - named and un-named - that have helped me add dimension to my stories. In any case: "To steal ideas from one person is plagiarism. To steal from many is research". And that will always be my defence.

The book is written roughly in chronological order so things that happened in any given year are bunched together in the same section. But it's not written as a "I did this and then I did that" monologue as that would be boring. But if you spot some flaws in the time lines, don't fret, just enjoy the story.

At the back of the book, I have added a Glossary as there are all sorts of bits of info that readers of various ages may need to help them understand some of the things in this book. These will be particularly useful to younger readers (i.e. anyone below the age of 25), who can't imagine life before Computers, the Internet, Facebook, Twitter, Instagram, Cell Phones, PS4s, Flat Screen TVs and all those things that we now take for granted. This information may also be especially useful to non-Brits, prop forwards and anyone with "cauliflower ears". So, if you suddenly think "Shit, I have no idea what the f*ck TSB is talking about!" check the Glossary and you may find the answer.

So far, it's been six years from being an immobile quadriplegic, to being able to walk with crutches and do most things that I want to do. The journey is not over yet, but I hope that I can inspire people to believe in themselves and their inner capacity to heal and make their bodies work again – whatever their disability or illness. The human brain is a fantastic organ and it can achieve miracles – as long as you "Don't Stop Believin'".

TSB
Abu Dhabi, UAE
April 2017

DON'T STOP BELIEVIN'

2011

DON'T STOP BELIEVIN'

1

THE ACCIDENT

The last thing I remember saying was "Stop pushing so fucking hard!"

What else would anyone say when his neck was being bent out of shape by three huge forwards in the front row of a scrum? I don't think that - "I say old chaps, would you mind frightfully if you just pushed a teensy weensy bit less? Cheers!" - would have had quite the same impact.

The expletive worked. They stopped. And then it went quiet. Completely silent, except for sort of a whooshing noise.

I had heard of people talking about having an "Out of Body Experience", but didn't think much of it. Until it happened to me. So, I guess I should apologise to everyone I had ridiculed regarding the experience.

I had a real sense that I was floating above myself watching what looked like a slow-motion video of me, slowly, very slowly, tumbling backwards with my arms in the air as they disengaged from around the shoulders of my two props.

Slowly, slowly, tumbling backwards with my feet slightly off the ground. So, "I" was floating but also watching myself floating in the air and my body was gradually getting closer and closer to the ground.

Then my body hit the grass, complete with that slight bounce you see on really slow-motion action shots in Quentin Tarantino movies. My head hit the ground and that bounced a little too. Luckily, I was wearing a scrum cap – otherwise I could have hurt myself. (Ha!)

I remember seeing myself, lying there on the ground, not moving. And then suddenly I was back in my body, laying on the grass and looking up at the sky.

I don't think I passed out. I mean, unless the "Out of Body Experience" was me passing out. But I have passed out several times before - usually due to nurses waving big needles at me and wanting to extract blood from my body. That passing out feeling is completely different to what I experienced that day.

Suddenly, the volume was un-muted and I could hear everything around me. Bill Middleton, the team coach and physio, was kneeling next to my head and talking to me.

"What can you feel Trev?" he asked.

"My arms are burning hot," I said and lifted them up into my range of vision to see if they were engulfed in flames, as that's what it felt like. "But burning from the inside."

"What about your legs? Can you feel your legs, Trev?" Bill asked.

"No, I don't think so" I replied.

I know that "I don't think so" may seem like a stupid answer. And it would be in normal circumstances. But when there is no sensation at all from some part of your body it's hard to tell if you can "feel" anything. Just think about when you have been sitting in one position for a long time and you get pins and needles. There is a certain moment in that scenario when the pins and needles stop but your muscle does not work properly, even if you tell it to do something. It's like an empty-nothing feeling. It was that "empty-nothing" that I was feeling.

He did all the touch and sensation tests on my feet and legs. Pricking, pinching, light stroking. But I could not feel anything. Nothing at all.

Then Bill did absolutely the right thing and probably saved my nervous system from permanent damage. He told the paramedics to get the neck brace and the compression board and strap me to it. That happened very quickly and the next thing I remember was being lifted up and put in the back of an ambulance with my sixteen-year-old- son, James who had luckily travelled up to Sharjah with me to the tournament.

But, as I was being lifted and carried to the ambulance, I saw the outline of the roof of the Sharjah spectator's stand silhouetted against the sky and it was like a flashback of some images I had seen in my dreams a few times over the period leading up to the tournament.

I remember thinking in the dream "What is that the roof of and why is it at a funny angle?" Now I knew. It was the roof of the spectator stand for the Sharjah Rugby Club and it appeared to be at a funny angle because I was laid on my back on a compression board with my head fixed in position by a neck brace. So, I was seeing it on a side view and not the normal view when you are upright on your feet.

Had I seen the future in my dreams? Or was it Déjà Vu? And what causes Déjà Vu anyway? Could the accident have been avoided if I had figured out what the dream meant and heeded what I saw? Can you change the future? Who knows? I certainly don't.

And then the doors of the ambulance slammed shut. Clunk!

2

EARLIER THAT DAY . . .

It was an unusual start to the day. It was Friday, 25th February 2011, and my son James and I were leaving the house early to go and play rugby. Nothing unusual about that of course as, like many rugby playing families, the alpha-males in the household will head to wherever their team (or teams) are playing. At that time, there were actually four of us in the family playing rugby. Colby (then five), Kyle (then nine years and 364 days) and James (then sixteen) were all playing for their respective age grades at Abu Dhabi Harlequins in the UAE Junior Leagues. On that day I was going to play for the Arabian Potbellies Vets Team in the annual Sharjah 10s Tournament. I was a bit older than the kids, (obviously) I had just celebrated my sixty-second birthday about seven weeks earlier on 5th January 2011.

So, what was unusual about a sixty-two year old dad and his sixteen year old son going off to play rugby together on a Friday? That's not a trick question. We were in the United Arab Emirates, a Muslim county that has its weekend on Friday & Saturday. Friday is the Muslim religious day. Friday is like Sunday and Saturday is, well, like Saturday. OK?

Well, the unusual thing that day was that my wife, Agnes, did not complain about it.

Normally, I would tell her well in advance about any game I was going to. And, to back up that conversation, game dates were added to the whiteboard monthly planner that was on the wall in the study.

This was a pain in the neck, of course, but it was good insurance in case I was accused of trying to cover over a last minute rugby event. All that my wife needed to do was read the board. So, much for systems! Agnes never read it (allegedly), and so would complain that she didn't know I was going to be out for the day.

Generally, she didn't say anything during the days leading up to a game or tournament even if I had made the extra effort of reminding her a few times. But, like most women, if the event began with an R for Rugby, my wife's usually active and highly retentive brain seemed to suddenly lose all cognitive powers.

Or at least it did right up until the moment I would be heading for the door! Then her brain would suddenly leap into action and I would get hit with a Spanish Inquisition. And no-one expects a Spanish Inquisition. Monty Python said so, so it must be true.

CUE YOUTUBE VIDEO: MONTY PYTHON
SPANISH INQUISITION

For the purposes of education I have given some of the stock answers to a rugby-related Spanish Inquisition, just in case you need them:

"Why are you so selfish?" *(Don't answer that. Keep silent.)*

"Why don't you want to spend time with your family?" *(I am doing. I am taking James. Do you want to come?)*

"How come you always say you are busy, but you always have time for rugby?" *(I am busy but this is the one thing I do for myself.)*

"How come you prefer to spend time with your friends instead of me?" *(Don't answer that. Keep silent again.)*

And of course, the special one she always managed to hit me with:

"When are you going to stop playing rugby? You are too old! You promised to stop when you were 60 and you are still playing!" *(But darling, this is not a UAERF League game; it's just a Vets friendly.)*

Of course, any keen sports person will tell you that all the above answers are true. Only the name of the sport and the age varies.

In my case I was still very fit. I had never stopped going to rugby training, I went to the gym regularly to work out and I was also an active member of the UAE Referees Society. I was still one of the fastest runners in the club and it was usually only the speedy twenty-five- year-old wingers who could beat me over a 100 meter sprint. I'd always had a great pair of legs – and I don't mean that in the Taylor Swift way or, for the older reader, the Tina Turner way (she had hers insured for a million dollars) – but mine were able to move me from A to B very quickly whether I was on a running track, bike or rugby pitch.

I am not bragging here. It was just a fact. Of course, you could always argue that it was this very fact that resulted in me having my accident, simply because I was able to run around on a rugby pitch at the age of sixty-two. But I don't think like that, so we won't go down that road.

So, rugby was a thing for me. It was something that kept me fit without feeling like it was a chore. In short, rugby formed a significant part of my life. Even if the other significant part of my life complained about it.

Except, on the day of the accident, Agnes didn't mention a word about rugby. James and I got our kit together, and I kissed her goodbye and that was that. It wasn't until James and I were actually in the car that I realized that, for the first time, my wife had been notably subdued about us going. I can't explain it, and I guess it could have been a premonition, but something inspired me to get out of the car and go back and kiss her again. She didn't ask why and I didn't offer any explanation, of course. I wasn't stupid. As weird as the day felt, I was almost away with a free pass, and I wasn't going to jeopardise such a rare rugby truce.

I jumped back in the car, turned the key and the big V8 roared into life and we burbled off through the houses trying not to make too much noise as it was still early on a Friday morning, and it being the holy day, lots of people were still sleeping and we had the road pretty much to ourselves.

My car was my pride and joy. I had only owned it for a couple of months, having talked myself into the idea that it would serve as an excellent Christmas present . . . to myself. It was a Schnitzer BMW M6 Convertible. Being a Schnitzer, it sat at the top of the performance heap, with everything you'd expect in a German sports car with 4.5 litres of highly tuned V8 power just waiting to be let forth through a sequential gearbox that felt like it had come straight out of an F1 car.

One of its most fun features was a small black button with "SPORT" written on it. When you pressed it the whole car metamorphosed from being a smooth, sophisticated, fast but refined sports car into a mean, rorty, street-racing monster that would burn rubber in third gear.

And – in a country where it rains about 2 days a year - it was a convertible. Perfect!

I am beginning to sound like Jeremy Clarkson here.

Of course, the real reason I bought it was that I am a family man and it was one of the few sports cars that had four seats. And being a considerate Dad, I wanted to be able to fit the kids in the back as well. Selfless, I tell you.

Schnitzer BMW M6 Convertible - Are those Low Profile Tyres or What?

Selfless and considerate family man aside, you have probably guessed from my enthusiasm for my beloved M6 that I am a "Petrol Head". You'd be right. It comes from many years spent (and many, MANY dollars spent) circuit racing, drag racing, slaloms, off-road rallying, karting and doing all things possible with fast cars.

But my M6 was probably one of the best and fastest street cars I had ever owned. That's saying a lot, as I've been lucky enough to have had a few great ones.

Despite having the road to myself, the perfect car, and a free pass for the day, for some reason, it just didn't feel right. Again, difficult to put a finger on, but it should have been an enjoyable drive, and it just wasn't.

Each time we passed an exit ramp I kept looking at it and I felt like it was somehow beckoning me to take it, cross the bridge and go back to Abu Dhabi. I had no idea why I had that feeling. But I just did. The trouble with those kinds of feelings is that they are usually very illogical so the logical part of your brain takes over and persuades you that you should do the opposite.

In my case, that morning, I should have listened to the illogical part of my brain – maybe it's what they call a "gut feeling".

So, I carried on up the Abu Dhabi – Dubai Highway, zooming along at 140 kph. The road actually has a speed limit of 120 kph for most of its length. It also has lots of speed cameras at very regular intervals to catch speeding cars. But, although all the circular speed limit signs say 120, there are huge billboards saying "Watch your speed. This road is controlled by Radar Cameras. Maximum speed limit 140 kph". Yes, you read it right, it's a 120 kph zone but the maximum speed you can drive at is 140 kph!! Jeremy Clarkson would love this and should recommend it to the Minister of Transport for UK motorways.

Eventually, we reached the Sharjah Rugby Club and parked. As I locked the car and walked away I glanced back over my shoulder and looked at the car. It's one of those involuntary things that you do when you have just got a new car and some uncappable sense of pride wells up in you. You turn back to look – just to make sure it is still OK in the last fifteen seconds since you got out of it – and a smile automatically crosses your face.

We have all done it, whether your new pride and joy is a BMW or a new Toyota Yaris. Although one might argue that Yaris drivers also look over their shoulder to make sure no one saw them getting out of it.

Little did I realise that it was going to be the last time I was able to drive that dream machine for well over eighteen months.

And on that bombshell . . .

3

THE GAME

The atmosphere was very strange in the team tent that morning. Normally, there is lots of chat and banter between all the players getting ready. But looking back on it there did not seem to be much talking at all. It somehow felt like I was in a sort of electrostatic cocoon or force field where I was doing whatever I was doing but everyone around me was somehow shut off from me. It was surreal.

When I was organising our entry to the Sharjah 10s I was pushing to get players interested as we were also committed (and paid up) to play in the Manila 10s in the Philippines a couple of weeks later. So, this was a great "warm-up" opportunity. But, there was a significant lack of responses from the players - not an unusual situation for many rugby clubs. Hence, when we got there we were short of players, as were the Das Island Vets, so we agreed to share resources and fill in the gaps for each other. In the morning, I played one game for Das Island and one for the Potbellies.

Then, in the early afternoon, we were scheduled to play the tournament hosts, Sharjah Wanderers Vets.

For those readers who don't play or don't understand rugby (or perhaps need a refresher – forward pack I am looking at you here) I had better explain what happens in a rugby tournament like this and how certain bits of the team work together. The objective of the game is to *"Outplay. Outwit. Outlast"* the other team - I think the Survivor reality

TV show stole that concept from Rugby - and score as many points as possible by getting the oval ball across the try line. The other team, while also doing the same, are doing their damndest to stop you doing it to them by as many fair or foul means as possible. It's the Referee's job to try and minimise the foul and maximise the fair. And it's the player's job to see how much foul he can get away with without attracting the attention of the Referee. So, it's like a battlefield at times.

Normally, in full rugby games you have two teams of fifteen players and seven players for each team on the substitute's bench. The game has two halves of forty minutes each way. In tournaments like the Sharjah 10s and the Manila 10s every team has, guess what, ten players on the pitch and five on the bench. The games are shorter, usually seven minutes each way or sometimes ten minutes one way – a decision made by the tournament organizer. This does not sound very long but when there are only ten in a team, the spaces on the pitch are much bigger and you do a lot of running. In most cases "rolling substitutes" are allowed, which means that players can come off the pitch at any time if they are tired and still go back on again later when they have rested. Having the players changing all the time helps keep the team fresh.

One very important feature of rugby is the scrum. In a game of 10s, the scrum is formed by five of the players from each team – known as the forwards. The other five – known as the backs – stretch across the field in a line and wait for the ball to come out of the scrum. When it does, they run forward and attempt to pass it along the line to the next player and eventually to the winger, who is then supposed to race over the try line and score. When I say "attempt to pass to the next player" I may be giving the reader the impression that the pass may fail. This is exactly what usually happens. One of the backs drops it and then we have to have a scrum again! So, the forwards have to trundle over to that point on the pitch and do it all over again. Ad infinitum.

I guess, from this sarcasm, you can tell that I was a forward. But, like many players, that's not where I started playing rugby. At first, because of my speed, I was put out on the wing. You may ask why did I start as a winger? The answer is simple. Virtually all coaches will put new players out on the wing because they have very little ability and were the lowest in the backline pecking order. They were placed as far as possible from the ball and, given the generally poor handling by the inside backs, were rarely given the opportunity to even touch the ball.

As I said earlier, I always had a great pair of legs. I wasn't ever a great rugby player, probably not even creeping into the "good rugby player" category, but I could run. It's a bit like Tom Hanks in Forrest Gump. He had no idea what he was doing, but he could run. I always love the clip of when he was playing American Football and he got the ball and then ran the full length of the pitch without anyone being able to catch him. Everyone is shouting "Run Forrest. Run!" and he gets to the end zone and instead of stopping he just keeps on running out of the stadium. It's magic!

CUE YOUTUBE MOVIE CLIP: FORREST GUMP
TOM HANKS

So, yeah! "Run TSB. Run!" But over the span of 35 years playing rugby, like many players before me, I gradually gravitated from the backs to the forwards, playing No. 8, then wing forward, and ending up in the front row of the scrum as the "hooker".

I think I have to apologise here to anyone who knows nothing about rugby and bought this book on the assumption that the word "hooker" in the title, coupled with the word "confessions" meant that they were going to read some salacious stories penned by an aging, former street walker/lady of the night. Possibly you thought it was the last-ditch naughty bits of Xaviera Hollander. But surely that book would have been called "*Call Me an Old Madam*"? Sorry for that, but if you have paid for the book and read this far you might as well carry on and get your money's worth.

Although, overall there is an intense camaraderie and team spirit between all players on any rugby team, there is always significant rivalry between the forwards and the backs. There is a reason for this.

Generally, the backs are short, skinny and foppish and more interested in their hairstyles and not getting mud on their shorts. Thus, they are very likely to drop the ball if anyone from the other team runs up to them and shouts “Boo!”. This provides the location for the next scrum. And the forwards are the engine-house of the team but get fed up going from side to side on the pitch every time the backs drop the ball.

“But”, I can hear the non-rugby playing readers saying, “What the hell is a scrum?” Americans call it a line of scrimmage – but in that the players don’t actually touch each other - just face each other a few inches apart.

Well, let me explain. A scrum is formed when the ball has been “knocked on” (i.e. as I said before, usually when one of the backs dropped it). In a game of 15s, there are eight forwards from each team in the scrum but in a game of 10s there are only five from each team as in the photo below. This picture is one of me in an Arabian Potbellies pack at the Manila 10s in the Philippines in 2010, the season before the accident at Sharjah. I am the good looking one in the middle of the front row of the team on the left, by the way. Of course, being good looking is relative and subjective when in comparison to the other two props in the front row. Maybe I have to apologise to Anson “PB Paris Hilton” Bailey and Peter “PB Roasty” Stubley to avoid libel action? But, surely, they must own mirrors and have a daily opportunity to appraise my claims.

Scrummaging 101 - Let It All Hang Out

So, the two packs face each other with three in each front row and the other two guys (the "back row") have their heads squashed between the buttocks of the guys in the front row. Now that may not sound a very pleasant place to be but the guys in the front row are always over-chunky sized, so there is plenty of padding down there. The two guys on each end of the front row are the "props" and the guy in the middle is called the "hooker". Ah, so now you know how I got the title for the book!

The scrum-half stands outside the scrum and throws the ball into the tunnel which is formed when the two opposing front rows bind together with their heads interlocked and they lean on each other forming a short, fat, hairy arch. *(And be careful how you say that. The last two letters are "ch" not "se")*

Lovely stuff, eh? Have you got the picture now? The two packs are interlocked, each side weighing about half a metric tonne (that's 500kg in simple terms, or 1200 pounds in even simpler terms for American readers). Each side is pushing against each other as the ball comes in and they are trying to gain supremacy over the opposition. Everybody is straining every muscle they have. It's not a delicate sight, but it is a delicate balance. A very delicate balance.

The stability of the scrum under these conditions relies on the grip of the players between each other, their relative weights and strengths, and very much on the props having a firm footing on the grass below their feet. And if one if those factors changes . . .?

In our team Arabian Potbellies team for the Sharjah 10s we had a front row that included me, at the age of sixty-two, plus two props in their late forties to mid-fifties. So, our combined age for the front row was about one-hundred and seventy years! Conversely, the front row players of the Sharjah team were all about thirty-five and one day. Thirty-five years being the minimum age for Vets rugby! They had a combined age of one-hundred and five years, or two thirds of ours.

This tournament was back in February 2011 and at that time the IRB Laws dictated that the referee told the players in the scrum to "Crouch…Touch…Pause…ENGAGE!" And on the final command, "ENGAGE", both front rows lunged at each other and the guys in the back row straightened their legs and pushed forward as hard as they could. This resulted in what we called the "Hit", with both packs each trying to make their hit the strongest one so they have instant dominance as the ball came in from the scrum half. What I do recall vividly that day was that at each scrum, the hit was the hardest hit I could ever remember – and I mean like ever in my whole rugby playing career!

I was in the starting squad for the game, but as a result of the Sharjah pack's hits, I was pretty happy to come off at the end of the first half and let Arthur Bell go on and take over my slot.

I walked off the pitch and, usually, any player who comes off will stand on the touchline in case he gets called to go back on. That's the general principle of rolling subs. But that day I felt really battered and my shoulders were aching from all the hits. So, as I was rubbing them, I started walking along the touchline in the direction of our team tent.

I recall looking across the Sharjah field at our tent about 100 yards away and somehow it had kind of a glow around it. Sort of like a halo effect – beckoning me towards it. In retrospect, I have no idea why I did not question what could be causing this as it certainly was not normal. I got to the corner of the pitch and then suddenly thought "What if the team needs me to go back on?"

So, I walked slowly back to the half way line and watched the game with the other subs. It got to very near to full time and they had had about four or five scrums almost one after another in a very short time – the backs were dropping the ball more than usual!

In fact, they were playing seven minutes each way, so to have so many scrums in such a short time is really tiring. Anyway, Arthur looked up exhaustedly and waved at me to swap with him again. It was the last minute of the game and the last scrum. To be honest, I really did not want to go back on. But it's a team game, so I did anyway.

Now to answer the earlier question: What if one of the factors making the scrum stable changes? Well, we scrummed down and, unfortunately, just as we took the hit, one of my props lost his footing and that destabilised the scrum and caused the other prop to slip as well. And, as you would expect, the Sharjah front row just kept pushing and pushing. That's what they were bred and trained to do!

But my props had both slipped. I had nothing to hold on to, and the only thing the Sharjah pack was pushing against was my neck and so it bent and then crushed in a downward direction.

And that was the very moment that a lot of things changed in my life.

4

SITUATION NORMAL . . . (BUT ACTUALLY AFU)

The weird thing was that I actually had no pain whatsoever, anywhere. You would kind of imagine that if 500kg worth of rugby players tried to break your neck, that there might just be some negative feeling somewhere. But no. Nothing at all.

So, James and I trundled off in the ambulance in search of a hospital that would admit me. I did not realize this at first – foolishly assuming that when you have an emergency case in an ambulance it would be easy to find a hospital. Not so. Not so at all.

We arrived at the first hospital and I heard the front doors open and slam shut as the ambulance crew got out. And then it all went quiet. Very quiet! After what seemed like an eternity we heard the front ambulance doors open and slam shut again and we drove off. No one bothered to tell me what was happening of course. Why would I be interested? After all, I was just the patient!

Then we went to the second hospital and it was "Déjà vu all over again"

As you can imagine, I started grumbling and shouting at James – even though, of course, it was not his fault. But when you are laid on your back on a compression board with your neck in a brace you have a very limited range of mobility and vision and you are left with only vocal power. So, you go for the metaphorical jugular of the nearest person.

"What the Hell is going on! What are the paramedics doing? Why am I not being taken into the hospital? This is a fucking EMERGENCY!!!"

James got out of the ambulance to go and see what was happening. And then the back doors slammed shut again and it all went quiet. Even more quiet than before! Suddenly I realised that I was all alone. No paramedics, no James, no one at all. What if I suddenly had a convulsion? Or, what if, like Jimi Hendrix, Bonn Scott of AC/DC, or John Bonham of Led Zeppelin, I threw up and choked on my own vomit because I couldn't move? So, I panicked. My heart was racing at a million miles an hour. I shouted but no one heard me, of course, because the ambulance was out on the driveway and they were all inside the building. Aaaarggghh!

Eventually, James and the paramedics came back. What a relief – at least for a moment. Apparently, the problem was that there was not an appropriately specialized doctor on duty at neither the first hospital nor the second one because it was a Friday which was the religious day in the UAE. What could we do about that? Not bloody much, was the answer!

So, we trundled off slowly to the next hospital. *Why did they not have the sirens blaring and the lights flashing*? I idly wondered, as I lay in the back of the ambulance staring at the roof. Wasn't this an EMERGENCY?

Sharjah is not a huge place, but when you are in the back of an ambulance with no way of seeing out and you have just been turned away from two hospitals, it seems to take forever to get somewhere. What I did not realize till several days later was that we were actually going around in ever-decreasing circles. This was because the third hospital we ended up in was the Al Qasimi Hospital which was actually in the same city block as the Sharjah Wanderers Rugby Club and they virtually shared the same boundary wall. Why didn't we come here in the first place? I am sure there is no answer to that question.

Then we had "Déjà vu all over again". All over again.

The paramedics got out, the front doors slammed shut and it all went quiet again. At that point I was becoming apoplectic, to put it mildly. I started shouting at poor James again and then realized we had better tell my wife Agnes what had happened as she was at home in Abu

Dhabi. James called her and it turned out that Bill Middleton, our team physio, had given her a call when we left the rugby ground – over an hour earlier – and we had been playing "Find the Hospital" ever since.

Of course, the first thing she asked James was "How's your Dad?" to which James answered "He is OK. He's shouting at me to do this and to do that!"

"Ah, OK," she said "That sounds normal!"

So, she thought that because I am grumbling and being grumpy with James, I must be OK. Well, at least my brain and my eyes and my mouth were functioning – even if little else was. Actually, as I was to find out later, over the course of my rehabilitation and physiotherapy, the fact that those things did still work perfectly was a major bonus in everything I did.

In reality it was Situation Normal, but actually, All Fucked Up. The famous army-style SNAFU.

Then, suddenly, the back doors of the ambulance flew open and the paramedics had come to get me and take me into the hospital. Yo! At last they found one with a doctor that was willing to accept me.

On the trolley and in we went to the high tech department where they did X-rays and scans. I ended up having all the tests, X-ray, MRI and CT scan. It all seemed to happen pretty quickly without much pain or heartache. I do remember feeling very claustrophobic in the MRI machine and for some inexplicable reason thinking that I hoped they had put me in the right machine and that I wasn't going to be zapped with radiation for cancer and have all my hair fall out. Maybe it was because I had been avidly watching Walter White in Breaking Bad.

CUE YOUTUBE VIDEO: BREAKING BAD
BRYAN CRANSTON

The doctor eventually appeared – he had been called in from his day off – and looked at the results. There was a long silence as he looked at things on a computer screen. And I mean a loooooong silence. Finally he pronounced that I had a Spinal Cord Contusion, one of my vertebrae, C5 in my neck, was slightly displaced, there were some fractures. It's what is called "breaking your neck" in layman's terms.

This was all said as though it was a "good thing" and that I should be happy about it. I asked if I was going to need an operation and he said that he did not think so at this stage. But, of course, he immediately covered himself by saying that we would have to wait till the swelling around the nerves went down to see the final picture. So, yes, that seemed at the time like a fairly positive diagnosis. I guess . . .

But, as I was to find out – over a long period of time – the doctors cannot fully know what is happening inside your spine and your nervous system. And particularly, they can't really tell how the brain works and whether some bits can reconnect and re-learn how to do things. I don't think anyone on the planet can do that yet. But the doctors do a good job with very limited information and – compared to the human body itself – with very primitive tools.

So, as I said, SNAFU, really SNAFU. And this is where the real story begins.

5

NIGHTMARE WARD

So, the good news was that my neck wasn't actually broken, but the bad news was it was somewhat bent out of shape, I was paralyzed and had no sensation from the waist down and could not move my arms.................Hmmmmmmm!

And there was more bad news – if that's possible. I was in the Al Qasimi Hospital in Sharjah. What's significant about that you might ask? Well you might ask, but even if you don't, I am going to tell you anyway. Imagine going back about 150 years to Victorian-era England and peeping inside one of the hospitals at that time. They all had dark green shiny tiles on the bottom half of the walls, flickering gas lights on the walls, nurses with starched uniforms and "that smell" peculiar to hospitals. It's a combination of antiseptic, floor polish, starch, infected bodies, and urine. It's the one that makes you shudder when you walk through the doors. I always hated going in hospitals as a kid – I only went a couple of times as a patient – but I hated "that smell".

While I may not be a spring chicken, the Victorian-era had long been over when I was a kid, *(It was from June 1837 to January 1901 for those of you with bad memories)* but, in England in the 1950s, the same old hospitals were still there and so was "that smell". Actually, I think that someone at the time had the franchise for selling aerosol spray cans of "that smell" to all the hospitals in the UK.

Maybe, that same person had done a deal with Al Qasimi Hospital too because "that smell" pervaded the whole place. It was all I could do to stop from gagging as they wheeled me from the MRI lab to the ward. Luckily I didn't throw up on the way as it was actually worse when we got to the ward. Good thing I saved a bit!

The Al Qasimi is not a specialist hospital; it's a hospital which seems to be run to match the requirements of the general population of Sharjah. For those of you not familiar with the UAE, Sharjah it caters primarily to the middle and lower income groups who work in Dubai but can't afford the sky high housing rents there.

As a result, there are not many western expatriates living in Sharjah so I think I was the only one in the Al Qasimi hospital. I never saw another white face while I was there! Also, normally in the private hospitals in the UAE, I would automatically be put in a private room but at the Al Qasimi I was put in what they (perhaps jokingly) called the Orthopaedic Recovery Ward. This had four beds in it, divided by curtains – so you could not see anyone but you could certainly hear everything that happened to the other patients.

One of them was in a coma from a car accident but being kept alive by equipment that continually beeped and buzzed and whooshed so that the nurses knew it was still working – and I presume at the same time they knew that the patient was still alive! The second one had a tracheotomy which meant that regularly there were these huge deathly gurgling noises accompanied by what I can only describe as "liquid coughing" as the fluids in his lungs were ejected. It was like the sound you get when you use a rubber plunger on a blocked toilet drain – and there is no way of writing that sound – you just know it when you hear it. I didn't know what was wrong with the third guy in the room. I never saw him as they always had the curtains drawn around him, but he had a constant stream of visitors who all talked and talked and talked. Not to him – just to each other.

So, as a result of this combination of patients, there was never a quiet moment in the room. The lights were on 24/7, there was a constant stream of nurses and doctors coming to attend to the patients, plus there was all the buzzing, clicking, whooshing, gurgling, coughing and "drain cleaning", talking, talking and more talking . . .

As soon as I had arrived in the ward the doctors – they always came in packs four – also fitted me with a big neck brace. They did not keep these in stock so they got one of the suppliers to come over to the hospital and try out a few on me. Naturally, as expected, they chose the tallest, stiffest, tightest and most uncomfortable one that was sampled. Really uncomfortable, believe me. They are OK when you are sitting up in bed looking straight ahead, but if you are in any other position they are excruciatingly painful. Oh, and then I had to pay cash for it too!!

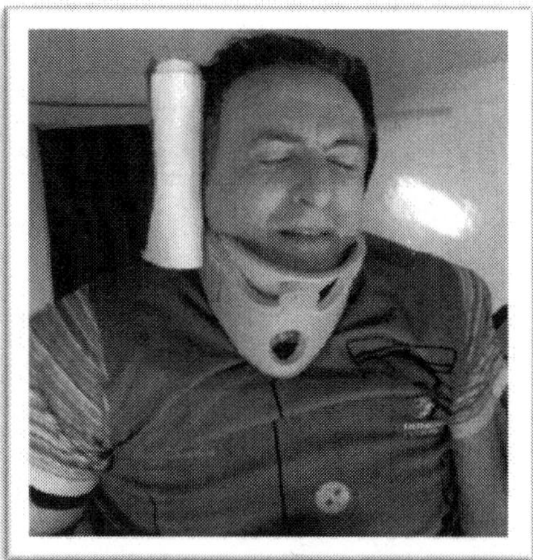

The Sharjah Strangler - And I Am Still Wearing My Rugby Kit!

This was not a place to relax and recuperate. Not at all. It was hard to sleep with all the lights on and the doors to the corridor were wide open. There were no emergency buzzers, and if I wanted something I had to shout! So, I kept asking the doctors if I could be moved to a private room. The response to this was garbled and nothing was happening. I kept saying “It doesn’t matter what it costs – just get me out of here”. It was a bit like the British TV show *I’m a Celebrity.... Get Me Out of Here!* Of course, I wasn’t a celebrity, so nothing happened for several days.

But eventually, one of the doctors confided in me that, because it was a government hospital, the only people who could have a private room were the sheiks . . . ! Ha! That was the problem. Then, without warning, on the fourth day, the nurses suddenly whisked in with a gurney and said that I was moving. Great! Yo! They put me in a double room but kept the other bed empty so, effectively, I had my own room. Brilliant!

Obviously, I was on a lot of pain killers – primarily because of the neck brace - and that was OK until they also tried to give me sleeping tablets too. This is a weird combination and NOT recommended at all. In me, at least, it seemed to produce the strangest sensations of discomfort throughout my whole body and actually had the reverse effect by keeping me awake instead of letting me go to sleep.

Somehow, I could never get to that point where the brain relaxes and everything shuts down and you drift into sleep.

The second day in my "private double room" I was awake after my sleepless night on the sleeping pills. I was feeling somewhat second-hand, as you can imagine, when I was treated to my first rolling bed sheet change. Two nurses/orderlies swept into the room and announced that they were going to change the bed sheets. One was a burly Egyptian male and the other was an even burlier African female. I had never been in hospital since I was a little kid, when I had my tonsils out, so I had no recollection what this would be like. If I had, I might have been more prepared. They slowly flattened the bed so I was laid on my back and then suddenly rolled me on my left side so that they could fold up the sheet for half the bed and replace it with another one. But rolling me on my side meant that my head flopped down to the left and – despite the huge neck brace – bent my neck a lot because no one had held my head!

I screamed out in pain. "Stop, it hurts!!!"

"No, it's OK," the guy said.

"No, it's not! It fucking hurts!!!!" I screamed back.

I had never felt so much intense, concentrated pain. It was obviously all the mangled nerves in my neck being stretched in a new direction that they didn't want to be stretched in. AAAaaaarghhh!!

But the two nurses just carried on despite me screaming at them. They had been told to change the sheets on my bed and that's what they were going to do and never mind the pain inflicted on the patient. Finally, they rolled me onto my back again – without holding my head – so it was a whole new batch of pain sensations and then at last it was over. Phheeeeeeeeew, my body just seemed to collapse in a metaphorical heap and I lay there exhausted from lack of sleep and that drained feeling you get when subjected to lots of pain.

Eventually, much against the doctors wishes, I managed to persuade them that I had to stop taking the sleeping pills so that I could get some sleep. As I will surely say again – I am only the patient. What do I know? Duuuuh! And in my waking hours all I could think of was:

"Even if I'm Not a Celebrity . . . Get Me Out of Here"

6

THUNDER ROAD

Finally, the medical insurance paperwork got sorted out and they said I could go back to Abu Dhabi to the Al Noor Hospital near to the Grand Mosque. This was great news as it was only about ten to fifteen minutes from our house in Sas Al Nakhl Village. Yo! It felt like going home!!

But - and there is always a "but" with these things - I could not be taken in one of the ambulances from Al Qasimi, which would have been free of charge as it's a Government hospital. I had to go in an ambulance from Al Noor which cost AED 4800 and that's equivalent to US$1,300 or £800. It's only about 130 km between the two hospitals so that's AED 37 per km = US$10 per km. When you consider that Dubai Van Taxi with a lifter for wheelchairs costs AED 2 per km = 57 US cents, that's a fair old mark-up. Welcome to the world of private medicine!!

Of course, it's not about the money – or so they told me – it's a responsibility issue. As soon as I left the boundaries of the Al Qasimi Hospital I was technically no longer their responsibility. I became the responsibility of Al Noor Hospital. So, if something happened to me on the way down to Abu Dhabi in a "free" Al Qasimi ambulance, the two hospitals would then have a bun fight over who should fix me up again. Of course, at that point in time, I was a bedridden quadriplegic with no feelings below the waist and arms and hands that didn't function. How much worse could it get????

I was wheeled into the back of the ambulance feeling some trepidation about the forthcoming trip. I am not sure if we had the flashing lights on but we did get into the fast lane and even the Toyota Land Cruisers seemed to keep their distance from the ambulance. If you live in the UAE, or have ever been here, you will understand what I mean by that comment. For those of you who have not had the "pleasure" of driving between Abu Dhabi and Dubai, it needs some explanation. That road is one of the major arteries of the country and its mainly 4 and sometimes 5 lanes in each direction. But it does not matter which day of the week or what time of day or night you go on it, it's always full of traffic.

So, why my comment about Toyota Land Cruisers? Well, they are one of the most popular vehicles in the UAE because they are big, V8 powered, fast, comfortable and can readily off-road into the desert when you need to. But, they also appear to be fitted with very large magnets behind the front bumpers and an accelerator pedal that sticks down at 150kph as, whenever you are in the fast lane doing 140kph, (which is already 20kph above the speed limit, right?) there will be a Land Cruiser that comes up behind you at 150kph and then sits about one inch from your back bumper "tailgating" till you move out of the way. I think that they are magnetically attracted to the back end of the car in front . . .

But, believe me, you do move out of the way because there is only one thing more frightening than a Land Cruiser up your back end and that is having one swerve around you either on the outside in the fast lane "hard shoulder" or on the lane inside you and squeeze by with millimetres to spare. Toyota Land Cruisers have about the same swerve-ability quotient as a pregnant hippopotamus, so it's safer to move over and let them pass in a straight line.

Michael McIntyre, the British comedian, came to Dubai in April 2014 and Kyle and I went to see him. It was probably the funniest two and a half hours of our lives. Our jaws ached with laughing so much. In all his shows he always makes observational jokes about the city he is in. For Dubai he commented that the UAE had the shortest "stopping distances" in the world as everyone drives around in strings of vehicles that are so close that they appear to be attached to each other!!

I have another theory. I think we are in a virtual movie set and everyone believes that we are rehearsing for *Days of Thunder 2*. You remember Tom Cruise as Cole Trickle in the original *Days of Thunder*? It's all about a rookie race car driver in the NASCAR championship races where they hurtle around the track at up to 340 kph with only millimetres between each car. If you are that close, in racing terminology it's called "drafting" as you use less power and fuel because you are being sucked forward by the car in front. In normal road driving, if you are that close, it's called "tailgating". In racing, if you bump the next car from behind it's called "rubbing". In normal road driving it's called "an accident".

There is a great scene in the movie when they are trying to teach Cole - race by race - all about racing. Cole angrily tells his head race car mechanic, that the car behind has just slammed into him and his response is "He didn't slam into you! He didn't bump you! He rubbed you! And rubbing, son, is racing . . .!". And it's all done to the tune of *Gimme Some Lovin'* by the Spencer Davies Group in the Steve Winwood era (1963-1967). Magic!

CUE YOUTUBE VIDEO: DAYS OF THUNDER – TOM CRUISE
MUSIC: GIMME SOME LOVIN' – SPENCER DAVIS GROUP

As you can see, Toyota Land Cruisers, Tom Cruise, NASCAR and Days of Thunder are all connected by *Gimme Some Lovin'*. What a coincidence! But, as you will see many times in the book, TINSTAAC - There Is No Such Thing As A Coincidence.

If you live in the UAE, next time you drive on the Dubai – Abu Dhabi Highway just play *Gimme Some Lovin'* and watch all the Toyota Land Cruisers "tailgating", "drafting" and "rubbing" I am sure you will know exactly what I mean. It's the Thunder Road.

As it turned out, the ride in the ambulance from Sharjah to Abu Dhabi was, thankfully uneventful, so I arrived at the Al Noor Hospital safely. They immediately put me in the Intensive Care Unit for observation for a couple of days where I had a one-on-one nurse 24 hours a day, and they hooked me up to a bunch of telemetry machines that checked my vital signs every nano-second. This was the opposite end of the medical spectrum to Sharjah where I had not had anything to check my vital signs except a thermometer under my tongue once a day! It was like going from the YMCA to the Ritz-Carlton

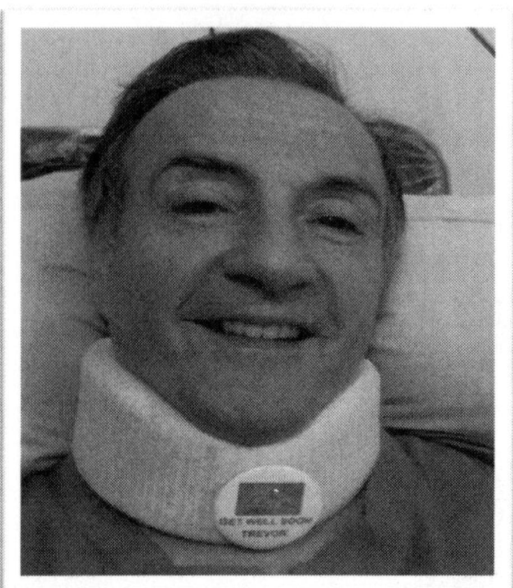

Back in Abu Dhabi - 20 March 2011
Al Noor Hospital

After a couple of days I was pronounced stable - and/or recovered from the stresses of the ambulance ride down the highway – so they moved me to their 'Step-Down Unit'. This is, as it sounds, one step down from an ICU (Duuuuh). And the little badge on my neck brace? It actually says "Get Well Soon Trevor". There was a whole batch of them made and sold by one of the guys at the Dubai Hurricanes RFC to raise money for me. Lovely "Feel Good" stuff!

So, I settled into the beginning of my sojourn at the Al Noor Hospital Step-Down Unit with no idea of what was coming next and high expectations of walking out of there in a fairly short time.

Little did I know . . .

7

DR. MOHAMMED

When you are lying in a hospital bed in a private room there is not much going on. Believe me! It's not like being on a big general ward in, say, a British National Health Service hospital. There you would have all sorts of patients from young to old with many different medical problems, so there would always be something happening, people moving around, nurses making beds, visitors coming in and out and doctors doing their rounds. However, in a private room anyone coming through the door is a significant point of interest to the patient, and I mean anyone!

The first person who came in my room every day was the cleaner. Now, in general we don't take much notice of the many people around us who do all the basic tasks. The cleaner in the office, the Xerox guy, the Pizza delivery guy, the tea boy etc. But when you can't do things for yourself - as I couldn't - you start to take note of the people that you need to help you to do simple things in life. It's human nature.

Anyway, the cleaner was a young, skinny Bangladeshi guy who came into my room every morning to mop the floor and clean the bathroom. But, like many people in that kind of role, he was very careful not to "disturb" or "impose" on the patient. So, he would always come in the room with mop in hand and swish it back and forth across the floor and at all times he would keep his head bowed and his eyes looking down at the floor. Maybe someone had told him not to stare at the patients.

Every day it was the same. Head down, look at the floor and go swish, swish, swish.

But, one day I asked him what his name was. He looked up, a bit shocked at first, because someone had actually spoken to him. But when I asked again he said it was "Mohammed". I should have guessed! I asked him a bunch of questions and his English was very good in all his replies. It turned out he was 26, the eldest of about 8 kids and the only wage earner in the whole family. He earned about Dhs 800 (US$200) per month, lived on about Dhs 300 ($80) of that and sent the rest home to support the family. Wow! That's a tough existence.

So, I started giving him my hospital food as they gave me three meals a day plus snacks but mostly I ate the food that arrived from home. As I mentioned earlier, my wife is a Filipina and it's a Filipino tradition in their culture to send food into hospital to feed your relative as hospital food in the Philippines is far from brilliant. Of course, Mohammed loved this. He was suddenly on three real meals a day, including soup, main course and dessert.

Then, one morning, he came into the room and he was wearing one of the surgical masks like the doctors and nurses have when they are in surgery or around infectious patients. I have no idea why he was wearing the mask and I didn't ask. Maybe he had been cleaning somewhere that was dusty or had just come from the room of a patient who had something infectious.

Anyway, instead of asking questions, I just said, "Good Morning Dr. Mohammed!"

He looked at me with wide open eyes above the mask. So, I said it again. "Good Morning Dr. Mohammed!"

"You look just like a doctor wearing that mask," I continued "From now on I'm going to call you Dr. Mohammed!" I said with a laugh.

You could see that he liked the idea of being a "Doctor". He visibly preened and stood more upright. And from that day on, he slowly changed his whole demeanour.

No longer did he come in to the room with his head down. It was always up and he was looking around. You could watch him walk down the corridor and he was proud and positive. Somehow, he had become a "real" person. He was saying "Good Morning" to other patients and people as he walked by. He was "Dr. Mohammed".

Mohammed - The Cleaner

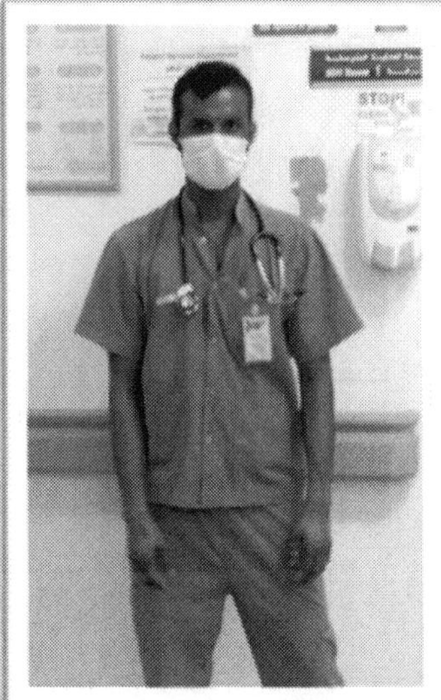

Dr. Mohammed

After being in the hospital about five or six weeks – stabilizing and recovering - it was decided that it was time to get me out of bed for the first time and put me in a wheelchair. Of course, (of course?), I had no muscle strength or means of activating them and I was like a floppy jelly. So, to get me out of bed and into the wheelchair they needed to use a small electric crane. They brought it into my room and it had a triangular base with three wheels and a big hammock-like sling hanging from the hook.

None of the nurses had done this before so there were about a dozen people in my room – including "Dr. Mohammed" - all giving advice to each other about the best way to go about it. Why the cleaner was involved, I have no idea. But he was there!

Basically, they had to put the sling underneath me and then wrap it around my body and hook the four straps onto the hook of the crane. To get the sling underneath me they had to do the "rolling back and forth changing the bed linen" routine as they couldn't lift me up. That was fun in itself . . .

Finally, I was all hooked up and they pressed the "Up" button and I was slowly winched out of bed. Of course, the sling does not stay flat as I was lifted up and I ended up in this big curved wrap-around like you see in pictures of a baby being lifted by a stork. Now this may be ok for babies and storks but it was no fun for me at all. This was the first time I had moved from the "safety" of the hospital bed. I was scared shitless . . .

There I was, dangling from this crane, above everyone's head about seven or eight feet from the ground!! Then they swung the crane around on its castor wheels and I was thinking that the damn thing does not look very stable at all on its triangular base. I was swinging back and forth as they moved me across the room to where the wheelchair was. Scary stuff, I tell you.

Then they all started talking again as they were trying to decide how to get me to "shoot" into the wheelchair. There was a huge babble of ideas going around the room. And I am still up in the air, swinging gently back and forth . . .

I was really scared by now and I could picture myself plummeting to the ground and causing more damage to my body than I already had. So, I started shouting down to them, "Guys, for fuck's sake get me down from here. I don't want to fall!"

And then Mohammed looked up at me and said, "Don't worry Mr. Trevor. You will be OK. Nothing is going to happen to you. Doctor Mohammed is here . . ."

They eventually did get me down without dropping me. So, it was OK in the end and I was wheeled down the corridor in the wheelchair and out into the fresh air for the first time in two months.

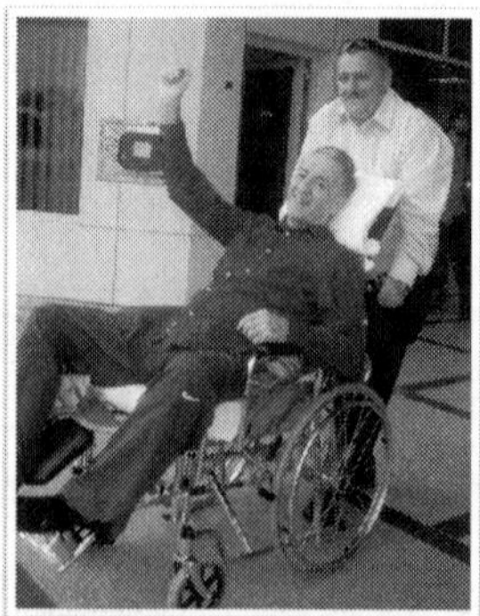

TSB & Arthur Bell - First Time Out of Jail

It was a lovely feeling – getting out of "jail" for the first time. But the star of the show was really Dr. Mohammed. That was just brilliant! "Don't worry, Doctor Mohammed is here".

And there was another very funny thing that he did. One of our family's favourite comedians at the time was Jeff Dunham. Well, he is not actually a comedian, he is a ventriloquist, but his act is hilarious. One of his dummies was called "*Achmed the Dead Terrorist*". I know that normally it is spelt 'AHMED' as I have lots of co-workers and friends in the UAE with this name. But the video title is spelt with a 'C' and in the sketch he actually spells it out. "Achmed, spelt 'A' . . .'C' . . . Phlegm . . ."

Achmed is actually a skeleton with a huge head (as all dummies do) and big popped-out eyes. The background story for him was that he was a terrorist who was a suicide bomber but the bombs blew up too soon before he got to his target. Ha! One of his favourite sayings when challenged (or if Jeff said something he did not like) was "Silence….! I keeiiiill you!" This, of course is even more amusing as Achmed is already dead. Anyway, one day I got Dr. Mohammed in my room and I showed him the YouTube video of *Achmed the Dead Terrorist*. He thought it was hilarious – and this was despite the fact that he is a Muslim himself.

The door to my room was always open to the corridor so the nurses could look in whenever they passed. So, after I had shown Dr. Mohammed that video, every time he went past my room he would stick his head round the corner of the doorway and say "Silence . . . ! I keeiiiill you!" What a hoot!

Just watch the YouTube video and see what I mean.

CUE YOUTUBE VIDEO: ACHMED THE DEAD TERRORIST
JEFF DUNHAM

Now remember, this is the same guy who, a month or so earlier, wouldn't even look up from the floor he was sweeping. And, all through my stay, he grew more and more confident. Whenever there was a group picture-taking he was always in it and he walked around the unit like he "owned" it. That small thing that I did, by naming him "Dr. Mohammed", had made a huge difference to him. I was so pleased with myself and very proud that I had been able to help him in some way and make it possible for him to feel more self-respect than he ever had before.

POST SCRIPT

All the above happened in late March 2011 and I wrote the chapter in September 2014. It was amongst the first ones that I did, mainly because it was such a funny story. But, now "fast forward" to the end of October 2015 when something interesting and unexplainable happened relating to the story of Dr. Mohammed.

By then I had "retired". Ha! That's a joke in itself. Agnes and I had set up a new company in the UAE called ASPIRE to keep me gainfully employed. For several months, I had been busier than I was when I was still working for Orascom and I had been rushing around like the proverbial blue arsed fly!!! One of the things ASPIRE does is staff recruitment of Filipino professionals in all sectors including healthcare, construction, hospitality, administration, IT etc. We have tied up with a Manila-based recruitment company called Orange International and Sarah McLeod is the Executive Vice President.

So, Sarah came over to Abu Dhabi for the Arab Healthcare and Recruitment Exhibition as there were about 40 potential clients all together in one room. On the first day we were zooming round the exhibition chatting up clients like there was no tomorrow. Of course, this makes you hungry and thirsty so I headed for the coffee shop inside the exhibition hall for some sustenance. But it was lunchtime so all the tables were full or partially occupied.

One had a bunch of Filipinos with a couple of spare seats and, normally, I would head for a table like that as its easy for me to make a connection with Filipinos – I only need to mention my Filipina wife and the fact that I lived there for 27 years and I am "in". But that day something drew me to another table where there was a bearded Sudanese gentleman sitting alone. I didn't know he was Sudanese, of course, till I sat down and we started chatting.

As it was a Healthcare Recruitment Exhibition I assumed that he had come looking for a new job but it turned out he was an "Intensivist" and interested in the lectures that were ongoing. I had never heard the term "Intensivist" before but it is someone who works in the Intensive Care Unit of a hospital. I had been in ICU when I first arrived in Al Noor Hospital so I knew something about it. So, we chatted and he asked how I had become injured. I told him briefly about my accident and the rehabilitation I had been going through. To that he responded by saying that I should write a book about my experiences!

"Funny you should say that," I replied, "as that is exactly what I am doing!"

Was the man psychic or what? I told him about how it was going and the style of the chapters etc. I then thought I would give him a sample so I randomly chose to tell him the story of Dr.. Mohammed. He laughed at the end and was obviously amused by it.

Then, as we had finished our lunch, I needed to get moving on to see some more potential clients. So, I belatedly introduced myself to the gentleman.

"Bye the way, it's been really nice talking to you and my name is Trevor."

"It's been my pleasure," he said, "and my name is Dr. Mohammed!"

Woooo! No, really! Then I looked down at the ID hanging round his neck, which was facing the wrong way. I turned it round and sure enough, he was Dr. Mohammed. The real Dr. Mohammed!

What were the chances of those things happening? A coincidence? But there is no such thing as a coincidence is there?

But then it got even more interesting when we went back to the exhibition the next day. We did the rounds again and then went for our lunch break to the same coffee shop and ended up at the same table (!). Sarah had missed the end of the conversation the previous day as she had left the table just before it happened. When I told her the story I got some raised eyebrows and sharp intakes of breath at the punchline.

By mid-afternoon we had covered all the booths so it was time to go home. But, as we neared the exit, Rowdah, our Ethiopian house-maid, who I had brought along to push the wheelchair and be my support if I needed assistance, asked if we could have a picture taken. So, we stopped and asked a young Filipino to take our photo.

Just then there was a shout "Can I join the picture too?"

It was the real Dr. Mohammed!! He just appeared, like out of nowhere, and joined us in the photo group. What were the chances of that happening? All those people in that big exhibition and he turned up at that spot just at that moment as we were about to take a photo. Was it a coincidence - an even bigger coincidence than the previous day? Or was it TINSTAAC – There Is No Such Thing As A Coincidence . . .

Will the Real Dr. Mohammed Stand Up Please?

8

NURSES, BED BATHS, CHOCOLATE CAKE & LBMs

What do nurses, bed baths, chocolate cake, and LBMs have in common? And what is an LBM anyway? Read on and find out . . .

The nurses at the Al Noor Hospital Step-Down unit were a great bunch - and I don't mean a great bunch of bananas! But some crazy things did happen and we had a lot of fun – well, as much "fun" as it's possible to have as a quadriplegic with your clothes on. There was a mix of Filipinos, some Indians and a Jordanian supervisor. Because it was the Step-Down Unit, the ratio of nurses to patients was very high. There were ten rooms and there were always five nurses on duty during the day and three at night. It was really 5-star service, believe me.

It was easy for me to get on well with them – especially the Filipinos – as my wife, Agnes, is a Filipina and I had lived in the Philippines for over twenty-seven years. So, I could talk about the country and things that happened there. Also, Agnes was always bringing in food for me to replace the standard hospital food. Of course, it was Filipino food such as Chicken Tinola, Mongo, Chicken Adobo, Nilaga and lots of other dishes, all of which arrived on a daily basis. My mouth actually started watering as I was writing the names of these dishes so I had to describe them in the Glossary. They are all really good!

Anyone who has been to the Philippines will know that it's impossible for Filipinos to cook exactly the amount of food required for a meal. Hence, there are always lots of leftovers. In fact, "Leftovers" is the favourite Filipino meal. Just ask my kids!

It's exactly opposite to that in the British culture. Growing up in England in the early 1950s, my mother, and the mothers of all my friends, would make a meal and serve the food in exact portions on the plate. There would always be just enough for however many people were in the family. No more, no less. If you brought home a friend unexpectedly for the meal there would be a huge flurry of activity (and a lot of black looks) to make some more potatoes or bread or something to stretch out the food. I think this was a throwback to food rationing in UK during World War 2 and in the post-war years.

Writing this bit about food rationing definitely reminds me of the "Four Yorkshiremen - You Were Lucky" sketch on Monty Python's Flying Circus all about "Living in't shoe box in't middle of t' road". The cast had obviously grown up in the same post-war period as myself.

CUE YOUTUBE VIDEO: FOUR YORKSHIREMEN
MONTY PYTHON'S FLYING CIRCUS

But the Filipino culture – and their intrinsic love of eating – demands that you cook a pot full of rice, whether you need it or not (because there is plenty more out in the rice paddy), and you make generally enough food for at least two, if not three, meals. There always has to be more than one type of food, served in big bowls on the table – usually some of it will be "leftovers" from the previous meal (or even the one before that) – and some of it will be "new" food. And some of that will become tomorrow's "leftovers", ad-infinitum.

Also, it's very important to have enough extra so if someone just drops in at mealtime they *can* be fed, because they *must* be fed. Plus, if you are having a party, the people in the kitchen will keep cooking food and putting it on the table almost faster than the guests can eat it so that there is as much uneaten food on the table at the end of the night as there was at the beginning!!

As you can imagine, the Filipino nurses loved Agnes as she was always bringing extra food for them. And lots of it. As a result, the attention and service that I received was brilliant.

One of the daily routines for the nurses is the changing of the sheets and the patient's bed-bath. For some people they had to have it at a specific time, probably because they liked the stability of it always happening at 10:00 am, or whatever. For me, I just told them to come whenever they could fit me in. The "surprise" was always a highlight of an otherwise hum-drum day.

But the "surprise" was always heralded by one of the female Indian nurses, Vigitha, bursting through my door dressed in full "head-to-toe-wet-suit-bed-bath" gear. This was not a scuba diving wet suit of course, but it was like an operating surgeon's long gown with a plastic apron in front, rubber gloves, facemask, and hat. The full works. And she always walked in with her hands up in the air like she had just "scrubbed up". It's important to know, when someone is about to wash your balls and your butt, that they are fully scrubbed up.

Vigitha was actually a young and very beautiful Indian girl and she had the most enormous eyes that you could ever imagine fitting on a human face without looking bizarre. But when she came bursting into my room for the bed bath all you could see were her eyes because of all the other gear, face mask, and hat. So, that seemed to make the eyes appear to be even bigger than usual.

As you can imagine, having a bed-bath administered by a young and beautiful girl was actually not a hardship. Far from it! It was just a pity that she had to have a couple of guys to help her with the heavy bits!

Given all this preceding scenario I was very amused about two years later when I went back to visit everyone in the Al Noor Step-Down Unit and wanted to have some pictures taken in my old room with all the nurses.

All the Filipino guys, the other Indian female nurses and Mohammed the Bangladeshi cleaner, were there and we were all sitting on the edge of the bed or standing behind. But Vigitha was really shy and she was very hesitant to sit down on the edge of the bed next to me with all the others. And this was the same girl that had seen me naked and given me bed-baths when I was a patient. Now she was shy . . . !

Birthday Girl!

I think you can appreciate the positive atmosphere that the nurses and I generated when I tell you that we had two birthday parties in my room while I was there. One was for Agnes as her birthday is 3 April. I won't say which year so I don't give away any secrets (and so I don't get a kick in the shins). The nurses even put some mini-posters on the walls to greet her when she came over for the party. I particularly like the little epithet they put on one . . .

"THINGS TURN OUT THE BEST FOR THE PEOPLE WHO MAKE THE BEST OF THE WAY THINGS TURN OUT"

The other party was for one of the nurses, Brian, as it was his birthday and also his last night duty at the Al Noor before he left to go to work at another hospital. We had a big bash for him and Agnes brought all the traditional Filipino food plus the most important one for birthdays and that's Pancit. Actually, it is usually pronounced "Panceeeeeeeet! This dish is important as the long noodles are supposed to indicate long life.

L to R - Ryan, Francis, Jason, Danilo, Sujith, Brian & Jemma

The second most important thing at a birthday party is a huge chocolate cake. So, we had one of those too.

All the nurses on duty were there, plus a few that came back for the party (of course!). We had food, "beverages" music, balloons, and chocolate cake. What more could we all ask for?

The party went really well and we all ate LOTS. And I mean lots. I won't tell you about drinking all the "beverages" out of paper cups because it was a hospital and I was a patient and you are not supposed to do that, of course. So, I won't mention it. Someone must have put the cup to my lips without me knowing it. I couldn't have lifted it with my (then) spastic hands, could I?

All this was great at the time but later, in the middle of the night, the situation changed. Remember, I was a quadriplegic at this stage and nothing worked below my waist. This included bladder and bowel functions. How does the hospital deal with this? Well, they fit you with a beautiful adult diaper. But what they don't tell you is that amongst the pills they give you are some to keep your bowels active. Actually that's Active with a capital 'A'.

Since I was not very far into my recovery, I did not yet understand the balancing act of interactions between medications and food. Also, I had not appreciated the full effects of a big Filipino food binge plus chocolate cake plus beverages. . .

Hmmmm! Anyway, what seemed to trigger things was that I was simply turned on my side by my nurse, Brian. This turning was to help prevent bed sores - but that night it had a much bigger effect than that. Suddenly, the heavens opened. Well, substitute the word 'bowels' for 'heavens'! Talk about LBMs . . . the Filipino acronym for Loose Bowel Movements. Need I say more?

Poor Brian! He had unknowingly hit the magic switch, and because of that he drew the short straw and had to clean it (i.e. me) up. I am sure that this was not what he wanted to do on his birthday and his last day at the Al Noor. It was a lot more chocolate cake than he was bargaining for!

So, in answer to the question at the start – "What do nurses, bed baths, chocolate cake and LBMs have in common?" Well, it's me . . .

9

BOYS WILL BE BOYS

Have you ever noticed how kids can multi-task? Both boys and girls do it incredibly easily and without fuss or fanfare. Allegedly, apparently - or at least according to women - the male of the species totally loses this ability about the time we go through puberty. It's something to do with the urban myth that men's brains are located somewhere in the testicular region and are inadvertently pre-focused on the naughty bits of women. Of course, it is not true that the adult male cannot multi-task. Certainly we can! Any adult male can think about making love to several women at the same time and could probably be able to walk along the street while he does so. And he may even be able to bend forward a little bit at the same time so that passers-by do not spot that he is getting tumescent. That's multi-tasking for sure!

Anyway, I digress, but only a little. My story is actually about Kyle and Colby, two of my sons. At the time when this happened, Kyle had just turned ten years old. In fact, his tenth birthday was 26th February 2011, the day after I had my accident in Sharjah. So, he missed his birthday party that year. Sorry Kyle! Colby was six at the time.

One day, a couple of weeks after arriving at the Al Noor Hospital, Kyle had come over to visit me after school. A while later, Joanne Mahmoud and Mohamed Abdel Latif, two of my work colleagues from Orascom Construction Industries, also came to see me. It was the first time I had seen them since the accident so I was telling them all about it and the things that had happened to me while I had been in hospital. Of course, when you are sitting in bed and your lower half is immobile, your brain and body compensate by doing other things. When you are telling stories, particularly dramatic or funny, you want to emphasize certain bits. If you are standing up normally - which I was not - you can move around or lean forwards and backwards as you tell the story. I could do none of that so I resorted to the Italian Technique - waving my arms around like crazy as I spoke.

Meanwhile, Kyle was very, very polite and quiet, sitting on a chair next to the bed playing computer games on an iPad. He just kept his face looking at the screen and - like all video game players - never blinked once.

Joanne and Mohamed seemed to be enjoying the stories as there was plenty of laughter in the room. But Kyle just kept his head in his game.

Eventually, my visitors left and a bit later in the evening, Agnes, came to pick up Kyle. On the way home in the car Kyle turned to her and said "Do you know, Mum, I think Dad has "lost it"". And he began to tell her about the visitors to my room and how I was waving my arms around in the air when I was telling them stories.

Kyle had not appeared to be taking any notice of what was going on in the room, as he was so focused on his video game, but in actual fact he was taking it all in. So, you see, boys can multi-task! And I think we generally underestimate our kids - they often have some insights that we would not imagine they would think about.

I will give you another example of this. One Thursday night about a month after the accident, we decided to have a "Boys Night In". Thursday night is Harlequins Junior Rugby Section training nights and they have about five-hundred and fifty kids of all ages from Under 5s to Under 18s. By coincidence, Harlequins' home ground is at Zayed Sports City, which is just across the road from the Al Noor Hospital. Colby was then in the U6s, Kyle was in the U11s and James was in the U16s.

So, the plan was that all the boys would go to rugby training and then come over to my room for Pizza and a movie. Great stuff. . .!

Now I am sure a few of you are thinking "Hey, wait a blooming minute! How come he lets his kids go to rugby training when he is in hospital suffering from a spinal cord contusion as a result of an accident while playing rugby?" Well, I work on this principle. Suppose you had a car accident and you were badly injured. Would you then stop all the rest of your family from ever driving a car? I am sure the answer is "no" to that one. An accident is an accident is an accident. So, why should I stop my kids playing rugby if they want to?

Anyway, going back to my story. The boys all came over and we ordered in the 3 Box Pizza, Chicken Wings, Wedgies (the potato kind not the underwear kind), Garlic Bread, Salad and Pepsi. The Pepsi is actually the most important ingredient when ordering a pizza – they just don't taste the same without it. Well, that lot lasted the usual several nano-seconds and then we settled down to watch *The Green Hornet* on my computer. To do this we were all lined up in a row on my bed, as you can see in the picture.

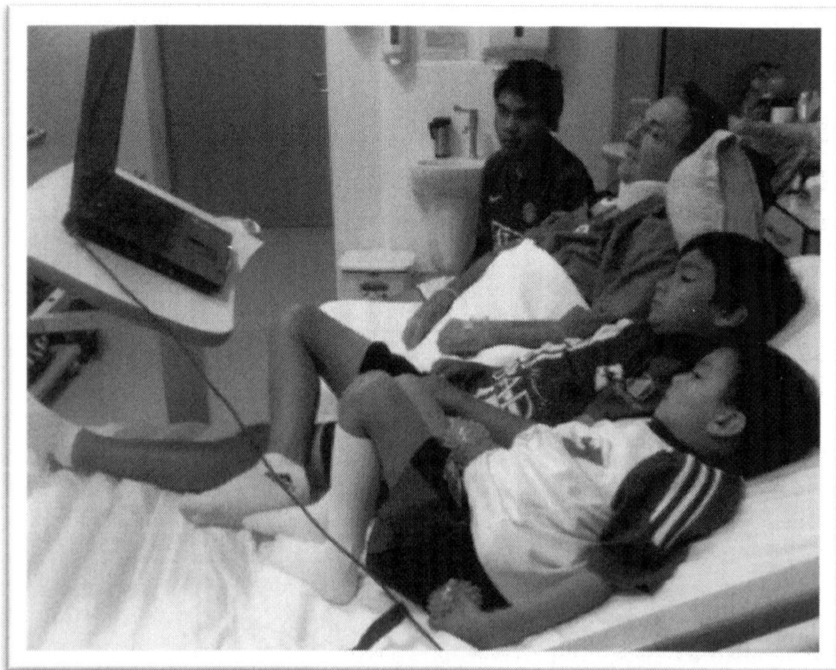

Boys Night In + Colby Holding My Balls

The balls referred to in the caption are, of course, my squeegee pink balls – though I am not sure that this explains anything. OK! They are the spiky balls that I should squeeze in each hand to satisfy my Occupational Therapist . . . Well, I am sure you can draw your own conclusions!

The movie was fun and we all enjoyed it. It's very spoofy and tongue-in-cheek of course but it's an easy-on-the-brain-cells way to pass a couple of hours. And Jay Chou as Kato is really the star of the movie . . .

CUE YOUTUBE VIDEO: THE GREEN HORNET (TRAILER)
SETH ROGAN/ JAY CHOU

After it finished, Agnes came over to pick up the boys. So, everyone was leaving the room and Colby was the last to go. But, before he did, when there was just he and I in the room, he came around to the side of the bed and stood there with his hands on his hips – like a school teacher in front of a class – and said "Dad. I don't think you should play for THAT rugby team again!"

Then he just turned on his heels and left.

As they say, "Out of the Mouths of Babes and Sucklings . . . Comes Truth and Wisdom"

10

OUCH! THAT 'KIN HURT

I had actually been putting off writing this chapter for a long while as the events that happened at that time remain a significant frustration to me. Just so you, the reader, are aware, although the story in this book is presented in roughly chronological order, I did not write it that way. Each time I wanted to write a new chapter I would scan the chapter list/outline and "cherry pick" a chapter that for, some reason, triggered a particular memory at that moment. I did not want to write the book in sequence, Chapter 1, 2, 3 . . . as I thought that approach might produce a "Then I did this and then I did that" kind of story, which could be boring. Remember, everything in this book actually happened to me so it's not like I am writing a mystery novel with a plot and a convoluted storyline that has to be written in sequence. OK, I admit that sometimes within a chapter the storyline is convoluted but that's because the memory of one thing triggers a memory of something else and then maybe a third thing. But the main story is all in my head and I am fortunate to have a humanoid RAM hard drive somewhere in my brain that can pick out facts and things in any order that I choose.

But I kept looking at the title for this chapter and passing over it to do something else.

And why was this, you might wonder? Well, there are many things that happened to me along the way as I have recovered from my accident. Some were horrendous at the time, but turned out to be funny when you looked back at them. But the two major things that happened in this chapter were not in that category and have had a lasting effect on me and my recovery.

As indicated by the title of the chapter, there was some significant pain involved. For the first month in the Al Noor Hospital no one did anything physical with me as I was basically under observation to let my neck and spinal cord stabilise. But this seemed to be going OK and I was not having any system shut-downs, so the doctor said I could start physiotherapy. This had to be a "passive" physiotherapy and all done on my bed in my room by one of the Al Noor physios. The Al Noor has a specialist Physiotherapy Clinic – which later I went to twice a week for PT and OT – and they have a team of physios and occupational therapists who deal with all the out-patients. But one physio called Leonard – or Leo for short – was assigned to work with all the in-patients.

Leo is a Filipino and he came to my room every day to administer physiotherapy to me. Because I had a lot of knowledge of the Philippines, having lived there for twenty-seven years, we could chat away about all sorts of places and things that we both knew well. At this point in time nothing much worked in my arms, legs, hands or feet so Leo did a lot of stretching and mobilization of my muscles and joints. It was amazing how tiring it was, even though I actually was not really doing anything. I was always exhausted at the end of the one-hour session.

Then one day Leo came in and, as usual, started with the stretches on my hands and wrists. This generally consisted of bending my wrist backwards at ninety degrees plus, and thereby stretching all the tendons on the underside of my wrist and arm. Unfortunately, that day he must have pulled just that bit too hard or too soon before the joint and tendons had warmed up. All of a sudden there was a sort of snapping noise and a sharp pain in my right wrist. Ooouuuch! It really hurt! Fairly quickly there was some swelling on the inside of the wrist just above the thumb joint. I think he must have snapped one of the tendons or pulled it off its mounting point on my wrist bone. And shit, it really did hurt!

I have heard a lot of Achilles tendons snapping when rugby players overdo something or they get tackled and their ankle gets rotated too far. The "snap" I had was similar to that.

Unfortunately, this accident meant that I had absolutely no strength in my wrist and it hurt a lot when I moved it in particular ways. So, I ended up wearing a wrist strap for about a year – particularly when I was doing PT and OT. This had a significant slowing down effect on the OT work we could do on my right hand. So, the OTs concentrated more on the left hand and wrist. That was fine for a while, but in the end, it has meant that my right hand lags behind very significantly in terms of full recovery since muscle atrophy is greater without constant use. I still cannot touch all my fingers with the end of my thumb and my grip is weak, so it's hard to hold a pen, pencil or knife.

To use one of my favourite paraprosdokians - I didn't say it was Leo's fault, I just said I was blaming him.

Another thing that happened around the same time significantly affected my right leg. This had nothing to do with physiotherapy, but rather, it occurred when one of the nurses came in to make the bed. I was lying in bed – what else would I be doing? – and he stood on the right side to lift the covers off my legs. He then lifted up my right knee and put my foot flat on the bed so my thigh and my lower leg were forming a ninety degree triangle at the knee joint. Then he walked round to the other side of the bed . . .

Remember, at this point, I am paralyzed below the waist. Nothing works. I have no muscle control and no muscle strength. Hence, my knee would not automatically stay in the upright neutral position the nurse put it. It wanted to fall down to a resting position on the bed. So, that's what it did, and by falling sideways it forced the hip joint to rotate way beyond its normal range. My right knee fell sideways and there was a huge "Craaaaaack". And, like my wrist, it hurt like hell!

Yeeeeeooooooowch! Oooooooooh! Shiiiiiiiiiit!!!!!!!

As there was no muscle strength to hold it up, the knee just fell down and ripped the hip joint to pieces in the process. Well, that's what it felt like and the subsequent problems I have had with my right hip would bear that out. The doctors don't seem to think there was anything wrong with it and did X-rays, MRIs and CT scans to prove it or - if I was of a cynical nature - perhaps to prove there was no negligence on the part of the hospital. But, as you read through this book, you will see all the recurring problems that I have with the right hip. I am convinced that if my right hip was as good as my left one I would be walking normally today. You can draw your own conclusions.

So, to use one of my favourite paraprosdokians again - I didn't say it was the nurse's fault, I just said I was blaming him . . . .

POST SCRIPT

Despite all the above, Leo and I are still friends. I saw him virtually every time I went to the Al Noor Rehabilitation Unit over a period of two years. At the time of writing, in 2015, I was there for back-to-back PT and OT sessions twice a week which took about three hours in total. The funny thing was that every time I was having a session I could virtually guarantee that Leo would knock on the door and want to come in to get some piece of equipment or other. In fact he did it so regularly and consistently that it became a standing joke between us.

11

THINGS START STIRRING

There is a tradition in the Philippines that if you are sick, someone must sleep in the room with you. This is true even if you are in hospital. I am not sure why, because Filipino nurses give excellent care, as I can well testify from my experience in the UAE. Perhaps that's the thing. There are so many Filipino nurses here in the UAE, UK, USA and many other countries around the world that there are not enough left behind in the Philippines to look after everyone there.

The person sleeping with you is usually family or a close friend of the family. So, it's lucky that most Filipino families are pretty large. In my case, my wife is the eldest of nine children – six girls and three boys.

So, what did this all mean for me during my hospitalisation? Well, it meant that I got to sleep with most of Agnes' sisters and friends. She even flew one of her sisters, Edna, who is a nurse, all the way from the Philippines to the UAE to sleep with me! Okay! Now I can imagine that most guys reading this – if they have any red blood in their veins - have at one time or another fancied sleeping with one of their wives' sisters or friends. They may never have done anything about it, and they certainly will not have mentioned this fact to their wives, but for sure they have all had such thoughts at one time or another.

Now, I can imagine all the women reading this turning to their partner and asking if they ever fancied sleeping with one of her sisters or friends. And, of course, all the guys are going to say, "Who, me? Naaaah! Never entered my head". Yeah right!

OK, you get to sleep with all the sisters and friends but there is a downside to all this, especially in my case, as my limbs did not work, I could not get out of bed and nothing – absolutely nothing – was working below the waist. So, it was a pretty safe bet that I could not get up to any fun and frolics – except perhaps in my head!

So, I was lying in bed and nothing was moving. Then, one day just six weeks after the accident, my wife noticed that my big toe on my left foot moved. She said, "Did you do that?" And, yes I had. It was not just an involuntary jerk; I was moving it by instruction from my brain. In actual fact, it was just a tiny, tiny movement. Only a fraction of an inch. But it was a movement nonetheless.

So, we called for my neurosurgeon, Doctor Salloum, and he came and had me move the big toe. Then he brought more doctors and said "Can you move the big toe?" So, I moved my big toe, just a fraction of an inch. But it moved on command and this was apparently a really, really big deal. It was the furthest extremity of the nervous system, from my brain to my toe, and if I could move that, the theory was that eventually I could move everything.

Then the next morning I woke up and I could move all the fingers on my left hand, individually up and down like I was playing the piano. The day before the fingers would not move at all and they were clenched up like a fist. So, something had reconnected on them as well.

As you can imagine, Doctor Salloum was ecstatic about this and called Agnes in for a meeting with him. He told her that, now he had seen these two movements, he was confident that I would recover. Of course, he was not able to say how long it would take and what level of recovery I would achieve, but the movements of my big toe and my hand were really positive signs. Yo!

We were both really happy to hear this, of course, but it was particularly good news for her to hear. I had been telling her from the start that I would be OK and I would walk again – but that was just me telling her – not a neurosurgeon telling her. What did I know? I was just the patient!

Shortly after this, one morning I woke up and something else was stirring. This time it was something stirring under the bed sheets! Luckily (!?!) it was my wife who was in the room with me that morning. Luckily (?) it wasn't one of the sisters or her friends. Well........I guess that's debatable, but we will never know!!

"Ness, come over here and put your hand under the covers!" I said.

"What for?" she queried.

"Never mind, "What for?" Just come over here quickly and put your hand under the covers." I replied.

So, she came and did what I asked. And straight away a huge smile came over her face . . .!!!

I can tell you now, that within 24 hours, everyone in the world knew I had had an erection!!! It was on Facebook, Emails, Twitter and SMS etc. etc. etc. You name it, she sent out the message on it!

I am probably lucky that she was not into Instagrams . . . And you ought to be thankful that I was not into Selfies!

12

HOW TO CONQUER THE WORLD

It was while lying in bed at the Al Noor Hospital Step-Down Unit that I first had the idea of writing this book. At the time I had absolutely no idea, of course, what I would write about or what style of book it would be. That concept would come slowly as time went by, but I have always liked writing and enjoy giving a story an amusing twist wherever I can.

I am not quite sure when I started writing for public consumption, but one of the first things I had "published" was a monthly newsletter called "The Barfine" for the Nomads Rugby Club in Manila way back in September 1987.

"Published" is in parenthesis as it was actually a couple of pages of typing, with a few pictures stuck on for good measure, which were faxed to all the rugby team members. But I did have a compendium of all the issues bound in a red leather hardback cover, so I guess you could say I am already a published author. (Ha!)

But, back to this book. My brain was working at a million miles an hour. Well, it's easy to do that when 75% of your body is incapacitated and my brain had much less to do since it didn't have to figure out how to move my limbs or any other multiple coordinative actions. On the basis that writing the book was the easy bit – ha! – I started to figure out how I could promote it. Who would buy it? What was my target audience, or at least how would I get sales going?

Of course, the answer was the rugby community as I have been involved in rugby for forty years and I know rugby people all over the world!

I started playing rugby in 1976 in Kenya with Nondescripts RFC, then went to the Philippines where I joined Manila Nomads RFC and played in senior rugby and vets and was on the Nomads Rugby Section Committee. I lived in the Philippines for twenty-seven years and was involved in playing in and organising the Manila 10s from its inception till the time I left the Philippines in January 2007. At that point I had been the Executive Director of the Philippine Rugby Football Union (PRFU) and the Tournament Manager of the Manila 10s for several years. I also became a qualified IRB referee and was a founder member of the Philippines Referee Society.

When I arrived in the UAE I became a member of the Harlequins RFC in Abu Dhabi and was a founder member of the Arabian Potbellies/Dubai Sharks. I have played in the UAERA Second Division Conference and subsequently in Vets Rugby. I have been a player in the Dubai 7s, a Fixtures Secretary and a Tournament Manager for the Arabian Potbellies. In addition, I was on the committees for the Abu Dhabi Harlequins and then the Arabian Potbellies. Plus, I was a Junior Rugby Coach for Quins and a qualified referee in the UAE Rugby Referees Society. That's a long rugby pedigree.

Consequently, in those forty years, I have built up a huge network of rugby contacts all across South East Asia, Asia, the Middle East, Africa, Austral-Asia, Europe, UK, and the USA. Some of these were presidents of Unions, which like the PRFU, were members of the Asian Rugby Football Union (ARFU) and others were Club Captains and players of teams that I had dealt with when they participated in the Manila 10s or teams that I have played against in Manila, the UAE or when touring.

Naturally, over time, this web spreads as virtually all the players are part of the international expatriate community who move from country to country as they change jobs. So, it is a huge, ever-expanding network of people that I know, or who know me or, at least, know of me.

The target audience was just an idea at that point in time, but I was soon to find out how real and effective the rugby community network actually was and I will tell you more about that in the coming chapters.

I wanted to have some visual way of seeing how far my rugby network spread – or at least the first level of the network. So, I got Joanne in the Orascom office to print out a map of the World for me and have it mounted on a polystyrene board so I could put it up on the wall. My idea was to put lots of different coloured pins in it wherever I had a rugby contact. I could not actually do this myself so I got Kyle (then ten years old) and Colby (then six years old) to stick all the pins in the various countries. This was actually a fun and educational thing to do between us as I would lie in bed and tell them which country I wanted the pin in and then they would have to find it.

When people came in the room they invariably asked what were the map and all the pins for. I jokingly used to call it my "Map of How to Conquer the World". It was always a great talking point and it was really good for me to see it every day as somehow it inspired me to think that I could write the book and in a small sense at least, "Conquer the World".

TSB - Ready for World Domination

Also, having the map on the wall motivated me to start the process of gathering book material. I had two white boards in the room and when something happened I would get one of the nurses or one of the kids to make a note on it to remind me; then when it was full I got someone to take a photo of it. Also, Arthur Bell from the Arabian Potbellies bought me a Sony digital voice recorder. I used it to record what had happened the day before when I was having my daily Occupational Therapy sessions as I could talk while sitting at a desk and doing things with my hands. Luckily, Agnes also loves taking pictures and videos and posting them on my Facebook page – *TSB-Trevor Stott-Briggs (Trevor at Rugby)* - so I had tons of good information to utilise and refer to as memory jerkers.

But, when I saw the picture of me sitting in front of the map it made me think of Peter Sellers in the 1964 movie "*Dr. Strangelove or: How I Learned to Stop Worrying and Love the Bomb*". It's a fabulously funny spoof, directed by Stanley Kubrick. It's a political satire, a black comedy that highlights people's fears of a nuclear conflict during the Cold War period when the US and Russia were constantly threatening each other with the relative power of each other's military might. Peter Sellers plays three characters in the movie – Dr. Strangelove, who was an ex-Nazi "mad scientist", the President of the USA, and a Royal Air Force officer.

The reason that picture of me and the world map reminds me of the movie? Well, Dr. Strangelove is crippled and in a wheelchair. He has a problem with his right hand as it seems to have a mind of its own and he can't control it. His right hand is always locking closed or trying to strangle him or shooting up into the "Heil Hitler" salute. That picture of me in front of the map was taken when I was sitting in my wheelchair and my right hand had a problem and I had trouble making it do things properly on command from my brain. Fortunately, it has not tried to strangle me yet!

Have a look at this scene where Dr. Strangelove is sitting in front of a map of the world in the War Room of the US Government explaining his "good idea" to the President (also played by Sellers) of how they can select people to be saved from the bomb and how they can live at the bottom of mineshafts for about a hundred years. Remember, this was a 1964 spoof but it's now certain that many of these ideas were considered in "Doomsday" scenarios. Sellers is brilliant in this.

CUE YOUTUBE VIDEO: DR. STRANGELOVE OR: HOW I LEARNED TO STOP WORRYING AND LOVE THE BOMB
PETER SELLERS & GEORGE C. SCOTT

But, getting back to the book. I had the map of "How to Conquer the World" but my hands did not actually function. So, how was I going to write the damn book? The answer was masking tape, rubber bands and splints. The masking tape and rubber bands were used to tape a fat Pentel Pen between my thumb and my first finger so that I could write stuff on paper.

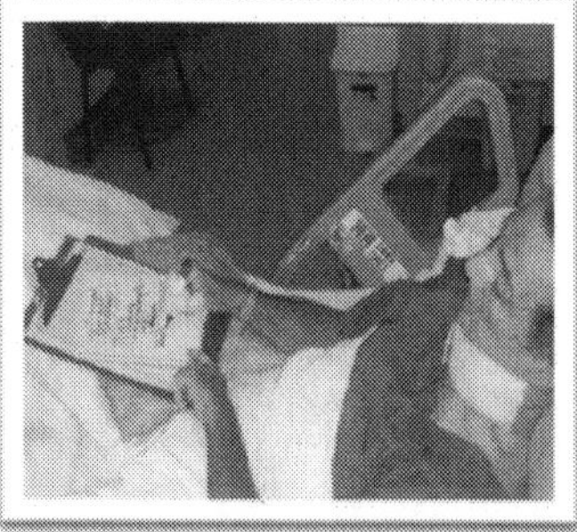

Learning to Write - Again

My wrist flexibility was virtually non-existent (it's not much better even now) so the paper had to be attached to a clip board which I could place on a cushion at an angle so that my words could follow the lines. Of course, at that rate of writing I was never going to get through 100,000 to 110,000 words of a book. So, the next thing was to figure out how I could use my laptop computer even though my fingers and wrists did not respond to my brain's instructions.

And the answer was - specially tailored hand/wrist splints. To do one finger typing – which is the way I typed before and am still doing today as I write this chapter – I needed to hold all my digits in specific positions. The thumb had to be sticking out to the side of the hand, the first finger had to be pointing down and the other three fingers had to be lifted up straight, out of the way of the keyboard. Finally, my wrist had to be slightly flexed back. The end result of all these conflicting design requirements are the two moulded splints that you can see in the picture. They looked like paddles but they really worked.

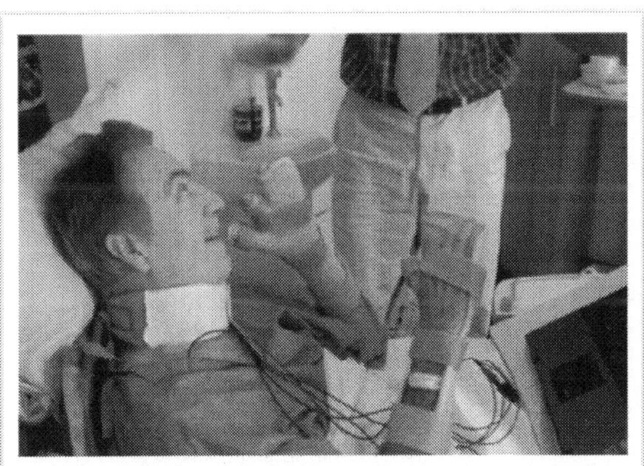

TSB with Splints a.k.a. Edward Scissorhands

The strange thing was that, after having the splints made and getting my laptop set up on an IKEA sloping platform, I still could not actually turn on the computer by myself. Really!

The on button was at the top left of the keyboard below the screen and the muscles in my arm did not have enough strength to push the button down when at full stretch. I had to ask someone else to do it! That's how much muscle strength and coordination I had lost in just a few weeks in hospital.

But at least I could type once the computer was fired up. It was VERY, VERY slow, letter by letter, but I was really feeling good, just being able to do it at all.

And I mean, feeling good . . .

CUE YOUTUBE VIDEO: FEELING GOOD
MICHAEL BUBLE

13

JUST TOO BUSY BEING FABULOUS

I always like the old adage "If you want something doing, ask a busy person." Watch any movie with an American diner and there is usually one waitress serving 20 tables. The opposite of this is when you go into an empty, haute cuisine restaurant and can't get any service from several waiters who are doing nothing and the food takes forever to come.

I think my wife Agnes is like that - a busy person I mean, not an idle one. She has a full time job as an Onboarding Officer with a Government Agency, helping new employees to settle in at work, to find their houses, choose schools for kids, and a myriad other things that someone new to the UAE needs. She has also twice been the Chairman of the Philippine Business Council which assists Filipino companies and individuals to do business in UAE. Note that there was none of the namby pamby, politically correct "Chairperson" title for her. It said "Chairman" on her PBC business card. So, there! On top of "just" these things she is also a qualified style consultant and interior designer.

Amazingly, she also finds time to be a great mother to three kids - and me too - as she reckons I am the fourth kid! And, of course I added a teensy weensy bit of extra load when I had my accident and she had to do double duty as a nurse on top of all the other things she was doing.

But all that hard work paid off in April 2011 as she received the "Woman of Substance! Award from *Illustrado Magazine.* It's an annual event giving recognition to Filipinas who have contributed significantly to the betterment of others or have achieved something extraordinary.

CUE ILLUSTRADO MAGAZINE: WOMAN OF SUBSTANCE
AGNES AQUINO STOTT-BRIGGS

One of the opening paragraphs in the Illustrado article says:

Agnes is one of those rare 'superwomen' who seem to be able to juggle managing a family, a beautiful home (with interiors done by herself and maintained without any fulltime household help), property leasing and expat relocations with personalized service, team supervision, social and networking events for the PBC, the International Business Women's Group, Expat Woman and various other clubs, throwing fabulous parties in her home, pursuing continued professional education to follow her dream, all the while always looking elegant and immaculately put together, without so much as breaking a sweat.

Agnes - Woman of Substance

And this is really true! Of course, the boys and I were all very proud of her achievement but the sad bit for me was that I could not actually go to the big event where they did the presentation. It's a huge ballroom bash with red carpet interviews and photos as you arrive, onstage presentations and "chat show" style conversations with guests and awardees. So, I sent the boys as my surrogates and then prepared a surprise for Agnes!

To make up for not being there myself I did a video. We recorded it in my room at the Al Noor on a digital camera and I sent it up to the Illustrado team just before the show. Agnes did not know anything about it and she was apparently very emotional when they ran it up on the big screen. Well, what else could I do?

CUE YOUTUBE VIDEO: TSB SPEECH
AGNES - WOMAN OF SUBSTANCE AWARD

Naturally, there is a flip side to this too. Every now and then – like everyone in the world – Agnes will overstretch things and take on a huge challenge or responsibility for the PBC or sometimes the Philippine Ambassador to the UAE and then the kids (or I) start asking "When is Mum coming home?" It's the usual thing with kids, when the parent is on top of them they want their own "space". As soon as the parent is missing they start asking for them. So, when this happens we have the joke thing that Mum is "Just too busy being fabulous . . ."

CUE YOUTUBE MUSIC VIDEO: EAGLES
TOO BUSY BEING FABULOUS:

Of course, this was just our family joke and, in reality, she was – and still is - always there for me and the boys. I guess we are just lucky that we can't change the fact that she is truly "fabulous".

Agnes and Three Boys of Substance - Colby, Kyle & James

An anecdotal story in relation to this came out just recently. One of the expatriate new joiners at Agnes' office had a problem with his landlord and she – as usual – managed to fix it. Then the guy said to her "No wonder they nicknamed you the 'Pitbull'!" Then he realised his gaffe and said "Oops, sorry. Maybe I shouldn't have let that out of the bag."

Agnes came home and told me the story and had taken it as a compliment but she did not actually realise what a Pitbull was. But the words sounded good to her. So, I explained that a Pitbull Terrier was actually one of the world's most ferocious dogs and that in some countries they are banned and you cannot have them as pets. They were originally bred as fighting dogs and can lock their jaws once they get hold of something. None of this seemed to faze Agnes, quite the contrary, she felt more complimented as I told her more about the Pitbull. She obviously liked the idea of having a reputation for being ferocious . . .!

So, Pitbull, Corporate Business Woman, Fashionista or Family Mother - take your pick. Sometimes, like British weather, we get all four seasons in one day!

Pitbull, Businesswoman, Fashionista, Mother – Take Your Pick

But, whichever version it is, we all love her and she is never too busy to be fabulous . . .

POST SCRIPT

And just to prove another point about her being busy, in October 2015 she decided, virtually single-handedly, that she would set up a new organization to promote the empowerment of Filipinas. So, she started the Philippine Women International Network (PWIN) in Abu Dhabi and has held networking meetings with many Filipinas of all ages and backgrounds. She would be really happy to have many more Filipinas join and ultimately wants PWIN to spread around the world.

CHECK THE PWIN FACEBOOK PAGE

But, as if all the above accolades were not enough, in October 2015, Illustrado did a special issue of the magazine called *100 Most Influential Filipinos in the Gulf*, showing that Filipinos in general have made a huge contribution to the development of this region and some have really excelled. There are over 3 million of them in the region and they have been active in many fields. So, it made us even prouder that Agnes was nominated into that top 100 and actually appears twice, on page 41 as Chairman of the Philippine Business Council and on page 96 as herself.

LINK TO ILLUSTRADO MAGAZINE – SPECIAL ISSUE

The Cover Says it All

1 in 3 Million - What a Girl!

What more can I say? She really is just too busy being fabulous . . .

14

YOU HAVE MY SUPPORT . . .

There are two types of support. One is the financial or emotional kind and the other is the one that sportsmen wear to protect their crown jewels (a.k.a a Jockstrap). Luckily, I got a lot of the former during my hospitalisation and later when having in-patient physiotherapy. Undoubtedly, because I had my accident while actually playing rugby, there was a huge positive connection to the rugby community. When the accident happened in February 2011, I had already been in the UAE four years and was very heavily involved in the rugby scene here. So, between Kenya, UK, Philippines and UAE I had a very large network of rugby people that I knew and who knew me

As a result, every rugby club in the UAE had some sort of fund-raising activity for me. Plus there were contributions from the UAE Referees Society, the Manila Nomads and several individual donations. The outpouring of support was amazing, and a real "life saver".

The money they raised was really needed and put to very good use as my medical insurance provider decided that their policy did not cover my physiotherapy costs. They paid for my initial hospitalisation and the operation on my neck, but they conveniently classed my physiotherapy as "rehabilitation" which they said was not covered by their policy. As you can imagine, I had many communications and arguments with them about this very grey area. Where does "providing a medical solution" end and "rehabilitation" begin? For me, people who have a stiff elbow or a sore shoulder need rehabilitation. I needed a medical solution to my injuries. Fixing my neck with a titanium brace was only part of that process. If I had stopped there I would still be totally paralyzed, a quadriplegic who would be bedridden for the rest of my life, needing full time nursing care to lift me in and out of bed, bath, toilet, and wheelchair. All of that would cost much more in terms of medical attendance than if I worked hard at my PT and OT and got my body functioning again - at least as much as possible, if not totally 100% working.

The in-patient care and PT/OT at the Rochester cost over Dhs 33,000 equivalent to US$9,000 per month. That really burns up money, and I was there for nearly two years! When I started at the Rochester we had fully expected that I would be able to claim back most of the expenses so that the money raised by the rugby community would keep rolling over and only deplete slowly. But that was not to be.

Fortunately, that money did make a huge difference and one of the biggest fund raising events was a Touch Rugby Tournament organised by the Abu Dhabi Harlequins at Zayed Sports City on 15 April, 2011. That was actually the first time I had been out of the confines of the Al Noor Hospital.

Poster Boy

It was a brilliant day for me. The weather was perfect, with the sun shining but not too hot. Lots of teams turned up and they had six half-pitches running continuously all afternoon. Quins had set the rules such that it had to be a mixed team. Seven players on the pitch at any one time but one of them had to be female and one had to be a junior – younger than sixteen. So, Kyle (then 10) and James (then 15) played for the Potbellies team and it was great for me to watch them playing in amongst the adults.

Kyle, in particular, used his small size and quick side-step to great advantage as he could easily dodge bigger, lumbering senior players. In a race for the line he was also pretty quick and again could out-pace many of the men. Generally, the only ones that could catch him were the sixteen to eighteen year old players because they had much longer legs!

Arabian Potbellies Touch Rugby Team - With TSB and Family

The funny thing is that, after writing the paragraph above, I then looked at the picture I have inserted and just realised how small Kyle was back then. He was only just about as big as me when I was sitting down (and leaning back) in the wheelchair! I was subconsciously thinking of him playing at the size he is now (at fifteen years old) and as tall as me.

One of the highlights of the day was when I was sitting in my wheelchair behind the try line watching the Potbellies play. They were on the attack and got to within about five metres of the try line but the opposition had a solid defensive line. Someone passed the ball to Kyle, he side-stepped one player, ran sideways around another, and then dodged in between two players to score a try right at my feet! Lovely! Don't they make you feel proud when they can do something like that?

I think Quins raised over Dhs 200,000 – about US$ 55,000 - that day and it was really good fun for everyone. That was a huge help.

A few months later, in August 2011, the Potbellies had a fundraiser at the Jebel Ali Shooting Club in Dubai. That was another big fun day, made even better by the fact that my eldest son, Elliott, had come to UAE from Australia to see me, so he could join in too. It was a knock out competition to see who was the best shot and cup winner. Amazingly, James did really, really well. He had never shot a real gun before but – like all kids his age - had spent plenty of time shooting things and people in video games like Call of Duty, Black Ops, etc. Well, it paid off! He got to the final and it was a target shoot-out between James and one of the Potbelly players who was ex-SAS and had obviously spent a lot of time holding guns and shooting – including probably shooting at real people rather than just video game ones! Sad to say James lost, but coming second to that guy was a great achievement. Well done that kid!

Lock & Load - Jebel Ali Shooting Club - TSB Fundraiser

Another cool one that happened in July 2012 was a sort of bench press marathon. Paul Gandy - former SAS, Paras or something similarly military and tough - set himself up to do as many bench presses as he could in a set time. Have a look at the poster below. He was sponsored by members of the Arabian Potbellies RFC and many other friends on a how-many-reps-could-he-achieve-before-he-collapsed basis.

I don't know what the final count was, but it was way more than the target, and he raised a chunk of cash to help pay my medical bills. Great!

Me Tarzan, You Jane. Ugh!

There were many other fundraisings done by the rugby clubs in the UAE, Philippines and elsewhere and I don't have space to describe them all. But I can tell you it's a wonderful heart-warming feeling when all those clubs, teams, and people lavish their support on you.

It reminds me of the regular banter between Ian, the Chief Engineer, and Ken, the Chief Architect, in the office of my first job in 1967 at the Engineer's Department of Skipton Urban District Council. They would often argue the merits of the design of something and whether one of them would back up the other when they went to a Town Council Meeting to get the project approved.

The common retort from Ken at the end of one of these inter-discipline discussions would be "Ian, you have my support. Wear it always!"

15

GLEE ON THE GOGGLEBOX

Eventually, on the 22nd of April 2011, the doctors at the Al Noor Hospital said that I could go home for the first time for the weekend. Talk about a "Get Out of Jail Card"! It was wonderful – after almost 2 months in the Al Noor - just to be in my own home surrounded by the family and all my own personal things instead of being in the clinical atmosphere of the hospital. It was party time at last . . .

If you a reading the E-Book and have the colour version of the photo below you will see that red is a predominant colour in our house. If you are reading the hard copy book with black and white photos, you will just have to believe me on this point. Whether it is for furniture, cushions, carpets, walls, kitchen units, candles or anything else, red features a lot. And I mean A LOT. It's Agnes' favourite colour by a huge margin.

Her other favourite colours are black and white. She has more pairs of black trousers and white shirts than I do. No joke. I always believe that colour choices are very much based on character and in the case of Agnes the linkage works perfectly. She is a very "Black" and "White" person. There are no "Grey" areas in her personality. Things are either on or off, never just possibly. The answer is either yes or no, never maybe. It's either good or bad, never just okay.

But red is definitely her "angry" colour. It has always amused me that whenever we had an argument she would go out and buy something red. Like a pair of red shoes or a red dress or red handbag. Once, back in Manila before we were married, we had a HUGE argument and I mean HUMONGOUS. We split up for a while and that meant I took back the car I had been lending her. So, what did she do? She went out and bought her own car to prove a point. It was a red car, of course . . .

So, I am not sure if a house full of red furniture and accessories means we have had a lot of arguments since we have been married. I think I will have to "Claim the Fifth Amendment" on that one! But when I rolled out of the big van-taxi and into the house in my wheelchair I was metaphorically "hit" by the mass of colour – after the monochromatic hospital room - and it was a lovely warm feeling to be home again.

I could not do much of course – I either sat in the wheelchair and sang Karaoke with Colby or just lay on the sofa watching TV. It actually took 3 guys - James, Garry (Agnes' brother) and a friend of ours, Spencer Hughes - to lift me out of the wheelchair and on to the sofa. So, once I was there I stayed there. Talk about being a couch potato . . .!

TSB & Colby - Singing Karaoke

I had heard a lot of hype about the TV series Glee but I had never seen it as, before the accident, I did not spend that much time watching the gogglebox. Anyway, as I was flicking through the channels I spotted it and started watching. For anyone "living under a rock" or "in't shoe box in't middle of road" between 2011 and 2015, the show is centred around a bunch of American kids in the High School Glee Club. They sing lots of current songs and have dance numbers etc. etc., have romances, fights, get pregnant, realise they are lesbians or gay and get verbally abused by the Sports Mistress but are never seen actually doing any academic lessons. They even have a kid in a wheelchair who can sing, play the guitar and "dance" better than most sixteen-year-olds with working legs. In other words, a typical day at any school in the world!

Actually, it was the Series 1 Pilot and "that episode" when they sang the song that became their first big chart hit. That song was *Don't Stop Believin'*. . .

I tell you, I was in tears!!!!!!!

I knew the song, of course, but had not heard it for years and years – and the band Journey, who did the original version - were in their "decline" period at the time too.

I listened to it and it just fitted me exactly. Exactly. I have replayed that song over and over in my mind so many times since first hearing their rendition of it. The theme behind the song is that it doesn't matter how tough the situation is, just don't stop believing in yourself and you will be able to achieve your goals. So, it's really become an "anthem" for me and my efforts to recover and walk again. Just listen to the Glee version and you will see what I mean.

CUE YOUTUBE VIDEO: DON'T STOP BELIEVIN' – GLEE

This song was also very inspirational in making me want to write this book – which I hope will help others in some small way. You will see it appearing several times in the book in different versions sung by different people. But, whoever sings it, the same feeling seems to come out of it. It's just one of those songs . . .

I was a bit sad to leave the house on Saturday night as I had to go back to Al Noor ready for another week bright and early on Sunday morning. But it was so good to have been home for a couple of days. And even better to know I would get another "Get out of Jail Card" next Thursday night.

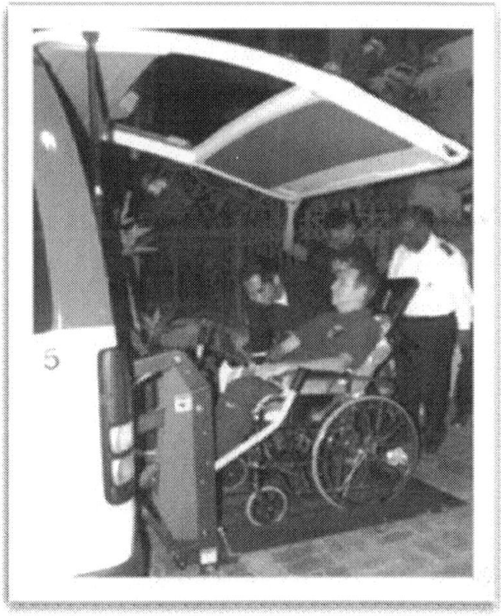

And at the End of the Weekend – Back to "Jail" I Go

16

NOSTALGIA ISN'T WHAT IT USED TO BE

I had not seen my only sister Lynn for about fourteen years. We are a somewhat disparate family (I said disparate, not desperate), particularly in terms of where we live. Some families cluster around the same area all their lives while others seem to want to "get out of Dodge" as soon as they can. We definitely fall into the second category.

My sister Lynn now lives in North Carolina, USA, where she is a teacher. But in June 1975, straight after University and Teacher Training College, she and John Pickles got married, left UK and went to South Africa to live for several years before moving to the States.

I left UK in 1976, stayed six and a half years in Kenya and then lived twenty seven years in the Philippines, while working in 30 different countries around the world. And, since January 2007, I have lived in the Middle East in the United Arab Emirates. My eldest son, Elliott, was born in UK, grew up in the Philippines, did his high school in California and now lives in Brisbane, Australia, which is about as far away as anyone can sensibly get. My next son, James, is now at university in UK. So, you can see that we are all over the place, geographically speaking.

This was part of the reason that I had not seen my sister for about fourteen years before I had my accident. There was also a contributory factor of a family argy-bargy – but we will dust that under the carpet as it's long gone.

But when she heard about my accident, as soon as her school closed for Spring Break in mid-March 2011, Lynn came "hot-footing it" over to Abu Dhabi to see me. Naturally, the boys were really excited to meet their – almost fictional – Auntie Lynn. But the most amusing one was Colby. Now, by coincidence (what?), Colby and Lynn have the same birthday – 4th March – so I was expecting some affinity. But I was not prepared for how much they instantly bonded. The night she arrived, Agnes and the boys went to pick her up at the airport and then brought her straight to the Al Noor Hospital to see me. It turned out that Colby had monopolised Lynn in the car and then when they arrived in my room she sat on a chair near the foot of the bed while we chatted. But Colby was all over her! He was lying over her lap, sitting at her feet, holding her hand, trying to get her attention and so on and so on. You name it he did it!

And he continued to do those things the whole time she was with us in the UAE.

Lynn has always been very good at keeping in contact with lots of people – old school friends, former work colleagues, people from wherever she has lived and, particularly, our family relatives. So, when she was in Abu Dhabi it was a constant updating for me about who had done what with whom back in our hometown of Nelson. And there were lots and lots of surprises in that.

You might think that a little town like Nelson - population 29,000 - in the heartland of industrial Lancashire, would be quiet and deadly boring. But, no! It's a veritable combination of *Peyton Place*, the *Bold and the Beautiful* and *Desperate Housewives* all played out in a setting just like *Coronation Street.* I would be surprised if you have never heard of any of these soap operas – you would have had to be living under a rock not to have heard of at least one of them – but, just in case, there is a short explanation for each of them in the Glossary. Actually, Nelson is really a lot more like *Haddock & Plaice, The Bald and the Bountiful,* and *Desperate Scousewives.* Almost every street in the town has terraced houses, a corner shop on one end of the street and some have a pub on the other. So it's like *Coronation Street Ad-Infinitum.*

Five Soap Operas - From the Sublime to the Ridiculous:

Peyton Place + The Bold and the Beautiful

+ Desperate Housewives + Coronation Street

+ Desperate Scousewives

Here is a special clip from Coronation Street so you get a feel for the show and you can imagine the backdrop of Nelson – terraced houses and smoky chimneys - and the goings-on there. But listen to the original theme tune and credits from 1960 – when I was eleven years old (!) - and a bit of classic Ena Sharples, one of the stars for many years, who was very caustic and always wore a hairnet . . .

CORONATION STREET - THEME TUNE (1960)

ENA SHARPLES – IN THE CORNER SHOP

But to get back to the story. Nelson was always a "lively" place even when I lived there. By lively I mean people seemed to be hopping in and out of the sack on a fairly regular basis. I will, of course, have to "Claim the Fifth Amendment" again on this. But, come on, it was the so-called "Swinging Sixties" where freedom had been granted to let your testosterone run rampant, the Pill had just been invented and no one knew about Herpes and Aids. Or if they did, no one talked about them. Plus, being gay was someone in a happy mood. So, you could have "Fun, Fun, Fun till her daddy took her T-cells away" to misquote a line from an early 60s Beach Boys song. Let's say, at the time, ignorance was bliss!

As I mentioned earlier I always had a companion sleeping in the hospital room with me, so one night Lynn took a turn. It became the "Nelson Nostalgia Night" as we stayed awake till the early hours of the morning telling "catch up stories". We even had a big slide show from her computer onto the room TV. It was fantastic as we had both gone to the same schools and we were only five years apart so we both know a lot of the same people from school and on the social scene.

The great thing about that visit was that it really made Lynn and I close again – as we had been when we were young. She now phones me on a regular basis and we communicate almost daily by email and Facebook. And, she has been very involved in helping me with this book, particularly by doing all the initial proof reading and making some suggestions here and there about things to highlight or otherwise. She deserves a really big THANK YOU for all the hard yards she has put in on this. It's great to have someone who is a teacher checking your work. You just keep hoping that there won't be too much metaphoric red ink on the pages and that you can get 10/10 for effort.

This photo below was taken in early April 2011 when I went home again from hospital for the weekend. We had a real family party and it was wonderful for us to be together after so many years. Lynn is on the back row, right side and Will the dog is at the front – the rest of the usual suspects appear all through this book.

The Bold and the Beautiful - Lynn and the TSB Clan (plus the dog, Will)

Besides believing in yourself, if I can add one piece of advice to everyone reading this book, it is not to let a stupid argy-bargy keep you apart from other people in your family. Remember what Forrest Gump said about "Laif" and not knowing "what you're gonna get". If something does happen – and maybe it's worse than what happened to me – then you might not get to see that person again. Believe me, it's not worth it in the end and you will regret all those "missed" years without them.

Whatever it is about birth signs and astrology, there is a really strong between Lynn and Colby. So, ever since she left, Colby has been nattering to go to "Ameerricah" to see her. We are always joking with him that he has a British father, a British passport, goes to a British school but he speaks with an "Ameerricahn" accent. How come?

I forgot to say this earlier, but I was also very pleased that Lynn and Agnes got on really well as – before Lynn's trip to the UAE – they had also never met each other. I had married Agnes and "somehow" developed a whole new section of family in the intervening years.

I did say at the beginning of this chapter that it was a long time since I had seen Lynn!!!

17

WELL, GOODNESS GRACIOUS ME!

Lynn had been very good at keeping me entertained while she was in the UAE, so I was very sad when she had left Abu Dhabi and gone back to the States. It went sort of quiet at the Al Noor as things settled back into a routine. The big problem was that I was not active as I could not move many of my muscles, so they were wasting away. And it was really noticeable that I was getting skinnier and skinnier as the muscles, particularly in my legs, were melting off me.

It made me think of Tom Hanks in the movie Philadelphia and the Bruce Springsteen song of the same name. In the movie, Tom is a young lawyer who gets Aids and is terminated from the law firm that he works for. But he takes them to court for wrongful dismissal and he looked thinner and thinner as the movie progressed. It's a very poignant video with short scenes from the movie mixed with Springsteen's song.

CUE YOUTUBE VIDEO: PHILADELPHIA
TOM HANKS + BRUCE SPRINGSTEEN SONG

I was not quite so bad but there was very little meat on my bones. Thankfully, for me, it was just muscle atrophy due to lack of usage and, although it was serious, it was not terminal.

So, I was really happy when, eventually, in early May 2011, Dr. Salloum said that I had stabilised and could be discharged and start full-scale treatment of my paralysed lower half and my spastic upper half. Sounds wonderful, yes? To do this I would need to be an in-patient at a clinic where they could give me Physiotherapy (PT) and Occupational Therapy (OT) several times a day, every day. But, and there is always a "but", there was no such clinic in Abu Dhabi. I could only get out-patient treatment in Abu Dhabi. So, this meant that I had to find a place that would accept me in Dubai. That turned out to be the Rochester Wellness Centre, which was then located in Al Safa 2 in between Sheik Zayed Road and Al Wasl Road.

In mid-May 2011, I finally got out of "jail". Well, the Al Noor Hospital was not really a jail but when you have been in the same hospital room for two and a half months, getting out of it feels like getting out of jail. Unfortunately, that was not the end of it for me. I was really transferring from one jail to another. Though, to be fair, The Rochester Wellness Centre was much less like a hospital and more like a small hotel/spa – at least that's how it looked from the outside as it had originally been designed as a guest house/hotel. So, maybe it was more like getting out of a maximum security facility and into an "open" prison where the inmates are allowed to wander around outside in the gardens.

I had done my "porridge" and was now supposed to be in the open prison on "good behaviour". Actually, the Rochester was a really nice place. It had twenty two rooms, a well-maintained garden – including a gazebo – and a swimming pool. The rooms were more like hotel rooms and mine was on the front of the building looking out onto the garden. Well, the windows looked out on the garden even if I was not able to stand up and see out myself! The PT gym and the OT room were out in the garden so I had to be trundled along the path in a wheelchair to get to my PT and OT sessions every day. But at least I got some fresh air and could pass the time of day with the other inmates – sorry patients - when we bumped into each other along the path!

When you are in "jail" it's the little things help you get through each day. This is actually the theme of one of the best-ever, British TV comedy series' called *Porridge,* starring Ronnie Barker as *Fletcher* and Richard Beckinsale as *Godber.* Fletcher was the "old lag" who tries to teach all the tricks to Godber the naïve, newly imprisoned, first offender to help him get through his sentence at HMP Slade. Have a look at this clip of their first day in prison.

CUE YOUTUBE: PORRIDGE
RONNIE BARKER AND RICHARD BECKINSALE

In case you are not aware, when Fletcher talks about adding something to the tea, he is referring to Bromide which is supposed to reduce male sex drive. I guess one of the major differences between HMP Slade and HMP Rochester is that in one you get porridge for breakfast every day – that being a hot oatmeal and milk breakfast cereal - and in the other I got muesli - that being a cold oatmeal, fruit and yoghurt breakfast. Oh, and I was careful only to drink tea that had been made straight from the packet without anyone adding Bromide to it. OK?

The opening title shot of the TV series Porridge at the door of HMP Slade

A shot of the front door opening for TSB's Muesli at HMP Rochester

What I did not know in May 2011 was that I was going to be at the Rochester for about two years. Almost eighteen months as an in-patient and six months as an all-day, out-patient! Although I did not realise how long I would be there I decided on Day One that I would try to make my stay there as enjoyable as I could by having some fun with the staff and other patients.

Physiotherapy at the Rochester started very slowly. By that I don't mean it took them a few days before they did anything to me – far from it. The first morning there, my daily schedule started with a bang. OK, maybe it was more of a whimper – from me - as I felt the first difficulties of trying to make my body work again. Trying is the exact word because in most cases my body did not do what my brain was telling it to do. When you realise that, it's a very strange feeling.

The first PT sessions started in my room on my bed. Often, this required two physios in attendance as I needed a lot of supervision and assistance. I can remember that, for a long time, the bed exercise that I hated the most was the one where I was laid on my back and was told to push my knee downwards onto the physio's hand that was under it. Honestly, when you have legs that work normally, this is really, really easy. But my quadriceps muscles had lost all their power in the preceding three months of inactivity. So, it was incredibly hard for me to move my knees in a downward direction and push onto the hand below it. It was like going NNNNNnnnnnnnaaaaaaaargh and using my entire body to try and create a downward force on the physio's hand – to no effect whatsoever! Herrruuumph!

The two physios that tried to do these things with me in the beginning were both Indian – from Kerala, naturally. One of them – Malar – was married to Velu, one of the Indian male physios. She was tiny – you can tell from the picture that I am as tall as her when I am sat down - and she was always dressed in a Rochester uniform. The other one – Kushbu – was tall and always dressed in traditional Indian clothing. I have no idea why! As you can see, I was in the middle and it was a sort of Indian "Push-Me-Pull-You" kind of teamwork by the two ladies. I could never tell whether I was coming or going, kind of like the Pushmi-Pullyu double-headed Llama in the film, *Dr. Doolittle.*

My name is Pushmi
and this is Pullyu

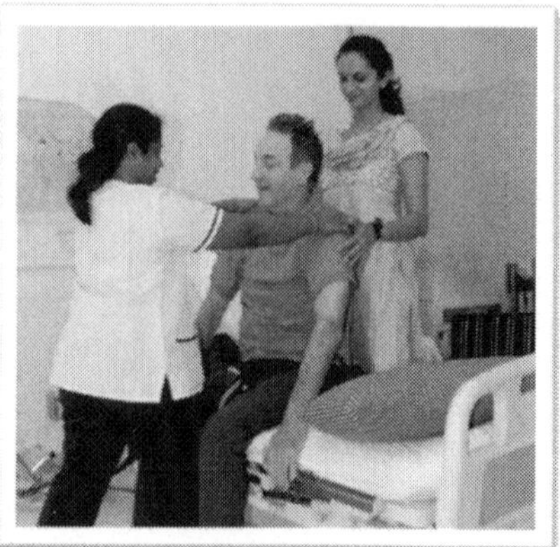

Can we do Push-You-Pull-Me
for a Change?

The other thing that featured in the early PTs was the Tilt Table. What I had not realised till they started me on this contraption was that three months on my back meant that my body had got used to being in a horizontal position. So, when you try to be vertical again the heart has to work harder and, at first, it's not very good at it so you feel dizzy. Very dizzy. As you can see from the picture, the Tilt Table name is appropriate and describes it very well. Basically, it's a flat table with a footrest and several large, wide Velcro straps to hold the patient onto the table.

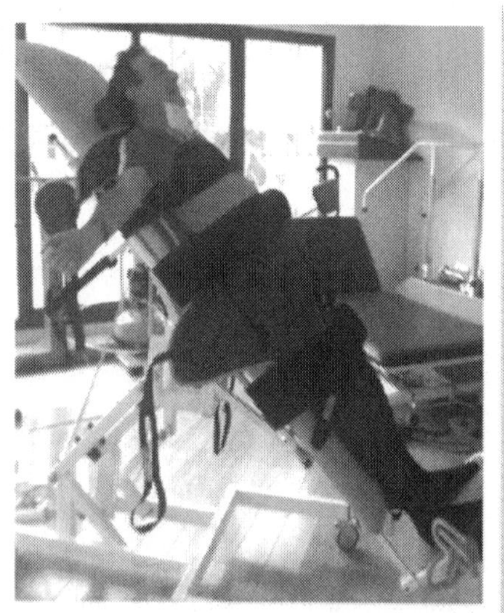

TSB - Taking it Easy on the Tilt Table

The angle of the tilt is fully adjustable. They start off with 10 - 15 degrees up from the horizontal and gradually increase it each session. It takes about 20 – 30 minutes per day for about 7- 10 days to get vertical. As you do this, you need the physio in attendance all the time as the dizziness comes and goes, so sometimes they have to lower the table so that you can quickly recover.

Once they get you vertical, the next stage is to do some basic exercises while you are in that position. These are only simple and easy like opening and closing your arms or doing bicep curls without weights. But it was amazing how quickly I got out of breath and started to feel dizzy again and I could feel my heart beating at what felt like a million beats per minute. It's a real boompety-boom-boompety-boom-boompety-boom-boompety-boomp-boom-boom like in the song *Goodness Gracious Me* by Peter Sellers and Sophia Loren in the 1960s movie *The Millionairess.*

CUE YOUTUBE VIDEO: GOODNESS GRACIOUS ME
PETER SELLERS AND SOPHIA LOREN

The amusing fractal in this is that Sellers was playing an Indian doctor in the movie – the title of the song being a well-known Indian phrase – and here I was at the Rochester surrounded by Indian doctors and physios. Well, goodness gracious me!

Sophia Loren is Italian, and just so you know – if you are less than sixty years old as you read this – she was well-known for having some of the biggest eyes and the biggest Bristol Cities in the movie industry at that time. And it was all natural. None of your face-reshaping plastic surgery and Double D silicone implants for Sophia Loren. Plus, she probably had the world's most naturally pumped-up lips in the pre-Botox era.

Eat your heart out Pamela Anderson - on all three counts!

When you were a pre-pubescent kid, as I was in the early 1960s, the scene where she undresses in the doctor's surgery and brazenly stands there in an hour-glass shaped black corset, stockings and suspenders was imprinted forever in your brain.

Take a look at the next clip to see what I mean.

CUE YOUTUBE VIDEO: THE MILLIONAIRESS
SOPHIA LOREN AND PETER SELLERS

Even now, aged sixty-six, there is a lot more than my heart going boompety-boom-boompety-boom-boompety-boom-boompety-boomp-boom-boom when I watch that clip . . . !! Just take an advance sneak-peek at the picture below just to get you started.

POST SCRIPT

Sophia Loren. One of the top-ten curvaceous, hour-glass figures of all time. Don't talk to me about Baywatch and Pamela who?

Well, Goodness Gracious Me!

18

HOW TO CHOOSE A NURSE

Now, when you are a long-term, full-time in-patient it's very important that you have the right nurse. And you can't wait until the prettiest nurse you've ever seen comes along and then say "I want that one!" You have to have one that works for you. There is, of course, the old Chinese proverb "Man who wants pretty nurse, first must be patient". It's very important to get the right nurse because he's the guy that takes you into the showers washes your balls and wipes your butt. So, you don't want the wrong one!

I was really lucky at the beginning as I had a Filipino nurse called Greggy. He was named after Gregorio Honasan one of the Colonels in the "Rebel" Philippine Army who instigated a number of coups against the Government. Honasan subsequently changed sides and now he's part of that same Government! Anyway, that's life in the Philippines. Greggy was great, he was fantastic. The perfect nurse, just right. A good, smart guy who did everything you wanted. But, he was part of the clinic's administration and they were always trying to get him away from me because he was a senior nurse and they wanted him at the nursing station to help run the clinic. So, they tried to give me lots of different nurses. It was really hard work and I went through about six of them. I mean some of them were too dumb, some of them were too "smart", some were too slow or some of them too fast and some were too gay!

Seriously, you don't want the nurse to enjoy giving you the bed bath more than you enjoy the bed bath! And then when it comes to going to the toilet he is the one has stick the suppository in your butt. Just imagine it . . .

"Sir, I think you need another suppository"

"But that's the third one today!"

"Yes, sir, I think you really need this . . ."

I think he wanted "To boldly go where no-one has gone before" to quote from Star Trek.

So, I kept turning nurses away and the Rochester management was getting really frustrated because it was taking a long time to find one I liked. Then, one day, I was in bed first thing in the morning. I was laid on one side facing Greggy and I suddenly felt a "presence" behind me.

Then, picture this. I was in bed only about two feet off the ground and I rolled over and stared up at this 6'- 2" or 6'- 3" tall person standing there in a blue shirt and blue outfit. He was massive. Now, it's important to remember that at this point in time, it was just after my spinal operation, I was still on a lot of drugs, painkillers, and other things. So I was still quite a little bit spaced out . . . I turned over and I said "What the fuck is Mr. Spock doing in my room!!!!"

This guy looked exactly like "the" Mr. Spock from the Starship Enterprise in the TV series Star Trek. He was Filipino and he'd got the thick black hair with a little fringe. He'd got the short eyebrows. He'd got the long face and he was very tall and slim. He had almost even got the pointy ears!

His name was Chris and, although he looked just like Mr. Spock, he had idea who Mr. Spock was because he was only 20 years old. Unlike me, I'd see the TV series in the late 60s and early 70s. I grew up on Star Trek. I am not a "Trekkie" but Star Trek was in its glory days then and since that time they have come out with several movies to bring it up to date. But Chris hadn't seen any of them so he knew nothing about Star Trek at all. So, all day I was taking the Mickey and joking with him and telling him this and telling him that. Telling him about the "communicator". About being beamed up by Scotty. I was telling him all about Mr. Spock. He was looking at me like I was crazy, but he knew I was on a lot of drugs, so he was taking it all.

Nurse Chris a.k.a Mr. Spock

I asked him how tall his mother was and he said, "About five feet two inches."

"And how tall is your Dad?" I asked. "Oh, about the same . . . five feet two, maybe five feet three," he replied

"Anyone else tall in your family?" I asked. "No just me," he responded.

At this, I told him I reckoned that, before he was born, his mother was abducted by aliens and she was beamed up into a spaceship and taken to the planet Vulcan and there she was impregnated by a Vulcan male. "Okay, so you're half Vulcan, half Filipino!" I said.

Chris was just looking at me like I'm off my head. And the day went on and on like that. Then, at 8 pm he disappeared and about ten minutes later he came back into the room and was changed out of his blue uniform. So, I said "Where are you going Mr. Spock?' And he said that he was going home.

"Why do you have to go now?" I asked.

He had his cell phone in his hand, and just at that moment he flicked open the lid, just like the Communicator on Star Trek and said, "Sorry I have to go now but it's because they are waiting to beam me up to the Starship Dubai Metro . . ."

And immediately I turned to Greggy and said, "That's the guy I want for my nurse!!!" Within one day he was "in the programme". That's how you choose your nurse. He was brilliant. Chris stayed with me for two years and he was fantastic.

Then, about six months later, we were at my house one weekend and the 2009 Star Trek movie started. I said, "Chris we HAVE to watch this". It's the one where they are going back and forth in time and there is the young Spock and Leonard Nimoy, the actor from the original TV series, playing Spock as a much older man, both in the movie together. It's cool.

We sat and watched it all the way through and at the end Chris said, "Now I understand what you were talking about on that first day. At the time I just thought you were going crazy."

CUE YOUTUBE VIDEO: STAR TREK (TRAILER 2009)
CHRIS PINE & LEONARD NIMOY

These were the words spoken at the beginning of each Movie and TV episode by the Captain of the Starship Enterprise:

"Space. The final frontier.
These are the voyages of the Starship Enterprise.
Its continuing mission: To explore strange new worlds.
To seek out new life or new civilisations.
To boldly go where no-one has gone before."

POST SCRIPT

Spock was a central character in the Star Trek TV shows and movies. Because Spock was half-human and half-Vulcan he was used as a means for the writers to examine humanity and what it means to be human. Leonard Nimoy was perfect in his portrayal of Spock. Sadly, he passed away in February 2015 at the age of 83.

RIP Spock – Let's hope we can all "Live long and prosper"

19

RADIO GA-GA

You will already have seen – if you have got this far reading the book and you're not just taking a freebie sneak peek in your local book store – that I have included lots of live internet links to You Tube "MTV" videos of songs that have "mind links" for me. I believe that music has that special ability to give us instant recall to some memory of something that happened in the past. Interestingly, it's usually a memory of something positive or pleasant. It seems that our brains have some sort of positive filter that only allows us to have a recall of something nice when we hear a particular piece of music. It might be a sunny day at the beach when you were a kid or the music that was played at a High School dance when you had your first slow smooch with your "crush".

The funny thing with music is that, for most of the songs that we recall, we don't know the words. Or maybe we just remember the chorus or punch line to the song. But, I have found that for me at least, although I don't "know" the words in my conscious memory, somehow, some part of my subconscious brain decides that I like that song because the words actually have some significance to me.

I figured this out because, when I was lying in bed recovering from my accident, I had plenty of time to listen to music on the radio. And I mean really, really listen. Normally the radio is on and you are doing something else so only your subconscious brain is listening to the song.

Your conscious brain is focussing on whatever it is you are doing. But I am convinced that your subconscious brain takes in and processes those lyrics and links them to some other activity that was going on at the time. Then it makes you feel happy when you hear it again years later.

Like me, right here, right now, I am typing this chapter of the book at around 12:30pm on Friday 13th March 2015. Radio 2 (UAE) is on and Accalia is the presenter. She just played a Barry White song from the mid-1970s which reminded me (or actually it reminded my subconscious brain as my conscious brain was doing the typing) of driving across the Sahara Desert in March 1976 in a Land Creeper with three friends, on an overland trip across Africa.

You might think, Barry White – a huge Afro-American singer with a phenomenally deep and sexy voice – and the Sahara Desert, how can those be linked? Well it's simple. For a few years preceding the trip across Africa I had my own place and I had fitted it out with a fantastic Bang & Olsen sound system - at a time when most people just had a tiny and tinny-sounding record player. Also, I was in a long-term relationship with a fantastic girl called Helen from Manchester. Barry White was "King of the Hill" and I played his music when Helen and I were together at my place. So, when I went on the overland trip – leaving her behind – I recorded a cassette tape (and yes, that was the "hot" technology at the time as iPods were still over 30 years from being invented) with lots of my favourite songs on it. And Barry White with *You Are the First, My Last, My Everything* was one of them and *Love's Theme* was another. Actually, I took a lot of shit from my friends in the Land Creeper as they thought it was very inappropriate. But, I did not care as it brought lots of good memories floating back to me. And, almost forty years later, it still does. That is the power of the subconscious brain.

CUE YOUTUBE VIDEOS: YOU ARE THE FIRST, MY LAST, MY EVERYTHING & LOVE'S THEME – BARRY WHITE

But, going back to me lying in bed recovering. Being in that state meant I was not really doing anything else except listening to the radio and so my brain tended to be more focussed on the music. So, I started to listen properly to the lyrics instead of them just being background sounds. And many of the songs had lyrics that related or moved me in some way.

In particular, this was the era of "The Kenny and Accalia Breakfast Show" on UAE's Radio 2. Kenny is an American with what I would call a mellifluous, soft drawl that reminded me of the voice of a radio presenter called Baby Bob Stewart on the infamous Radio Caroline "Pirate Radio" ship in the mid-1960s. There is now a fun film about it called *The Boat that Rocked* and it has Phillip Seymour Hoffman playing the part of Baby Bob Stewart. Just have a look at the trailer to see what I mean. Magic stuff and absolutely loaded with memories and memorable songs.

These are actually three different trailers for the same movie – but sometimes, on one or other of them, the person who posted them tries to get people to pay for the pleasure of watching them. So it might say "This Video Is Unavailable". It's a bit like the British Government trying to stop people listening to Radio Caroline. Bah! Humbug!

CUE YOUTUBE VIDEO: THE BOAT THAT ROCKED (TRAILER)

The third trailer features interviews with Richard Curtis, the Writer/Director of the movie and some of the stars and they make comments about the great influence that music has on people. I am glad they agree with me . . .

Note that the trailers feature the song *Gimme Some Loving*' by the Spencer Davis Group that I wrote about in Chapter 6 – THUNDER ROAD. See how this stuff just keeps popping up again and again!!! TINSTAAC???

And then there is Accalia. She is a Brit with a great sense of humour – as long as you like yours served on the sharp edge of a scimitar – and a fabulous, deep laugh that just rolls out over the radio waves. And when you put Kenny and Accalia together, as they were on the Radio 2 Breakfast Show, the synergy was brilliant. Definitely, two plus two equals five. They were on the air from 6am to 10am every day and it was always a fun-filled few hours with lots of stories, competitions, listener phone-in slots where they joked about all sorts of things. But, for that period when I was in the Rochester, every morning they seemed to be picking songs just for me. The accuracy with which they were selecting songs that musically had some "mind link" for me and had words that were significant was almost spooky.

A typical example of this was James Morrison and Jessie J and the song "Up". Just watch the video and listen to the lyrics of this song. . .

CUE YOU TUBE VIDEO: UP
JAMES MORRISON FEATURING JESSIE J

As the song says, when you fall down, the only way is up. That is very appropriate for me. Listening to and singing along with the song promotes a really strong, positive mind-set. And, by the way, anyone who has a major, life changing injury has quite a few "demons" running around in their heads and it really does not help to bury them in the ground. They will only surface again later. It's much better to shake them out in the open and put them behind you. And doing something like writing this book has a huge therapeutic effect as it gets the things that are in your head out in the open and, in my case, down on paper or, rather, up on the computer screen. You will have already listened to some and there were many, many of these significant songs which you will find scattered through the book in places where they relate to a particular piece of the story.

It was really mind-blowing how every day I would wake up and so often the first song I would hear on the Kenny & Accalia Breakfast Show would mean something to me in some special way. As a result of that I often "participated" in the show by texting (OK sending an SMS, if you prefer using an acronym that's longer that the word it replaces) or calling in on their open hot line to voice my opinion or answer some question that they were asking on the show. And then, because of my regular participation, I also ended up having an off-air dialogue with Accalia which resulted in her and Kenny coming to visit me in the Rochester Wellness Centre - and that is described later in Chapter 29.

Probably, the one song that encapsulates almost all of the things I have been saying in this chapter is *Radio Ga-Ga* sung by Freddie Mercury of Queen. Just watch the video and listen to the lyrics and you can see and hear how he is paying homage to radio and its influence on people.

CUE YOUTUBE VIDEO: RADIO GA-GA – QUEEN

Obviously, Freddie Mercury believed strongly in the power of music played on the radio. And I do too. So, I am definitely Radio Ga-Ga. I am certain that Kenny and Accalia are. I hope that you are also!

POST-SCRIPT

The interesting thing about the MTV Video of Radio Ga-Ga was the use of footage and symbolism from Fritz Lang's 1927 classic movie *Metropolis*. The symbolism of the workers marching in and out is also featured in the Pink Floyd song *Another Brick in the Wall – Part 2* where they do the same thing with children going in and out of school.

The *Metropolis* black and white movie used to be shown on BBC on quite a regular basis when I was a teenager. That was so long ago that TV was still in black and white anyway – and I always liked to watch it as it had a very strong message. I must have been "deep" as a teenager (ha!).

The movie is all about the vast differences between the rich and poor in a futuristic dystopia. It features one very tall tower with lots of lights on it, lots of skyscrapers all built very close together, roads full of nose-to-tail cars, tramways and overhead metro railways. Does this remind you of anywhere in particular . . .? TINSTAAC?

20

WHEN THE GOING GETS TOUGH . . .

After about six weeks of bed-based physiotherapy I "graduated", if you can call it that, to gym-based physiotherapy. This was massively different, of course, but it was enjoyable for me as it was like all the gym workouts I had done for years prior to my accident. It's funny that nowadays doing gym workouts is considered the norm. But when I was in my mid-to-late teens I had a yearning to work out and build some muscles as I had read the Charles Atlas "Dynamic Tension" adverts on the back of the Marvel Comics. Especially the "I was a 97 pound weakling and had sand kicked in my face" and "I can make you a man" adverts. Back then, I was a skinny kid too and the Charles Atlas theme was that you attracted more girls when you had a big buff body. So, I was up for that - and there was a money back guarantee. Though this probably did not cover failure to attract the girl of your dreams!

Charles Atlas Can Make You a Man

One of the biggest cult movies of all time and one of my personal favourites, *The Rocky Horror Picture Show*, even did a very tongue-in-cheek parody song about building muscles called "I can make you a man".

CUE YOU TUBE VIDEO: ROCKY HORROR PICTURE SHOW
I CAN MAKE YOU A MAN – TIM CURRY

But, in the mid-to-late 60s, there was no Fitness First or Gold's Gym and really nowhere to do any workouts except what I would call boxing gyms. It just seemed that they were set up for, and populated by, really tough kids and underprivileged youths who probably wanted to use the boxing skills to beat up more privileged members of society and steal their money. This is a generalisation, of course, but gyms at that time always seemed to be in the tough parts of town and not in the wealthier suburbs. There was one in Brierfield, where I lived at that time, but it was at the top of a flight of very steep stairs in a commercial building above a greengrocer's store and a pawnshop. Even in movies they always seem to be at the top of a flight of stairs above some other business. I often looked up those stairs but I never dared to go up them and open the door at the top.

The boxing gyms of that era seemed to espouse the classic *Rocky* syndrome. Rags to riches through training, body building and fighting. And this time I don't mean the *Rocky Horror Picture Show* syndrome as that was all about Dr. Frank N. Furter – who was just a sweet transvestite from transsexual Transylvania. I'm talking about the Sylvester Stallone

Rocky not the Tim Curry one. Don't get them mixed up as I am sure they would never want to swap places! I must say that Tim Curry looks really at home in his black silk corset, stockings and high heels in *The Rocky Horror Picture Show*. But I somehow can't picture Sylvester Stallone swapping roles and wearing that gear. I don't think it would match his "*Rocky/Rambo*" image.

CUE YOUTUBE VIDEO: ROCKY IV – SYLVESTER STALLONE
EYE OF THE TIGER - SURVIVOR

The training scenes in all the *Rocky* movies are very inspirational such as in *Rocky IV* he uses the basics of Mother Nature, like deep snow, logs and hills – because they cost nothing – and his opponent used all the latest techniques and high-tech equipment. I must tell you that, to any casual observer, my physio training scenes looked nothing like the ones in *Rocky*. Look as me in this picture doing a pectoral press – assisted by Isaac. The equipment was simple, the weights were small and the pace was slow. But the amount of effort I had to put into them – because my muscles were only partially functional – was massive. And I had to do them sitting in my wheelchair.

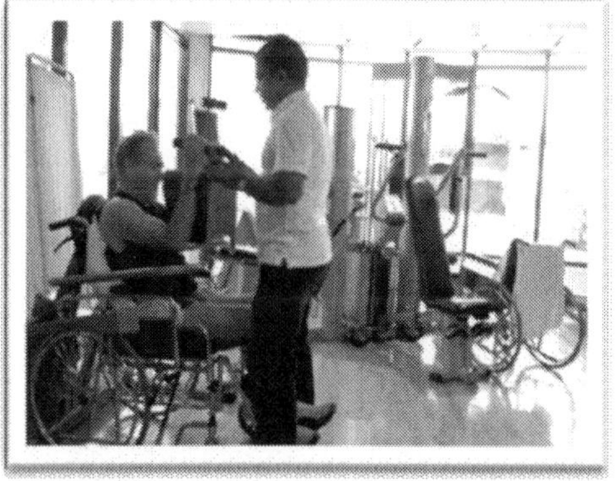

Rocky Bilbriggsy - Working Out

In addition to the gym machine exercises, they also started me doing a basic cycling exercise. Fortunately, the machine they used was designed specifically for people like me with almost zero muscle strength. In other words a motor drove the pedals around as my legs would not do it themselves. It's a clever system as, over time, it lets you take over and the dials show how much effort is yours and how much is coming from the machine.

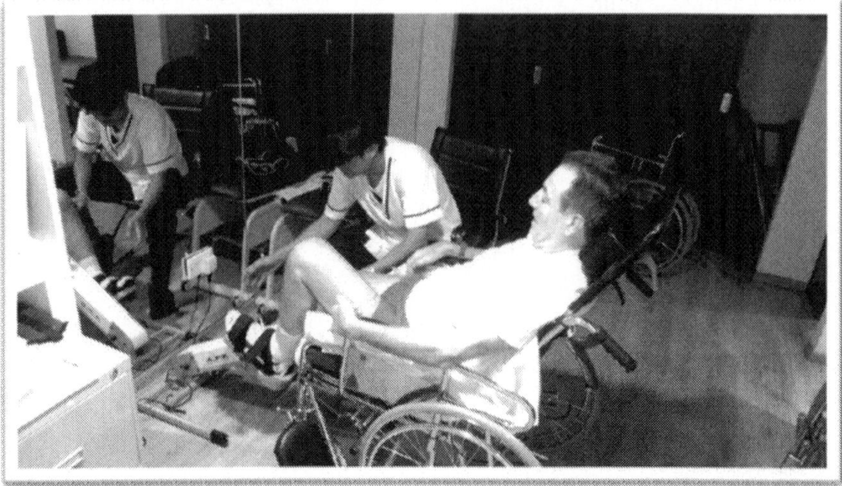

TSB - Training for the Tour de France

The other thing they had me start doing is what they call "Bridging". This is basically the male version of trying to have a baby as they want the patient to have his knees up and feet flat on the bed then thrust the pelvis upwards as far as possible. At first it was impossible and, in September 2011, the physios would need to pull on my knees to help lift the pelvis off the bed. I am still doing this one in my PT sessions in 2016 but now I can lift up my pelvis and hold for five seconds when doing three sets of ten. So, it's a huge improvement. The baby still has not come out yet, but the exercise really makes me want to go for a pee!

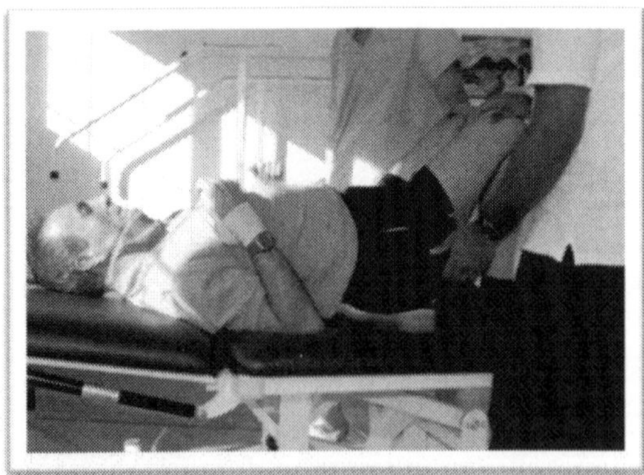

Have the Waters Broken Yet?

Things were also improving on the Occupational Therapy side. The OT ladies were working on my left hand as it was, by far, the better of the two and, by about the end of July 2011, I could just about touch my thumb onto the ends of all my other fingers. That meant I could hold things in my left hand. So, Agnes and I went to the Social Café in Dubai Mall and I chose Japanese Sashimi that required me to use chopsticks. My OTs were very proud of me when they saw this photograph.

Waiter, I'm trying to catch a fly in my Miso Soup

There is a lovely scene in the first *Karate Kid* movie (from way back in 1984) where Mr. Myagi says to Daniel (his young protégé) "Man who catch fly with chopsticks can accomplish anything". I was not quite at the fly catching level with my chopsticks – stationary tuna sashimi was about my limit – but I did believe that I could accomplish anything.

CUE YOUTUBE VIDEO: KARATE KID
PAT MORITA & RALPH MACCHIO

They did a spoofy reprise of that scene in the 2010 remake of the *Karate Kid* with Will Smith's son, Jaden, and Jackie Chan. The janitor (Chan) is trying to catch a fly with his chopsticks but eventually succumbs to using a fly swat which does not impress the young kid.

So, this entire initial daily exercise regimen was the foundation for my recovery. I can tell you that three times a day, six days a week is tough going. But, as the Billy Ocean song says, "*When the going gets tough, the tough get going*"

CUE YOUTUBE VIDEO: WHEN THE GOING GETS TOUGH
BILLY OCEAN

I like the jokey bit in the video where he has Michael Douglas, Kathleen Turner and Danny DeVito as back-up singers because they starred in the movie *Jewel of the Nile* which featured the song. It must be the most expensive line of back-up singers in history. And I love the fact that, despite this being an 80s song, the three of them are doing the 60s Tamla Motown "Four Tops" style of stage dance with left and right shuffles and chugging arms.

As they say – when the going gets tough, the tough go dancing . . .

POST SCRIPT

When I was just about finished writing this chapter in November 2015, Colby (then ten) came to me and asked if I could send an email to Miss McLoughlin, the music teacher at Al Yasmina School. It turned out she had asked him if he wanted to be in the Gifted & Talented Choir again this year and he had turned it down. But then he found out what the two songs were and he wanted me to ask her if he could change his mind and be in the choir. So, I agreed to do that and then he asked me to print out the lyrics of one of the songs. It was *The Circle of Life* by Elton John from *The Lion King* movie and he sang it for the rest of the night. The interesting thing about that movie is that the phrase "When the going gets tough, the tough get going" is used in one of the scenes.

Later, I asked Colby if he wanted me to print out the lyrics of the other song. He replied with "No, the other song is *The Eye of the Tiger* and I already know the lyrics to that." And launched into it. "Risin' up, dah de de dah . . ." And kept on singing!

What a coincidence that the two songs that Colby wanted to sing in the G&T Choir have some links to the chapter I had just written! But then, TINSTAAC, there is no such thing as a coincidence, is there?

And one of the most memorable intros in rock music is . . .

Dahh…….....Dah..Dah..Dahh
Dah..Dah..Dahh
Dah..Dah… Daaaahn

The Eye of a Tiger – the *Rocky* theme tune!

21

WOULD YOU LIKE SOME KIMCHI WITH THOSE X-RAYS, SIR?

After about six weeks at the Rochester I went to the Wooridol Centre, which is a Korean-run clinic with lots of really high-tech specialist equipment. The Korean doctors looked at my x-rays and shook their heads in the way that Koreans do. So, we had more x-rays done. And they still shook their heads . . . ! The shattering conclusion from all this was that the Korean doctors would not let me do any physiotherapy in their clinic unless I had an operation on my spine. They said that one of my vertebrate had moved out of place and if I continued doing physiotherapy it might move more and create even worse problems. Of course, that really worried me, given that I did not relish having to "go under the knife".

So, I decided that I had to get a second opinion… and a third opinion in case I didn't like the second one . . .! You know the old adage – always choose a lawyer or a doctor who tells you what you want to hear. I got the second opinion from another doctor at a different spinal hospital in Dubai, but he said the same thing as the Korean doctors. That was no good. Finally, I asked my own neurosurgeon, Dr. Antoine Salloum, back at the Al Noor Hospital in Abu Dhabi, for his opinion. The conclusion from Dr. Salloum was that, yes, my C5 neck vertebrae had moved and, if I wanted, he could do an operation to fix it. Alternatively,

I could wait and see if it moved any more. I thought. “No way Jose! I'm not waiting for it to move some more in the event that one day I wake up and I am permanently paralysed because the nerves are trapped”. So, I agreed that he should do the operation as soon as possible.

One of the “amusing” things at the time was that Dr. Salloum said that he would have to pack up the C5 vertebrae with some bits of bone and that the options were to take them from my own hip bone or to use cadaver bones. I didn’t fancy the additional operation to take bits of my hipbones so I opted for the cadaver bones. Then he started talking about the brace he was going to put on my neck. Originally, he said that he would attach it to three vertebrae, but during the operation, it turned out to be five and, as a result, I was about eight hours in the surgery. He also told me that the brace, which is bolted into each of the five vertebrae, is made out of titanium. This, of course is the stuff they use in the NASA spaceships and space shuttles.

So, basically, I am held together with bits of dead people's bones and scrap metal from old spaceships!!

Agnes had been delaying her planned trip to the Philippines for several weeks, waiting to see when I would get approval from the insurance company for my operation. Eventually, I told her that she should just go as we had no idea when the approval would come through. Of course, “Sod’s Law” (a.k.a Murphy’s Law) then kicked in as usual. In mid-August 2011, on the same morning that Agnes and the two youngest sons, Kyle & Colby, got on the plane to go to the Philippines, I received the call from the insurance company giving the OK to proceed with the operation. Great timing!!

It was too late to stop them going as they were already on the plane with their seatbelts fastened when I got the call. So, they went on holiday while I looked forward, with significant trepidation, to a huge operation on my spine!!

The following day, I went back down to Abu Dhabi to the Al Noor Hospital for the operation. It was performed the second day I was there and all I remember was being taken down to the operating theatre and the anaesthetist giving me an injection and I just drifted into a blissful sleep.

I woke up afterwards in the ICU to the smiling face of the Filipina sister who wiped my face with some (probably) cheap cologne and it felt like the most wonderful thing anyone had ever done to me.

I was feeling fine because, of course, I was on a lot of drugs and painkillers. To be sure, to be sure . . .!

22

I DIDN'T KNOW WHETHER TO LAUGH OR CRY

The first few days after the operation were "interesting" to say the least. I was in no pain at all – of course – because I was stuffed full of pain-killing drugs. The day after the operation I actually did an interview with Nick Marsh, one of the journalists at The National newspaper. I remember I was bubbling over with ideas, telling Nick about writing this book and setting up a charity fund to help others who faced similar problems but could not afford the proper treatment.

THE NATIONAL: VETERAN RUGBY PLAYER INJURED
NICK MARSH - 26 AUGUST 2011

After a couple of days recuperation I was taken back up to the Rochester Wellness Centre in Dubai and back to my "own" room. Of course, all the Rochester's doctors, physios and nurses wanted to come in and have a look at my operation scar.

As you can see from the picture it is five or six inches long and was held together by some sort of special staples. Not sure what kind of stapler they use for putting them in . . . ! I have visions of one of those big professional staple guns that builders and furniture makers use. You squeeze the trigger and they shoot staples out like bullets. Kerchunk, Kerchunk, Kerchunk, Kerchunk . . .

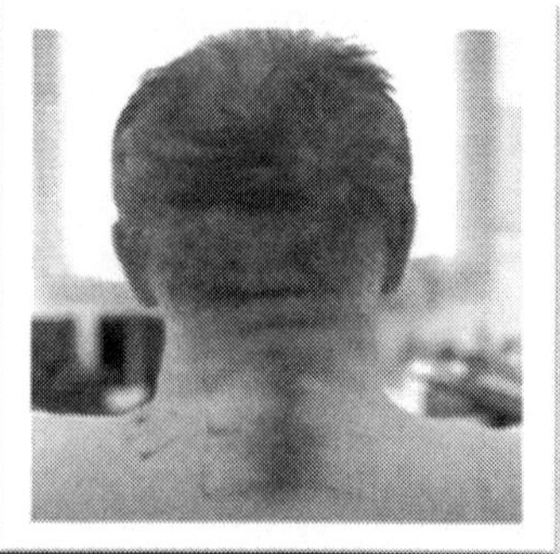
Wanna See mv Battle Scars?

The first couple of days back at the Rochester were fairly eventful. Because I was undoubtedly on a myriad of painkillers I was able to sit up and talk to everyone around me – whether they wanted to listen or not. Apparently, my brain was running at a million miles an hour and I could talk non-stop for hours.

Nick had not been able to take any pictures when he interviewed me shortly after the operation, so it was arranged to be done in the Rochester when I got back. When The National photographer came to my room to take the photos for the article I insisted that I had my hair brushed to look respectable.

Arthur Bell was there at the time and he commented, "You are the vainest man on the planet."

Quick as a flash I retorted with, "Yes. But which planet?"

And it didn't stop there. For a couple of days I was regaling Edna, Chris, the physios, the other nurses and anyone else that would listen, with funny stories about my childhood and they were howling with laughter. Then my mind would do an internal flip and I would start talking about the members of my family and relatives that were deceased. This included my Mother, Father, and my favourite uncle, Uncle Roy. This made me cry bucket loads. This was something that I had not really even done at the time they had died. So, I was alternately laughing and crying . . .!!!

What was making me do this? I never normally opened up about my family and relatives that had passed away. The only thing I could think of was that now I had, in my neck, pieces of bone from someone who was actually dead. As this was right next to my brain and my whole nervous system was running through there, I wondered if maybe I was somehow getting a spiritual connection from these bits of bone!! Woooooooooo!

And why did I make that crack about "Yes. But which planet?" Maybe it had something to do with the titanium brace being used to hold my spine together. Who knows?

As I said in the previous chapter – I am now held together with dead people's bones and bits of old spaceships. But, this seems to have given me an additional weird problem. It's like the Apollo 13 mission when all sorts of things started to go wrong with the NASA spacecraft and they radioed back to earth "Houston. We have a problem."

CUE YOUTUBE MOVIE CLIP: APOLLO 13 – TOM HANKS

While all this laughing and crying was going on and my brain was working on overtime, my body was not actually doing much. I had to be fed my breakfast by Agnes' sister, Edna. This was not "peel me another grape" decadence, it was necessary because of my incapability. My hands were curled up, with my fists closed, so I could not do it myself.

One morning, as always, we were listening to the Kenny and Accalia Breakfast Show on Radio 2 and they were doing the "Movie Spoiler Quiz". This was so-called because Accalia would tell the audience the ending of a movie and you had to guess what the movie was and text in the answer. Of course, if you had not seen the movie, telling you the ending was real "spoiler".

That particular day the clue was something like "After being marooned on a desert island with only a picture of his wife in an old pocket watch, he was finally rescued and reunited with her". Both Edna and I knew the answer. It was *Cast Away* starring Tom Hanks and he was the FEDEX courier in the plane that crashed into the sea during a thunderstorm. Luckily, he was washed up on the beach of a deserted tropical island. As the movie went on he got thinner and thinner and more and more ragged looking and he grew a stubbly beard. So, I sent an SMS with the answer and pulled up the trailer on YouTube while we were waiting for Accalia to announce the results.

Part of the trailer shows Tom Hanks sitting on a beach and looking despondently out to sea. As we watched it, Edna turned to me and said, "You look just like Tom Hanks in that movie!"

And it was true, I did. I had lost a lot of weight due to muscle wastage over the preceding six months, my hair was all messed up as I had not washed it since the operation for fear of softening the six-inch-long scar that was healing on the back of my neck, and I had not shaved for about 10-12 days since the operation. I looked really rough and just like I had been cast away on a deserted island for months!

This "Movie Spoiler" quiz was the spark for a whole bunch of mind linkages for me as a theme running through this book. At the time there was no book, of course, it was just one of my other "crazy" ideas. But, the biggest mind link at the time – well more of a mind leap really – was that I had the idea of Tom Hanks playing me in the movie made about the book that was three years away from even being started. See how crazy it was. I had not even written one word of this book and I already wanted to make a film about it starring one of the world's most popular actors! Yeah right!

Now, remember that my wife Agnes and the two younger kids were still in the Philippines "on vacation". In reality Ness was, of course, really worried about me and frustrated that she was not with me in the UAE at this critical time. However, it was supposed to be some consolation that her sister Edna – who was also a nurse – was looking after me. You might have thought that, being a nurse, Edna would be diplomatic and be telling Ness that the operation went fine and I was recovering well and in "good spirits". But no! She was telling her that I was going crazy and laughing and crying and talking about dead people and all sorts of strange stuff that only made Ness more worried. Gee thanks Edna . . .

And then there were the long international phone calls. With the emphasis on "long". I had several two-hour phone calls to Agnes in the Philippines, my sister Lynn in the States, Elliott, my eldest son, in Australia, and his mother, my former wife, in UK.

I said earlier that the medications were making me talk for hours and the phone calls were no exception.

Agnes told me – after the fact - that the calls to her were really crazy-sounding. She also loves to tell other people the same thing too! We had two completely different scenarios, of course. She was sitting in a tropical beach resort called Puerto Galera on an island south of Manila, Philippines. But, although I was telling her about Tom Hanks sitting on a beach on a deserted tropical island, I was actually sitting on bed in the Rochester Clinic in Dubai, UAE with a six-inch scar in my neck and a line of staples holding me together.

Apparently, allegedly, I told her about doing the book, setting up a charitable trust fund, having Tom Hanks star as me in the movie of my book (yeah, think BIG), having a big charity rock concert with one of the bands that would be featured in the book and – wait for it – meeting the Queen of England! On top of that I talked about my deceased parents and uncles and aunts, the dog we had when I was a teenager which I carried around on my paper round because it was pregnant and the Lambretta scooter that I had when I was a "Mod". Not bad for one phone call . . .

It obviously sounded like I was really off the wall as Agnes then called my sister Lynn to see if any of the things I had told her were actually true. So, another long international call. This time from the Philippines to USA!

Next on my list was a similar conversation with my eldest son Elliott who was in Brisbane, Australia.

Then I called up his mother, Helen, my former wife, who was in UK and had another long conversation with her telling her about all the things I was planning to do. On top of all that, I tried to persuade her to get married again! This time, to her long-time friend, Paul, who she had known since we broke up. Apparently, he had kept asking and she had kept dithering. He is a really great guy and something in my slightly medication-altered synapses was trying to make sure Helen would be looked after!

Not yet satisfied with all the phone calls so far, I sent my sister an SMS to give me a call and then ran her through the whole story again. For good measure, I told her that I was planning to come to her place in

North Carolina, USA with the family at Christmas, fly over to California - taking James and her son Leon with me - and meet up with Elliott at his mother's place in Sacramento. Then the four of us "boys" would drive down the Pacific Coast Highway from San Francisco to LA and deliver the outline script of the movie to Tom Hanks. And why not?

That call was apparently so long and expensive that Lynn's husband, John, said that she was the crazy one!

The funny thing was that I was telling all of them about Tom Hanks starring in the movie of this book and I was really convinced that I could just write to him and he would say "yes". This was based on the chance viewing – while I was in the Al Noor in about March 2011 - of one of the last Oprah Winfrey shows. Normally, I never watched Oprah but the channel choice was very limited in the Al Noor and I had NOTHING to do - and actually could do NOTHING –all day except watch TV.

This particular show featured Tom Hanks and Julia Roberts talking about their, then, latest movie together, called Larry Crowne. As they talked he mentioned that he was answering some of his online fan mail. And Oprah incredulously said "You answer your own fan mail!?!" To which Tom replied, "Yes, why not? I was sitting at home on the computer . . .! So, this convinced me that I could "just" write to Tom Hanks and get him to star in my movie and then deliver the script to him. Easy peasy, yeah!

CUE YOU TUBE VIDEO: LARRY CROWNE
TOM HANKS AND JULIA ROBERTS

It was a hilarious interview. Both Tom and Julia were on top form. I have been looking for a clip of the interview where he talks about answering fan mail but I can't find one. But the next best thing is Tom Hank's confession about what he does when he is at home and he I not answering his fan mail . . .

CUE YOUTUBE VIDEO: TOM HANKS CONFESSION
OPRAH SHOW (MARCH 2011)

Seeing that Oprah episode was just another coincidence, of course. But, there is no such thing as a coincidence (TINSTAAC). Is there?

But laugh . . . I could have wet myself! (And maybe I did, but we won't talk about that just yet)

23

DIE ANOTHER DAY

The "not knowing whether to laugh or cry (or wet myself)" phase turned out to be "small potatoes" compared to what happened next. After a couple of days back at the Rochester I started getting massive spasms running through my entire body whenever I was moved. And that happened a lot as the nurses at the Rochester were always very conscientious about making patients lie and sit in different positions all the time in order to prevent bed sores. Those nasties appear very quickly and take months to heal as they create a really deep hole in your flesh.

But for me, I think the problem was that bits of my nervous system were starting to reconnect as a result of the surgery on my neck. Another factor in this – I am sure – is that the effects of the anaesthesia and post-operation, heavy-duty pain-killers were starting to wear off. Big time!

It's hard to describe what it felt like but, as soon as someone tried to move me, the nearest thing I can tell you is to try to imagine what it would feel like if someone connected about 1,000 volts to your toes. That's where it always started and my feet would kick one way – say to the left. Then it moved up my legs and my knees jerked to the right. Next my hips would thrust in the opposite direction, to the left. Then my upper torso would jolt to the right. And, finally, my neck and head would whiplash to the left. It was like having thunderbolts rip through my entire nervous system. AAAAAAaaaaaaargh!!

This was staggeringly painful as those thunderbolts zapped me every single time I was moved. And, of course, each time it happened, it left me exhausted.

In 2014 I saw a re-run on TV of the *2013 Royal Variety Show* at the London Palladium Theatre where Jessie J did a stunning live performance of the song *Thunder* and it reminded me of all the thunderbolts I had endured for days after my operation. Click on the link below and you will see what I mean. Just make sure your body is properly "earthed" . . .

CUE YOUTUBE VIDEO: JESSIE J - THUNDER
ROYAL VARIETY SHOW

One night the nurses and James tried to turn me over from my back to my side but the pain was so intense that I was screaming out in agony. So, they stopped turning me and left me half on my side and I drifted off into an exhausted sleep.

Sometime later, in the middle of the night, I woke up but I was choking and could not breathe. I think it was the mucus that collects in the lungs when you have an operation. Whatever it was it was choking me and I could not get it out. I really could not breathe at all - it felt like the back of my throat and my nasal passages were completely clogged up.

The natural reaction in this circumstance is to try and turn over onto your front but my muscles did not work and any attempt to move sent the thunderbolts zapping through me. It was pitch black in the room so I could not see anything nor could I reach the emergency button to press it to call the night nurse. All sorts of ideas flashed through my mind but I could not do anything. At all!

Couldn't breathe, so I could not speak. Couldn't move, so I could not turn over to clear the throat blockage. Couldn't reach the emergency call button, so could not summon the nurse. I really thought I was going to die . . .!

But, luckily, James was sleeping on the sofa in my room and he must have somehow heard my gurgling and gasping and he woke up. This is amazing, of course, as he was a sixteen-year-old-teenager and usually they sleep like logs. But whatever it was, sixth sense, morphic resonance or just plain luck, he heard me and got up to help. He was able to grab some tissues and turn me a little bit on my side so I could cough up and clear my throat and nasal passages. I felt like it was one of those water torture things, that you have seen on TV or movies, where they hold the prisoner's head under water till their lungs are bursting and then pull it out again. You see the prisoner coughing and spluttering as they try and get the water out and get air into their body.

It was just like the scene in *Die Another Day* where James Bond is tortured by having his head dunked in a bath of ice-cold water. But the torture scene "replica" MTV video of Madonna singing the title song is actually more graphic and violent than the movie!

CUE YOUTUBE VIDEO: DIE ANOTHER DAY – MADONNA

But the main thing was that James (my son James, not James Bond!) was there and he probably saved my life by waking up at the right moment. Then James and Greggy, the night duty nurse, sat up for the rest of the night watching me to make sure I kept breathing. Thanks guys. Lifesavers!!!!

As the song says - it wasn't my time to go. I guess I'll die another day.

24

IN YOUR DREAMS!

One of the interesting side effects of all the medication I was being fed with was that my dreams were incredibly vivid and intense. They also seem to have made a significant impact on my brain as I can still remember them even now, whereas normally dreams are forgotten very quickly - if they are recalled at all - even the next morning.

For example, one night I was dreaming of being able to see inside someone's house as though I had X-ray vision. I can picture myself standing outside in the garden and being able to see through the walls. And why was I looking through the walls? It was because I wanted to see the beautiful girl inside, of course. The X-ray vision also meant that I could see through the clothes of the girl inside – which gave an intriguing erotic slant to the dream. Then she came out of the door and started walking slowly towards me – very, very slowly - as this bit of the dream seemed to last for an incredibly long time. As she walked, I could hear her breathing heavily and in a very sensual way. But in actual fact what I could hear was myself breathing as I was slowly waking up.

Now, normally, it always feels like you wake up from dreams just when you don't want to. It always seems to be just before you win the race or get to kiss the beautiful girl. So, you turn over and try to go back to sleep again but the "moment" has passed and you can never "replay the video" and get back to that place or that moment in time. But, here is the weird thing. During those first days after my operation I could wake up – so the dream stopped – and then when I went back to sleep, the dream would start up again exactly where it had stopped. It was brilliant! I did get to win the race and I did get to kiss the girl.

Of course, I cannot disclose here which girl it was that I kissed as that might be grounds for divorce or castration at least – and I am not sure which is more painful. Or maybe it would be "Divorce or Death"? And that might also be a difficult choice, particularly if you were married to an American woman. The rule of thumb in the USA seems to be that the divorce court awards her 150% of everything you have ever had since childhood and they cut your balls off too. So, the answer may be, "Er, I'll take Death please." It's probably the opposite of the Eddie Izzard sketch where he discusses mass murderers, religion and how "soft" the Church of England religion was in the late Middle Ages. Other religions were tough and had torture and subjugation. Like the Spanish Inquisition – which no-one expects! The Church of England, according to Eddie Izzard, would ask religious prisoners if they wanted "Cake or Death?" Have a look for yourself.

CUE YOUTUBE VIDEO: CAKE OR DEATH – EDDIE IZZARD

Anyway, back to my dream. And yes, as I said, I could re-join the dream and pick up where it left off, which was wonderful. But, in order to have dreams, you first need to be asleep. Duuuuh! At that time the hard part sometimes was actually the falling asleep bit. It seemed like I could just not let my brain relax and allow myself to drift gently into sleep.

Amongst the concoction of pills that I was being fed was one called Neurobion, which was simply a Vitamin B complex. Apparently, Vitamin B is very good for nerve regeneration and I needed lots of my nerves regenerated at that particular point in time. But what I began to realize was that when I was taking the Neurobion I was in a really good mood and talking and joking. When I did not have them I was a bit grumpy and fidgety. OK, to tell the truth I was VERY grumpy and VERY fidgety.

As a result, I kept having huge arguments every night with Agnes' sister Edna, to try and get her to give me a Neurobion so I could go to sleep. But she would not agree as the Doctors had said I should only take them during the day. It was driving me crazy (OK, crazier!). I was screaming at her to give me the pills and she would not.

I was telling her, "Look, you are giving me all sorts of pills every day to do this and to do that. And who knows what they are doing to my body. Neurobion is only Vitamin B. It's not going to kill me! It's only fucking vitamins!!!"

Eventually, as a result of a round-robin of phone calls between Edna (in Dubai), Agnes (in the Philippines), my sister Lynn (in USA), Doctor Salloum (in Abu Dhabi) and the in-house Physiotherapy doctor at the Rochester, they all agreed that I could have a Neurobion at night before I went to sleep.

CUE YOU TUBE VIDEO: IN DREAMS - ROY ORBISON

Yo!! Magic. I just put my head on the pillow and I was gone. Back in my dream with the x-ray vision and the beautiful girl. What more could I ask for? And she never once made that caustic woman's retort "In your dreams!"

If I could have recorded those Neurobion dreams I am certain I could have made a fortune selling them to one of those hotel Pay-Per-View porn channels . . .

25

THE CAST AWAY

So, because of the Tom Hanks *Cast Away* movie spoiler quiz on Radio Two that I talked about earlier, I had this crazy idea! Actually, it was just one crazy idea among many at this point in my recovery. I will blame it on the pain killers and the drug cocktail that I was being fed on a daily basis.

"Let's go to the Miramar Hotel then I can sit on the beach and have my picture taken looking like Tom Hanks," I said.

The Miramar is on the east coast of the UAE in between Fujairah and Dibba and looks out onto the Gulf of Oman. It's a lovely hotel, built on the beach in a low-rise, Arabic-Mediterranean style of architecture. It's all in a big semi-circle around a huge pool with a restaurant in its centre.

The Eid Al Fitr holiday was coming up so I booked a room at the Miramar and off we went. The "we" in this case was my son James, my nurse Chris, our driver "Bernie the Bolt", and myself. For those of you who have never been, Fujairah is about a three and a half hour drive from Dubai over the mountains. These mountains are not the picturesque type with slopes covered in fir trees etc. They are 100% rock from base to tip. But they are very dramatic to look at especially in the late afternoon sun when there are lots of shadows and haze. It's one of the few places in the UAE that has roads with bends in them; most roads here are a straight line between two points across the desert. On the way

I was trying to teach "Bernie the Bolt" to drive faster round the corners – racing and rally style – but he was useless at it and the car kept falling off the asphalt road onto the gravel hard shoulder. Discretion is the better part of valour, so I gave up on the lessons as I did not want any more injuries as a result of a car crash. I had quite enough of them already!

We arrived at the Miramar and were given a fantastic ground floor room with a veranda looking out over the beach. What more could we ask for? Well, a pitcher of Margaritas for a start, please. So, we sat at the beach bar and drank our Margaritas and it was wonderful. The best experience I had had since my accident! There was only one slight, but amusing, problem. Bernie and Chris had never drunk Margaritas before and were unaware of the significant effect they can have . . . They taste sweet-sharp and innocent, but they really pack a punch.

After the Margaritas, getting me on the beach for the photos was an interesting exercise for the boys. I had to be lifted out of the wheelchair, carried down the steps and across the beach to a big rock where I could sit and have my picture taken looking like a castaway. It was a bit like a couple of drunks trying to carry a dead body and get it in the boot/trunk of a car without attracting any attention. But of course they can't help but attract attention. Have you ever walked in soft sand? It's hard work. Have you ever walked in soft sand when you are drunk? It's really hard work. Have you ever walked in soft sand when you are drunk and carrying a dead body? Probably not, but it's really, really hard work. And this was not helped by the fact that one of the boys was about six feet three inches tall - and a *Star Trek* Mr. Spock look-alike - and the other was like a dwarf - from *Lord of the Rings* - on steroids.

Tote that barge! / Lift that bale! / Get a little drunk and you land in jail . . .!

Anyway, I eventually made it, but it's a good job the sand was soft when they finally dropped me on it! You can see the similarities in the picture below. I looked rough, my hair was a mess and I had plenty of stubble. But, unlike Tom Hanks, I did have several Margaritas on the inside.

TSB on the Beach
Full of Margaritas

Tom Hanks on the Beach
Hoping for a Margarita

Did I get those captions right for the pictures above? Maybe not, but who cares after a pitcher of Margaritas!

CUE YOU TUBE VIDEO: CAST AWAY (TRAILER)
TOM HANKS

I was still having "thunderbolts" charging through my body so I was having difficulty sleeping. Even the Margaritas were not able to produce enough soporific effect! I found that the only way I could get to sleep was to have someone squeeze and massage my feet till I drifted off.

Amazingly, it turned out that "Bernie the Bolt" was the best at this. He would squeeze and squeeze till I drifted off into oblivion.

It also turned out that he was the best at eating breakfast next morning too. The Miramar breakfast was a Filipino's dream as it was a huge multi-cultural buffet. Bernie and Chris seemed to have a battle each morning to see who could have the most food. And then James, being half - Filipino and a growing teenager, was not very far behind. If you didn't already know this, Filipinos just LOVE eating. It's a national hobby for them. So, we would sit out on the terrace in the morning and the boys would go back and forth till they were sated. Then they would go back for some more! It made me full just watching.

Clockwise from left - Chris, TSB, Bernie & James

We managed to get into the gym a couple of times while we were there as it's always important to keep all my body-bits moving. It feels like it is nice to rest sometimes (and I need to) but, if it is for too long, my body starts to remember that it is 66+, and not the 35+ that my brain thinks it is, and everything starts to seize up again.

But each evening we went back for another pitcher of Margaritas at the Miramar Beach Bar at sundown. I can highly recommend them. Even better than a session in the gym, they loosen up your body and your brain to just about the right level of "loosidity"

26

ROCKY MOUNTAIN EXORCISM

All too soon we had head for home and so we loaded ourselves back into the trusty Cadillac SRX SUV and set off on the road to Dubai via Fujairah. As always, I was listening to music as we drove along. We got about half way to Fujairah and I looked out of the window and saw the late afternoon haze in the mountains alongside the road. Just as I did that, the Eagles' *Long Road Out Of Eden* track started playing. I asked "Bernie the Bolt" to quickly pull over and stop so we could look at the view, turn up the volume and listen to the music at the same time. If you know the track it is quite surreal as it's all about unfortunate US Army soldiers fighting in the deserts of oil producing foreign countries so that the fat cats in the US oil industry can keep eating their pecan pie in the "Petroleum Club". It starts off with the desert wind blowing across the dunes and a plaintive wailing Arabic flute . . .

Is This the Last Exit to Brooklyn or Eden?

And here we were in an oil producing, desert country with palm trees and lots of sand, so the lyrics were very pertinent.

And the lines in the middle of the song are all about music blasting from an SUV on a bright and sunny day. No kidding! Listen to the song on the video and take note of the imagery projected behind the band. There is a fantastic guitar solo by Joe Walsh in the middle of the song, with a clip of some mountains that look just like the ones in my picture. TINSTAAC, surely? What could be better than that?

CUE YOUTUBE VIDEO: LONG ROAD OUT OF EDEN
EAGLES

Well, about half an hour later we found out what could be better than that.

We went back a different way to the one we had come as I wanted James to drive up a fantastic piece of winding road and go through the mountain in the tunnel at the top of the road. But I wanted him to drive it while listening to yet another great piece of music – *Rocky Mountain Way*" by Joe Walsh. What could be more appropriate than that? It's one of my favourite "10 miles per hour faster" tunes. And what do I mean by that? It's simple. When you listen to one of them you can't help but drive 10 miles per hour faster just because something in the beat is urging you to do it.

This piece of road starts at the foot of the mountain. It's a dual carriageway (two lanes up and two down) with a concrete wall divider. There are no straight bits as its one continuous winding snake up a steep incline. There is a rock face on one side and long drops on the other! At the bottom of the mountain I told "Bernie the Bolt" to sit in the back and let James drive. I was sitting in the front passenger "Shotgun" seat as usual. Just so you can appreciate the significance of this I will tell you that this was the first time James had driven on a real road!

He had driven karts on race tracks before and driven cars a little bit on private roads and tracks etc. But never on a real highway before. And what did I want him to do? Just go up this winding road as fast as we could hustle the SRX – despite the road having a 40kph limit. So, before we set off my instruction to James was "Just to listen to what I tell you to do and do it – without question or thought – just do it".

Gentlemen, Start Your Engines!

I had done this before with my eldest son, Elliott, when he was just starting to learn to drive. We had gone down Highway 1, the Pacific Coast Highway, between San Francisco and LA and it's a fabulous, fast, winding road right along the coastline. The views are fantastic – if you have time to take your eyes off the road!

CUE YOUTUBE VIDEO: ROCKY MOUNTAIN WAY
JOE WALSH WITH THE EAGLES (1977)

So, I cued the *Rocky Mountain Way* track, pressed start, told James to go for it and turned up the volume at full belt on the car's Alpine sound system. Just listen to it for yourself and think about driving up a mountain pass as fast as you can.

Up the hill we blasted. OOOOOOoooooohhhh! Big intakes of breath from Bernie and Chris in the back seat! I was telling James when to go faster, when to brake, when to turn, how much to turn, where to cut the corner, how to aim for the apex and how to let the car drift wide as it came out of the corner. But, one of the most important things about driving fast is to continuously assess what the next bend is going to be so the car comes out of one bend well-placed and ready for the next one. These were all things I had learnt over many years on racing circuits and rally stages but I was teaching James to do it by asking him to follow my instructions to the letter. Remember, of course, we are not in a race car or even a sports car. We are in a fully loaded SUV, so we were a bit more "on the edge" as I was pushing James hard to go as fast as possible. He did a great job – way, way better than Bernie had on the way to the Miramar. He exactly followed my instructions. You may think I was a bit crazy for doing this but, in reality, I love my cars (and my son and myself) and I had no intention of letting James crash.

Then it happened! SHIT! And no, we did not crash(!). Just as we went around the last bend before entering the tunnel I spotted a police car parked on the side of the road. So, I told James to slow down and then said to everyone, "Do NOT look at the policemen. Whatever you do look straight ahead as we drive by. If one of us looks at them they will assume we are guilty of something and pull us over!" We drove slowly past the police car at 40 kph and I kept smiling while looking ahead and saying between my clenched teeth, "Do NOT look at the police! Do NOT look at the police!" Then we disappeared into the dark mouth of the tunnel. Phew! It's about a kilometre long and as soon as we burst out into bright sunlight on the other side I told James to pull off the road, stop the car and let "Bernie the Bolt" take over again.

Yeeehaaaa! We did it! It was tremendous fun and we were all laughing and joking like a bunch of schoolkids.

As we cruised down the sweeping curves of the road on the other side of the mountain I had yet another crazy idea.

"Let's go to Sharjah." I said, "To the Sharjah Wanderers Rugby Club where I had my accident!"

Silence - everybody sort of looked at me with "that" expression. It was the "Oh, here he goes again" expression. But we were on the road that lead straight into Sharjah so how could we not do it? So, that's what we did.

About 30 minutes later we arrived at the Sharjah Wanderers Club, which, by the way, is actually still British Territory since it used to be the site of the British Army Barracks when they first came to UAE (i.e. even before it was the UAE). Sharjah is a "dry" emirate – which means no alcohol whatsoever – except for at the Sharjah Wanderers Club which serves alcohol to its members. As you can imagine, it's a very popular place with the Sharjah expatriate community.

I was wheeled into the Club by the boys and there were lots of people that knew me. We had a drink then I suggested that we go out onto the rugby pitch and have some pictures taken. The first ones were of me standing up (well, being held up by the people on each side of me, actually). Notice also that I have the leg braces to stop both my knees buckling . . .

With a Little Help from My Friends!

Then I wanted a picture taken where I had had the accident. So, I was laid out on the field in the exact place where the scrum had collapsed on me so that the guys could take lots of pictures. Especially with the roof of the spectators stand in the background.

For me, this was a kind of exorcism . . . exorcising the ghost of my accident by lying in that self-same spot as I had on 25th February earlier that year. This wasn't the Linda Blair vomiting green bile, floating in the air and having the words "help me" appear on my stomach kind of exorcism. It was more of an internal "cleansing of the soul" for me and I can recommend it to anyone who has an accident. Go back to where it happened and let all those demons out of your mind and your body. Don't let them sit inside you, gnawing away at your sanity and giving you nightmares. It's a really good way to shake off the "What if I hadn't done this or hadn't done that?" syndrome that we all go through when something traumatic happens. It's no good feeling angry or guilty for the rest of your life. That's not going to change things. We can't turn back the clock and replay the video with a happier ending. When you have a life-changing accident or event just accept it and get on with making yourself better.

Demons Get Thee Hence!

If you have never seen *The Exorcist*, which came out in 1973, take a look at this trailer. At the time, it was the most graphic portrayal of possession by demons that had ever been shown in the cinema. So watch it, but don't do it just before you go to bed . . .

CUE YOUTUBE VIDEO: THE EXORCIST
LINDA BLAIR

After the "exorcism" session on the pitch, we left the Rugby Club and went over to Peter Baron's house which was close by. He had offered to feed us and, as his wife is also a Filipina, the boys were very happy with the huge spread that was instantly conjured up when we got there.

Peter and I ended up talking for hours (while the boys ate for hours) and, in particular, he introduced me to the concept of "Morphic Resonance". The theory of it is that we all emit "brain waves" when we think. But, they don't just stay in our heads or our bodies; they float all around the world like radio waves or internet transmissions. This means that there are billions and billions of thought waves running all over the world all the time. This is the explanation for the very common phenomenon of you thinking that you need to talk to, say, your wife about something and the phone rings and it's her calling you. Likewise, parents get "feelings" when something has happened to one of their children when they are separated from them. These sorts of things happen to me all the time, so I believe that my Morphic Resonance is very strong. But, I am sure it has happened to you too.

So, in a way, this is one of the recurring themes in this book; I believe that if the people close to you think positively all the time Morphic Resonance will transmit those positive thoughts and they will reinforce your own positive feelings and help you recover.

It was about midnight when Peter and I forced ourselves to stop talking as the boys were full, tired, and falling asleep. We left Sharjah and drove back to the Rochester Clinic and, with the combined effects of my exorcism and Morphic Resonance, I slept like a proverbial baby. And I didn't need "Bernie the Bolt" to massage my feet even once . . .

27

TRANSFORMERS – THE TRUTH IS OUT THERE

I just had to write this chapter today, Sunday 01 June 2014. There are already a number of references in the chapters so far to TINSTAAC. This is actually my own acronym for the phrase "There Is No Such Thing As A Coincidence". I am a firm believer in this and some people have written whole books about it.

What is it? Fate? Someone (who is that someone?) telling you something? Is it something that you "willed" to happen? Does it happen because of Morphic Resonance? I don't really know. But I do believe that "There Is No Such Thing As A Coincidence" - TINSTAAC - and because of that and what happened last night and today, I just had to write this chapter now.

Last night when I was going to sleep I kept thinking about the need to write another chapter of this book because I had been slipping behind in my programme. And, for some reason, the one about my "Who-is-watching-over-us-religious-theories" kept coming to the front of my mind. I have no idea why. There are plenty of other things that would have been easier to write about, but this morning when I woke up and was having breakfast I "involuntarily" (?) thought of it again. Then, on the way to work, it happened . . . I saw one of the 1994 Mark 1 Toyota Previas!

Let me explain. I am not a religious person in the sense that I go to church and pray and sing hymns. I have never really been keen on that. Going to church doesn't make you a Christian any more than standing in a garage makes you a car. But, nonetheless, billions of people in the world do have religious beliefs. And so that's fine by me.

There are many types of religions and religious beliefs. The major ones include Christianity, Islam, Buddhism, Hinduism, and many more. There are also various disciplines within each of the major ones, for example, Roman Catholic, Church of England, Methodist, and Coptic Christianity, etc. are all variations of the Christian religion.

Scientology is also on the fringes of these. Of course, Scientology is the famous religion where, if you are a movie star who is madly in love with your partner, you go on a TV talk show and jump up and down on a sofa. And then, later, when you fall out of love with her you go and make a couple of movies about life on Earth after the aliens have taken over. If you don't believe me, ask Tom Cruise and watch him on Oprah Winfrey and then in *Oblivion* and *The Edge of Tomorrow*.

But there are many other theories too. One significant one is that we (humans) are an "experiment" and that we are being watched over by aliens who, every now and then, come down to earth and pluck a few of us off the planet for a closer inspection and then return us when they are done. There have been quite a few movies with this theme, the most famous being *Close Encounters of the Third Kind* and others such as *Fire in the Sky* and *The Fourth Kind*. You might remember that I tried to convince my nurse, Chris, that this had happened to his mother and that, as a result, he was half-human and half-Vulcan.

More recently, we have had the *Transformers* movies. These movies basically hypothesise that there are machine-like alien beings looking after our planet and these beings can transform themselves into any vehicle or piece of machinery to hide their true shape, thus allowing them to blend in with our 21st Century World.

So, where am I going with this, you might ask? One day, shortly after my operation, I was lying in bed (what else could I be doing?) and I had a bit of an epiphany; I came up with a similar theory based on the Transformers' principle. I make a point here of emphasising that this idea came up shortly after my operation, at a time when I was taking a significant amount of drugs to stop pain, spasms, muscle jerks and thunderbolts through my body (though they were not doing a very good job with this latter problem!). Basically my Transformers' Theory was that I was being watched over by my own personal Transformer in the form of a 1994 Toyota Previa.

Was I being a space cadet? Maybe I was. But subsequent events over a five year period have made me wonder, more than just a little, if my theory could be true. Is there someone out there listening and watching? And this song by Snow Patrol, where the chorus is "We are listening", kept playing on the radio at the time . . .

CUE YOUTUBE VIDEO: CALLED OUT IN THE DARK
a.k.a. WE ARE LISTENING – SNOW PATROL

Going back in time – no time machine here, just me telling you what happened previously – I need to set the scene. So, rewind to 2004, we were still in Manila, Philippines. It was a tough period for the country. More than the usual run of political scandals and other economic problems meant that there was no influx of investment money coming into the country. I was in the business of project development so there was not a lot of work around for me. As a result, we had to be very, shall I say, "economical" in our choice of transport, and the best deals around at the time were the imported, second-hand Japanese people-carriers. They were cheap because there is a law in Japan that bans the use of vehicles older than ten years. So, they had to junk them or sell them on to "3rd world" countries that did not have such age-related regulations. So, LOTS of these used vehicles came to the Philippines where guys made a small fortune out of converting them from right to left hand drive. But, you did NOT want to look under the car to see how they did this – believe me. Bits of old scrap cars were welded together to re-fashion parts. It's a "Chop-Chop" car thief's dream come true.

But we needed a people-carrier – one with seven or eight seats and big sliding doors and plenty of space - and the best available vehicle that fitted that description was a "Mark 1" early 1990s Toyota Previa. So, I scoured the junkyards. Yes, you read it correctly, the junkyards. These vehicles did not come from forecourts of certified, accredited manufacturer's dealerships. No way Jose! When you found one it was usually in the middle of the junkyard surrounded by all the useless bits that they had chopped off to convert the car from right to left hand drive. Of course, this included the interior too as they had to chop out the dashboard and patch together a new one on the other side. Are you getting a picture of this assembled mass of botched together car bits? Well you should. They are a bit like some of the crazy cars that Clarkson, May and Hammond patched together when they were doing their *Top Gear* shows.

Transforming a Toyota Previa – Right to Left

The one thing on these vans that they could not change was the sliding side door. Naturally, this was supposed to be on the curb side so you step out on to the sidewalk (using the American terminology so I don't confuse any Americans). This meant that, in Japan, the sliding door was on the left side of the vehicle. Okay! But when you drive on the right side of the road, as you do in the Philippines, and then pull over to the curb, it means that the sliding door is on the outside – nearest the passing vehicles!

So, your kids jump out into the middle of the road and usually into the path of an oncoming Jeepney overloaded with about 30 passengers and possessing the braking distance of a super tanker. AAAaaarrrgh!

If you don't know what a Jeepney is, then GOOGLE it. But, in simple terms it's like a World War Two, US Army Willys Jeep on steroids and LSD. By this I mean that the Filipinos make the front end look like a Willys Jeep and then streeeetch the chassis till it's about twenty-five feet long, put some pick-up sides on it, add a roof (but no windows) and fit plastic seats down each side of the interior so that passengers face each other like paratroopers in the back of a C-130 Hercules Transport Plane. But it does not stop there! Now the Filipino love of bright colours, lights, horses and slogans kicks in. The whole thing is painted in the brightest array of colours you can imagine with hand painted pictures in every available space. To complete the recipe: add a few bits of shiny chrome, lots of spotlights, bolt a few cast-iron horses to the top of the bonnet (aka "hood" for the Americans) to give the vehicle more "horse-power", then stick on a big, big straight-through exhaust pipe to make your Isuzu Diesel engine sound like a Pro-line Dragster. To complete the transformation, make some funny slogans for the mud flaps and the big flap below the rear bumper (usually "King of 'd Road").

But Who is Paying the Electricity Bills?

It's also important to stack all your cassette tape boxes and other décor on top of the dashboard (to show you have lots of them), leaving just a narrow slot at the top of the windscreen so that you can just about

Did I Say There Was a Bit of a Blind Spot?

see through, just like a Sherman Tank. Then, pump up the volume on the stereo . . . and you are away. Ah, but I forgot one thing. No self-respecting Jeepney driver would turn a wheel without some very loud air horns – usually screwed to the bonnet/hood between the legs of the horses. Now he's really "King of 'd Road" Yeeeehaaaaa!

CUE YOUTUBE MUSIC VIDEO: PUMP UP THE VOLUME
M.A.R.S.

Then you put hundreds and hundreds of these Jeepneys on every major road and street in the city and allow them to stop instantly – and I mean instantly – in the middle of the road, or wherever they happen to be, whenever a passenger taps on the ceiling (which is very often). So, now you get the picture? Chaos and mayhem! Brightly coloured chaos and mayhem, but chaos and mayhem none the less.

The point of all that explanation is so that you can appreciate that wherever and whenever you stop your ex-Japanese Toyota Previa and open the door to let the kids out, there will be a Jeepney bearing down on them at high speed with the horses' nostrils flaring, the music blaring, the driver peering out through his tank slot, the air horns blowing, and the brakes doing very little at all to slow down his progress. Add to this the fact that the streets are narrow and congested and there will be another Jeepney going past in the opposite direction. There is not much room for Jeepney No. 1 to swerve across the road to avoid your kids! But . . . somehow they do. Somehow they always missed. Somehow!

Now that time has passed, and I know some things that I didn't know back then, I believe that it was possibly, the Toyota Previa that somehow had a hand in this. Maybe there was a "force field" around it. Perhaps, even then, it was my own personal "Transformer". Read on to understand why I think like this.

My 1994 Toyota Previa people-carrier was metallic maroon, had five spoke alloy wheels, three rows of seats in the back and, significantly, the first row of these were actually two “Captain’s Seats”. In other words they had arms and swivelled around like Captain Kirk’s seat in the Starship Enterprise. Shades of *Star Trek* here.

When I went to the junkyard in Bulacan looking for a vehicle, “my” Previa was sitting in the middle of the yard surrounded by scrap metal and old car parts and there were a few other Previas ready for sale sitting by the office. But I was somehow drawn to this particular vehicle and, no matter how often I sat in the other cars, I kept going back to the maroon one. It was just like in the first *Transformers* movie when Sam Whitwicky’s dad is buying him his first car. Somehow, the old, battered Chevrolet Camaro “chooses” Sam. I think the Toyota Previa “chose” me!

It was an old, but brilliant vehicle and it cost peanuts. It had about 200,000 km on the clock but it never missed a beat. And it was soooooo comfortable and quiet. It swallowed up the whole family, our two live-in house guests, plus the maid and it never complained.

Now, you have read all the build-up and the scene setting, here is the intriguing part of the story . . .

Ever since I had that “spiritual epiphany moment”, lying in bed at the Rochester, we kept seeing old “Mark 1” 1990s Toyota Previas <u>everywhere</u> we went. We would drive from Abu Dhabi to Dubai and somewhere along the journey would pass a Toyota Previa. Nearly every morning when I went to work, there was one parked outside a building site near our house. I came home from work along Al Salam St and there would be one cruising near me, in amongst the rush hour traffic. It became quite a thing in the car amongst the family – spotting the Toyota Previa.

Now, some of you may be thinking, “What’s the big deal? There are lots of Toyota Previas around in the world.”

Well, yes, there are. But we are talking about Abu Dhabi and Dubai between 2011 and 2014 and seeing early 1990s Mark 1 Toyota Previas. That makes the vehicles 20 to 24 years old . . .

And how many 24 year old vehicles do you see on the roads of the UAE? Apart from the Previas that I see following me, there are virtually none. That’s because UAE is one of the richest economies in the world and every day you see more Ferraris, Lamborghinis, Bentleys, Rollers,

Range Rovers, Porsches, and BMWs than virtually anywhere in the world except maybe Monaco and Hong Kong. So, why do I keep seeing Toyota Previas? How many can there be in this country? How come they are still running?

I said earlier on in this chapter that something made me want to write this story today. Well, this is what happened. I was turning on to Reem Island from Al Salam Street at 11th Street, where the flyover is, as my office is in the middle of the island. When you make that turn you can see a long way in front of you to the crest of the bridge onto the island. It was unusual that there was nothing else driving over the bridge with me at all. But when I went over the crest of the bridge suddenly a Mark 1 Toyota Previa appeared in front of me. No other cars – just this one. So, I ended up driving alongside the Toyota Previa and we pulled up at the next set of traffic lights together.

I looked over at the Previa and there were two guys in it. The driver was rocking back and forth and gesticulating madly at the other guy in the car. They appeared to both be Pakistanis as they were wearing the usual Pakistani, pale-coloured, long shirt. Then they both turned together and stared hard at me! Woooooo! Spooky!

I thought this was too good an opportunity to miss! I wound down my window and signalled the other driver to do the same. I said "Nice car!" And he just stared at me . . . So, I said it again. And he just stared at me . . . Then I asked "What year is your car? What model?" At this the driver started rocking back and forth and waving his arms again. It was just like he did not understand me. But it was not like we were just two people from different countries. It was like I was speaking some alien tongue. Just like in the *Men in Black* movie when one of the aliens, who looks like a human, has forgotten to switch on his Alien-English translator module.

I said it again and the other guy answered, "1994". What could I say? It was a "Mark 1" 1994 Toyota Previa!! So, I just gave the thumbs up sign and said "Aaahh, good car, good car!" Then the lights changed, and I drove away. The Previa moved forward slowly then pulled over to the curb. The last thing I could see was that they were both waving their arms at each other inside the Previa. Then it disappeared from my sight as I went around the corner.

What an odd experience!!!! But I had to do it. And I was right about the age of their Previa. 1994. So, it was 20 years old. Yeah right!

What can I say about this strange phenomenon of 20-year-old Previas everywhere I go? Are they for real? Or are they actually "Transformers" watching over me? Of course, I am assuming that these Previas are Autobots (i.e. "good" Transformers) as opposed to Decepticons (i.e. "baaad" Transformers). I have no idea . . . but it's a great theory.

But I do know that "TINSTAAC – There Is No Such Thing as A Coincidence"

CUE YOU TUBE VIDEO: TRANSFORMERS 1 (TRAILER)
SHIA LABEOUF & MEGAN FOX

Actually, the real reason I want to believe in the "Transformers' Theory" is that I keep dreaming that one day a 1994 Toyota Previa is going to pull up next to me in some dark and secluded place. Then the sliding door and Megan Fox slowly steps out and walks over to my car. I wind the window down, she leans forward on the edge of the door looking hot and beautiful, and I say "Need a ride?"

She looks at me with those huge . . . eyes (You thought I was going to say something else there, didn't you) and just slides into the passenger seat. My car responds by turning on its own radio as we drive away, playing *Sexual Healing* by Marvin Gaye, just like Sam Whitwicky's Camaro did in the first Transformers movie when Sam and Megan Fox drive off to a romantic spot together. And couldn't I just do with some sexual healing . . .? "In your dreams!" as young and beautiful girls are wont to say to older and greyer men.

CUE MUSIC VIDEO: SEXUAL HEALING
MARVIN GAYE

Of course, there is the nightmare version of this dream too. In that one, as Megan Fox steps out of the sliding door - on the left of the Previa remember – I hear the chorus of *Pump up the Volume* and a Manila Jeepney roars past, splattering her all over the bonnet/hood and she is impaled on the horses and the air horns............................AAAaaaargh!

I have got to stop eating cheese before I go to bed – my parents always reckoned that it gave you bad dreams!

The strangest part about this story is that, after I wrote this chapter on 01 June 2014, I did not see another Mark 1 Toyota Previa in the UAE for about three months. Not one. So, I thought that maybe I had broken the "magic spell" or whatever the connection was. But, you can catch up with the Previa phenomena later in the book.

I don't know what to think about all these different things. But, I do know that, as they often said in the X-Files, "The truth is out there".

28

WHILE YOU'RE DOWN THERE

September 2011 was a busy, but fun time. I am not quite sure what created the humour but all sorts of things seemed very funny to me and I would start making jokes about them. Maybe, it was the effects of the medications, as mentioned previously, or maybe it was a sense that my neck had been fixed - literally and figuratively – and that this was the beginning of my recovery.

One thing in particular that seemed to make me happy was the action of standing up – which I had not been able to do before. So, I guess it set off positive vibrations in my brain. I use the term "standing up" somewhat loosely as, at that point in time, it was more like a "drag, heave, lift and push me up"

Also, at that time, the Rochester was hiring a lot of new male Filipino nurses and they always started off with a probation period where the new nurses were tested and observed to see if they were OK. But, what seemed to happen was that they sent each new nurse into my room for a few days to "assist" Chris or give him a well-earned day off since he was looking after me seven days a week. I think the basic idea was that if they survived a few days with the "crazy Brit" then they would be fine with anybody else. Without a doubt, there was some truth in this theory as I was very particular about who did what and how with me and - unlike many of the other patients – I was able to verbalise it in great detail.

It worked out quite well for everyone concerned. They had to do an official assessment of the probationers, so after a couple of days, one of the senior Rochester staff nurses would come and ask me what I thought about the new guy. I always tried to be fair, as I knew that a lot of hopes were resting on securing a permanent position at the Rochester. But I always looked at it from the viewpoint of the safety of the patient. If there was an emergency and something happened to a patient in the middle of the night when no one else was around, would that nurse be able to deal with it or would he panic and do the wrong thing – or nothing? This was the baseline from which I gave my evaluation.

In part, this was also a matter of personal survival. What if something happened to me in the middle of the night – like when I was choking and I thought I was going to die? Would I trust that particular nurse to save me? It was often a simple gut feeling, but nevertheless, an important one. So, I always gave my honest opinion to the administrative staff at the Rochester since it was also for their protection as they would be ultimately liable if something bad happened.

But, OK, that was the serious part of the story. As I said, we had a lot of fun with the new recruits too.

There was one new nurse called Rex. Now, prior to meeting this guy I only knew of two Rex's. One was my best friend back in Nelson and the best man at my wedding to Agnes in Boracay, Philippines. And the other was Rex Harrison, the movie actor. Actually, there was one more Rex but he was not a person. It was *Rex the Wonder Dog* from Marvel Comics! Unfortunately for him, we teased Nurse Rex incessantly without ever telling him about the Marvel connection. I would say things like "Rex, you are a really good boy!", "You're a marvel Rex", "Sit Rex", "Stay Rex", and so on.

Rex the Wonder Dog

He was a lovely guy, but not the brightest crayon in the box so he never caught on! It was perhaps at its funniest when he was part of the action to get me standing up. As previously noted, it was really a "drag, heave, lift and push me up" by three nurses because I did not have enough muscle strength to stand by myself. I also needed braces on my knees to stop them buckling. Two nurses would lift me up and the third would kneel on the floor in front of me and push on my knees to keep them straight. Take a look at the picture to see what I mean.

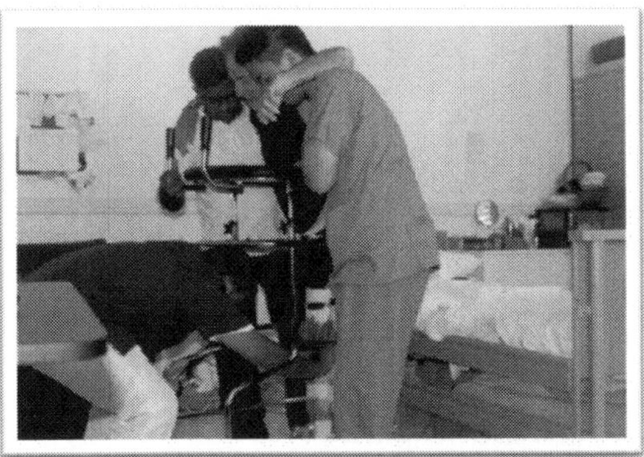

Who'se a Good Boy Then, Rex?

So, if it was Rex that was part of the trio helping me I would be saying things like "Stay down boy", "Good boy Rex", and so on and the two other nurses would be having a lot of difficulty lifting me up as they were laughing so much.

At other times Edna, Agnes' sister, would be part of the trio. You can see her in this picture. This was actually the one taken by the National photographer for the article about me as mentioned earlier. Chris and Greggy were holding me up with my arms around their shoulders and Edna was on the floor in front of me. The funny thing about this was that, as you can see, her face was right in front of my groin area. So, I jokingly said "While you are down there, how about a blow job?" Edna was looking up at me saying "Trevor, shut up!" And I was saying "How about if I say please and pretty please?" Naturally, all the boys, including the photographer, were cracking up at this, so it was difficult to compose ourselves and take a serious-looking picture.

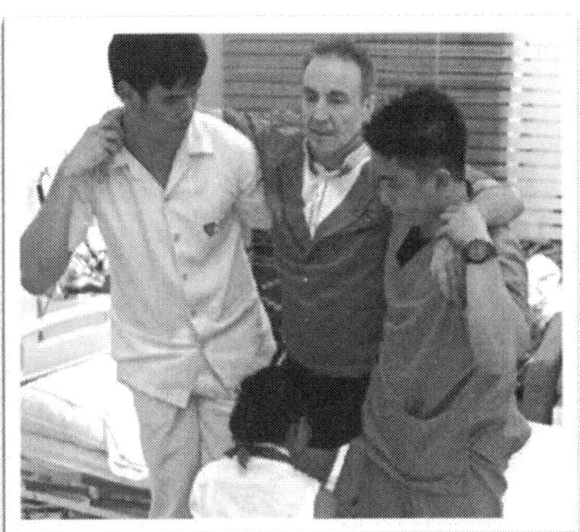

While You're Down There . . .

Eventually, Agnes and the two boys came back from the Philippines - so I had to stop asking Edna for BJ's. Well, you can't have everything!

Then we found out it was Greggy's birthday on 5 September. Party Time! Greggy had not planned anything so we organised a big party in the garden/pool area of the Rochester. All the staff and patients were invited plus we had lots of friends, the guys from the Potbellies Rugby Club and work colleagues. The whole garden/pool area was full. We even got Dennis de Castro, the Philippine Business Council's in-house DJ and music man. So, it really was Party Time!

CUE YOUTUBE VIDEO: GET THE PARTY STARTED
PINK

Although it has got nothing to do with the actual functionality of your body, having parties and a bit of fun while you are doing all the hard yards for your physiotherapy creates some sort of positive mind-set which really helps on the physical side.

Happy Blow Job to You!

And yes, we did get Greggy a cake and he did blow out the candle. So at least he had a BJ in September, even if I didn't . . .

29

KENNY & ACCALIA AND THE ROCK 'N ROLL KID

Kenny Jones and Accalia Hipwood, the UAE's Radio 2 DJs. What more can I say about those two? Finally, as a result of all the chat with them on the show, lots of SMSs and emails, they said they would like to come and visit me at the Rochester Clinic. This was great! Yo! Big Time!

On the appointed day I got myself set up to look relatively human, sitting in a big leather chair in my room when they arrived. There was a bit of behind-the-scenes cheating as I had to be lifted into the chair by three male nurses – I didn't tell them that, of course!

They arrived mid-morning after finishing the show and when they came in Accalia gave me a Radio 2 Goody Bag but said "Don't look at that now, you can open it later".

OK. So, we talked and talked about a whole bunch of things for almost 2 hours.

I told them that they had been a "life saver" for me and how the music they were playing was really uplifting every morning and that there were so many songs that somehow had links to me, my life and my current situation.

I said that I was really a first generation "Rock 'N Roll Kid" as I was thirteen to fourteen years old when rock/pop music as we know it today suddenly hit the radio airwaves. The Beatles and Elvis Presley were obviously the big contenders, but there were so many others too.

The Beatles were my idols, of course, as they came from Liverpool which is only about fifty miles away from where I lived. *Love Me Do* and *Please, Please Me* were their first two releases and were being played non-stop on the radio. I grew my hair and fringe long – well, it was long for those days – to copy their hairstyles and got caned a few times by the school Headmaster for it! And yes, corporal punishment was allowed – even encouraged – back then.

CUE YOUTUBE VIDEO: PLEASE, PLEASE ME
THE BEATLES (LIVE ON ED SULLIVAN SHOW IN USA)

As we talked, I told Kenny and Accalia that the big event in the summer of 1963 was that the Merseybeat Roadshow, with the Beatles as the headline act, came to Nelson, Lancashire, which was only a mile and a half from Brierfield, where I lived at the time. I managed to get tickets – I think they were about ten shillings at the time (half of one pound sterling!!!) – and persuaded 3 of my friends to come with me. We were like the 4 Musketeers – Peter Skirrow, John Stephenson, Alan Storton and I.

It was a Saturday in early July and this was "Wakes Week" in Nelson. That meant that all the cotton mills were closed, everyone went on holiday (usually to Blackpool) and the fair (carnival for the American readers) came to town. We had some rides at the fair in the afternoon and then went - very early - to the Imperial Ballroom where the show was to be held. The Imperial was then tagged as the largest ballroom in the North of England. Actually, it was a converted World War Two bomber hangar! It was big enough to fit a few Lancaster Bombers in it. I worked it out that we had to go early as I wanted us to be one of the first in the ballroom so we could be at the front, near the stage. We were just fourteen year old kids, so I knew we would not be able to see anything if we were in the middle of a crowd of older teens and twenty-somethings.

We went there about 3:30pm and "finally" at about 6:30pm the doors opened. We were the first in! And we all ran across the huge floor to get to the front where they had placed a big semi-circle of leatherette sofas in front of the stage as a sort of rudimentary protection for the performers. We leapt over the back of one sofa and plonked ourselves down. We had made it! We were literally only a few feet from the stage in what would be VVIP seats in any concert today and which would probably cost several hundred pounds/dollars. We got ours for ten bob!!

Then we had to wait a couple of hours till the show started. There is nothing new in concerts. Fifty years later you still have to wait a couple of hours before the band turns up! But what a show it was . . .

There was Gerry and The Pacemakers, The Merseybeats, The Searchers, The Fourmost, Billy J. Kramer and the Dakotas and, topping the bill, The Beatles.

We had never been to a rock concert before so we had no idea really what it would be like. None at all! We were really lucky to have those seats as the rest of the several thousand people in the audience were all standing. Of course, the noise level was phenomenal - our eardrums had never encountered anything like it. And when you were only a couple of feet from the speakers you felt every note. But I am not sure which were louder, the bands or the screaming from the girls in the audience!!

As you could see (and hear) in the *Please, Please Me* clip of the Beatles on the Ed Sullivan Show in the USA all the girls were screaming and waving and fainting. Apparently, they were also peeing their pants too!! I saw a documentary recently with old footage of the Rolling Stones and Mick Jagger commented in an interview about their first American tour that girls were fainting everywhere and there was always the strong smell of urine! I don't remember the smell of urine that night with the Beatles so maybe British girls from Northern cotton mill towns had stronger bladders than American girls at the time . . .

But I do remember the fainting girls, for sure. All night there was a constant stream of young comatose girls being passed from the audience, over our heads, to the "bouncers" waiting in the semi-circle, who then took them backstage or outside to recover. This was amazing stuff for fourteen year-olds and the flow of fainted girls built up to a crescendo when the Beatles came on stage for their set!!

It was brilliant, for sure! John, Paul, George and Ringo in their Cuban-heeled boots only a few feet away from you can never be forgotten . . .

Live bands, rock music, huge amplifiers, tons of adrenalin, huge audience and that feeling of being wrapped up in the music. I was hooked! I have been to loads and loads of concerts since that first one but the feelings are still the same.

Kenny and Accalia seemed to love this story and I got lots of the famous Accalia laughter and the follow-on rumble from Kenny Jones.

So, we talked and talked and talked about all sorts of stuff and I told them about my personal belief that I would fully recover and that the song *Don't Stop Believin'* by Journey was what it was all about for me. I told them about seeing it for the first time on Glee and how it made me cry.

Eventually, they had to go so I asked if I could open the Radio 2 Goody Bag before they left. They were OK with this and Accalia explained that they had just grabbed a few things off the stockroom shelves before they left the studio, so it was just a mish-mash of stuff.

So, I opened the bag and the first thing I pulled out was a CD of the Beatles *A Hard Day's Night* album. Was this a coincidence or was it TINSTAAC – There Is No Such Thing As A Coincidence?

Then the next thing I pulled out was a copy of the Radio 2 Compilation Album and the first track on that was – wait for it – *Don't Stop Believin'* by Journey. Whoooooooooooo! Spooky stuff, what! I am getting goose-bumps just writing this and its three years later. Just listen to the track on that album which is the original version with the legendary Steve Perry.

CUE YOUTUBE VIDEO: DON'T STOP BELIEVIN'
JOURNEY WITH STEVE PERRY

What could I say? This was just amazing. How come they picked those two albums? They had no idea about the stories I would tell them. I had never mentioned any of it in previous conversations and communications. Yet another example of my TINSTAAC concept!!

This video is actually the opening sequence of the Beatles movie *A Hard Day's Night* and gives you some idea of "Beatlemania".

CUE YOUTUBE VIDEO SONG: A HARD DAY'S NIGHT
THE BEATLES – MOVIE TITLE SEQUENCE

Anyway, a BIG THANK YOU to Kenny and Accalia, who lifted me up at the start of every day, even when it had been "A Hard Day's Night" for me. There were lots of nights after my operation when the pain and the spasms and the thunderbolts rocketed up and down my body. But there was always a good song on the radio to wake up to. And they continued to do that every day, without fail, for another three years. Their music, chat and laughter did make the pain go away and it always felt like they were doing it just for this particular "Rock 'N Roll Kid".

POST SCRIPT

I have to say that when I wrote this chapter - in early August 2014 - I was very sad that the Kenny and Accalia early morning partnership on Radio 2 was no more. Kenny was still on the early show, but with Daisy and various others. And Accalia had her own afternoon show. But the magic "something" that worked between them was fantastic at the time and I hope it can be repeated someday.

30

HERE WE GO ROUND THE MULBERRY BUSH

Here we go round the Mulberry Bush
The Mulberry Bush
The Mulberry Bush
Here we go round the Mulberry Bush
On a cold and frosty morning.

Somehow, this period and the activities that I was doing always made me think of this kid's nursery rhyme. I am sure that most kids who sing this nursery rhyme have never actually seen a Mulberry Bush, I certainly haven't! By November 2011 my life at the Rochester had settled into a fairly regular routine. Six days a week I had three sessions a day; Physiotherapy from 10:00 - 11:00am, then two hours of break until Occupational Therapy from 1:00 – 2:00pm, then another two-hour break before my second Physiotherapy from 4:00pm – 5:00pm.

The morning PT session was usually in the Gym doing a workout on the equipment there. The OT session was always in the OT room (not surprisingly!) and then the afternoon PT session was usually focussed on making me walk. The walking was primarily around the balcony of the atrium. This was a pleasant place to learn to walk as it was light and airy due to the roof window and a big, double-storey window on the stairway. It had a waist-high wall with a rail on it which I could hold if I needed to.

The great thing about the atrium walkway was that it was exactly twenty five meters for one circumnavigation. I know that was correct because we measured it as my walking psychology needed to know how far I had walked in any given set or on any given day. The good thing about a twenty five meter loop was that four of them were a one hundred meter walk (*no kidding Mr. Genius!*) - which is the length of a rugby pitch. Knowing I had walked that distance – or multiples thereof - always had a positive psychological significance for me.

At this point in time I was just starting to learn how to walk again so I had to use the high rolling frame. You can see what I mean by "high" when you take a look at the pictures below. Basically, it was a u-shaped frame that more or less came up to my armpits. On the top of the frame there were pads on which to rest my forearms and two vertical handles at the front for me to grab. It moved on four castor wheels.

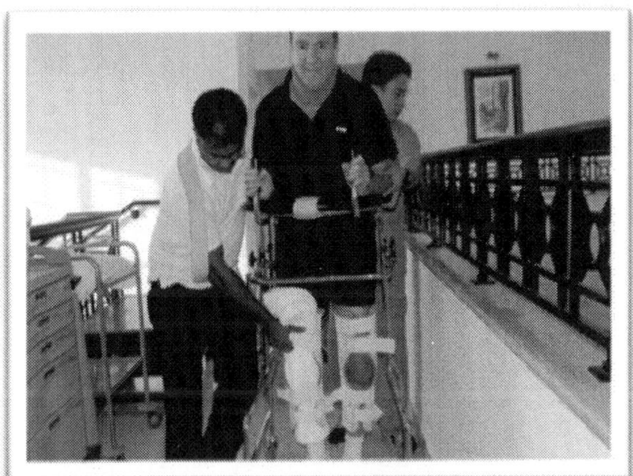

Rocking 'N Rolling Along

As you can see in this picture I needed the knee braces to make up for the missing strength of my thigh's quadriceps muscles. Without those braces I would have just crumpled to the floor. Previously, I talked about what an effort it was to get me up from the bed or the wheelchair and into a vertical position. Even with the knee braces, I needed help to swing my right leg forwards for walking as my hip problem meant that my own weak muscles could not do it.

So, round and round we went. Day after day. It really was like the nursery rhyme – *Here we go round the Mulberry Bush*. But there were never any cold and frosty mornings – it was always hot. We were in a desert, after all.

But it was strange, as some days I walked for, say, two hundred metres in one go. That was eight times round the atrium (Duuuuh!). But other days I could hardly manage once around without a rest. That really is the nature of the beast. Some days your body is ready and responsive and others it just does not want to respond despite all the urging of the brain to do more.

I have to admit that this was a tough time. I felt just the beginnings of muscle movements but with very limited strength. So, everything I did I needed assistance. It needed three people to lift me out of bed and into the wheelchair. Three people to get me stood up and into the rolling frame when I got to the atrium. It actually felt like I was having my arms pulled out of my sockets every day when they pulled me up from the wheelchair into the frame. My upper arms really hurt like hell and then I had to use those same muscles to support my elbows on the rolling frame when I walked. Every walking session needed four or five rest periods, which meant that each time I had to be pulled up by two of the nurses and needed a third one to push on my knees to stop them buckling.

This was really tough stuff, and there was virtually no respite as it happened six days a week. But one morning I heard the (then) new Kelly Clarkson song on Radio 2 – *Stronger (What Doesn't Kill You),* and I thought "Yeah, right!!" It just gave me a bit of a boost so that when I was tired, and my arms were hanging off my shoulders like jangling wind chimes, and my legs felt like jelly, I thought of that song and sang the chorus in my head. See what you think . . .

CUE YOU TUBE: STRONGER (WHAT DOESN'T KILL YOU)
KELLY CLARKSON

So, there were good days and bad days, and there was no telling which days were going to be which when I woke up in the morning.

The other thing about this period of my recovery was that I had to get used to being on my own. Not totally, of course, there were always nurses, physios, and doctors around me. But it was my wife and family that I was missing. When I was in the Al Noor Hospital in Abu Dhabi I was only about ten to fifteen minutes from the house, so I had lots of family visitors every day and at all times during the day. But when I started at the Rochester I was in Dubai and they were all in Abu Dhabi. As a result, I only saw them at weekends when they would come and visit me and sometimes stay over.

The good thing about the room I had at the Rochester was that it had originally been a large office divided into two by a glass wall and glass door. When I was there, I stayed in one half which was furnished with a big TV, leather sofa and a couple of leather armchairs. In the other half, there was a double bed, wardrobe, a small table, a couple of stand chairs, cabinets and a big fridge. So, we brought our own microwave, kettle and stack of food so that we could make our own meals, zap food in the microwave etc. and generally be fairly self-sufficient. It also meant that Agnes and/or the whole family could stay with me for the weekend or overnight whenever they wanted to.

Naturally, Agnes was still working in Abu Dhabi and the kids were in school there, so I spent a lot of time on my own staring at the ceiling or practicing Omphaloskepsis, something like the four naked gentlemen in the photo. Well, what happens when you have done about as much navel contemplation that you can manage for one day? In my case I would communicate with Agnes by email.

The Art of Contemplating One's Navel

Actually, a lot of the email communication between us was initiated by her and I got sucked into the habit due to my situation. I am not sure how many people know this, but the Filipino culture is very "non-confrontational". You go into any office in the Philippines and the chairs for the visitors are always placed sideways – so the visitor is not directly facing the host. Also people there will often tell you what they think you want to hear rather than what you really need to know. And Filipinos will very rarely argue back when someone shouts at them – my wife being a significant exception to this - but they may then never, ever speak to that person again, and will take any opportunity to make "tsismus" about them to verbally stab them in the back. However, the "Chinese Wall" provided by the internet means that they can be much more direct with emails.

There is a similar situation with phone texts (or SMS to some people). I have known people in the Philippines break up relationships of several years using texts. That was in the days before smart phones with QWERTY keyboards and smart predictive text. At that time everyone used the short form of words as they were pressing the number keys on the phone one, two or three times to get the appropriate letter. So, you got "I luv u" for "I love you" or "I h8 u n dnt wnt t b ur GF n we r fnshd" for "I hate you and don't want to be your girlfriend and we are finished". Good Aah!

So, yes, I would get these long emails from Agnes saying we need to do this and we needed to do that and the other. There was a period when she went through the "anger" phase in the trauma psychology syndrome, so I got quite few emails where I was blamed for having my accident. This was despite the fact that an accident is an accident is an accident. But it was my fault for being there. It's a bit like the well-known theory in some countries that if a foreigner has a car accident involving a local person, then it must be the foreigner's fault as, if he had not been in the country, the local person would not have crashed into him. Right?

Of course, the combined accident, hospital, surgery and rehabilitation put a huge pressure on the whole family. Being in two different cities added to the stress as Agnes had to do all the things to look after the family as well as work and be involved with my recovery. So, as you can imagine, the contents of the emails were many and varied!

It was a bit like the love-hate relationship thing that went on between Tom Hanks and Meg Ryan's characters in the movie *You've Got Mail.* In case you forgot, Tom Hanks played Joe Fox, the owner of a mega-chain of bookstores and Meg Ryan played Kathleen Kelly, the owner of a little independent bookstore called "The Shop Around the Corner".

They communicate on line using anonymous pseudonyms, getting more and more interested in each other – but without realising that in the business world they are arch-enemies. Maybe I should have used a pseudonym when I was emailing Agnes!

CUE YOUTUBE VIDEO: YOU'VE GOT MAIL
TOM HANKS & MEG RYAN

Some nights when I was on my own I would be restless and unable to sleep. My medications obviously had an effect on that. So, I would grab the attention of whoever was around or on duty and talk them to death. One time James was staying with me but the rest of the family was in Abu Dhabi. It was a school break as his holidays were often miss-aligned with the other two boys as he was in Choueifat School and they were in Al Yasmina.

One night I could not sleep and I started talking and talking and talking to James. Well, not so much to him as at him. I was telling him all about my youth – not so much about the misspent bits – more about the good bits. I did not want to give him any ideas about ways to misspend his time!

I was also telling him about my previous marriage and about the growing up years of his half-brother, Elliott who is about 10 years older. And I told James about how I met his mother, Agnes, and how we ended up getting married on the beach on the island of Boracay on Millennium New Year's Eve.

Of course, what you are getting there is the short version. The very, very short version! What James got was the very, very, very long version. In fact, it was so long it lasted all night and the sun was coming up when I finally let him go to sleep.

I drifted off to sleep for a while and then woke up about 8:00 am when Chris, my nurse, arrived and started making my breakfast.

As always, one of the first things he did was turn on the radio and the Kenny and Accalia show was on. And, amazingly, the first song they played when the radio came on was *Marry You* by Bruno Mars!

CUE YOUTUBE VIDEO: WANNA MARRY YOU
BRUNO MARS

Of course, it must have been TINSTAAC – There Is No Such Thing As A Coincidence. Yet another bulls-eye by Radio 2. Even more so when you consider that, like James, Bruno Mars is half-Filipino.

POST SCRIPT

Sometimes a combination of TINSTAAC and Morphic Resonance produce some slightly spooky things. I was going to call this chapter something related to the *You've Got Mail* movie till I had finished it and thought that the Mulberry Bush thing was more appropriate as it started with the nursery rhyme. When it was done I sent it to my sister Lynn to do her usual first proofread of my chapters. But, she sent an email back saying she couldn't do it right then as she was in Arromanches in Normandy, France. She lives in North Carolina, USA, so she was a long way from home! She had previously told me she was going to UK in October, but had never mentioned France, so I asked her why she was there. Her reply was that she wanted to see where our Dad had landed during the WWII when he was in the Royal Corps of Engineers. The retreating Germans blew up all the bridges, so they replaced them with floating pontoons called Bailey Bridges. And he built those new bridges.

She said I should have a look at the history of Arromanches as it was a significant factor in the war and an amazing engineering feat.

So, I took a look on Wikipedia and found that the story was all about the "Mulberry" Harbour that had been built by the Allies from floating and submerged caissons that they manufactured in England and then towed across the channel to make the harbour. The Allies needed a harbour to be able to unload all the troops, trucks, equipment and supplies to support the D-Day assault. "Mulberry" was just a code name.

On top of the obvious connection between the rhyme and the code name of the caissons, the really spooky thing was that I was doing all the above stuff about Arromanches and Mulberry Harbour on the 4th October which - if he had still been alive – would have been my Dad's 93rd birthday. Have you ever had the spirit move you? TINSTAAC. There is no such thing as a coincidence . . .

RIP - Dad

31

CLOUD NINE - HAMMAD AND JOYZ

Of course, there were lots of other patients in the Rochester Wellness Centre. It had twenty two rooms and the patients were there for many, many, many different reasons. Spinal injuries, strokes, road traffic accidents, post-operation rehabilitation, speech therapy etc. etc. One of the patients was a young guy called Hammad. He was an Arab kid and he had, I am guessing, some quite serious problems. He was confined to an electric wheelchair so that he could get himself around as all his limbs were very small, and his hands and arms were always bent up.

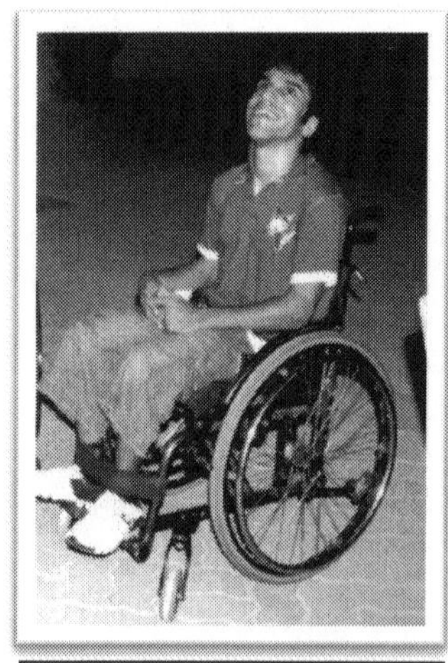

Always Happy Hammad

He also had a speech impediment. He spoke like he was talking down his nose, through clenched teeth, out of the corner of his mouth, if you can imagine that! Unfortunately, because of this, people thought he was a bit stupid. But Hammad was far from that. He was not stupid at all. In fact, he was very smart. He used to come to my room often because he had the one across the hallway. So, he would come over and watch television and, of course we would talk, so I got to know him quite well.

The funniest thing about Hammad was he was madly in love with Joyz. She was a young Filipina, small and pretty and Hammad really, really fancied her. She was one of the Clinic administrators and she was often in the reception area. If Hammad wasn't doing his physiotherapy, he was usually to be found sitting in reception staring at Joyz. So, naturally, I used to joke with both of them about this. Unfortunately for Hammad, despite the fact that he really fancied Joyz, he could not really do anything about it, but he would sit in his wheelchair and just stare at her anyway with big "puppy dog" eyes.

One day it just so happened that there was only Hammad and I in the gym and there were no other patients around. Usually, the gym was full of people and there would be a mix of patients, family and physiotherapists, all doing different things. But on this particular day we were the only two there with our respective physios. I was sitting in my wheelchair doing pectoral exercises on one of the machines with my physio, Velu. And Hammad was opposite me on a big, high, exercise table. It was a bit like a massage bed, but much bigger and wider.

His physiotherapist, Isaac, was trying again and again to get him to do a particular exercise. But he just didn't want to do it at all. I don't know whether he really didn't like it or he didn't think he could do it. Either way, he was refusing point blank to cooperate.

"No. No. No. I'm not doing that," he was saying in his Hammad-down-the-nose-through-clenched-teeth-out-of-the-corner-of-his-mouth kind of way. So, it came out like "Nnnnnuh. Nnnnnuuuh. Nuuuuuuuhh. I'mmm nouuuttt doooinnnnnn thaaatt!"

Now, this particular exercise required Hammad to be on his knees on all fours on top of the bed. Basically, his hands and forearms were on the bed in front of him, his knees were on the bed, and his backside was stuck up in the air. Actually, I am sure that you can all imagine this; he was in what we would call the "Missionary Position". And, for those of you who still don't get it, the Missionary Position is the standard position described in "How to Make Love 101". It's the one generally adopted in most cases, by most people, or so I'm told!

Of course, Hammad has never had an intimate relationship in his life so he didn't really know what the physio wanted him to do which was to push forward and down, push forward and down, push forward and down, basically as though he was making love to someone. However, as I said, Hammad has never made love to anybody and on that particular day he did not want to do this exercise. So, I looked over at him and said, "Hammad, why don't you pretend you're making love to Joyz and enjoy the exercise?"

Straightaway he starts! WAP, WAP, WAP WAP! Hammad is going hammer and tongs . . .!!

He finished the exercise and everybody clapped and cheered and had a big laugh and I said, "Hammad, did you enjoy that?"

"Nnnyeeeth!" he said

"I bet you're on cloud nine", I said

"Nnnnooough," he replied " I'mmm onnnn ccclllowwwd tennnn!!!"

CUE YOUTUBE MUSIC VIDEO: CLOUD NUMBER NINE
BRYAN ADAMS

We all cracked up and we howled with laughter. It was just a very funny thing. Like I said at the beginning, he was actually really smart.

Then there was a follow-on to the story. The next day I was in the Occupational Therapy room which had a similar bed to the one Hammad was on the day before. My physiotherapist that day was Isaac and he was asking me to do the same exercise as he had done with Hammad. So, I got on the bed and into the same "missionary position" on my hands and knees. My occupational therapist, who was a young Indian girl called Kriti, was also in the room with her patient plus a couple of the patient's relatives. It also happened that my wife Agnes was there too. I started telling them all the story of the previous day with Hammad and I'm explaining how it went. They all thought it was hilarious and so did my wife, Agnes.

But, of course, I was on the exercise bed in the "missionary position" while I was telling and demonstrating this story. So, I tried to persuade my wife to get on the bed and get underneath me so I can do the exercise "properly", and everyone was cracking up because I am saying "Please and pretty please . . .!"

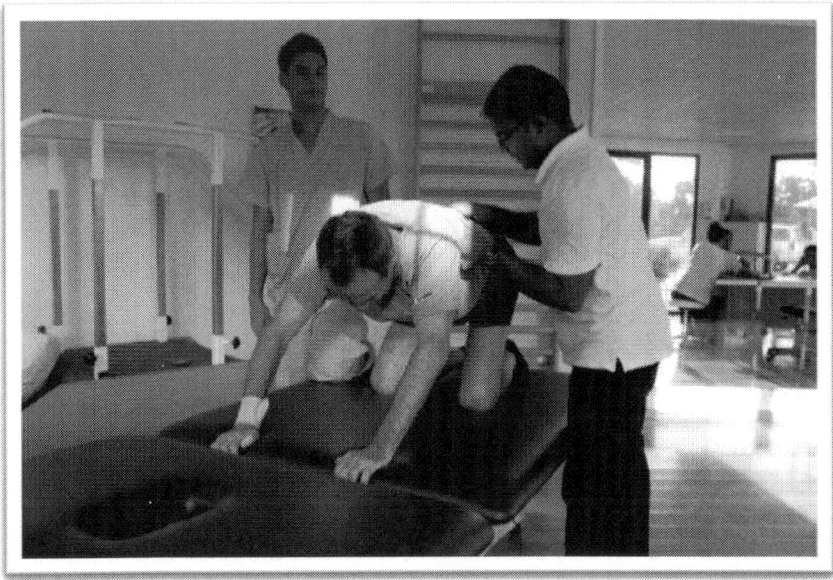

TSB - Adopting the Position - But Where Did The Girl Go?

But, unfortunately, there was no "Happy Ending" for me in this story. But that's life in the physiotherapy fast lane.

CUE YOUTUBE MUSIC VIDEO: LIFE IN THE FAST LANE
EAGLES

32

MACCA, THE BOSS AND ME

The Abu Dhabi Formula 1 Race is held at the Yas Marina Circuit each year in late November or early December. This is a huge event for the city and they always have fantastic after-race concerts for the three-day race weekend. In November 2011 it was American pop princess Britney Spears on the first night, then US rockers Incubus plus veteran British rock band The Cult on the second night. Topping the bill for the final night's concert was former Beatle, (Sir) Paul McCartney.

Back in Chapter 29, I talked about seeing the Beatles in 1963 on their first big tour when I was a whipper-snapper of only fourteen summers. So, despite my inabilities and temporary disabilities, I really wanted to go to the race and the concerts. I just had to do it.

What started it off was a small competition in the newspaper a few days before it was officially announced that Paul McCartney was headlining the F1 concerts. There was a picture of a pair of eyes and eyebrows and you had to guess who it was. It was obvious to me that it was The Macca.

Way back (waaaaay baaaack), when I was in my teens and early twenties, I was told that I looked similar to Paul. My long/Beatle cut hair had a significant impact on that, of course. It also had a significant impact on my hands and fingers as I was caned a few times by the Headmaster at school for having long hair. It wasn't really, really long, but it did cover my forehead and part of my ears so it wasn't the regulation "short back & sides" or (worse) the "bowl cut".

And now a SPOT THE DIFFRENCE competition. Have a look at the two pics below. One is yours truly and one is Macca. What are the differences?

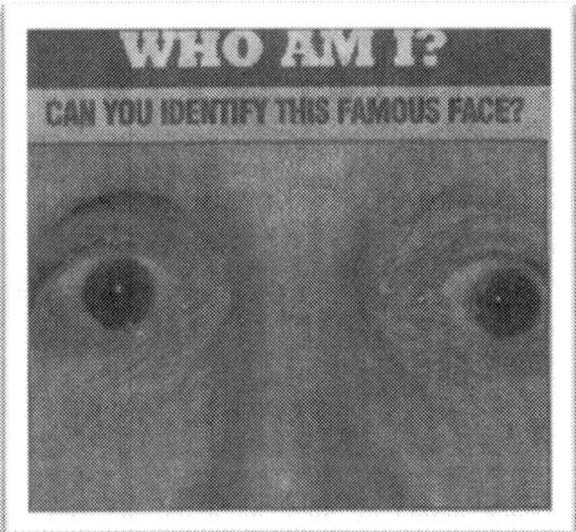

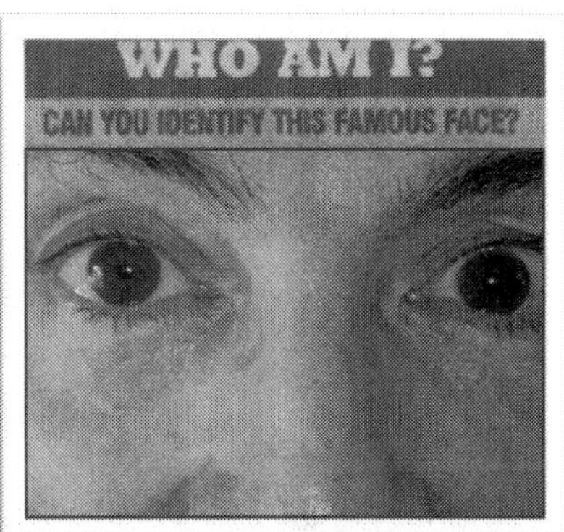

The differences in the pictures are that Macca has lots of money and musical talent and I, unfortunately, don't have either. But at least I don't have to speak with a scouse accent. (If you are not sure what that is, see more about scouse and scousers in Chapter 41). Oh, and he is the one on the left.

When I found out about the Paul McCartney concert I called one of The National reporters who had done an earlier article on me and I told him the story of me seeing the Beatles 50 years previously, as I had told Kenny & Accalia in Chapter 29. So, the reporter and photographer came to the Rochester and did an interview and took a bunch of photos. I have put the link to the on-line version of the article below. The nice touch was that they put a photo of Paul and one of me in there (click on the arrows at the bottom right of the main pic to shuffle) and they chose ones where we are both holding up our arms and pointing. And even better is the fact that there is also a picture of The Boss, Bruce Springsteen, (Do I have to say his name? Surely, everyone knows who The Boss is? Duuuuh) in a related article about him and Macca – and he also has his arm in the air and pointing!

So, there you go, my big claim to fame is that I shared the headlines with Macca and The Boss. Can't be bad for a guy with zero musical talent . . . !!!!

CUE THE NATIONAL ONLINE NEWSPAPER LINK
TSB AND PAUL McCARTNEY STORY

And to prove it, here are the pics!

Macca, The Boss and Me. All Giving "The Finger"!

I actually tried to get to meet Macca while he was here and my friends, Kenny and Accalia at Radio 2, were in discussions with "his people". But they could not manage to make it happen. Ah well, it was a big opportunity missed – for him I mean. Well, how often in the UAE would he get the chance to meet a fan who had watched him 50 years previously? Maybe, he did not want to appear that old!

But that meeting would have been a great promo for him (Oh, and just a teensy-weensy bit for me too) and I could then have written nice things about it in this book. As it is, all I can say is that his concert became a huge pain in the arse for me. Literally!

In case you are not aware, to go to the after-race concerts at the Abu Dhabi F1 you have to have a ticket for the actual race. You can't just buy tickets for the concerts. Naturally, as a true petrol-head, I wanted to watch the race anyway, as well as the concerts.

The best deal is to get a 3-day ticket then you can watch the race practice sessions, qualifying, and the race itself. It also means you get automatic entry to all the concerts. I wanted to be there every day and see each of the artists, so I bought two tickets so that I could take different family members on different days to the track and to different concerts.

I was very much confined to my wheelchair at this point in time so I had also to take Chris, my Mr. Spock-look-alike-nurse, along with me to push me around. So, that's what we did. Colby (then 6 years) came with us to see Britney Spears, Kyle (then 10) came to see Incubus and The Cult, and Agnes came with me to the Paul McCartney one. James (then 16) also came to see Macca as he had been working at the Yas Marina Circuit over the summer and had an official ID that got him in.

I sat in my wheelchair for three days non-stop from 8 am to virtually midnight when we got home from the concerts. And that's a looooong day - particularly when you are out in the heat and going up and down elevators in the stands and then back and forth across the brick-pave that is the most popular surfacing here. I can tell you that it looks nice but the cracks between the bricks every six inches make it a very jolting ride in a wheelchair – particularly when wheelchair manufacturers seem to think it's necessary to have solid tyres, no springs, and seats without any cushioning. I bet they never ever rode in one of their products from 8am to midnight!

As a result of all that punishment, by the end of the Macca concert, my arse was grass! It was not comfortable to sit down and I was holding myself in a semi-prone position, lifting my arse off the seat by pulling on the rail on the front of the raised disabled-persons platform.

It's a good thing that the Macca concert was brilliant, just brilliant. The man may have been 69 years old when he did the Yas concert, but, as James remarked, "He's still got it". He went through a whole repertoire of songs from virtually all the different Beatles albums. The big finale was Macca at the piano for *Live and Let Die,* the 1973 James Bond movie theme, from his Wings days with Linda McCartney and Denny Laine (formerly of the Moody Blues – another great band).

Of course, I had heard the song hundreds of times but never live and at full volume. And then when you throw in a chunk of exploding fireworks, pyrotechnics and lighting effects as a backdrop it turns into a huge, show-stopping, anthem. Just fantastic!!!!!!!

CUE YOUTUBE VIDEO: LIVE AND LET DIE
PAUL McCARTNEY

Yesssss! Fantastic, but very painful!!!

By the end of the concert I could hardly sit down! When we got home, Chris checked my butt (at my request) and he found that I had a deep bedsore just on the crease of my arse at the top of my leg. These little mothers take about three to four months to heal and are no fun – at all. It was just too much constant pressure from the bumping around in the wheelchair that brought it on.

So, as I told you, the Macca concert became a huge pain in the arse for me. But I would undoubtedly do it all again if I was given half a chance . . .

POST SCRIPT

Before the concert started they were showing a constantly changing collage of photos and images on the big stage screens, running from the early Beatles days in Liverpool up to the present day – but more on the old stuff. I was watching this as it was very interesting because many of the photos were from an era when I was a teenager back in a mill town in Lancashire, UK. But suddenly "that" picture came up on the screen.

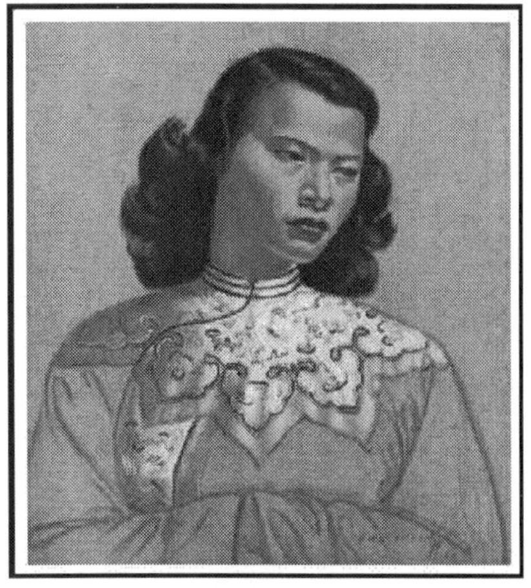

It was *The Chinese Girl* by Tretchikoff. And why was it significant? Well, when I was about 11 or 12 and living in Brierfield, Lancashire I used to go to the Boy Scouts every week on a Friday night. Oh, yeah, I could "Dib, Dib, Dib" and "Dob, Dob, Dob" with the best of them. On the way, I had to walk past an art shop - yes, surprise, surprise, we actually had one in Brierfield - and in the window, for what seemed to be forever, was a picture. "That" picture. I have no idea why, but I was incredibly drawn to it and would stop each time I passed – going and coming home – and just stare at the picture. I had never done that before and had no previous artistic pretensions. But I really thought that the girl was very exotic and incredibly beautiful. I don't think I had ever seen a live Chinese or Asian girl at that time, but I found the one in the picture hugely attractive.

Many years later I went to live in Asia and I am now married to a Filipina. She does not look quite like the girl in the picture but she has the high cheekbones, the Asian eyes plus that same exotic aura and, naturally, I think she is incredibly beautiful.

Is this a coincidence? But TINSTAAC, There Is No Such Thing As A Coincidence . . .

POST-POST SCRIPT

While we are talking about pictures, have a look at these two. Paul McCartney in 1970, aged twenty-seven, with long hair and a beard and TSB in 1974, aged twenty-three, with long hair and a beard.

1970's Style. Beard & Long Hair.
But Macca's Parting is On the Wrong Side

I'm the good looking one on the left, by the way. Maybe, I should have applied for a job as his body double . . . or learned to play the damn guitar!

33

XMAS 2011 – JINGLE WHAT? JINGLE WHERE?

Christmas is coming
The geese are getting fat
Please put a penny
In the old man's hat
If you haven't got a penny
A ha'penny will do
If you haven't got a ha'penny
Then God bless you

Christmas 2011 crept up on me very quickly. One minute it was February and I was running around on a rugby pitch. Next I was in hospital with a spinal cord injury. Then it jumped to August when I had my spine operation. And suddenly it was December and Christmas was upon us. Normally, I start to sense it coming way, way ahead as all Filipinos – and particularly my wife, Agnes – absolutely love Christmas. As soon as the months have a "BER" in them, it's Christmas. Like, SeptemBER, OctoBER, NovemBER and DecemBER. Plus, when you go to the Malls they also start putting up their Christmas décor much earlier than you would at home.

But, in the Rochester Wellness Centre I was somehow cocooned from all that. So, it was a big surprise when one of the admin staff came into my room to announce that there was going to be a Rochester Christmas Party. Oh, and they wanted me to suggest a party game! OOooooh, this had possibilities! What could I suggest that no one would have played before?

After a bit of thought I sent Chris to the medical equipment store to buy a stainless steel bedpan and to the supermarket to buy some non-alcoholic beer. For those of you who have never seen, or used, a bedpan take a look at the picture. It's a large stainless steel, oval-shaped, flat dish with the top edges bent inwards to form a seat – like a toilet seat. There is also a gap in the seat at the front of the bed pan so that you can pour the contents away easily. It's designed so that bedridden patients do not have to get up out of bed. They can just stay in bed and sit on top of the bed pan to have a pee or a poo.

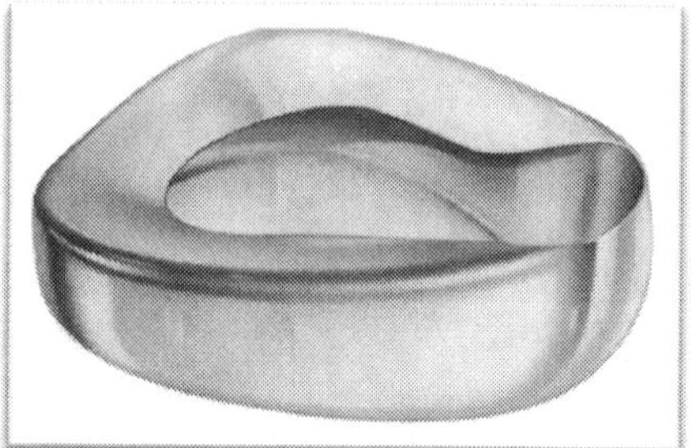

The Bedpan
a.k.a "The Holy Grail"

Every hospital ward has at least one of these. So, does the Manila Hash House Harriers (MH3), which is where I first encountered the alternative use for a bedpan. The link between Christmas parties, hospitals, bedpans and the MH3 may seem somewhat tenuous but there is one, trust me. Just read on!

The general principle of Hashing is that each week the members of the Hash meet at a designated location chosen by the Hare for that week. The Hare has previously set a trail using chalk arrows, flour, toilet tissue etc. around streets or countryside pathways, hills, forests, rivers or whatever location he has chosen and all the hashers have to find their way round and back to the beer truck.

The Hash was started by A.S. Gispert in Kuala Lumpur in 1938 and after the run they used to go to a place called the Hash House for the food. Hence, the name Hash House Harriers. Everyone is given a Hash Name. Mine was Briggs & Stratton as every pump boat in the Philippines had a Briggs & Stratton single piston engine to propel it from island to island.

SEE WEBSITE: MANILA HASH HOUSE HARRIERS (MH3)

And where does the bedpan come in? Well, once everyone is back, a Circle is formed and the Grand Master (GM), assisted by the Religious Advisor (RA), dispense fines on various runners for whatever transgressions they can think up – and most of these are fairly tenuous, believe me. But no one cares as that is all part of the fun as the "fine" is to drink a "Down-Down" of beer as quickly as possible out of the bedpan – also known as "The Holy Grail" in Hash terminology. So, now you can see why the Hash is a drinking club with a running problem! Life's tough in the MH3! For people new to this kind of "torture", there is generally some psychological reluctance to drink out of a bedpan especially when the contents are yellow and a little bit frothy. Just look at this guy's face. Yes, beer in a bedpan looks exactly like urine! And you have to put your lips to the edge of the bedpan where you know that its previous contents were poured out of……….. MMMmmmmmm!

Hash Name "Nancy Boy". Staring into the Holy Grail for Inspiration

But, don't assume the Hash is just for simple minded souls with merely a modicum of intelligence just because Hashers are a crepuscular bunch waiting for some afflatus from the RA before they head off to participate in celebrations of pure venery at their favourite nightspots.

The Hash Trash is full of big words – like the ones in the preceding sentence. So you need to have your Wiktionary handy at all times. To take a quotation from the MH3 HASH TRASH No. 2114 for the run held on 23 March 2015: Septic Yank gave us this paraprosdokian: "Manila hashers are a bunch of phat aulde pharts, but you can catch up to that high standard over time."

So, my idea for the Rochester Christmas Party was to have all the Filipino male nurses drink the non-alcoholic beer out of the bedpan while being timed against a stopwatch to see who was the fastest. Ha!

It worked wonderfully. We had all the usual party games like Pin the Tail on the Donkey – good practice for Occupational Therapy – and Musical Chairs, which is twice as difficult when you are somehow physically disabled! Have you ever tried Musical Chairs on crutches? People are getting entangled and off-balance and falling all over the place. It's WAY better to watch than if you have fit and healthy people doing it . . .

Then I got all the Filipino male nurses together for the bedpan game. We had kept the game a secret, and especially the fact that we were using non-alcoholic beer. It was being poured into the bedpan outside the door of the party room so they did not see it come out of the bottle. When they were given the bedpan and looked inside, it looked just like someone had peed in it. Remember, they are nurses and we are in a medical rehabilitation facility with lots of bedridden patients! So, to get the game going I did the first "Down-Down". Actually, I am really good at doing "Down-Downs" as I had lots of practice over twenty-seven years in the MH3 – including a stint as the Grand Master. I can just open my throat and

Hash Name "Egg on Legg".
He Knows How to Drink it Down
Like a Zulu Warrior!

pour it down really quickly. It never touches the sides. But you have to picture the scene to fully appreciate this game. All the patients and many of their family members were all in the OT room and most of the patients were locals so there were a lot of Emirati wives there too. Of course, they were not in on the secret either, so they probably thought that we were drinking urine from the bedpan.

Then it was the turn of the Filipino male nurses. One of the subliminally amusing things about this scene was that, while it was going on, Christmas tunes were playing to give the party atmosphere. One of the main ones, of course, is Jingle Bells and "Jingle" is the Filipino terminology for going for a pee. So, there were all the Filipinos drinking what looks like frothy urine out of a bedpan to the tune of Jingle Bells . . .

CUE YOU TUBE VIDEO – JINGLE BELLS

You can't make this stuff up!

Jingle bells, jingle bells
Jingle all the way
Oh, what fun it is to ride
In a one horse open sleigh

It was really funny to watch as each of them was initially quite reluctant to take a sip – they didn't know that I had bought the bedpan brand new the day before and it had never been used for its real purpose. But, once they realised that the yellow liquid was non-alcoholic beer and not urine, you could see the look of relief pass over their faces as they drank. So each of them took it in turn to drink and I got all the patients, families and other staff to chant "Down, Down, Down, Down . . ."

And Greggy, my first nurse, won the time challenge to the cheers of all the other Rochester staff. Good man!

POST SCRIPT

Here is a more normal Xmas scene. The Stott-Briggs family 2011 Christmas Card photo. Well, as normal as the Stott-Briggs family ever can be!

But How Come James Doesn't Have a Santa Hat?
Doesn't He Believe in Santa Any More?

2012

34

GLITZ, GLAMOUR, GARAGES, GRUNGE & GREGGY'S GIMMICK

February 2012 was an incredibly busy month for all of us in the family. Perhaps I could even go as far as changing the word "incredibly" for "excruciatingly". As I have said earlier, I had been living as an in-patient at the Rochester Wellness Centre since May 2011, but Agnes and the boys were still living in Abu Dhabi. This was very far from ideal as I did not get to see the family much and Agnes was left with the double task of working every day and also dealing with all the boys on her own. So, we decided to bite the bullet and move everyone to Dubai.

If you have not lived in the UAE, you might not appreciate that Dubai and Abu Dhabi have completely different characters. Dubai is all about "Glitz and Glamour" and it has a "Bright Lights, Big City" image. This is because, unlike Abu Dhabi, it does not have massive oil or gas resources, so it relies on trade, tourism, shopping and the hype of its glamorous lifestyle. Abu Dhabi is much more conservative. It has massive oil and gas reserves which enable it to do things at its own pace. Generally, Dubai has a younger, first-time expatriate crowd looking for exciting nightlife, whereas Abu Dhabi is more family-orientated with lots of parks for family picnics. You can still have all the nightlife in Abu Dhabi but it's on a "whenever you want it" basis. Dubai has a big social scene and it's almost obligatory to be part of it.

CUE YOUTUBE VIDEO: BRIGHT LIGHTS, BIGGER CITY
CEELO GREEN

The song *Bright Lights, Bigger City* by CeeLo Green, which was playing on the radio all the time in late 2011 and early 2012, describes it perfectly. Just have a look at this and tell me if it doesn't make you want to buy your girlfriend/wife/significant other a pair of diamond studded sunglasses!

But, the nightlife wasn't the reason for the family moving to Dubai. Far from it! But even so my personal night life was going to change quite radically for the better. Instead of chatting to the night nurse and/or watching MBC 2, the only English-speaking TV channel available on the Rochester cable TV package, I was going to be able to go home at night and sleep in my own bed. Well, sort of, as it turned out.

Doing that entire house move at a million miles an hour – and me only partially mobile – was a bit of a struggle. Trying to find a place that matched our requirements, was in the right place, was available at the right time, and for the right price was far from easy! Luckily, Agnes' twenty plus years' experience in the real estate market really paid off to get us what we needed. She found us a place in Garden View Villas behind the Ibn Battuta Mall, just off Sheikh Zayed Road, the main artery of Dubai. Location, location, location!

But the lease on the Abu Dhabi house ran out at the beginning of January and the new place was not available till the end of February. And, on top of that, we had to get the kids in a new Dubai school for the start of the January term. Luckily, we managed to get Kyle and Colby into the Winchester School, which was located only five minutes away from the new house and James got into Choueifat, Dubai on Hessa St, only a short metro ride from the house. So, that was all great – once we could move in!

Fortunately (ha!), I had the divided room with the extra double bed etc., etc., etc., at the Rochester so we all ended up living in my room for almost two months. You can imagine the panic and pandemonium every morning getting the kids up, ready and fed in time for school, get me showered, dressed and ready for my first PT session – the latter which needed assistance of the nurses - and Agnes off down the road to Abu Dhabi to her office. Wwwwoooo!!!! I used to joke with her that, as we were in a medical facility, she could get one of the nurses to give her an Inoculatte Coffee . . . !

The new house was great. Perfect. Well . . . almost perfect! It had three bedrooms upstairs, a decent sized living area and dining area, a downstairs bathroom and a big garden. What it did not really have – and what I really needed as I could not walk upstairs – was a downstairs bedroom. But it did have a real garage with an American style, electric up-and-over door. This was unusual as most houses in the UAE have either a car port or just a space in front of the house to park your car – as it never rains or snows. This one actually had car parking spaces as well as the garage. So, we converted the garage into a bedroom for me.

The Grunge Patient's Bed.
Somewhere to Relax Before the Next Jam Session

Of course, it had a rough floor and breeze block walls, so we put a carpet on the floor, painted the walls white and covered most of them up with the wardrobes and a chest of drawers plus a big mirror. The other thing it lacked was air-conditioning, but that was solved with a portable unit in the corner of the room near the door. Have a look at the picture and you will see that it's not bad – for a garage. You can also see the back of the up-and-over door on the right of the pic.

I used to tell people that I had become a "Grunge Patient" like the "Grunge Bands" that proliferated in garages in Seattle in the late 80s. I always reckoned that this happened because it rained a lot in Seattle and there was nothing to do and nowhere else to go except into the family garage and perform angst-ridden songs about the fact that it was raining all the time and they could not play outside. Kurt Cobain of Nirvana was one of the most famous of these, probably because he committed suicide by shooting himself, becoming some sort of a cult figure as a result. I blame the rain and all that angst! I am not sure if the gun in the *Come as You Are* video is the one he used to kill himself with, you must make your own judgement on that, but he obviously had a "thing" about them.

CUE YOUTUBE VIDEO: COME AS YOU ARE
KURT COBAIN & NIRVANA

The only other thing of note about Seattle is the very famous movie, *Sleepless in Seattle,* starring Tom Hanks and Meg Ryan. Probably, the real reason Tom Hanks couldn't sleep was due to the sound of the rain constantly drumming on the roof. It's the ultimate chick flick, but I reckon lots of guys have gone a bit wishy-washy at the ending on the view deck of the Empire State Building. That's probably because it just never happens like that in real life to ordinary guys!

I like to hypothesise that the gestation of the music scene in Liverpool in the 1960s and Seattle in the mid-1980s had certain similarities due to them both having cold weather and lots of rain forcing the young kids to stay inside and be creative. But I don't think that they could have done the same with the movie. Can you imagine *Sleepless in Scouseland* and the final scene being shot on the view deck of the Blackpool Tower? You can just imagine the elevator operator trying to get Tom and Meg – called Jim and Velma in the Scouse version - to get on with it and go back down. In the Seattle version he does a discrete cough. In the Scouse version he would say something like:

"Ee baay gumm, Scouser! Shurrup lad! Grab 'old of 'er 'and 'n gerrint' bluuddy lift. Me tea's gerrin cold!"

It does not quite seem to work the same magic . . .

Scouse Housing
Like Tom's House in Seattle (not).
With a View Over the Mersey.
Oh, Sorry Tom, is That Your Car?

Blackpool Tower
A Very Romantic Spot (not).
But Where is King Kong Hanging
Off the Lightning Conductor?

Getting back to the main story - Agnes and I were having a bit of angst of our own around this time as she was on my case about buying an electric wheelchair. Her reasoning for this was that it would make me more independent and less reliant on people pushing me around. I was resisting this strongly as my walking was slowly starting to happen and I did not want to take the easy route and drive myself around with a little joystick. Plus, they were heavy, difficult to lift in and out of the car, and very expensive. For me, I saw those electric wheelchairs as something that permanently disabled people used, and I was never going to admit to being permanently disabled. No way Jose'!!

As a result, there were huge arguments about having an electric wheelchair, but fortunately the physios were all on my side. They all said "Don't get one". So, I stuck to my guns - luckily not one of Kurt Cobain's - battened down the hatches and waited for the storm to subside. It never really did subside, but I held out despite that.

Meanwhile, back at the ranch, or rather the Rochester, my daily walking around the atrium was improving and I had graduated to using the Zimmer Frame. On St Valentine's Day I did a total of 24 laps = 600 metres. Wow! It must have been all the love in the air. I was having a rest at the end of all that and my sister Lynn called me from the States and, while we were chatting, she remarked that she was walking too - in her suburban neighbourhood. She has a dog and was in the process of picking up her dog's poop - because that was the law so you had to do it! I was silently chuckling to myself that the "American Dream" has a few drawbacks.

Then on 26 February 2012 I set a new record and did a total of 27 laps = 675 metres. It took an hour as I did it in stages of 7+6+4+5+5 laps and rested in between each set, but at least I did it. Wwwwwoooooooo!! That was Kyle' birthday and a year and a day after my accident.

As I was writing this chapter I was eating lunch - KFC Chicken Strips - when a bit of the crunchy batter got stuck in my throat. I was coughing, coughing, trying to drink water and turning red in the face. Kyle was with me and offering to help so I was thinking about the famous Heimlich Manoeuvre - hands under the sternum from behind and shake/squeeze the patient so that whatever is blocking the throat spits out of the mouth. But luckily, I eventually managed to cough enough to dislodge the bit of batter and I was OK again.

There is a very funny sketch about the Heimlich Manoeuvre in one of Eddie Izzard's *Dress to Kill* shows. As you saw earlier in the *Cake or Death* sketch, Eddie was in his high heels, kimono, eyeliner and red lipstick period at that time but, amazingly, does not talk in a gay way. A little "camp" perhaps, but then Michael McIntyre is even more camp and he has a wife and two kids. Eddie Izzard describes himself as "A straight transvestite or a male lesbian" if either of those oxymorons are actually possible. His comedic style is like a rambling, whimsical monologue and self-referential pantomime. He often takes several parts in his sketches, successfully talking back and forth to himself. And he uses a stream-of-consciousness delivery that jumps between topics. Hmmm, sounds a bit like this book! Anyway, just enjoy the sketch . . .

CUE YOUTUBE VIDEO: THE HEIMLICH MANOEUVRE
EDDIE IZZARD

But this also reminded me of another manoeuvre that was being applied to me in 2011 and 2012. Actually, at first it was not referred to as a manoeuvre, not even as a gesture. It was called Greggy's Gimmick. In case you had forgotten, Greggy was my original full-time Filipino nurse and Filipinos like the term "gimmick". In England we use the term generally to mean a clever ploy or strategy but the Filipino's use it to mean a trick or device used to attain some end. This latter meaning was probably more appropriate for this particular Greggy's Gimmick!

Right from the beginning of my incarceration I was suffering from significant constipation. Well, I wasn't suffering too much as I was having a regular dose of Greggy's Gimmick. And if you have to make a choice between constipation and LBM's, I would choose constipation every time. (See Chapters 7 and 43 for more on that subject).

So, what exactly was Greggy's Gimmick? Well, for some reason doctors in general are paranoid about constipation so they always want you to be "regular". My problem appeared to be that the neurological release button for my anal sphincter was not working very well, if at all. Have you ever tried to figure out which bit of the brain actually opens and shuts your sphincter? I have, but it's not at all easy. Stop reading for a second and try it and you will see what I mean. I think it's one of those subconscious things that you learn at the age of two and half and never, ever really think about again. You go in a bathroom, sit on a porcelain pedestal and – bingo – the gates open. But for me they didn't. I needed some assistance. That was where Greggy came in . . .

There had to be a planned strategy to make it work. First, there was the insertion of a suppository in the appropriate cavity. Wait for forty five minutes or so for a reaction. Then head for the bathroom. But, usually nothing happened. So, you wait a little longer. Next I would try pushing and thrusting and whatever other neural/physical actions I could achieve. Nothing happened. The next tactic was to spray the buttocks with hot water from the flexible showerhead. Nothing happened. So, if everything else failed, I had no choice but to ask Greggy to perform his gimmick – which, wait for it - was to push his finger, lubricated with soap, into where the sun does not shine – and wiggle it about (!!!!). And, just in case you are wondering – yes, he did wear rubber gloves!

What a gimmick! But it usually, immediately, had the required effect. So, what can I say . . . ?

One day I asked him if there was a proper medical term for what he was doing and he said it was called the Valsalva Manoeuvre.

Ach, so. Yet another manoeuver! Ze Heimlich Manoeuver ist verry strichtforvart und kann be performet in resturands und public platzez. Haweffer, ich do nicht rekommendt performink ze Valsalva Manoeuvre eggcepdt in ze privissy auft yur owvn bassrom!

But I looked it up and Wikipedia says that *"The Valsalva Manoeuvre is performed by attempting a moderately forceful attempt at exhalation against a closed airway. This is usually done by closing your mouth and pinching your nose shut while pressing out as if blowing up a balloon*". The end result is to make your ears go "pop".

Even after changing my full time nurse and having Chris instead of Greggy, the procedure was still always called Greggy's Gimmick. It was sort of much easier to ask Chris for Greggy's Gimmick than to say "Please put your finger up my butt".

So, while not quite medically correct, I guess Greggy's Valsalva Gimmick did have a similar effect as it made my sphincter go "pop" and my bowels open up and the pressure was relieved.

What more can I say, except always heed the Government Health Warnings!!

35

FUN, FUN, FUN

Having a house in Dubai meant that I was no longer on my own so much. The kids could come over after school and Agnes could come over in the evening when she got back from work in Abu Dhabi. So, we could all eat together. Also, it was much easier to go home for the weekend as it did not entail the long trek to Abu Dhabi in a van taxi with a wheelchair lift on the back. That was a nice feeling, believe me.

The PT and OT sessions at the Rochester were designed to improve my strength, muscle and nervous system activity, plus build up my stamina. And it was working. Three sessions a day, six days a week was a hard slog, but necessary to make gains. When I started that regimen I was really, really tired after each session and needed to rest. But as my stamina improved I recovered much quicker. Usually, a cup of Earl Grey tea and a biscuit did the trick – it's a sure British remedy for most things.

So, it meant I had more time in between sessions to do my Orascom work, but I did not want to be sitting up in bed doing it as I was likely to generate bed sores – and they are no fun at all. Luckily, one day, Agnes spotted a second Tilt Table that was not being used. As described earlier, the Tilt Table is actually for patients who have been horizontal for a long time and their bodies need to be reintroduced to being vertical.

But we thought of an alternative use for it. I could be strapped onto it and then made vertical. My laptop could be placed on a rolling bedside table in front of me, allowing me to work easily. Yo! We have the technology! And I had the legs! The straps were able to stop my legs and body from sagging but there was also the huge advantage that my legs were actually holding up most of my weight. My muscles were forced to have to work, and thereby gain strength, even though they were not moving.

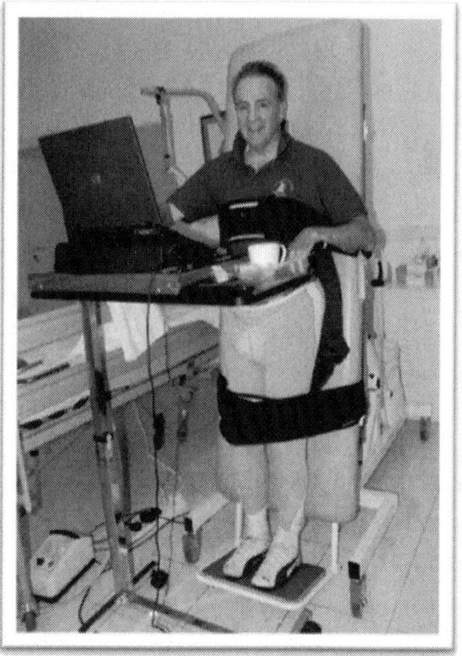

All Strapped In and Ready for Blast Off

Doing my job as Business Development Manager meant that I had to do a lot of emails related to projects for Orascom. Those, of course, can be done anywhere and there is no obvious sign of where you were when you wrote them. The internet is the internet is the internet, wherever you are. The fact that I was strapped upright to a Tilt Table - in my room or a quiet spot next to the gym at a physiotherapy clinic - would not show on an email. But I also had to make and take a lot of phone calls . . .

Most people I talked to would have probably been surprised if I had told them where I was at the time when I was making the call. I only told a few close clients about my situation as it was not necessary for most of them to know. Often, I would be in the PT Gym or in the OT Room – but I would always take the incoming call and the therapists understood that it was business, so I had to do it. I could always deal with the matter by sending an email, or make a few calls, within a very short time after finishing my PT/OT session. If it was urgent, I could be back on my laptop in a few minutes. So, it was fairly easy to carry on working, despite the nominal hindrance of having only a partially functional body.

Then, as I slowly regained my functionality, I was able to start going to meetings and interacting with people. This meant I had to get dressed up in a suit and wear a shirt and tie. Yo!

The dressing up process was slow and complicated at first. Getting into fitted, long sleeved shirts with lots of buttons instead of pull-on polo shirts, tying the tie, wearing trousers with zips, buckles, and belts instead of elasticated waist jogging pants, plus putting on proper lace up shoes instead of trainers, all took a lot of time and an amazing amount of energy even though Chris was helping me. But, naturally, it made me feel good to be dressed up in "real" clothes again. That small thing felt like a lot of progress had been made.

As part of this re-assimilation process, in mid-March 2012, I went to a Foundation Piling Conference at the American University of Dubai (AUD) as Orascom was one of the sponsors. I had never been to AUD before, just driven past it many time along Sheik Zayed Road. However, when I drove in I thought WOW!!! First of all the students' car park was full to overflowing with fancy, expensive cars - Porsches, Lamborghinis, BMWs, Mercedes-Benz and several American muscle cars – well, it was the American University of Dubai! Also, the campus buildings were really beautiful. The "feel" of it reminded me of the University of Queensland in Brisbane, Australia where my eldest son Elliott had studied. They don't have the huge UQ quadrangle but they do have lots of 3-4 storey buildings in American Neoclassical style architecture, old trees, grass, coffee shops, and bistros. AUD even has a building with a dome on it like the US Capitol building in Washington DC – that one being the central auditorium where the conference was being held.

At lunchtime, Chris and I went out of the conference to one of the bistro coffee shops as the March weather was perfect – sunny but not hot. In doing so we found another bonus point for AUD and that was the fact that while we sat and ate our lunch there was a non-stop parade of some of the most beautiful girls in the world that Chris and I had ever seen. And I mean non-stop. Chris and I could not get over it. I just can't remember when I have seen so many beautiful girls in one place at one time and this was just an ordinary Tuesday lunchtime, not a star-studded cocktail party on someone's yacht in Monaco on Formula 1 Race weekend.

I thought to myself that James must see this as it would show him it was worth studying hard and getting into university. He was at home that afternoon studying for his school exams, so I told him to jump on the metro and come over to AUD. When he arrived I took a coffee break at the bistro where Chris and I had lunch and I said,

"James, you can have this - or the equivalent anywhere in the world - though perhaps with fewer beautiful girls - if you just focus and pass your final exams. If not – McDonalds is hiring. . ."

He just smiled – a typical James' smile – one that makes his whole face light up. I am happy to say that the imagery and mind association did work – though it took a while. I am sure James' constant attendance on me, plus the psychological traumas for him dealing with my situation did have an effect on his ability to focus on his studies. During those times, when I needed a lot of assistance, James was always there for me and he never complained, whatever I asked him to do.

So, you can imagine how pleased we were when he passed his Finals and in September 2015 started university in UK doing a BSc. (Hons) in Motorsport Technology – a course on racing cars and sports car design.

I wish that they had a course like that back in the early '70s when I went to university!!!! My choice was to be a Civil, Mechanical, Electrical or a Production Engineer. You could take any course back then, as long as it was to be some sort of engineer. It was a bit like Henry Ford's colour options for the Ford Model T "Tin Lizzie" - you could have any colour you want, as long as it was black . . .

The whole scene at AUD – nice cars, beautiful girls, classically styled buildings, sunshine - was in sharp contrast to my memories of being a teenager in cold, wet Lancashire and jealously listening on the radio to the Beach Boys songs about "*California Girls*" and driving their daddy's T-Bird and having "*Fun, Fun, Fun*" instead of studying.

CUE YOUTUBE VIDEO: FUN, FUN, FUN – THE BEACH BOYS

The Original T-Bird.
You Could Have Fun, Fun, Fun
Till Your Daddy Took it Away

If you're not a petrolhead, the T-Bird they are referring to is a Ford Thunderbird. Even though it only had two seats, it wasn't what the Brits would call a sports car as it was a full-sized car with soft suspension and terrible handling. But really cool to cruise around in if you happened to live in California in the 60s. My California dreaming did eventually turn into reality as, in the late 90s, I worked for a company that was based in Sacramento. I had a house in Folsom and Elliott went to Junior and Senior High School there.

Amazingly, despite the external AUD distractions, I did do some work and manned our stand with Joanne Mahmoud and the other guys from the office. And I have the picture to prove it.

TSB in Best Bib and Tucker with Joanne.
In Conference at the AUD

At the end of the day, back at the Rochester when I was doing my atrium walking, Chris and I told Greggy all about the AUD and that we were going back the following day so that Chris could become a Permanent Undergraduate – he did not want to study a subject, just be a Permanent Undergraduate.

I had been doing quite a lot of my PT sessions in the OT Room. That may not seem to make sense unless you know that the parallel bars are in the OT room. The parallel bars are like the ones you see in ballet dance studios. I always wanted to be ballet dancer like Rudolf Nureyev – wearing tights and having a big bulging crotch box. Yeah right!

I had been trying to stand up between the parallel bars for well over a month. The PTs were counting the seconds. Naturally, I was very wobbly at the beginning; I had to hold onto the bars and could not get anywhere near 100 seconds duration. But slowly my strength was building up. Then one day I was in there with Velu and for some unknown reason everything was working in synchronicity. First, I managed to stay standing for 2 x 100 counts while holding onto the bars. Then Velu wanted me to stand while sliding my hands forwards & backwards.

Then he told me to let go of the parallel bars – so I did while still moving my arms forwards and backwards. Of course, I fell back into the wheelchair! So, he said do it static. I locked my knees – both of them – and then, one by one, took my hands off the parallel bars till I was balancing myself and standing up on my legs. Whoa! What a feeling. Immense! You can see the happiness on my face!

Happiness is . . .

I sent an SMS to loads of people - over 100 at least. They all replied with really great comments and I sat in the chair. Tears were in my eyes while I was saying in my head thanks to everyone who had helped me. I even uttered a little prayer for the miracle that had happened. Finally back on my feet! That was Sunday, 25 March – one year & one month after the accident.

Next, I just had to learn how to move my legs so that I could walk. Easy peasy, lemon squeezy!

At the end of the rugby season Harlequins always have a Summer Ball. It's a big night. A black tie event and an excuse for the WAGS to go and buy another fancy dress that they will probably only wear once. My wife would always say that she could not wear "that" dress as people have seen it before . . .

We decided to go as it would be a bit of a challenge for me and also an opportunity to let the Harlequins club members see how I was recovering. As with all these events it's a one price deal for food, wine and all the beverages you can consume. Some people take that literally and really do try to see how much they can drink – without regard for the consequences!

Is This What They Call "Dirty Dancing"?

And as it was a Summer Ball some of my "friends" who shall be nameless – Tom White and Terry Rooke – decided that I needed to go dancing. So, they grabbed me, one each side, and lifted me up and dragged me out onto the floor. The overall feeling for me was a combination of adrenalin and fear! The adrenalin was pumping as it was exciting and fun, and the fear was there in case these two very inebriated guys dropped me or we all fell on the floor in a heap. I know I was being careful about my liquid consumption as I still had the catheter, the tube and the urine bag strapped to my leg so I was really worried about it spilling if we all fell over . . .

I think the photo says it all!

Remember, at this point in time I had not learnt to walk and could only just about stand for 100 seconds if I had knee braces and if was concentrating very hard on staying as still as possible. And these two lunatics had me on the dance floor swaying and moving around.

I am happy to say that I survived the night – but I'm not sure how Tom and Terry felt the next morning as I am certain they drank a lot, lot, lot more than me. But at least I had my first dance!

And it was "Fun, Fun, Fun". I guess that's what friends are for . . .

36

REIKI AND HIGH SPIRITS

Most people have heard of the Bermuda Triangle. It's that area out in the middle of the Caribbean where – allegedly – unusual, ghostly and spiritual things happen. Ships and planes disappear or get "lost" forever. Navigational systems malfunction. Ships float around with no crew. And so on. Well, I think we have a place similar to that in Dubai. But in this case, the ghostly and spiritual things that happen are positive and healing – not frightening at all – and it's called Reiki.

Bill Middleton, our team physio who came on the pitch when I had my accident, happens to be a qualified Reiki Grand Master. What is Reiki, you may ask? Well, for those not in the know, it's a form of healing via energy by means of the Reiki Master putting their hands close to you or above some area on your body that has a problem. They don't actually touch you, the hands are just above the surface of your body, but you can feel what they are doing. Sometimes the feeling is hot, very hot. Sometimes it's cold, very cold. And sometimes it's a bit like an electrical sensation, tingling but not shocking.

Bill came to see me shortly after I transferred to the Al Noor Hospital in Abu Dhabi and, while he was there, he gave me my first introduction to Reiki. He put his hands close to my lower legs, but always kept a gap between them and my skin. But in a few seconds I could feel the heat he was generating in my muscles. It was very hot and very intense and very localised. There was no doubt at all that something was happening even though he was not even touching me. Amazing! But Bill said that he could not really treat me because we were very good friends, he had been at the accident and there was a strong emotional bond between us which would somehow affect his Reiki abilities. But he recommended another Reiki Grand Master and Spiritualist Medium to me. Her name was Rachel Beavan.

I couldn't get to see her for over a year as I was bedridden in the Rochester doing my initial physiotherapy and generally trying to get mobile again. But by about mid-2012, once I was able move around in the Dubai Taxi-Vans with wheelchair lifts, I set up my first appointment.

I had never heard of the residential estate where she lived. It was (then) new and you virtually never saw anyone moving around in there. It was like a ghost town. But an all-new ghost town. You can feel the spirits moving already!

Rachel is a lovely lady and always bubbly and chatty. And, every time I went there I would lie on her treatment bed and she would tell me what was wrong with me that week. Of course, there were plenty of things wrong with me. Half of my body didn't work at all and the other half was only partially functional! But each week, as my physiotherapy progressed, there would be something different that was on the top of my critical list. I never told Rachel what it was, but she always told me. And that was without touching me and always as soon as I had lain down. She was amazingly intuitive and accurate – every week! I wish "real" doctors were as good at this kind of diagnosis. They usually send you for loads of expensive, time consuming and sometimes painful tests. Rachel just looked at me and told me what was wrong.

She started off by treating me with Reiki and sometimes brought in another Reiki Master to give a double boost to the treatment. And, WOW, that generated some massive sensations. Hot, cold, tingling. You name it, I felt it.

After several weeks of this she asked if I was willing to try something different. The Reiki was already in the "something different" category, so "What the Hell – go for it" I said.

Rachel wanted to try spiritual healing on me . . .OOOOoops! Maybe I should retract and rephrase the "What the Hell" statement!!

So, when Rachel said she could get the spirits of doctors and medical experts to help my body recover I was happy to agree to it. And why not? There are many things we don't know about our bodies and the world we live in. There is a lot going on out there that we can't even imagine. For instance I have already told you about the "Transformer" Toyota Previas that follow me around, the TINSTAAC coincidences and Morphic Resonance. So, let's just accept that we cannot explain everything and take whatever is offered with an open mind.

This was at the end of August 2012. For the preceding few weeks it had been a bit frustrating. "Things" really get in the way of progress sometimes! There had been Ramadan for a month with short Physio hours, the Eid Holiday - 5 days without Physio - but I went in the pool at the Miramar Hotel in Fujairah and Rachel had been away on vacation. I had been on too many antibiotics due to UTIs and those really debilitate you for several days. I had been busy at work and having meetings. Busy having arguments with my wife etc., etc., etc.

On 28 August, at the Rochester Clinic, I had managed six rounds of the atrium at twenty-five metres per round. That's six in total but a stop for a rest in between each one. And it was really, really hard work! That night when I was just going to bed, Agnes and I were talking as she was helping me get ready for bed. Suddenly, she switched subjects and "attacked" me saying "What's wrong with your right leg?" fuelling a huge argument and the usual storming out of the room – by her of course, not me.

Then the following day I went for my session with Rachel. She immediately said that my right side looked weak. And, in fact, that has been my problem recently with standing & walking. My right knee wouldn't lock, my right thigh/groin muscles were not as strong as the left and my right foot would not lift properly so the toe would be catching on the ground.

Normally, Rachel would sit on my left side, but that night she sat on my right side and put her hands on my spine and my right thigh then she must have weaved some special magic spell that night . . .

The following day, walking with Isaac the Indian physiotherapist, started off inauspiciously – just one round then a rest, and it was hard work. He had also got me standing up by holding one crutch in the right hand, pushing off the wheelchair with the left and when I was up I would take the left crutch from him. Then we would go walkies! So, for the second set, I got up as just described and started walking and, somehow, the rhythm just came.

After a couple of rounds I went through the "pain barrier" and just kept going. I did eight rounds of the atrium without stopping. That's two hundred metres!! A personal best – my previous best was three rounds without stopping. And the eight were easier than the one round in the beginning. And Isaac said that he thought I could do more . . .

So, after only a short rest, I stood up like before and did another eight rounds - another two hundred metres. In other words that was four hundred metres in one session. That was brilliant. It was a major miracle. And I am sure my session with Rachel the previous night had a lot to do with it. I could just feel the energy running through me that day as I walked. And I said to Isaac "I won't get better sitting in the wheelchair. The more I walk the easier it will become!"

So, as soon as I had done the four hundred metres with Isaac I called up Agnes and said "Do you know what's wrong with my right leg? Fucking nothing................!! I just walked four hundred metres!" Click.

Rachel's spiritual healing had a lot of positive effects and I continued to go to her virtually every week till I moved back to Abu Dhabi. If you want to know more about what she can do, check out her Awakened Soul website on the link below:

WEBSITE LINK: RACHEL BEAVAN - AWAKENED SOUL

The next day I had to go to the Occupational Therapy room at the Rochester. Just as I went in, the Rob Thomas song *Little Wonders* started on the radio. And I sat and listened to it.... One line near the beginning of the song is "And the hardest part's behind you now" And the song is all about believing in yourself and doing it. Soooo appropriate. And then, as a result of that, I walked up and down the four steps on the stair trainer for the first time. Yo!!!!!!

CUE YOUTUBE VIDEO: LITTLE WONDERS
ROB THOMAS/MATCHBOX 20

And the comment at the end of the video from the person who put the words on YouTube is . . .

"Believe in yourself, follow your dreams, and never EVER give up".

37

GRUMPY EILEEN

One day in October 2014 I was listening to Radio 2 from Dubai when I heard the song *Come on Eileen* by the Irish band, Dexy's Midnight Runners. It's an old song. It came out in June 1982 when I was thirty-three and working in Kenya. It's a great, fun song and at the time a friend and I ran a mobile disco called the "The Electric Wotta Gas Company" in our spare time, and we played the song a lot at dances, parties and events. It was a perfect song to get everyone up and moving on the dance floor. Aaah those were the days . . . TSB the DJ!

CUE YOUTUBE VIDEO: COME ON EILEEN
DEXY'S MIDNIGHT RUNNERS

But that is not what the song reminded me of when I heard it that day. It reminded me of a funny thing that happened in the Occupational Therapy room at the Rochester about two years earlier in mid-2012.

There was a patient there called Eileen who happened to be Irish. She apparently lived in Oman and was married to an Omani. She had suffered a stroke so the limbs on one side of her body did not function very well. She also had Alzheimer's Disease which meant that one day she would talk to you like a long-lost friend and the next day, ask who you were. She was probably in her late 70s and thin and bony like some older ladies are. But mainly, she was really, really grumpy. And I mean grumpy with a capital G.

Most days, I would see her in the ground floor reception of the Rochester main building and she would be arguing with her nurse and her physiotherapist that she did not want to go and have her physio session. If it was one of her good days I would joke with her and say "Come On Eileen – you can go for your physio session". I had asked her – on one of her better days – if she knew the song by Dexy's Midnight Runners, and she had told me "To be sure! Of I course I do!" in no uncertain Irish terms. So, the phrase "Come on Eileen" was a bit of a thing between us. At least on the days when she remembered who I was!

Anyway, one afternoon I happened to be in the OT room at the same time as Eileen. I was sitting in my wheelchair at the OT desk having things done to my hands and fingers to try and get them functioning again. OT is incredibly hard work. Superficially, you assume it's going to be easy, but it's not. The Occupational Therapist said make an "O" with your thumb and first finger and touch all the other finger tips in succession. At the beginning, it would take a massive amount of energy and muscle pressure to even try and do it. And, at first, I could not do it at all. No joke! In terms of effort it was like lifting 200 pounds on a barbell just to move your fingers together. If you, the reader, try it now, I am sure that it's hardly any effort at all. But for me, back in 2012, it was huge.

Velu, one of the Indian Physiotherapists, was working with Eileen. Well, he was trying to work with her but not succeeding at all. They were standing inside the set of "ballet" parallel bars in front of the big wall mirror where I had done my first 100-seconds stand up. Except that Eileen was no ballet dancer and she was never going to do Swan Lake. In fact, that day she was determined not to do anything at all, at all.

The two of them were arguing and Eileen was refusing point blank to let go of her grip on the parallel bars. So, I said to her "Come on Eileen, you can do it. Come on Eileen" And she just looked at me and stared. But there was just something in that look. It wasn't bloody mindedness, it wasn't defiance. It was like "I'll show you . . ."

So, then I started singing the chorus of the Dexy's Midnight Runners song. Slowly at first . . .

"Come on Eileen, dah dah de dah"

And, amazingly, she took her hands off the parallel bars and started to walk slowly. So, I kept singing. I did not know all the words but that didn't matter. I just kept singing.

"Come on Eileen, dah dah de dah"

She kept going, down the length of the parallel bars. So, I sang louder and started banging the side of my fists on the desk to the beat . . .

"I said come on
Come on Eileen, dah dah de dah"

By now she was at the end of the parallel bars – but she kept walking! It seemed like the more I sang, the more she walked. So, I just kept on singing!

"Come on Eileen, dah doo dah day
Dooda doo dye day"

And she kept going, all around the room in a big circle. Till eventually she got to the big exercise bed on the other side of the room and plonked herself down on the edge of it with a big smile on her face.

So, I said to her "Well, that was really great Eileen! I bet you could just drink a pint of Guinness right now?"

And, like a true Irish colleen, she replied "To be sure, to be sure, I really could . . . !"

We all laughed and cheered and clapped and Eileen was obviously really happy and proud of herself.

It was yet another example of how music can bring back memories and subconsciously inspire you to do something you thought you could not do. Velu, the Physiotherapist, told me afterwards that she had never, ever, done that before. She had never tried to walk outside the parallel bars at all.

Unfortunately, we never got to see Eileen do it again as shortly after that her family took her out of the Rochester and she went back to Oman.

I just hope that someone gave her a copy of the Dexy's Midnight Runners, *Too-Rye-Ay* album for Christmas that year. If they did, I am sure she will be dancing Irish jigs around the house by now!

38

FROM ROCK OF AGES TO SEVEN DWARFS

That seems like a quantum leap – from Rock of Ages to Seven Dwarfs – but the third quarter of 2012 was a busy time for me. Busy but good.

In August, my eldest son, Elliott, came to the UAE to visit me at the Rochester. He was living and working in Brisbane, Australia at the time so it was a long haul. But "somehow" he managed to combine the UAE visit with a trip around the night spots of Europe with a bunch of his Aussie friends. Now, which came first on the agenda, me or the tour, I didn't ask. Apparently Ibiza and Prague were significant highlights. Having been to Prague and witnessed, first-hand, the local beauty parade on the city streets during the day, I can only imagine what it must have been like when those same girls were dressed to kill and out on the town.

His friends also came to Dubai but only passed through for about 24 hours. Naturally (sic), and of course, he asked if he could borrow my Schnitzer BMW M6 Convertible to take them around. It was somewhat better than a rented Toyota Yaris for sightseeing as you could put the roof down, put on your shades, look cool and cruise around feeling fully involved with your surroundings. If you have ever been on one of those open-topped city tour buses it's that same sort of feeling of being able to see absolutely everything – except that the BMW is a whole lot faster! And it has a fabulous deep-throated exhaust note from the four exhaust pipes. That, in itself, makes any guy with red blood in his veins feel good.

Elliott did say that one of the highlights of his Dubai city tour was when they were coming back from having lunch at the Atlantis Hotel on the Palm and he changed down a couple of gears and gunned it through the tunnel with the exhaust sound reverberating off the tiled walls. OOOOoooooohhh! Wonderful!

I wasn't even there, but just listening to him telling me about it made me feel great. They all agreed that the exhaust note from the big V8 was absolutely magic. There is something like a 60 kph speed limit in the tunnel so my car undoubtedly got caught speeding on one of the cameras – I probably got at least a Dhs 300 (= $82) fine for that little bit of fun. Ah, but boys will be boys!

Another highlight for me was an invite to The 7s rugby ground to meet the Chairman of the Dubai Exiles Rugby Club and to be presented with a cheque. I earlier talked about the significant amounts of money raised to help pay for my physiotherapy by all of the rugby clubs in the UAE plus my old club, Manila Nomads. It turned out that the Exiles had continued with an ongoing fundraising by simply asking members to add a little bit to their annual subscription payments. A simple idea that really worked as they raised Dhs 18,200 (US$ 5,000), which was no small potatoes. This, again, was typical of the huge support that I had received from the rugby community and why I want my TSB Trust Fund to be able to raise money and help others who get injured playing the game.

The National newspaper had previously done a couple of articles on me so we invited them along to cover the presentation. I was now walking around with the help of a Zimmer Frame and you can just see the front legs peeking out from below the giant cheque. The National journalists did a video taping of the interview so that they could have both the written article in the newspaper and the taped one up on their website.

It's What You Call a BIG Cheque

THE NATIONAL – ARTICLE ON EXILES PRESENTATION

LINK TO VIDEO:	LINK TO ARTICLE:

The most fun event of the third quarter of 2012 – for me at least – was watching and listening to the Tom Cruise movie, *Rock of Ages*, with my other three boys – James, Kyle, and Colby. Of course, the title, *Rock of Ages*, is a play on words as many people will recognise the phrase as being the name of a very well-known hymn.

Hey Man. Let's Rock 'n Roll

The *Rock of Ages* hymn was written in 1763 by a guy called Reverend Augustus Montague Toplady – and that's a name and half for anyone, never mind a Methodist minister. But the *Rock of Ages* that is a hit Broadway musical, and now a movie, is a totally different kettle of bananas. The movie is set in the mid-1980s and stars Tom Cruise as Staycee Jaxx, an over-the-hill, really-lost-the-plot, alcoholic, run-out-of-ideas, but-very-randy, rock star. It also stars Alec Baldwin, Russell Brandt, Paul Giammatti, Bryan Cranston and Katherine Zeta-Jones. Oh, and a baboon called "Hey Man"

If you like rock and roll it's a fabulous movie! It features the 1980s music of Def Leppard, Night Ranger, The Scorpions, Poison, Foreigner, Bon Jovi, Guns N' Roses, Pat Benatar, Joan Jett, David Lee Roth, Twisted Sister, Starship, Whitesnake and – of course – Journey. And, and, and, the movie heavily features *Don't Stop Believin'* both as a song and as a central theme. Till I went to see it, I had no idea that this song was featured in the movie as it not shown in any of the trailers. So that was an added bonus. But TINSTAAC, of course.

CUE YOUTUBE VIDEO: ROCK OF AGES (TRAILER)
TOM CRUISE

Apart from featuring all the above well-known stars, the basic story is about a boy (Drew) and a girl (Sherrie) who both go to Hollywood to try and find fame and fortune as singers.

SPOILER ALERT – I am going to tell you the story!

Drew fancies Sherrie and starts to write a song for her - but about himself and her. It's called *Don't Stop Believin'* of course! He sings the first verse to her . . .

Just a small town girl
Livin' in a lonely world
She took the midnight train
Goin' anywhere
Just a city boy
Born and raised in South Detroit
He took the midnight train
Goin' anywhere

And then tells her "It goes on and on and on", which is a link in the actual Journey version.

Eventually, Drew and Sherrie get to perform *Don't Stop Believin'* on stage at the Bourbon Room and Staycee Jaxx hears it and loves it.

A singer in a smoky room
The smell of wine and cheap perfume
For a smile they can share the night
It goes on and on and on and on

The final scene is at the Hollywood Bowl with Drew and Sherrie on stage along with Staycee Jaxx and Arsenal all singing *Don't Stop Believin'*. So, Drew and Sherrie have their fame and are obviously a couple, Staycee Jaxx is smiling, cleaned up and back on track and his girlfriend is significantly pregnant. Happy ending!

CUE YOUTUBE VIDEO: DON'T STOP BELIEVIN'
ROCK OF AGES - TOM CRUISE AND CAST

It's a fabulous, fun movie! Plus, the theme of the story - believe in yourself and you can make it - and the songs in it are very significant for me. And as a bonus, Tom Cruise actually sings all his songs in the movie and he is pretty good at it too. I have a copy of the movie and whenever I need a pick-me-up I just sit and watch it and listen to the music as it goes on and on and on . . .

But the biggest event of the third quarter of 2012 was that I "discharged" myself from the Rochester Wellness Centre and officially became an out-patient. Yeehaaa! That really felt like progress. It meant that I could sleep in my own bed, in my own house (well, garage actually), with my own family. And there is no substitute for that.

So, instead of living in at the Rochester I went there all day for my three sessions. And in between sessions they gave me a quiet space so I could sit at my computer in my wheelchair and do my Orascom work.

Going back and forth to the Rochester felt like I was going to work. At first, my trips every day were in a taxi. Then, later, when I got the hand control conversion for the BMW, we could use that, which was much more satisfying.

So, at the end of each day of physio sessions and work, Chris and I would jump into the BMW M6 Convertible. Well, Chris would jump in after he and a couple of other nurses had lifted me in! Then I could drive home to our house in Garden View Villas and my Grunge Patient bedroom in the garage. Once I was home, he would leave me with the kids and go to his own place to sleep and come back in the morning.

It really felt as though I was driving home from work like a normal human being. *"Heigh-ho, heigh-ho, its home from work we go"* as they sang in the Disney Cartoon, *Snow White and the Seven Dwarfs* when I was a kid. It just made me feel good!

CUE YOUTUBE VIDEO:
HEIGH-HO, HEIGH-HO, IT'S HOME FROM WORK WE GO
SNOW WHITE AND THE SEVEN DWARFS

It really was like a daily routine of going to the office and it made me feel much more like a "real" person instead of an invalid.

And you cannot put a price on that feeling! As they say in the credit card advert . . .

- Having a pair of cool-looking Ray-Ban shades - $200
- Wearing a well-fitted Giorgio Armani suit - $2,700
- Checking the time on a Rolex Oyster Perpetual watch - $5,000
- Driving a Schnitzer BMW M6 Convertible, top down - $135,000
- Feeling like a real person instead of an invalid – Priceless!

39

I ONLY HAVE ONE PENIS . . .

Like most males on the planet, I only have one penis and I have never met anyone who admitted to having two. So, working on the law of averages, remembering a picture of Michelangelo's "David", and having been showering with other rugby players for about 40 years (and, no, I don't mean I spent 40 years in the showers!), I think it's safe to conclude that most men have the same number of penises (or is that penii?) that I do. Namely, one and one only.

One "prick", one "dick", one "willy", one "gentleman's sausage" (Jeremy Clarkson's favourite terminology), one "plonker", one "cock", one "pud" (as in pounding the . . .), one "chopper", one "dong", one "percy" (as in pointing at the porcelain), one "one-eyed trouser snake", one "schlong" . . . and one of many more nick-names. Actually, according to the Wikisaurus, there are 214 different names for the penis. But I know two more! So, that's 216 and counting. See the Glossary for the full list, if you are interested or suffer from subliminal penile envy.

In general, I have been pretty happy with mine. It was not too big that girls would say "You are not putting that thing anywhere near me" and not too small that they would say "Is it in yet?" No one laughed at it and no one (in this case I mean no one female) ever complained about it. It responded to all the right cues and never let me down. And, based on the fact that I have four boys it definitely was not "willy-nilly".

So, everything was fine until it stopped working properly after the accident. Hmmmmmnn really . . .

I said earlier that nothing worked below the waist. And when I say nothing, I mean absolutely nothing. As I described in Chapter 11, it was a big smile day when I had my first erection back in the Al Noor Hospital, but other regular functions were still not controllable. It seemed that my bladder did not send signals to my brain to say it was full, and the "valve" controlling the bladder did not respond either. I could not keep it closed and I could not make it open on command. So, what happens in that situation is that the nursing staff put diapers on you. These are not the cute, baby-sized, wrap-around baggy pants. They are huge, man-sized things that look like they have been made from slightly cut down garbage bin liners. No joke, no joke at all. See for yourself in the picture.

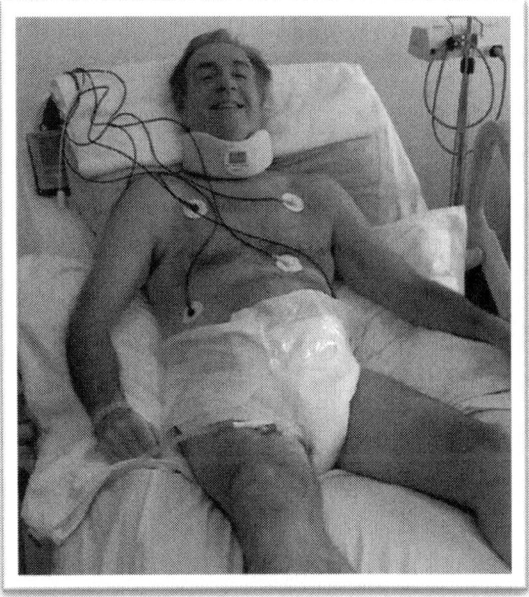

Wired For Sound & Sartorially Elegant (Not)

And then you start getting visits from hospital urologists or the doctors recommend that you go and see a urologist if there isn't one in the hospital.

The trouble with urologists is that they all have different ideas on how to solve the problem. "On the one hand we could do this . . . On the other hand we could do that" Guys, these are not my hands we are talking about – it's my pride and joy that needs fixing. There is only one thing that they seem to agree on and it is that, in cases like mine where you have a spinal cord injury, the bladder and penis functions are the last to recover. Thanks for that guys. That's just what the patient wants to hear!

Over a period of three years I had a total of eight different urologists. All with different ideas on how to solve my problem. As I said at the beginning, I only have one penis - but I had eight urologists poking and pulling at it (easy there, Doc!), sticking things up it, on it, over it and, in one case, cutting it out of the action altogether.

Most of them were men, which sort of helps as at least they have the same basic equipment as I do. But one was a woman . . . and this created a basic problem as she did not have the same kind of fishing tackle. So, how could she tell what a male patient feels when she decides to push a piece of plastic tube the "wrong" way up the hole in the end of your penis? It's like women going to a male gynaecologist – he can never know what it's like to have a baby – so why trust him with your husband's favourite plaything?

Let's face it you have to mistrust male gynaecologists right from the get go. I mean, what would you think if you said to your eldest boy, "What do you want to be when you grow up, son?" You are expecting something like, lawyer, airline pilot, architect or civil engineer and he came back with, "Oh, I want to be a gynaecologist, Dad." That would be a real show stopper . . . !!! Or if your sixteen year old daughter came home from school one day and said "Mum, I want to be a male urology doctor when I grow up". Just what are they teaching her at that school, or rather behind the bike sheds of that school???

Anyway, going back to my problem, Urologist No. 1 came to see me while I was still in the Al Noor Hospital, shortly after I had the accident, and he decided I needed a catheter. This is the most common solution for a non-functional bladder and it's basically a long piece of plastic tube connecting your bladder and urinary system to a big plastic bag strapped to your leg to catch the urine. Lovely concept, yes? But there are several versions of those too, and none of them are what you might call "fun". They have ones that they call intermittent catheters and others they call permanent catheters. The big difference with these is the frequency which they insert them. Intermittent means 3 times a day and permanent means it stays in for two or three weeks. So, you can guess which one is preferable – the one they mess about with the least, of course.

Both of these are basically long tubes that they insert into the hole in the end of your penis and then push them all the way through the urethra till they enter the bladder. Now all men reading this are allowed to suck in their breath, to cringe, close their eyes, grimace and hold their groin as they "feel" the pain that this activity is very sure to generate. And believe me it does!

If you have never had a catheter inserted you won't know that there are actually two very important dimensions that the urologist needs to know when he is selecting the correct size of catheter. One is the diameter of the hole in your penis. And just how do they measure this? I am not sure, but they don't use a set of internal callipers - which engineers use to measure internal diameters of tubes and pipes – so invariably they get it wrong and choose a size that is too big. I know (now) from experience that mine is a Number 12 sized hole (and please don't ask me what the units of the 12 are as I have no idea) but they always wanted to start with a Number 16. Believe me, a Number 16 tube does not want to go into a Number 12 sized hole, but the urologists will keep pushing it in, however loud you scream! Masochists!

The other important measurement for a catheter is the length, because it has to go all the way up your penis, inside the urethral tube, along the pipework inside your body, past the valve on the branch tube connecting to your testicles, then push past your bladder valve and end up inside your bladder. That's a loooong way, and you feel every millimetre. But everyone is sized differently ranging from little kids to ridiculously well-hung porn movie stars. So, the "rule of thumb" (now that's an unfortunate choice of nomenclature!) for measurement for the length of the catheter tube is the distance from the tip of your fingers to your elbow. When you look at it, that's a long piece of plastic . . .!

This "rule of thumb" holds good except in cases like Robbo, the Captain of the Dubai Sharks in 2013-2014. He is a Scotsman who was reputed to have one of the smallest penises on the planet. Maybe it was something to do with wearing a kilt in cold weather when he was a teenager going through puberty.

Once the catheter is inserted you actually can't feel anything but it has a plastic coupling to join with the other tube coming from the big plastic bag that collects the urine, which is strapped to one of your legs.

The bladder and your urinary system just act as a flow-through conduit and nothing is retained in the body. The bag is not a problem when it's empty but, of course, it gradually fills up with your own urine. This is body temperature when it comes out – naturally – but then it goes colder. So, you have a bag of cold urine strapped to your leg and, by the end of the day, this is fairly heavy and fairly unpleasant. And you need someone to empty it for you because – for me at least - I was still moving around in a wheelchair and not independently mobile.

For about two years I had Chris – a.k.a Mr. Spock – as my full-time nurse and for the first 18 months of that I was an in-patient in the Rochester Wellness Centre, so there was always a nurse on duty to do it after Chris had gone home for the day. But, eventually, I had to let Chris go as he was an expensive luxury and I needed to become more independent. That meant I had to get my kids to help me with this. And this is when you find out that, actually, you have really good kids if they come and empty your urine bag without complaint whenever you shout for them to do it!! Most kids are expected to take out the garbage. Mine are overachievers!

James was then about seventeen and I have to give him credit here, he was the mainstay of this activity; he even took over the changing of the bag every day and recoupling the new one to the long catheter tube. Not something most seventeen year old boys would relish! But Kyle was also pretty good at it too and he was only ten at the time.

One of the problems with this set up is that you have to tape the tube that goes from the end of your penis to the bag, onto your leg. It needs really strong tape to do this so they use something that's a bit similar to Duct Tape. Gentlemen, picture this: the catheter tube comes out of the end of your penis and then is taped to the top of one of your legs.

The problem is that it creates a constant sideways tension on the tube which, in turn, pulls down and sideways on the hole in the end of your penis. Just in case any of you male readers have never checked, I can tell you that this hole is generally round or possibly slightly oval. Are any of you going to put down the book to check? Maybe you should ask your wife, girlfriend or significant other as – if you are lucky – she may have had her face closer to the end of your penis than you ever have!

The reason for this shape is to get a nice smooth flow of urine when it comes out of the end of your penis when you are having a pee. Just like a hosepipe watering the garden. But, if you have ever squeezed the end of the hosepipe or if it had a nick in the end of it, you will know that this affects the flow and water starts to spray in different directions. So, it's like that when the catheter tube causes a distortion in the hole in the end of your penis. You don't get a smooth flow any more. It sprays around a bit and sometimes bifurcates (i.e. splits into two flows).

Trick or Treat? Open Wide . . .

So, because I had an intimate relationship with a catheter for about two years, the hole in the end of my penis is very far from round. It ended up being shaped a bit more like the mouth on the "Ghostface" mask used by the killer in the movie series *Scream*. That mask was inspired by the face of the person in the painting, *The Scream*, by the Norwegian impressionist painter Edvard Munch. Did any of you know that? See, you learn something new every day reading this book.

Of course, I did not realise any of this till much, much later. But before I talk about that, let me go back to the urologists. Correction, my eight urologists. As I said earlier they, all had different ideas about how to solve the problem and here comes Number 2.

Urologist No. 2 gave me a prescription for pills that relaxed the muscles in my bladder – because when you have a through-flow catheter it shrinks in size as it never gets full. But the dosage was so high that it relaxed all my other muscles too. At that time I was just starting to get mobile with the big under-the-armpit rolling frame and then the Zimmer Frame, but with this new medication, I suddenly found that I could hardly walk – even with the frames. The muscles in my legs were just too relaxed!! But the urologist wanted me to keep on with the medication as it was "good for my bladder". Eventually, I stopped going to see that one as the treatment was having a negative effect on my walking recovery. I wanted to pee, but I wanted to walk even more!!

Urologist No. 3 was the one I nicknamed "The Crazy Professor". He looked like Doc Brown, the professor in the "Back to the Future" movies with his hair sort of sticking out and a wild look in his eyes. But his urological ideas were even wilder than his looks. His favourite plan to solve my problem was to insert a small electronic valve to open and close the bladder. This seemed like a good idea until he mentioned that the on-off switch would be placed in the lower fraenum - the small space between my scrotum and my asshole. I was trying to visualise myself reaching into my underwear and trying to find the switch. Imagine the looks I would get in a public toilet!! Another thought . . . where do you keep the batteries and what happens when they run out??? It was just too crazy to think about.

CUE YOUTUBE VIDEO: BACK TO THE FUTURE (TRAILER)
MICHAEL J. FOX & CHRISTOPHER LLOYD

The biggest problem with catheters being inside the urethral tube is that, naturally, the body does not really want them to be there. Basically, they are foreign objects and when you are messing about taking them in and out, it's not done in a sterile hospital operating theatre. It is done on your bed or in the Doctor's consultation room which hundreds of sick people pass through every day. Hence, there is always a high risk of infection and this generally means that you get a Urinary Tract Infection (UTI). Usually, its women that get UTIs if they don't drink enough water and the concentration of the urine is too high. It's only a "man problem" when you get them as a Sexually Transmitted Disease (STD) due to playing out where you shouldn't and being a big and brave "Bareback Rider". UTIs are not fun and, because of the catheters, I probably had a higher incidence rate than a New York streetwalker. The treatment is a huge dose of knockout-strength antibiotics which used to take me about three days to recover from. So, I wanted to find an alternative solution.

It turns out that there are a couple of other types of catheter in addition to the urethral tube kind. One of these is the "Condom Catheter". This seems a perfect solution at first. It is, as it sounds, just a condom with a hole in the end of it. This may seem like an oxymoron. Condoms are usually used because you want to contain the sperm that you ejaculate during orgasm and stop it entering your partner's body. Therefore, what use would a condom with a hole in the end be except to probably guarantee that your partner would get "a little pregnant"? But, in the world of dysfunctional bladders, it does make sense as you can use a plastic tube to connect them to the urine bag. Great, you think when you first hear about this. No more catheters being pushed up your fragile equipment. Yeah!!!

But, and there is always a "but". A normal condom is used when the male is in a state of tumescence and raring to go. So, it's easy to unroll it along the shaft. When you are fitting a condom catheter neither you or your penis are raring to go, particularly if the procedure is being done by your male nurse. You really don't want to get an erection at that moment in time as he might get the wrong idea! But once you have got it on, there is the problem of keeping it there, and the answer to that is the same sticky tape they use to fix the tube to your leg. However, the place where they need to put the sticky tape to hold the top of the condom in position is where you have your pubic hair. That's nice, yes? No!

Sooooo there you are, condom on taped up to your pubes and connected to the bag with the tube stuck to your leg. All systems go. Well, for a while anyway. Any man will tell you – in confidence of course – that if you leave a penis alone for a while it gets smaller. It might be the cold weather or some primeval subconscious protective thing to protect your manhood but, whatever the cause, the fact is that it gets smaller. The problem with this is that when you move your legs the tube pulls on the condom and then it starts to come off and the (very) sticky tape tries to pull out your pubic hair. It's like having your pubes waxed. I must have been the only guy in Dubai with a "Brazilian".

This is bad enough during the day when you are awake and can feel what is going on but it's much worse during the night when you are asleep. Ever so slowly the condom will slip off and all the urine that it contains and all that is in the tube spills out onto the bed. So you end up laid in a pool of your own pee. Lovely, really lovely! And what is even less fun than lying in a pool of your own pee, is waking your wife up at 3:00am and telling her she is laid in it too. This is not recommended.

Having this happen several times is a driving force to make you want to explore some other solution. So, I went to see Urologist No. 4. He was a very jolly, Syrian doctor and he listened to all my trials and tribulations and said he had the solution. Yet another kind of catheter. Yeah right! Just what I needed. But he explained that this one did not need to be pushed up my penis, nor was it pulled over it, in fact my penis would not be involved in this catheter at all. It was called a Supra Pubic Catheter (SPC) and it went straight into my bladder just above my pubic bone.

"And how do you do this?" I asked innocently. "Oh, I will just make a hole through your abdomen straight into the bladder. Then I will insert the SPC through the hole and tape it in place. Then the urine comes straight out of the bladder and into the bag." he said with a big smile. Love that word…JUST!!!

"I assume that you do this in an operating theatre under full anaesthetic, of course?" I queried.

"Oh no, I just do it with a local anaesthetic in the ER room. It only takes a few minutes," he replied with an even bigger smile. There's that word again…JUST!

HMMmmmmmnn! The thought of someone sticking a tube through my skin and keeping going through the wall of my bladder did not fill me with joy and abandon, believe me. I hate having injections and have been known to faint when they want a blood sample for a medical test. But at this point I was willing to try anything and he promised I would not get UTIs since this method avoided the urinary tract.

So I agreed to go for it – there and then before I chickened out - and the most amazing thing was that he was right. I did not feel anything, it was quick and I did not pass out. Yo! The weirdest bit of it all was, after he had made the hole through my abdomen and into my bladder, and before he inserted the catheter collector tube, the urine flows out of the hole and across your stomach – of course it would, wouldn't it.

I have to say that of all the catheter options I had tried so far, it was, surprisingly, the best.

It was non-penis-invasive and therefore not painful. It did not leak. It did not hurt. I did not get UTIs. It only had to be changed every eight to ten weeks – and that was a five-minute job. And the sub-conscious knowledge that I did not have a tube sticking out of my penis just made me feel so much better.

This was not the end of the urinary saga – far from it – as I am only at Urologist No. 4 and there are four more to go. Being happy about having a piece of tube permanently sticking out of your body may seem a bit odd but, it's amazing what can make you happy when you have had an accident like mine. So, I will leave it there for now as I had the SPC for about 6-7 months without any problems. But this epic penile chronicle goes on into 2014 - and beyond - so I will come back to it later in the book.

40

THE FASTEST INVALID CARRIAGE IN THE WORLD

When your legs don't work, mobility and independence is a really big deal. This may seem obvious, of course, but the human brain tends to crave the thing it cannot have. Ask anyone who grew up in the US Prohibition era. Everyone wanted to have a drink - and I mean an alcoholic one - because they were illegal. So, when you are disabled or even "temporarily unable" and you cannot quickly run down to the corner store, you really want find a way to do that. And you want to do it by yourself without the assistance of your nurse/caregiver/wife/children.

Back in the 18th Century they solved the mobility part of this problem by having the invalid sit in a Bath Chair. This was shaped like a light carriage, but it was just for one person and had a folding hood, which could be open or closed. It was usually mounted on three wheels and pushed by hand. It got its name from being invented by James Heath in Bath, England, and possibly also because it resembled an old-fashioned bathtub.

And How Fast Do You Think This Guy Can Run Without His Straw Boater Falling Off?

If required, the chair could also be mounted on four wheels and pulled by a horse, donkey or small pony. So, you were limited to a 1 HP (one human power or one horse power) invalid carriage in the 18th century.

From what I can gather, things didn't change much for invalids for about a century and half (It just shows how much people cared!!!) as bath chairs still seemed to be around in the 1930s and early 1940s. The only thing I could find that (slightly) improved on a bath chair was the Harding "Spinal Carriage" of 1932 (see picture). But it was not very successful as it looked a bit too much like a coffin on wheels and most invalids wouldn't be seen dead in one (Ouch . . . sorry, I could not resist!).

At Least it Saved on the Undertaker's Bills

Then, after World War 2 and in the caring, rosy glow surrounding the beginning of the National Health Service (NHS) in UK, it was felt something was needed to make injured ex-servicemen and disabled people more mobile. So, in 1948, the first accessible motor-driven "Invalid Carriage" was invented by engineer Bert Greeves by simply fitting a lawn mower engine to the wheelchair belonging to his paralysed cousin.

He then designed a "proper" invalid car, formed the Invacar Company and the NHS gave out contracts to various companies to build them. Although this was a step up from the bath chair, it still only had three wheels (why do they think invalids can't cope with four wheels?) and a tiny 147cc engine with a chain drive. But hey, it was a convertible. So, the invalids who had them could cruise up and down the High Street with the roof down looking for chicks if they felt so inclined (Not!).

Invacar Mk 1 Convertible. One Front Wheel and One Headlight

The problem was that even if you managed to pick up a chick she had to sit on your knees (if you were lucky enough to still have any knees - think of Douglas Bader), as there was only one seat in an Invacar (invalids weren't supposed to have friends) and it had a tiller steering mechanism like at the back of a boat (yes, they also thought invalids whose legs did not work could not manage a steering wheel either). So, the tiller would get seriously in the way if the driver and his new "inva-chick" contemplated any kind of fornication in the car.

For anyone who has never heard of Douglas Bader, or Sir Douglas Bader to give him his proper title, my comment about "no knees" is not a cruel or sarcastic remark. He actually lost his legs in a flying accident doing aerobatics before the WW2. So, he had prosthetic legs fitted. But these were not like today's prosthetics. I think they were carved out of wood. But they did not have any joints at the knees so they could not bend at all! As a result, he walked with two stiff legs. He re-joined the RAF when WW2 broke out and became a Squadron Leader, flying Spitfires so he could shoot down a few Jerry's and get even. Kenneth More starred in the 1956 movie about Bader called *Reach for the Sky*.

CUE YOUTUBE VIDEO: REACH FOR THE SKY (TRAILER)
KENNETH MORE

Gosh, they don't make them like that anymore! I'm not quite sure that nowadays we would describe someone as having "tremendous energy and gay good humour". But he did play rugby for Harlequins – before he lost his legs of course – and he did campaign for the disabled. So, he has to be some sort of hero for me. Hey, but what about Tom Cruise playing Kenneth More in the remake of the trailer of *Reach for the Sky* - he already knows how to fly as he was the star of *Top Gun*. Then he could have a cameo appearance in the movie about this book starring Tom Hanks playing me . . .???

Anyway, metaphorically jumping back to earth from Spitfires to invalid carriages. Though this is not recommended in the physical sense. Slowly the design had evolved by the 1960s – I wouldn't go so far as to say it improved. OK, it had two headlights instead of one! The power was now from a 500cc or 600cc BSA motorbike engine with about 17 HP. Plus, it had graduated to having a solid roof, a reverse sloping rear window copied from a 1960s Ford Anglia (yeah, cool, man!) and two sliding doors like today's people carrier vans. I think my "Transformer" Toyota Previa and other van designers copied this idea!

1960s Invacar. Sliding Doors and Two Headlights. What Progress!

Oh, and you could have the fibreglass body in any colour – as long as it was Arctic Blue. The cars were not overly stylish (British understatement), even their own drivers referred to them as "Noddy Cars".

One of the companies that won an NHS contract to build Invacars was AC. Yes, the very same company that gave the world the iconic AC Cobra. For anyone who does not know, an AC Cobra was a small British sports car, originally called the AC Ace, which then had a 4.7 litre Ford V8 engine stuffed into it by famous American racing driver Carroll Shelby (Sorry, for our American readers, he was a famous <u>race car</u> driver). Look at the picture and I think you get the idea. Note that it's the same Arctic Blue as Invacars.

The Car is Arctic Blue with Orange Racing Stripes. It Did Not Actually Need Them. The AC Cobra Was Too Fast, Even Without Them

Same Colour Scheme. Arctic Blue & Orange Racing Stripe. Only One Wheel at the Front Though. But You've Just Got to Love the Registration Plate!

In fact, I have a sneaky feeling that Carroll Shelby actually stole the concept for the Cobra from the AC Invacar. Well, think about it. The Invacar was small, had a lightweight fibreglass body, minimal creature comforts (read no padding, no radio, no air conditioning and no electronic gadgets as they had not been invented yet) and each car was painted in Arctic Blue. Look at the photo above and compare it to the AC Cobra in the preceding paragraph. Some amazing similarities, yes? Bulging wheel arches, wide rim wheels, orange racing stripe etc. Yeah, right!

The major difference was that the AC Invacar (luckily) did not have a V8 engine. Instead, it was powered by an air-cooled motorcycle engine with a chain drive to the rear wheels. But even this tiny engine propelled the car to an unlikely 130 kph (82 mph). Yep, you read that right - 130 kph. Due to the lack of virtually everything, it probably had a power-to-weight ratio to rival a current BMW M5. The only (??) other problem was that the AC Invacar was actually missing two wheels as only three wheels kept it off the ground and it had a tiller instead of a steering wheel. Can you imagine doing 130kph on three tiny wheels and steering it with a stick? I cannot believe that you could attempt that and live to tell the tale, especially if you tried to turn at all. In fact, I have read that many Invacar owners put a 112 pound sack full of King Edward potatoes in the back of the car to make it more stable and stop it falling over on its side. And, to top off these design errors, the drum brakes were activated by a bicycle type hand-brake lever on the tiller making braking yet another exciting, cross-your-fingers-and-hope, feature. Whooooooh! Big intake of breath!

I have two images in my mind. The first is of the AC Invacar barrelling along the Dubai – Abu Dhabi highway (a.k.a. Thunder Road) at 130 kph with a Toyota Landcruiser tailgating it with a one inch gap between the bumpers. Go back and re-read Chapter 6 if you have forgotten about Thunder Road. And second, I keep remembering the episode of Top Gear where Jeremy Clarkson was driving a three-wheeled Reliant Robin and it kept falling over on its side. Just how do you get out when the car is on its side and you are disabled?

CUE YOUTUBE VIDEO: RELIANT ROBIN – TOP GEAR JEREMY CLARKSON

The other "slight" problem with the Invacar was that they had a tendency to burst into flames and, of course, the fibreglass was flammable, so they quickly became a bonfire on the side of the road. So, all the disabled driver could do was to stop and hope that other motorists would drag him out as the thing went up in flames. Take a good look at the photo. Oh, the joys of being disabled!!

I Don't Think This is Quite What is Meant by the Term "Hot Hatchback"

Anyway, eventually, the NHS cottoned on to the fact that these things were actually a lethal weapon, potentially causing more accidents and creating more problems than they solved. Finally, on 31 March 2003, they were banned in UK because of "safety concerns". It had only taken the NHS fifty-five years to work out that one!

Nowadays, in the UK, they have a lot of rules as to what a Class 3 Invalid Carriage should or should not have. Notice that they still call it an Invalid Carriage! These rules include that its maximum unladen weight is 150kg, its maximum width is 0.85 metres, it has a device to limit its speed to 4mph(!), it has a maximum speed of 8mph(!!!), an efficient braking system and, most important of all, an amber flashing light if it's used on a dual-carriageway. But, why would you want to be on a dual-carriageway on something that only goes 8 mph, anyway?

Though this is not as unlikely as it sounds. Pensioner Stanley Murphy drove his Class 3 Invalid Carriage (a.k.a mobility scooter/quad bike) along the six-lane A27 in West Sussex, UK after taking a wrong turning. Luckily, he was rescued by a passing truck driver. His problem? He did not have an amber flashing light on the vehicle! (True story)

At Least he was Going in the Same Direction as the Rest of the Traffic!

If you look at the picture, you will see that all the above rules translate into what looks like a "Sit-up-and-beg" version of a Quad Bike. People in the UAE use Quad Bikes for zooming up and down sand dunes in the desert and frequently breaking their legs while doing so - and thereby perpetuating the need for more invalid carriages!

Anyway, I am not living in UK so all those rules – and particularly the one about a maximum speed of 8 mph - fortunately don't apply to my personal invalid carriage . . .

Getting my own invalid carriage actually started in the simplest and most obscure way, as many of these things do. It was in October 2012 and every day I would be wheeled out of my room and across the car park to either the PT Gym or the OT room. Every day, Chris would push me past a Mercedes-Benz E63 AMG sedan. The E63 stands for E-Class 6.3 litre V8 with 507 horsepower, by the way. It was black, had 20 inch wheels with low, low profile tires and four big, fat exhausts. This thing was a beast among beasts! And I assumed it belonged to a relative of one of the patients, but it turned out I was wrong about that – in a big way.

At that time I was always in a wheelchair, therefore my head was too low and I could not see the inside of the car through the window. So, I was not aware of the magical secret lurking there. But one day, the driver's side door was open as I passed and I spotted something inside. It was a mechanism to operate the accelerator/gas pedal and the brake pedal using only the right hand. Whoooooooo!

Just Twist for Go and Push for Stop

And it was so simple – just a bunch of levers, ball joints, tubes and rods. To increase speed you just twist the big wooden knob clockwise and to brake, you just push it forwards towards the dashboard. The bottom end clamps on to the pedals and moves them as you turn or push the knob. But the best bit is that anyone else can still drive the car normally using the pedals. Yes!

It turned out that the car actually belonged to a patient, not a relative of one. That guy had suffered a Road Traffic Accident (RTA) and had a complete spinal cord severance somewhere around his C5 vertebrae. It was a more serious version of my own C5 injury. It meant he had total paralysis of everything below the waist and he could not recover at all as his spinal cord was cut, not just damaged like mine. So, he was a brave (or crazy) man! He had a RTA that rendered him totally paralysed, and then went out and bought a 6.3 litre AMG Mercedes-Benz. Wow!

When I saw the mechanism, my own crazy brain began racing at a million miles an hour too. Remember at the end of Chapter 2, back in February 2011, I got out of my "pride and joy", my Schnitzer BMW M6 Convertible, and walked into the Sharjah Rugby Club. It was the last time I was to walk anywhere properly and it was the last time I had driven the car. Since then, it had been sitting outside my house for eighteen months doing nothing except reminding my wife that she needed to grumble at me. "Sell that car. It's no use to you at all. Sell it and buy a van with a big rear door so that we can fit a lifter/ramp to it and you can roll into it while sitting in the wheelchair." Blah, blah, blah!

Yeah, right! In a way she was correct, of course. But rationality and logic rarely enter the equation when men are deciding which car they want to buy. With sports cars in particular there is an over-production of testosterone and ones cojones get a certain feeling that I cannot describe (partly for fear of censorship), though I am sure every male reader knows exactly what I mean without me describing it in mere words.

A few years ago, when the BMW M6 Convertible first came out, Jeremy Clarkson did one of his Sunday Times columns about it. As with all of those columns, a huge chunk of the blurb is about other things that may or may not (and its usually not) be directly (or even indirectly) related to the car being tested. It's a bit like this book actually. He loved the car and decided he wanted to "... marry it, move to a croft in the Highlands and spend the rest of his life making M-powered Jezza babies". So, his cojones were obviously buzzing at full throttle that day.

He also said – and I absolutely agree with him, "The M6 never feels light, agile or sporty. But the speed. Oh my God. The speed. It's hyperspace fast. And that's more addictive than watching *Deal or No Deal* on crack".

He concluded, "I don't know what you do for a living. But . . . if you're making enough to buy an M6 Convertible. You should".

Then, imagine giving Schnitzer (the BMW equivalent of the Mercedes Benz AMG tie up) an Arctic Blue M6 Convertible and telling them to make it go faster, change gear quicker, have a louder exhaust and handle better. Yo! And that was the car sitting outside my house gathering dust and nasty stares from my wife. But not for long. At least not for long after I saw the hand control in the 6.3 AMG Mercedes. I quickly found out from the owner that it had been fitted in Ras al Kaimah and cost only Dhs 2500 (US$ 680) complete. A bargain!

Quick as a flash – or as quick as flashes can be when you are disabled – I made an appointment to have one fitted the following Thursday evening at their workshop in Ras al Kaimah. So, Bernie "The Bolt" drove me up there from Dubai and then I drove the car back. It was that easy. Easy Peasy! It's hard to describe the sense of liberation that I felt during that drive back to Dubai. Suffice to say, I could not wipe the ear-to-ear-silly-Cheshire-cat-grin off my face even when I was falling asleep that night.

As luck and good planning would have it, the following day was the start of the Eid Al Adha holiday so I had booked a family room for us at the Miramar Hotel on the beach between Fujairah and Dibba.

It's the same place that serves potent Margaritas to Tom Hanks' look-alikes, Trekkies and LOTR Gnomes (See Chapter 25 if you have forgotten what I am talking about). Remember, it's that great drive through the mountains on winding roads with big drops on one side and a tunnel to cut through the top of the mountain.

Now, for some unknown reason (ha!), my wife would not let all the boys travel in the BMW with me and she insisted that they went with her in a different car. Anyone would think she didn't trust me to drive slowly and sensibly. I mean I was in an invalid carriage, right? It had four seats, right? It was Arctic Blue, right? The only difference between it and real invalid carriage was that it didn't have a bright orange stripe over the bonnet/hood and it had a 450 horsepower V8 engine, right? So, why might I be tempted to drive fast on a mountain road when I had been either sitting in a hospital bed or being pushed around in a wheelchair for the previous 18 months, right? Yeah, right! She was perhaps, probably, possibly, right . . .

Ah, I have omitted to tell you about the best feature of that car. Because it was a convertible, it meant that the roof could be electronically folded down in 20 seconds at the touch of a button. At this point in my recovery I did not have any real strength in my lower half and I was still being lifted in and out of the bed and the wheelchair. So, to get me in the BMW we would put the roof down and one nurse would stand on back seat, another would stand on the front seat and the third would stand outside the car next to the wheelchair and then they would all lift me into the car. Same in reverse to get me out.

This was great as it meant that all Agnes' grumbling about selling the car and exchanging it for a van stopped due to the fact that I could be lifted in and out of the car easily – just because it was a convertible. Yo! A winner! Yep, give me three strong people and I can do it myself!

Actually, my biggest fear when I first started driving the BMW again was not about crashing, but about hurting my neck due to the acceleration as my neck muscles were still weak even though I had my C3 - C7 vertebrae fixed with a titanium brace. When you pressed the

"Sport" button, amongst other things, the gear changes on the DSG Sequential Gearbox stopped being soft and smooth and became faster like an on-off switch, resulting in a neck-snapping jerk. I was scared that if I hammered it going up through the gears it would jerk my head backwards and do some new damage. I am happy it never happened, but I did bang the back of my head quite often on the headrests!

The best bit was that when I was driving no one could tell that I was disabled. But I can tell you that I used to get some funny looks, particularly when I was on a Zimmer Frame or crutches and could get in and out of the car myself. As I zimmered or hobbled across the car park I could see that people were thinking. "That guy is disabled and can't walk properly but he is driving that car. And it's an M6 Convertible!"

Now I Could Cruise Up and Down the Boulevards

All this talk of cars reminds me of the very first morning when Agnes and I arrived in Dubai. It was 7 January 2007 and we had flown overnight from Manila, Philippines. It was about 6:00 am as we got into the airport taxi to go to the hotel. As the taxi went over the flyover the song called *Drive* by *The Cars* came on the radio. I had always liked it so I asked the taxi driver to turn it up loud. Agnes and I rode along a fairly quiet Sheikh Zayed Road, with the sun coming up, listening to *Drive* and feeling very happy to be starting a new life in the UAE. As a result, it became "our song" and we always turned up the radio when it came on.

But when I could drive the BMW again, that song had a new significance. Just listen to it, especially the words.

CUE YOUTUBE VIDEO: DRIVE – THE CARS

Somehow, we have managed to progress from 1 HP Bath Chairs, through 17 HP Invacars and 5 HP Mobility Scooters, to 450 HP BMW M6 Convertibles. That means the travel time for invalids can be reduced - and the fun factor increased quite a bit - if you step outside the "disabled" mould that other people want put you in and make your own choices. So, the best thing about getting the hand control in the BMW was that it gave me back my mobility and my independence. And, even better, Agnes liked being chauffer driven in the fastest invalid carriage in the world.

And – as it says in the song – "Who's gonna drive you home tonight?" Well, it's me!

41

ON THE FIRST DAY OF XMAS . . . I WANNA BE A ROCK STAR

The Christmas Party at the Rochester in 2011 was all about drinking yellow frothy liquid, which looked like urine, from a stainless-steel bed pan. And that was fun – at least for those watching. See Chapter 33 if you are cherry picking what you read and missed that one. But I did not want to do that again and I was racking my brains trying to think of something different to do for Christmas in 2012. Fundamentally, Christmas is all about carols, choirs and music, but how could I do something musical?

Then one day, in the middle of the night it came to me or, should I say, he came to me. Does that make any sense? Probably not! It's a bit like the first line of the Beatles song "*It's Been a Hard Day's Night*". So, let me explain. In the early and middle stages of my stay in the Rochester I was pretty much incapacitated. I could hardly move my limbs and had to be lifted in and out of bed by two or three nurses. This meant that when I was sitting in bed – as I was for most of the day – I had a high likelihood of getting bed sores. So, the nurses always wanted to be moving me every couple of hours to change the pressure points on my butt and hips. But this constant repositioning of my body had to go on 24/7 not just in the day time. Even in the middle of the night, someone had to come and turn me from my back to my side or vice versa.

Virtually every night it was the same night nurse who was on duty. He was an Indian from the State of Kerala (of course!) and he was a really lovely man who was always smiling and laughing. And he had the perfect name – Ajoy.

Every day, in the middle of the night, every two hours, he would come into my room to turn me over. Of course, this has a significant impact on your sleeping pattern, particularly if you are a deep sleeper as I was. And quite often I would be so disturbed that it would be difficult to go back to sleep so I would end up in the middle of the night chatting to Ajoy trying to find the answer to "Life the Universe and Everything". No, not the serious stuff, but the crazy stuff – remember I was on a lot of "medication" at the time – just like the story lines in the second amazingly funny book by Douglas Adams. And if you have read that, or taken the time to watch the video clip below, you will know the answer.

CUE YOUTUBE VIDEO: LIFE, THE UNIVERSE & EVERYTHING
HITCH HIKERS GUIDE TO THE GALAXY- MARTIN FREEMAN

Ajoy really surprised me one night as he admitted to being a closet rock star. He actually had a drum kit and played in a band with a few of his fellow Keralites (Is that the correct derivation? Or maybe it should be Keralonians or even Kerapudlians). Yes, really! I was amazed. I just had to wonder how his father reacted when, sitting in Kerala in the middle of India, he asked his son what he wanted for Christmas and, expecting to hear "A sitar", the answer instead was "A drum kit".

So, this set me thinking about the Christmas Party. What about Ajoy bringing his band to the Rochester and playing for the patients and the staff? He thought it was a great idea. And so did I as it meant that I could also come out of the closet and be a rock star too – for one night anyway. I had always wanted to be the singer in a rock band, right from the time when I saw the Beatles live on stage when I was only fourteen years old.

At the time, way, way, way back in 1963, I actually persuaded the three friends who had been with me to see the Beatles that we should form a rock band. I mean, if some scousers from the scruffy end of Liverpool could do it, so could we. At that time the music scene in Liverpool, Manchester and the North of England in general was exploding. Somehow there seemed to be an endless mass of talent just waiting to burst onto the world's record players, TV screens and juke boxes.

But, my friends and I never did manage to form a rock band, mainly because, even though we bought guitars, none of us had any musical talent, whatsoever. I only found out many years later that I could actually sing pretty well!

There I was, fifty years later, in the middle of a desert, a long way from Liverpool. But, with Ajoy and his Indian musician friends, I had a ready-made rock band! Yo! And I had my wheelchair. So I could really rock 'n roll, ha! All we needed now were some appropriate songs for the party. Oh, and some appropriate stage costumes so that we looked like a real rock band – or at least like a real rock band from the 1960s when all bands played in matching outfits. Not like today, when most band members look like they are wearing what they slept in.

I soon had an idea to solve that problem. I called a few of the Arabian Potbellies/Dubai Sharks rugby players and asked to borrow their "Pinkies". This is a very important part of the Potbelly/Sharks culture and ethos. A "Pinkie" is the formal attire to be worn at dinners, dances, special gatherings and whenever it's "called" by the Captain of the Team or the Chairman of the Club. And a "Pinkie" is a pink, shiny silk jacket with the club logo on the pocket and the most outrageously coloured or patterned lining that you can get the tailor to put in it. This is because, on a regular basis at a club event, the call may be issued to turn the jackets inside out for a while. You might think that you would feel gay or poncy wearing a pink silk jacket, but other peoples' reaction to them is generally very positive and you get some great comments from other people wherever you go. You just have to be a bit careful when you go to a bathroom in case anyone hanging around in there gets the wrong idea!

So, now we had a stage outfit, and I had a pink wig, all we needed were some songs. My first thought on that one was the song *Pink*, sung by Steven Tyler of Aerosmith. I have done this Karaoke-style at several Sharks and Potbelly rugby club functions and the words are perfect for a rugby club - or a band - wearing pink jackets. Just take a look at the video and listen to the words. It's like Steven Tyler wrote it for us.

The Song is Pink, the Jackets are Pink
and so is my Wig

CUE YOUTUBE VIDEO: PINK
STEVEN TYLER & AEROSMITH

But, it was a Christmas Party so we needed a Christmas song as well. And what could be better than *The Twelve Days of Christmas?* It needed a little tweak of the words, of course, so I re-wrote it, fitting in verses about the doctors, nurses and related things that happen at the Rochester. Then I persuaded all the Filipino nurses – male and female – to be the choir and sing with the band. And we did it. Yeah!

CUE YOUTUBE VIDEO: THE TWELVE DAYS OF CHRISTMAS
INSTRUMENTAL

If you don't know it, just listen to the tune on YouTube and sing along with the lyrics of *The Twelve Days of Rochester.*

THE 12 DAYS OF ROCHESTER

On the first day of ROCHESTER,
My true love sent to me
A WHEELCHAIR in a pear tree.

On the second day of ROCHESTER,
My true love sent to me
Two RUBBER GLOVES,
And a WHEELCHAIR in a pear tree.

On the third day of ROCHESTER,
My true love sent to me
Three TIMES A DAY,
Two RUBBER GLOVES,
And a WHEELCHAIR in a pear tree.

On the fourth day of ROCHESTER,
My true love sent to me
Four MEDICATIONS,
Three TIMES A DAY,
Two RUBBER GLOVES,
And a WHEELCHAIR in a pear tree.

On the fifth day of ROCHESTER,
My true love sent to me
Five..... OT.... THINGS................!!!,
Four MEDICATIONS,
Three TIMES A DAY,
Two RUBBER GLOVES,
And a WHEELCHAIR in a pear tree.

On the sixth day of ROCHESTER,
My true love sent to me
Six PT SESSIONS,
Five..... OT.... THINGS................!!!,
Four MEDICATIONS,
Three TIMES A DAY,
Two RUBBER GLOVES,
And a WHEELCHAIR in a pear tree.

On the seventh day of ROCHESTER,
My true love sent to me
Seven DAYS A WEEK,
Six PT SESSIONS,
Five..... OT.... THINGS................!!!,
Four MEDICATIONS,
Three TIMES A DAY,
Two RUBBER GLOVES,
And a WHEELCHAIR in a pear tree.

On the eighth day of ROCHESTER,
My true love sent to me
Eight CONDOM CATS,
Seven DAYS A WEEK,
Six PT SESSIONS,
Five..... OT.... THINGS................!!!,
Four MEDICATIONS,
Three TIMES A DAY,
Two RUBBER GLOVES,
And a WHEELCHAIR in a pear tree.

On the ninth day of ROCHESTER,
My true love sent to me
Nine NURSES NURSING,
Eight CONDOM CATS,
Seven DAYS A WEEK,
Six PT SESSIONS,
Five..... OT.... THINGS................!!!,
Four MEDICATIONS,
Three TIMES A DAY,
Two RUBBER GLOVES,
And a WHEELCHAIR in a pear tree.

On the tenth day of ROCHESTER,
My true love sent to me
Ten PHYSIOTHERAPISTS,
Nine NURSES NURSING,
Eight CONDOM CATS,
Seven DAYS A WEEK,
Six PT SESSIONS,
Five..... OT.... THINGS................!!!,
Four MEDICATIONS,
Three TIMES A DAY,
Two RUBBER GLOVES,
And a WHEELCHAIR in a pear tree.

On the eleventh day of ROCHESTER,
My true love sent to me
Eleven HOMECARE VISITS,
Ten PHYSIOTHERAPISTS,
Nine NURSES NURSING,
Eight CONDOM CATS,
Seven DAYS A WEEK,
Six PT SESSIONS,
Five..... OT.... THINGS................!!!,
Four MEDICATIONS,
Three TIMES A DAY,
Two RUBBER GLOVES,
And a WHEELCHAIR in a pear tree.

On the twelfth day of ROCHESTER,
My true love sent to me
Twelve DRIPPING DAIPERS,
Eleven HOMECARE VISITS,
Ten PHYSIOTHERAPISTS,
Nine NURSES NURSING,
Eight CONDOM CATS,
Seven DAYS A WEEK,
Six PT SESSIONS,
Five..... OT.... THINGS................!!!,
Four MEDICATIONS,
Three TIMES A DAY,
Two RUBBER GLOVES,
And a WHEELCHAIR in a pear tree!

But, as you can see from the photo below, all this singing with Ajoy's rock band turned me into a real rock star. Just like in the Nickelback song . . .

Bbutt Whyy Aam I Sseeiingg Ddoubble??

Hey, hey, I wanna be a rock star. But isn't it funny how the drugs make your vision go blurred around the edges!

CUE YOUTUBE VIDEO: I WANNA BE A ROCK STAR
NICKELBACK

I just love the line about "We all have a drug dealer on speed-dial". I actually had two of my own personal "drug dealers" on speed-dial. Well, sort of. One was called Dr. Rehan and the other was called Dr. Adham, the resident Physiotherapy doctor and GP at the Rochester. Their medications kept me happy and pain free through some tough days during my recovery.

Good guys! Rock on Tommy!

2013

42

WHEN I'M SIXTY-FOUR

It was 2013 already. Wow! Time was zapping by faster than you could say "Daily Physiotherapy". For Agnes and I, every New Year always starts with our Wedding Anniversary as we got married on the beach at Boracay, Philippines on Millennium New Year's Eve. The great thing with that is that I never forget our anniversary – even though I'm a man!

It's also my birthday on the 5th January, which always happens five days after our anniversary every year for some unfathomable reason. But 2013 wasn't one of those "big" years – like when you are forty or sixty or sixty-five – so I just quietly turned sixty-four without a lot of fuss or favour. But my sister Lynn – who often seemed to be late with birthdays – reminded me that Paul McCartney had written a song about my birthday. Well, it wasn't just for me but *When I'm Sixty-Four* was very apt and this video made me smile – some very funny pics in it.

CUE YOUTUBE VIDEO: WHEN I'M SIXTYFOUR
HAPPY BIRTHDAY - THE BEATLES

Once we got over the excitement of our anniversary and my birthday we started thinking what to do next. Having had a couple of month's experience as an out-patient, we decided that we could move back to Abu Dhabi. I had been cutting back on the nurse/caregiver support from Chris to get used to an eventual full severance. So, he would just come in the morning at 8:00am to help me get showered and dressed before we went to the Rochester for my three PT/OT/PT sessions for the day. While I was there, Chris would attend to other patients and, in between the sessions, the Rochester gave me a quiet space to sit and do my Orascom work on my computer. Chris was always around so he would get me a drink of tea whenever I asked and zap my lunch in a microwave. Then after my last PT session, which was generally 4:00pm – 5:00pm I would drive myself home. Depending on his schedule, I would pass by Choueifat School to pick up James. Even if James was delayed, the other two boys were always at home, so there was always someone around to assist and do important things - like make me another cup of tea!

All that was working well, so it was bite the bullet time again and move back to Abu Dhabi. After moving out of Sas Al Nakhl Village only a year earlier, all the rents had gone up significantly in price (Surprise!). We liked Sas but to get back in would have cost us more to get a medium sized, three-bedroom, bungalow than what it had previously cost for our large, five-bedroom, two-storey house. Hence, it was a no-brainer. Find somewhere else! So, in late February 2013, that is what we did.

Like many other Abu Dhabi people, the answer was to move further out, away from the city centre. Khalifa City A, which is a big triangle of land between the road to the Airport and the Dubai Highway, was the place to go. Rents were cheaper and the houses bigger and we - well, substitute Agnes for "we" – found a great place in the Al Shamsi Compound. The compound had eighteen houses, well-maintained gardens, and a communal swimming pool just outside the house we chose. It was like having our own pool, without the hassle of maintenance!

Being back in Abu Dhabi also meant that I could go back to working at the Orascom office every day. Since I had been able to drive (with my adapted car), I had been going down to the Abu Dhabi office twice a week and the rest of the time I was working from the Rochester between

PT/OT sessions and in the evening at home. It meant that I was always busy and able to keep up with my work responsibilities. But being in the office was much better.

I was happy to be out of Dubai and back "home" in Abu Dhabi. It's an interesting phenomenon in the UAE that people who live in Dubai initially don't really like Abu Dhabi if they move there, and vice-versa. We were all glad to be back, especially the boys who were reunited with all their friends in Harlequins Rugby Club and at school. We managed to get Kyle and Colby back into the Al Yasmina School and James went back to Choueifat, both schools being in Khalifa City within a ten-minute ride from the house.

The other good thing, of course, was that it meant that Agnes did not have to drive up and down the very scary Thunder Road every day as it was now just a twenty-minute drive to work. That was a huge relief for me as I used to worry every day in case she might get involved in one of the many crashes that happened almost daily. The Thunder Road syndrome is ongoing 24/7 and 365 days a year.

The new house in Abu Dhabi was great. Really great! For starters, it had a downstairs bedroom with an ensuite bathroom. Woooooowooooo! So, I did not have to sleep in the garage any more. No more a "Grunge Patient"! Well that was a good thing really. Especially as there was no garage, just a sun-shade tent roof over the parking spaces in front of each house.

I would have looked funny sleeping out there – a bit like sleeping out in the open in the Sahara Desert when I did my overland trip to get to Kenya. But the upside of that is that the desert sky is very clear at night, so if you sleep outside, you can see lots of shooting stars.

I must say that the one spooky thing about sleeping in the open in the Sahara was, that when you woke up the next morning, there were always lots of antelope hoof prints in the sand around each bed. And really close too. So, at some point in the night there had been desert antelopes sniffing around us and staring at our faces from only a couple of inches away. A good thing that antelopes are generally not carnivorous!

Anyway, I can tell you that in the new Abu Dhabi House it was fantastic to have an ensuite bathroom. This is not a snobby thing but – obviously – garages do not have bathrooms, ensuite or otherwise.

Every morning in Dubai, because I was sleeping in the garage, I had to strip off, "transfer" out of bed and into my wheelchair, put a towel across my loins, be wheeled up the little ramp into the house, across the hallway, through the kitchen and the pantry into the maid's bathroom. Luckily, as I was only wearing a towel and a wheelchair, we did not have a maid, so there was never a clash of bodies in the shower!

But, Wow! Having a real room and my own bathroom was a fantastic luxury, I can tell you.

Also, our dog, Will, would come in the room every morning and stand by the bed with his face a few inches from mine and stare at me till I woke up and spoke to him. Then he would go and lie at the foot of the bed. Maybe he thought he was an antelope!

On the downside, I couldn't see any shooting stars from in there, but you can't have everything – even when you're sixty-four . . .

POST SCRIPT

After I had written this chapter I was checking through YouTube that the particular videos that I wanted had not been taken down – for whatever reason. I came across another *When I'm Sixty Four* video. But this one is a cartoon parody on the original. I think it's very funny and Stu Churchill has really hit the nail on the head with the new words. He's got them all – incontinence, flatulence, aches & pains, losing hair and many more . . .

CUE YOUTUBE VIDEO: NOW I'M SIXTYFOUR
CARTOON – STU CHURCILL

43

BLITZKRIEG

There was one big hiccup with moving back to Abu Dhabi, and that related to my physiotherapy. I had been having three sessions a day as an out-patient at the Rochester but I could not continue that kind of regimen in Abu Dhabi – however much I would have liked to do so. Primarily, I wanted to go to work every day so that meant I could only, realistically, have one PT or OT session per day. But it was problematic trying to arrange even that on any sort of consistent basis. Basically, all the physiotherapy clinics in Abu Dhabi were fully booked all the time. There were two frustrations for me with this. First, most of the other patients were people with what I would call very minor issues. They had a stiff elbow or an aching shoulder – whereas I was trying to learn to walk again! Actually, I had stiff elbows and aching shoulders too. In fact, every day several parts of my body had aches and pains either *from* the exercise the previous day or *the lack of* exercise the previous day.

So, I would watch 95% of the patients walk into the PT clinic waiting rooms with nothing apparently wrong with them. But they were taking up time slots from the limited number that were available. I once asked one of the PT's at the Al Noor Rehabilitation Centre how many patients did she treat in a week with my kind of problems and needs? The answer was that I was the only one. The rest had minor aches and pains. QED. Point proven.

There was a second problem generated by having many patients with minor issues. They would come for a few sessions then the pain would go away – as it does over time when the body heals itself. So, then they would not come back for their next booked sessions – usually without advising the clinic - and the PT would be left with an unannounced empty slot that could not be filled at short notice. This created a mind-set in the clinic receptionists that they would not let patients schedule sessions well in advance. They would only book say two sessions in one week and would not book the sessions for the following week till you had completed your two for the current week – because you might not come back! It did not seem to matter how many times I would say "Of course I will come back. I am trying to learn to walk again!!!"

This modus operandi was endemic across all the hospitals and physiotherapy clinics in Abu Dhabi in 2013 and it meant that I had a really hard time trying to get back into the "groove" of daily PT or OT sessions. If you detect a significant air of frustration here, you are right on the ball. I basically lost two months of physiotherapy progress. And it does not take long for regression to set in with muscles and joints. Phhheeewww! It's fast!

After getting very, very frustrated (a.k.a. pissed off) with this situation, in the end, I went to see Dr. Antoine Salloum, the neurosurgeon who put the titanium brace in my neck, to see if he had any suggestions. Fortunately, he did! He set me up with an appointment to see Dr. Baroumi, the head of Physiotherapy and Rehabilitation at Sheik Khalifa Medical Centre (SKMC) as they had previously worked together.

At that time, I was moving around with the Zimmer Frame but it was a very ungainly movement. My right leg was still dragging behind due to the longstanding hip problem that was not really getting any attention. Everyone kept telling me that there was nothing wrong with it as it looked OK on X-Rays, MRI's and CT scans. I was just the patient, what did I know? Well, I knew that it did not work like the other leg for sure.

So, in mid-April 2013 I zimmered and limped into Dr. Baroumi's surgery. Sort of clunk, step and scrape. Clunk, step and scrape. Clunk, step, scrape. A bit like someone at an old people's home Xmas Party impersonating Long John Silver, but without the parrot on the shoulder.

In case you never read the book by Robert Louis Stevenson or saw the 1950 *Treasure Island* movie, Long John Silver was the infamous one-legged pirate with poppy-out eyes who became the model for all kids playing pirates in the 50s. "Arrrrr, Jim Lad!! Shiver me timbers!!"

CUE YOUTUBE VIDEO: TREASURE ISLAND (TRAILER)
ROBERT NEWTON

Nowadays, if you want to impersonate a pirate it's got to be Johnny Depp playing Captain Jack Sparrow in *Pirates of the Caribbean.* And he specifically does not have a parrot on his shoulder.

But, even without a parrot on my shoulder, Dr. Baroumi quickly diagnosed that I needed serious help to get back on track again. He recommended that I was admitted immediately to SKMC for at least one month to have intensive physiotherapy and occupational therapy. He told me that he appreciated the fact that it probably was not what I would really like to do but that it was the best way to make up for the lost time since I had been back in Abu Dhabi.

Naturally, I agreed as I also could not see any better way to break the stalemate over trying to get regular PT and OT. So, back in to hospital I went for a Physiotherapeutic Blitzkrieg. . .

The new rhythm was very quickly established. It was PT in the morning at 9:30am with Elmer. Then OT at about 1:30pm in the afternoon with Rashid, followed by a session on the cycling machine with Elmer at about 4:30pm, before the end of his shift.

The morning PT sessions were probably the most interesting as Elmer had me using the NASA Spacewalking Machine. This was worth about US$1 million and had apparently been donated to SKMC by one of the Abu Dhabi Sheiks. It had been developed by NASA to get astronauts used to walking on lower G-force planets like the moon. All I can say is thank you very much to the Sheik who donated it.

It was a big machine with a frame over the top of a driven, rolling belt that you walked on like the treadmills on walking/running machines in fitness gyms. But the difference with this machine was that there was a harness suspended from the overhead frame and you were strapped into that to take the weight of your body off your legs. And also, there were multi-jointed leg braces – strapped on your thighs and calves - that were attached to the machine. These were also driven by the machine itself and moved your legs in a perambulatory motion. The machine was also loaded with sensors so that it could tell if you were walking properly on the moving belt and if your legs were performing the correct actions.

It took about half an hour to get me strapped into the machine but it was worth it as it simulated the proper walking action in my legs. You really did feel like an astronaut "walking on the moon" and it always made me think of the Police song of that name sung by Sting!

CUE YOUTUBE VIDEO: WALKING ON THE MOON
THE POLICE/STING

And as the song says "I hope my legs don't break – walking on the moon" It was a weird feeling at first. "Walking" properly with knees bending and hips rotating like they are supposed to do. And you are hanging up above the treadmill so you have this weightless feeling as you walk "forward". But eventually you get used to it and the machine is designed to be adjusted so that you take more and more weight on your legs over time and the motor action of the leg braces assists you less till eventually you can walk without them.

When it came to the overall diagnosis and monitoring of patients, most hospitals just have the doctors who are directly appropriate to your type of case. But, the SKMC approach was to have several different specialist doctors on a team that looked after you.

Also, at SKMC they were very interested in monitoring and checking my other bodily functions too. For instance, the nurses had a small portable ultrasound machine that could instantly read the amount of urine in my bladder before and after I had a pee.

Remember, when I got to SKMC I had the Supra Pubic Catheter (SPC) sticking out of my lower abdomen and that was connected to a plastic bag to collect the urine. But, Dr. Shin, the urologist at SKMC, was not happy about me having the SPC. So, he had me keep a list of the volume of everything that I drank each day. Then he had the nurses shut the valve on the SPC pipe for a few hours so that my bladder had to fill and then they would open the valve to let it empty and take note each time of the volume of urine in the bag. This was followed by an ultrasound scan to see what was left in my bladder. All good stuff. "And how much did you pee this time, sir?"

What I did not know was what he was planning to do when he got all that information. For more on that you will have to wait till you get to Chapter 49. My gosh, it's like wanting to pee really badly, but holding it till you get home. OOOOoooooohhhh the antici.......pation, as that other famous doctor, Dr. Frank N. Furter, says in *The Rocky Horror Picture Show . . .*

TRHPS - Frankenstein meets the Folies Bergere

CUE YOUTUBE VIDEO: SWEET TRANSVESTITE
ROCKY HORROR PICTURE SHOW – TIM CURRY

Of course, if the doctors wanted to know all about my bladder functions you can also imagine that they wanted the same information about my bowel functions too. Lovely people!

They decided that I needed a "fresh start" and to do this meant completely emptying my bowels and my associated organs. They made me take Cod Liver Oil every day plus various bowel-loosening laxative pills. Don't ask me their names – I can only remember the Cod Liver Oil! That stuff was an instant throw-back to my childhood. My mother used to make me take it when I was a kid. Not every day of course, but it seemed to be done on a regular basis – to keep me "regular". The trouble is that it tastes abso-bloody-lutely awful. If you have never had it, just imagine drinking a mouthful of Castrol GTX engine oil with some long-dead fish sauce added. It would be just about the same smell, flavour and consistency.

The problem was that nothing happened for several days. Nothing at all. Not even a squeak or a blip or a fart. Nothing. Nada. Zero. Zip. Zilch. Maybe, this should have been a warning to the doctors and nurses. Maybe, it would have been better if I had stopped taking the Cod Liver Oil and laxatives. Maybe was right!

Suddenly, without warning, chemistry and lubrication overcame bowel capacity and sphincter muscle strength. I felt a gurgling sensation, a deep rumbling and shuddering. OOOOOOooohhh!!!! I pressed the buzzer for the nurse but there was no response. I kept pressing and shouted. But they were down the corridor and no one was in the nurses' station. And more rumbling. OOOOOOOOOOOooooooooohhhhhh! Press the buzzer. Buzzzzzzzzzzz. Buuuzzzzz. Buuuuzzzzzzz!

I could not wait any longer for the nurse, so I struggled to sit up in bed, which also put pressure on my abdominal muscles and made it harder for my sphincter muscles to stay shut. I grabbed hold of the Zimmer Frame and just then the nurse arrived. So, I took a big breath and squeezed shut everything I could possibly squeeze shut and started a "rush" for the bathroom. Rush is a relative term for me, of course. For most people in that situation it would have been a quick dash while undoing buckles, belts and trouser zips to make the "docking" on the toilet bowl as fast as humanly possible. But for me – I was less than a week into my Blitzkrieg – it was still clunk, step and scrape. Clunk, step and scrape. Clunk, step and scrape.

I must tell you that the combination of Cod Liver Oil and laxatives is a lethal and remorseless cocktail. You might almost compare it to a Molotov Cocktail. Once you have lit the fuse and thrown the bottle you know it's going to explode. It was like that for me. I was on my way to the bathroom but I knew my anal sphincter muscles were under massive pressure and I was about to explode. The only saving grace in the situation was that, very luckily, I was wearing an adult diaper! It was the one time in my life I was pleased about that.

I would like to tell you that it all went to plan and I made it to the toilet with a successful docking. I would like to proudly tell you that, but it would be a distortion of the truth. In actual fact, I got about half way there and then I "exploded". Nothing I could do about it. Nothing whatsoever! And in that situation, the next thought that goes through your mind is "I wonder what the capacity of an adult diaper is before it overflows?" Well, I can tell you. It's about three steps short of the toilet bowl . . .

Of course, it was not my fault that I went into a diaper overload situation. It was the Cod Liver Oil and the laxatives. But that somehow does not make any difference. I still felt angry (with myself), embarrassed and ashamed that I was not able to get to the toilet quick enough and managed to leave a trail behind me on the way there! Fortunately, the nurses were very "jolly" about it and just got on with the job of cleaning up.

Not surprisingly, the following day, the team of doctors were all very happy to hear that I had done a total "file dump" (to use an IT terminology) and was now ready for a fresh start. Plus, I was excruciatingly happy to know that I was not going to have to take any more Cod Liver Oil. And the attending nursing sister just looked on, said nothing, but nodded and smiled a little knowing smile . . .

Jawohl, meine Damen und Herren. On with the Blitzkrieg!!

44

DEM BONES, DEM BONES, DEM DRY BONES

The SKMC Blitzkrieg was successful in getting my body moving again but I was still having problems with my right hip. It ached when I sat down, it ached when I was standing up and it ached when I walked. But the doctors kept insisting that there was nothing wrong with it. Why the f**k did it ache then? Duuuuh!

As a result, I decided to try some alternative medicine and the first on the list was a bit of chiropractic treatment. So, I went to the Canadian Medical Centre on the corner of Airport Rd and 13th St/Delma in downtown Abu Dhabi and had a consultation with Dr. Ahmed who is another Lebanese-Canadian like my neurosurgeon Dr. Salloum. They seem to get everywhere those guys!

The basic principle of chiropractic medicine is to somehow manipulate and "pop" the affected joint or joints to mobilize them or reduce pain. It's most often used on the spine to relieve back pains and associated problems. In my case I did not have any back pain but the area at the back and side of my hip bone - which connects the spine and the legs - was where my problem was most evident. As I have said before, it all seemed to stem from the day my knee fell sideways and my leg dropped onto the bed with a massive clunk emanating from my upper leg/hip ball and socket. And that was way back in April 2011!

The chiro doctor had this funny chair in his consultation room. Not funny ha-ha. Funny strange. It looked like a combination of a dentist's chair and an obstetrics-gynaecology chair if you can imagine that. Just imagine having your legs up in the air in the stirrups and the doctor says "Open Wide!" Confusing ha! Of course, all females can relate to this chair design but it's a bit harder for men to get to grips with it!

But the trick with this special chair is that it can impart a sudden jerk to your body so that your stiff joint gets "popped" mechanically. So, for me, I was positioned on the chair in a semi-reclining posture and then the doctor pressed the pedal and the seat of the chair suddenly dropped an inch or so. It really is sudden and I could feel the "pop" on my hip joint.

This was repeated a few times during each session I had with him and gradually I could feel the improvement.

The funny thing was that every time I sat in that chiro chair and had my joints popped I thought of the African-American spiritual song, first recorded in 1928, called "Dem bones, Dem bones, Dem dry bones . . . ", which was used (or at least used to be used when I was a kid in the early 50s) to teach kids about which bone was connected to which in the body.

CUE YOUTUBE VIDEO: DEM BONES (EZEKIEL BIBLE STORY) DELTA RHYTHM BOYS

Unfortunately, despite the song having biblical origins, I did not experience a miracle, where after one session in the chiro chair – like one of those American-Bible-Belt-preacher-laying-of-hands cures – I could suddenly jump up and run down the aisle waving my arms in the air shouting "Hallelujah!" But there was an improvement and my right leg started to swing forwards a little easier.

When I started going to the chiropractor I always used the Zimmer Frame as it gave me stability. But the downside of that stability was the fact that it really slowed down the pace of walking – whether I wanted it to or not. Just think about it. Have you ever seen an OAP in a retirement home on TV or the movies? If you have, I guarantee that someone has walked across the screen using a Zimmer Frame. They always do that for effect. I think it's to provide the viewer with some basic mental signal that says "This scene is in an old people's home". (Duuuuh). I also guarantee that it usually takes longer than length of any scene for the person with the Zimmer Frame to enter from the left side of the screen and disappear from view on the right side of the screen. In the first scene the old person gets about half way across and then when they shoot the second scene you see the old person in the middle of the screen and slowly making their way to the edge where they eventually exit from it. Zimmer Frames are <u>that</u> slow, believe me!

Prior to the chiropractic bone popping I had no choice but to use a Zimmer Frame as my right leg would not swing forwards and it was always dragging behind causing me to walk with a half-limp. I was still doing the clunk, step and scrape. Clunk, step and scrape. Clunk, step and scrape. Also, I did not have a lot of stability when just standing as both legs needed to be constantly adjusting to balance properly. If one leg does not react to your body movement, then you easily become unstable and fall over. But once the hip joint started freeing up I could ditch the frame and start using crutches.

The funny thing about Zimmer Frames and crutches is that other people look at the users of the two things completely differently. If you have a Zimmer Frame it is automatically assumed that you are old and infirm – so there is a certain stigma attached to using one. Whereas, if you are using crutches, it is assumed by the onlooker that you had some sort of accident and maybe broke your leg or something. More importantly, you are not assumed to be old and infirm as young people break legs, in fact people of all ages break legs.

So, I was much happier when I could ditch the Zimmer and start using crutches. I know that the walking action using crutches is far from perfect but it is significantly more natural than that with a Zimmer Frame. With crutches, your arms end up swinging backwards and forwards like when soldiers are marching. That action also triggers subconscious brain linkages to your legs and the whole forward movement is much faster than zimmering.

I found a video clip on YouTube that really highlights how slow Zimmer Frames are. It shows an old man and his wife "rushing" to get to the bus stop before the bus arrives. As it happens, this clip is set to the song "Eye of the Tiger" by Survivor. I featured this song earlier in Chapter 20 because of its association with Rocky Bilbao and his training to be the World Champion boxer. But it's equally appropriate to this clip. Take a look and see for yourself.

CUE YOUTUBE VIDEO: OLD MAN "RUSHING" TO BUS STOP
SURVIVOR – EYE OF THE TIGER

If you look at the distance he walks it's about fifteen metres and it takes him two and a half minutes to do it. Computing that to a speed it equals 0.4 km/hr or 0.25 miles/hr. According to Wikipedia (so it must be true) most humans walk at 5.0 km/hr or 3.1 miles/hr. So, a Zimmer user is travelling at less than one tenth of normal walking speed.

I did say they were slow!

POST SCRIPT

Here is another one that's more of a Zimmer spoof, but fun to watch anyway! This guy, John Woloski, had a really serious heart attack and was given very little chance of recovery. But his personal spirit and determination, plus a huge amount of support from the nurses and physios, got him through it and out the other side. This Zimmer Dance is done to the hit song *All About the Bass* - itself a spoof on girls with big butts - and it's a hoot.

CUE YOUTUBE VIDEO: : ZIMMER DANCE
JOHN WOLOSKI

Riverdance it's not, but it sure is a lot more entertaining and adds to my personal credo of *Don't Stop Believin'* in what your body can do.

2014

45

HAPPY BIDET

Some say that your 65th Birthday is a special occasion that should be memorable and well-remembered. For many men – and for me at least - it signals the age of retirement which has some plusses and some minuses. Luckily, I was still firing on all four cylinders, and so my 65th birthday on 5 January 2014 came and went without me retiring - or being retired.

And we did have fun on my birthday . . .

Agnes invited a bunch of the usual suspects over for a party at the house and prepared tons of food. As I said before, it's a Filipino tradition to have as much food left at the end of a party, after every one has eaten, as there was at the beginning of the party. If you don't do that how else can you have "leftovers" for the next few days?

Significantly, for the first time since my accident, I got back in the groove of making my world-famous Margaritas. I say that they are world-famous as I have made them all over the world including Philippines, United Kingdom, United States, United Arab Emirates, and Germany. Well, OK, maybe that's not <u>all</u> over the world but I have many happy imbibers from a very large number of nationalities which should just about make my claim for fame just about legitimate.

Margaritas are a wonderful drink. Usually, they are either ice cold or "frozen" and there is a combination of bitterness from the Tequila, a mellow sweetness from the Triple Sec, as it's an orange-based liqueur, and a sharp-sweet tanginess from the lime juice. This carefully balanced combination makes them appear almost harmless to the first-time drinker. But they are far from harmless - more like a time bomb set to slowly explode in your brain – a bit like the Pan-Galactic Gargle Blaster drink, which was invented by Zaphod Beeblebrox in *The Hitch Hiker's Guide to the Galaxy.* The HHGTTG describes the drink as "the alcoholic equivalent of a mugging - expensive and bad for the head". Margaritas are not quite that bad, but they do have devastating effects as Chris and "Bernie the Bolt" found out at the Miramar. Watch the HHGTTG trailer - probably one of the funniest and most truthful movie trailers ever made - to see what I mean about devastating effects. Like the world being blown up to make way for an intergalactic super highway . . .

CUE YOUTUBE VIDEO: THE HITCH HIKERS GUIDE TO THE GALAXY (TRAILER) – MARTIN FREEMAN

Despite the Government Health Warning about devastating effects, as with many of our parties in the past, the best way to get things going is to make several pitchers of frozen Margaritas and get plenty of people to drink them. Different alcoholic beverages have remarkably different effects on people. Gin is a well-known downer; somehow it has a depressant effect. Beer is a fighting drink – check outside any Glasgow pub at closing time on a Saturday night. Liqueurs and other shot drinks are good at making people throw up. But Margaritas have the ability to loosen tongues. You give someone a Margarita and they become very talkative, which is great for a party atmosphere.

Well, the TSB Margaritas did have the desired effect. Later on in the evening people began singing Karaoke – not a good thing when you are sober - but it always seems a lot better after several Margaritas. We actually bought the Karaoke machine for our youngest son, Colby, as he loves to sing and he requested it for his Christmas present in 2010. He was about five and a half when we got it and his favourite movie at the time was *Mamma Mia!,* the musical featuring the music of Abba. Now that he is eleven, Colby vehemently denies that this was true – but it was.

CUE YOUTUBE VIDEO: MAMMA MIA!
MERYL STREEP & PIERCE BROSNAN

As a result, his favourite karaoke song was *Gimme! Gimme! Gimme! (...a man after midnight).* He used to sing it over and over and over again, so he knew it very well. But then he would get frustrated when he did not get a high score – I think that was just because he had a light kid's voice – so one day I started joining in with him. Yes, really! Now, maybe it's because in the late 70s and early 80s ABBA was hugely popular and wherever you went their songs were on the radio and hence, I was some sort of closet fan. Not something one should readily admit in public – but I did think that Frida, the brunette, was way more attractive than Agnetha, the blonde one. Whereas most guys were having wet dreams about the blonde – but I think that was just because she had big boobs. As a result, I enjoyed singing the song with Colby, so much so that he and I once got 98% on the Karaoke doing a duet of *Gimme! Gimme! Gimme!* (Ha!)

That night at my party, I had obviously been drinking my own Margaritas – along with everyone else – so it suddenly seemed like a good idea to do the Abba song with Colby. Now, normally, we are doing it just the two of us together, alone, no audience, no hecklers and no one to be embarrassed in front of. But that night a whole group of friends were in the room in front of the TV. Anyway, thanks to the mind-bending effects of the Margaritas, I was the one pushing Colby for us to do it together.

But, when we started singing, all Agnes' Filipina friends started dancing crazy dances to the music. What a blast it was! The louder we sang, the crazier they danced! Colby and I were giving it all we had – and the girls were certainly matching us. It was great fun and quite bizarre at the same time. We were singing *Gimme! Gimme! Gimme!* at the top of our voices while the girls gyrated, bopped and twerked all over the room.

CUE YOUTUBE VIDEO: GIMME! GIMME! GIMME!
(A MAN AFTER MIDNIGHT) – ABBA

Yeah! Yeah! Yeah! So, it was just like a normal, quiet, cut-the-cake-and-have-a-glass-of-sherry-before-you-zimmer-off-to-bed-at-9:00pm kind of 65th birthday party . . . Really?

I tell you, Margaritas are way, way more fun than sherry!

Happy Bidet to you!
Happy Bidet to you!
Happy Bidet dear Trevor
Happy Bidet to you!

46

WE'RE ALL GOING ON A SUMMER HOLIDAY

In January 2014, Molly Scragg the (then) Under 9s Harlequins Team Manager, sent out an email asking who would like to go to Sri Lanka on a junior rugby tour. The (then) Under 13s Team Manager, Dorian Digby-Johns and Head Coach, Dominic Whiting, had arranged a tour with several games against local opposition in Kandy and Colombo. The plan was that the Under 9s would latch on to that tour itinerary and games would also be set up for them.

At that time, Colby was playing in the Under 9s and Kyle was playing in the Under 14s. We all wanted to go on the tour so it was agreed with Dominic that Kyle could play for the Under 13s if there was no objection from the opposition team to him being from a higher age grade. Fortunately, Kyle was fairly small for his age at that time and played with some of the Quins U13s in the Al Yasmina School U13s side as they had differing birthday cut-off dates. So, he did not stand out as a huge U14 kid in a U13 team, but he had the extra year of development and experience, so he was bringing some useful skills to the touring side. Everybody wins!

Dorian had set up a really good tour itinerary for a whole week in Sri Lanka, from 8 – 14 February 2014, and the package included the flights, transfers, hotels in both Kandy and Colombo, all food, several sightseeing trips by tourist bus and, of course, the rugby.

Both the U13s and the U9s would have two mini-tournaments against school sides in Kandy, then a one-day tournament against several teams from the Colombo Rugby Academy. The best bit was that all the family - Colby, Kyle, James, Agnes and I - could go for a total cost of about Dhs 10,000 = US$ 2700. What a snip!

With me being in hospital and significantly less than mobile, we had not really done any major trips since before my accident, when we went to Germany in July 2010. We knew the Sri Lanka trip was not going to be easy – with all the games, trips, and travelling – but we wanted to do it anyway as it was a bit of a test for me. The big advantage was that there would be two bus-loads of friends around if I needed help, and that was very reassuring.

We were all excited and we knew that there was going to be quite a bit of bus riding – little did any of us realise exactly how much – so it reminded me of the 1963 movie called *Summer Holiday* starring Cliff Richard. I was 14 years old when it came out and so impressionable that I wanted to do the same when I was old enough to drive. Just look at the graphics on the poster. That and the trailer tell you the whole storyline so you actually don't need to go and see the movie. It was sort of the *Mama Mia!* of the early 60s but the reference in the trailer to being "gloriously gay" was nothing to do with homosexuality, even though the female lead starts off as a boy in the movie. How times change!

Is that the No. 9 to Piccadilly, Paris, Switzerland, Austria, Yugoslavia and Greece? GPS had not been invented in 1963 so they were completely lost!

CUE YOUTUBE VIDEO: SUMMER HOLIDAY (TRAILER)
CLIFF RICHARD

But back to the story. We all arrived in Colombo airport and the culture shock was phenomenal. Gone were the big, wide multi-carriageway roads of UAE, with lots of fancy cars moving at high speeds; they were replaced with narrow, winding two-lane roads (one lane each way, not dual carriageways) and lots of old Toyotas and Nissans bumbling along slowly. It turned out that the fastest vehicle on the Sri Lankan roads was a big white Volvo Tourist Bus. Even better than a London double-decker. Luckily, we had two of them. One for each team!

That was no joke. A Volvo Tourist Bus really is the "King of the Road". It's important to believe in that, even though the roads are not quite wide enough for the bus, especially when you get another one coming in the opposite direction. Because I did not want to walk far inside the bus, I always had the "shotgun" seat next to the driver so I had a front-line view of the road at all times. Talk about scary! It was very good exercise for my sphincter muscles. How those things missed each other, I have no idea. They never slowed down at all and it felt like it was a Sri Lankan version of "Chicken". Each of them had one wheel on or over the centre white line and at the very last moment they both seemed to drift ever so slightly towards the edge of the road and they passed with millimetres in between them. I was breathing in to make the bus thinner all the time, on every journey!

The first games were up in the mountain resort of Kandy, which is about a five-hour drive, constantly climbing uphill. Well, it would have been a five-hour drive but we made a huge detour to go to the Pinnawala Elephant Orphanage for breakfast. And no, it was not elephant steaks for breakfast . . . Just the usual bacon and egg while we watched the elephants bathe in the river. A wonderfully surreal sight!

Luckily, when we eventually arrived in Kandy, we found that the Quins Rugby Tour party completely filled the Hotel Suisse. So, the kids could run around, take over the dining room, monopolise the pool, and generally wreak havoc without upsetting anyone else at all. Just perfect.

The following day we had the first games against the local school teams. It turned out that their kids were generally older than ours and some were stunningly fast runners. So, they had the home advantage and were used to playing in the thinner air at 1600 feet above sea level. Oh, another home advantage was that they didn't wear rugby boots, so our boys also had to run barefoot, which they were not used to at all. As a result, we lost the first day's games but there were more scheduled for two day's hence. And all our boys were up for winning the re-match.

Kandy is a very pretty place with lots of tourist spots to visit in the city and the surrounding area and we did them all. For sure! We went to the gemstone factory shops, the batik stores, the spice gardens, the Temple of the Tooth, and the Cultural Show. So, it was on the bus and off the bus for me. Each time, that meant climbing up and down the steep bus steps and walking around the place we were visiting, which was like doing my own physiotherapy. Get on the bus and get off the bus. Drive down the road. Squeeze past the buses and trucks coming the other way. Breathe in every time one passes. Arrive at a new tourist spot. Get off the bus and get on the bus. Repeat, ad-infinitum.

Kandy - Rugby Tour Central HQ

On the fourth day of the tour we went back to play the schools again and the Quins coaches had some new game strategies - one of which was putting Kyle as an attacking fullback, a position that he liked playing as he had the freedom to move all over the pitch. We didn't win the game but only lost by a 2pt conversion and really had the Sri Lankans worried.

On Wednesday, we left Kandy and headed for Colombo, but by yet another circuitous route. First, we stopped at a tea plantation and then headed for Kitulgala where everyone – well everyone except me – went white water rafting, and loved every minute of it. While they were doing that, the tour guide took me to a beautiful hotel overlooking the river.

It turned out that it was the location where they shot the 1957 movie *The Bridge on the River Kwai,* which starred Alec Guinness. It was about WW2 POWs being forced by the Japanese to work on the Burma-Siam Railway. It won seven Academy Awards, including Best Picture. They actually built a bridge over the Kitulgala River to make the movie and there were lots of photos on the hotel walls. I saw it with my father when I was a kid and it made a significant impression on me regarding the unnecessary cruelties of war.

I Think the Japanese Copied the Design of the Forth Rail Bridge in Scotland. But Used Bamboo Instead of Steel

CUE YOUTUBE VIDEO: THE BRIDGE ON THE RIVER KWAI (TRAILER) – ALEC GUINNESS

We eventually arrived in Colombo and checked in at the very fancy Galle Face Hotel. It's one of those old colonial-style buildings just oozing character and charisma. Of course, it meant that all the kids had to be much better behaved than they had been at the hotel in Kandy!

Next morning I decided to try the world-famous Ayurveda style of massage treatment as it is supposed to be very beneficial for people with major injuries like mine. So, James and I went off to a nearby hotel so I could have the Ayurveda treatment. I must admit it was very pleasant experience but it was obviously tuned and sanitized for the tourist palate. And, moreover, in no way did it prepare me for the "real thing" when I had a course of Ayurveda massage in Abu Dhabi when I got home. It turned out to be a bit like having curry and chips from an Indian take-away in Manchester compared to ordering a Chicken Vindaloo in a Calcutta restaurant! But more on that later.

That day both the U9s and U13s were entered in a tournament against teams from the Sri Lanka Rugby Academy. For our players, it was a much better day of rugby since the U13s won all of their matches and the U9s won most of theirs. Everyone was very happy.

One particular moment in one of the U13's games made me really proud. Kyle was playing fullback again and the Sri Lankan fullback kicked a long clearing kick from deep in their half to deep in our half. Kyle was waiting for the ball, caught it, and then set off on an attacking run. It was amazing, as he ran, sidestepped, jinked, and dodged his way through all the other players without anyone touching him. He crossed the try line to score a really impressive one-man try. As a rugby player, it's fantastic to watch something like that being done, but it's even better as a parent when it's your own 13-year-old son doing it.

The Tourists and Their Opposition – Colombo Rugby Academy

The whole tour was brilliant. We, as a family, had a great time, and the boys had non-stop fun both on and off the pitch. But there was one incident when we were leaving that will go down in the TSB history books.

We all went on the buses to transfer from the hotel to the airport. Just as we got there, and before we had got off the bus and gone inside the terminal building, James decided that he really needed to go to the bathroom. Like he really needed it instantly – it must have been one of the Sri Lankan curries that had caught up with him. So, the tour guide pointed to a building across the road and off James went. We all went into the terminal building and were waiting ages for James before he eventually turned up. But he was in a real mess as his jeans and his shirt were all covered in shit. His own shit! He said he flushed the toilet and it "exploded" and everything in the bowl shot upwards over him. Luckily, we had not yet put his suitcase through the check-in so he could get some clean clothes and change inside the bathroom in the terminal. Luckily that one did not explode!

The "get on the bus, get off the bus" physiotherapy I had when I was in Sri Lanka was a good exercise routine especially as there was a reason for each of those movements. When recovering patients are doing the same routines every day in the sterile confines of a physiotherapy room, the exercises seem much more laborious and at times, demoralizing in their repetitiveness. Being out in real situations really helps make these somewhat tedious tasks more bearable; being surrounded by compassionate and understanding friends, plus the boys having their first-ever rugby tour, made the experience one I shall never forget.

POST SCRIPT

Interestingly, in late 2015 as I was writing this chapter, I saw the movie *The Railway Man* starring Colin Firth and Nicole Kidman. It was an updated *Bridge on the River Kwai* type of story about POWs working on the Burma-Siam railway. But it was set in the late 60s when an ex-POW realises that one of his former Japanese guards is still alive.

It puts a new perspective on the prisoner-guard relationship. Watch it if you get the chance.

CUE YOUTUBE VIDEO: THE RAILWAY MAN
COLIN FIRTH AND NICOLE KIDMAN

47

MOTIVATION IS A FOUR-LETTER WORD

When you are recovering from an accident like mine you have to do all sorts of things that you may not really want to do. In addition, the physiotherapists tell you to do many things that you may not think you and your body can do. It does not matter how strong-willed you are, or how much you want to recover, there are always going to be things that you baulk at doing.

The brain is a very clever organism. It will always try and do something the easy way. For example, in my case, my right hip was not as strong, nor did it work as well, as the left one. So, the brain took the easy way out and, when I tried to walk, instead of trying to lift my foot up off the ground by raising and bending the knee, it would make my leg swing in an arc to the side with the knee kept stiff.

On top of that, due to my age (shhhhh, don't mention my age in front of my brain!), it would decide that I did not need that particular muscle to do that particular task. "No, you don't need to be able to do squats at your age" it would think to itself and try and forget about using a certain muscle combination. I would have to be constantly trying to outwit my own brain to make some things happen. It's a bit like *Survivor*, the very long-running TV reality series, which has the motto "Outwit, Outplay, Outlast". I continually had to outwit, outplay and outlast my own brain. That sounds crazy, I know, but it's the only way I can describe it.

The best "non-event" that happened every so often is that I would suddenly realise that my body had just done something without me particularly thinking about it. When your body is fully functional, you only need to consciously think "I need to go now". And then your sub-conscious brain does all the rest. You stand up, walk around your desk, open the door and walk out into the corridor. And you keep on going. I can tell you that 99.9999% of that was done by your sub-conscious brain. All you did was think "I need to go now". The rest happened automatically.

With me, and people like me, recovering from neurological and physical damage, we have to very consciously think about every tiny action to make it all hang together. Think, push this muscle, pull that one, stretch here, and squeeze there. You must do that because many of your minor muscle coordinative actions do not work. But this is much harder than when your sub-conscious brain controls the whole thing. Much harder. Believe me! It is a bit like "walking meditation" where you consciously order and observe each minute movement and feeling of parts of your foot as you walk ever so slowly. But in my case I have to do it when half of my muscles don't want to do anything.

So, it's a fantastic feeling on the day when you, say, stand up without thinking about it - except for consciously thinking "I need to stand up now". You stand up and then think "I didn't think about that". Sometimes you don't even realise it at first till you think back about what just happened. And, when you do, you realise that you have just got one step nearer to recovery . . .!!

But, to do all these things that you and your brain want to do but your body doesn't, you need some motivation. And motivation comes in many forms, so I will tell you about some of the ones that worked on me.

The senior physiotherapist at the Rochester was called Isaac. He was an Indian from the state of Kerala, India, as they all are. He would tell me to do something. Then tell me to do it again and say it in a very convincing way so that you believed you could do it just because he told to do it. Then afterwards he would say "You know, I didn't think you would be able to do that". Ha! What a brilliant con-man he would have made.

Then there was Elmer at Sheik Khalifa Medical City. He was a Filipino physiotherapist who was in charge of my daily sessions when I went into SKMC for a "Blitzkrieg" in April 2013. He had a long-time British "partner" so some words he would say with a soft British accent. In particular, if you did something well he would tell you "That was l-o-v-e-lee . . ." It was like being coached by Professor Higgins when he was trying to give elocution lessons to Eliza Doolittle in *My Fair Lady*. I thought that any minute he would ask me to say "The rain in Spain stays mainly on the plain" Followed with "By George he's got it!"

CUE YOUTUBE VIDEO: MY FAIR LADY
AUDREY HEPBURN & REX HARRISON

Hamzah, the Gym Manager at the Burjeel Physiotherapy Gym, was completely different. Completely. He did not have a "lovely" in him. But his motivation was a stopwatch and a killer smile. He would have me do something really tough then tell me I had one minute to recover. He would time that minute on the bloody stopwatch. Then he would say, "OK, Mr. Travis, the break is over." He would give me the killer smile and then I had to do the next set.

It was like the joke about new entrants choosing the room in Hell where they wanted to stay for their purgatory. The latest entrant is shown one of the rooms by the Devil and everyone is standing up to their knees in shit but being served cocktails and canapés by beautiful, scantily clad girls. So, the new guy chooses that room. Then the Devil says, "OK folks. Break over. Back on your heads!" He – Hamzah not the Devil – was like that. It always felt like "Back on your head" when he wanted me to do another set of something that was very difficult. He also had me walking the 250 metres around the Burjeel atrium against the stopwatch and he always expected me to be faster every time.

Gilbert was another one who liked to inflict pain on me under the pseudonym of motivation. He was a Personal Trainer at Fitness First in Dalma Mall. The interesting thing was that, although he was a young, twenty-three-year-old Brit, he had recovered from prostate cancer, which is usually an older man's affliction. He therefore had a strong motivational streak in him. He knew what it was like to have a body malfunction problem and beat it. So, he would try all sorts of different exercises and watch me closely for minute transgressions from what he wanted. "Lift that left shoulder!" "Posture!" "Keep that arm straight!" "Don't slack off!" "Breathe!" And always, just when I thought I was finished, as he counted "Nine and Ten" he would say "Trevor, two more, go to twelve" Aaaarrrgh! Was that motivation? Well, it certainly worked on me.

More recently, in May 2015, I got a new Italian physiotherapist at the Exeter Medical Centre. He decided that the way to motivate me was to be tough on me and make me do lots of reps at a high intensity rate. This is great at the beginning but then my half-powered muscles would weaken and get tired. Then, instead of bridging properly, my knees would fall open and I would be laying there, legs akimbo like a mother who had just delivered her first baby. And Giulio's response to this would be "Don't piss me off! Keep your legs straight!" Funnily enough, it worked. I was motivated to not piss him off . . .

Then there was my wife, Agnes. Her motivational style was - and continues to be - completely different. And I mean completely. I am not sure to this day if it was carefully orchestrated or just a sub-set of her character. Her motivational style usually kicked in when one of the boys was not around to assist me so I had to ask Agnes to help me instead. Often, it was something simple like getting me a clean pair of jogging pants or a shirt out of the wardrobe so that I could get up and get dressed. You might wonder why I could not do that myself. Well, the reason is that it's very tricky to stand in front of a wardrobe supporting yourself on crutches while at the same time lifting a pile of clothes to get something that is not the top item. Then how do you carry it when both hands are holding the handles of the crutch? Try it yourself one day if you don't believe me!

So, she would get me the pants and a shirt and then she would invariably start moving things on the bedside table. Of course, I had not asked her to do that at all and everything on that table was in a particular place so that I could reach out, in the dark, in the middle of the night and get whatever I wanted. I had to be able to do it in the dark on auto-pilot using the body's natural proprioception capability to locate something as it was not easy for me to move around, sit up or stretch too far. I never wanted things to be moved. But Agnes, like most women, had a burning desire to re-arrange things the way they would have it. I would make a small comment to her about not moving things. But it did not matter how I phrased this request, it would always be taken the wrong way.

Back would come the retort, "Ha, you ask for my help and then you criticise what I am doing!"

"Nooooo. I just don't want the stuff on the bedside table moving."

Any guy will tell you that there is no way back from this point. You can't win. Whatever you say your partner does not want to hear it.

The end result is usually "Oh, well you can do it yourself then . . .!" Which is the throw-away line as your partner storms out of the room.

For me, lying in bed trying to get help getting fresh clothes, I would have the usual alpha male response, which is "Well, fuck you! I will do it myself then!" Then I would have to struggle to get up and do it myself, however hard it was. But I would do it just to prove a point. Therefore, I guess that this was Agnes' own style of motivation. And it obviously worked on me . . .

All these examples of motivational techniques make me think about Jordan Belfort, the Wolf of Wall Street. He was incredibly good at motivating people and had no qualms about using the "F" word to do it.

CUE YOUTUBE VIDEO: THE WOLF OF WALL STREET INSPIRATIONAL SPEECH - LEONARDO DI CAPRIO

You see what I mean? I counted fifteen "F" words in a three-and-a-half-minute speech. That's pretty good going. An "F" word every 14 seconds. You don't often get that rate of expletives down on the docks or the building sites.

So, motivation really is a four-letter word . . .

48

AYURVEDA - BOILING OIL AND OATMEAL

At certain points in time during my recovery – March 2014 being one of them – I felt like I was on a physiotherapeutic plateau. In other words, I was having my daily PT and OT sessions but I didn't seem to be improving as much as I would have liked. These peaks and troughs have been recurring throughout the whole period of my rehabilitation.

Sometimes you feel like you are "Coming on like Gang Busters". But, to appreciate that phrase you must have been listening to the radio, reading DC Comics, or watching a postage-stamp sized TV screen with a black and white picture - well, actually, 50 Shades of Grey - between 1936 to 1957 (or you read the Glossary). At other times, progress seems to be glacially slow. In fact, global warming means that many glaciers are retreating. So, sometimes I feel that I am retreating too. Some days my muscles are weaker, the joints stiffer and aerobic progress grinds to an apparent halt. That is very frustrating – especially when I was doing physio six days a week!

Coming on Like Gangbusters

Because of the rugby tour to Sri Lanka in February 2014 my interest in Ayurveda treatments was heightened. Ayurveda is a big deal in Sri Lanka and they have many claims to success. They even promote Ayurveda holidays where you go to a sort of retreat/resort and have daily Ayurveda treatments and special diets of "healthy food". So, I thought I would give it a try. What the hell . . .!

I managed to find the one and only Ayurveda Clinic in Abu Dhabi. It's always like that. Abu Dhabi has one Ayurveda clinic and Dubai has about six. Abu Dhabi has no in-patient physiotherapy clinics and Dubai has lots. Why is that? Anyway, Abu Dhabi's one and only Ayurveda clinic is the Al Falah Clinic which is above the National Printing Press on Airport Road opposite the big (30 ft. tall) "coffee pot" on the central reservation. The entrance to the building is "from the backside" which I always think is an amusing, though misused phrase.

Would You Like to Come Back to My Place for a Quick Coffee?

So, I went there and had an appointment with the doctor and he recommended I had one of their special, month-long, treatments which meant going there for six sessions a week for four weeks. This seemed like a tough call at first hearing, but as I was not making progress with the more formal physiotherapy approach I decided to give it a whirl. Now, you might think that they would just wheel me into the treatment room and start ayurveda-ing me. But no, it took them about a week to buy all the special oils needed for my particular treatment. Apparently, there were about ten ingredients to make up a special recipe for me. "Wow!" I thought. None of your simple, "We used Mazola cooking oil for this boy . . ."

Dhanvantari, the Hindu God for Ayurveda. And Having 4 Arms Really Helps with the Massage!

I finally got the call to go back to the clinic for my first session. When I went into the treatment room, it was dominated by a long, high table with a sort of galvanized sheet steel tray on top of it. The tray has little edges about one to two inches high and a drain hole. Of course, eventually, I realised that the big tray with edges is there to catch all the oil as it runs off my body and then it flows out of the drain hole into a pan so it can be recycled. But my first impression was that this table and tray looked like something in a Filipino fish market where it would be filled with ice and have lots of red snapper, tanguige, big shrimps, and squid for sale. Maybe I was in the wrong shop? Maybe I had inadvertently walked into the fishmongers by mistake?

But, there was no mistake as, shortly, two strong looking Indian guys came in the room and ordered me to take all my clothes off and get onto the tray! I have to admit that I was not quite expecting that. Where was the woman with four arms? In most places where you can go for a massage, anywhere in Asia, it would be done by a beautiful woman who you had personally selected from a batch of maybe twenty or thirty sitting on tiered seating behind a one way mirror, each with a number tag. The girl with number 69 was always a good choice. You are guaranteed to get a "Happy Ending". The only time you had to be really careful of this scenario was in Thailand as, if you picked a really, really beautiful masseuse, it was more likely to be a (former) man than a woman. In that case, you might just not get the kind of "Happy Ending" you were expecting. But I think I have to cite the Fifth Amendment here once more. Yes, siree!

The funny thing was – well, it wasn't so funny the first time – that they produced a tiny, tiny loin cloth garment made out of white bed sheet material torn into strips about an inch wide. They started off with two pieces tied in a T shape, wrapped the top bit around my waist and then the other bit went down across my fishing tackle, between my legs, up the crack of my butt and was tied at the back – but don't ask me what kind of knot it was. This attempt at a modesty garment was somewhat laughable as – I don't know about you – but a one inch wide strip of cotton bed sheet does not adequately cover my penis and testicles. The damn bits kept falling out of the sides!

Now I know what a problem it is for the Masai warriors in the Serengeti of Kenya. They appear to have the same Ayurveda fashion designer for their traditional clothing. But the favourite pastime of the Masai is jumping straight up and down in the air on the same spot. They just spring off their toes and go really, really high, but I have no idea how they keep their personal heaven and earth together!

Apart from the obvious concerns about what was going to happen next, I noticed that the receptionist kept coming in and out of the room every few minutes. This might not have been so bad if the receptionist had been a beautiful woman who just happened to fancy me and wanted to get in the room for some free eyeballing. But that was unfortunately not the case. It was a tall Indian guy who talked with a slight lisp . . .

There I was, virtually stark naked – except for my micro-mini loin cloth – lying on a fishmonger's galvanized steel-topped table, and then suddenly without warning everyone disappeared, including (thankfully) the receptionist with the lisp. It went very quiet. Very quiet. Even the receptionist stopped coming in and out. The only noise I could hear was the gentle bubbling of the massage oil in the pan on the electric ring next to the massage table. But I thought to myself "DON'T PANIC".

Something is Sure to go Horribly Wrong. But DON'T PANIC

These are the words written in large friendly letters on the back of *The Hitch Hiker's Guide to the Galaxy* in case something goes horribly wrong as you hitch rides from planet to planet. It's one of my favourite books of all time. But, unlike Arthur Dent, I did not even have my own towel for reassurance . . .

Suddenly, the two Indian guys burst back into the room chatting away in their own language (I assumed it was Hindi) and talking about something that I obviously did not understand. It sounded like garbled gurgling, but the word "cricket" – which in Indian/English/Hindi sounded more like "krikkit" - kept coming up. And Krikkit features significantly in all Douglas Adams books. What sort of coincidence was that? TINSTAAC surely! Apparently there was some big game ongoing – between India and Pakistan, I think - and they had nipped out to their break room to listen to it on the radio. Never mind the almost naked patient waiting there on the slab!

Also, them being out of the room for a while allowed the massage oil on the electric cooker to get really boiling hot . . .

And then, they started. And what a start. They took the pan and just poured the boiling oil over my body. OOOOOooooooooh – big intake of breath!!! Well, it was actually almost a scream and could well have been if I had not had the fortitude to suck it in with the big breath. When you have been lying virtually naked in an air-conditioned room, with just a few square inches of thin cotton between you and Mother Nature, your skin surface gets very cold. So, when someone pours boiling oil over you it's fundamentally a massive temperature reversal. Whhooooooooooooh!

But that wasn't the real start. That came next. One of the guys was standing on each side of the table and they commenced what I can only describe as synchronised, heavy duty, pummelling of my body. I was lying face down at the beginning and their clamp-like hands started at my ankles, came up my legs, across my back from butt to neck, and then down my arms to my hands. It was perfect symmetry. Like poetry in motion, except it hurt like hell. These guys were physically very strong and they had hands like vice grips. Plus, they exerted a massive amount of downward pressure. Remember, I am not lying on a cushy soft massage bed. I am on a galvanised sheet steel tray. So, there was no "give" at all. The muscles on my back were being battered like Jamie Oliver tenderizing a steak, and my front was being reshaped into a flat pancake. Like the tough guy in the movie said, "The last thing I want to do is hurt you, but it's still on my list".

Finally, finally it was over. I made it through. But only just! Of course at this point in time I am covered from head to toe - and a few orifices in between – in rapidly cooling oil. I looked down at my Ayurveda loin cloth and, as it was soaking wet with the oil, I could see right through it. So, what was all the modesty fuss about?

I slowly climbed down from the tray and the guys wiped me down with warm towels – which was probably the best part of the whole event so far. Then they removed the oily loin cloth and helped me to get dressed as after one of those sessions I was abso-bloody-lutely exhau-bleeding-sausted.

I did that six days a week for four weeks and they gave me some special tablets and medicine to take at home. That stuff had a terrible taste - it was one of the vilest liquids I had ever put in my mouth – and, having been on tour with several rugby clubs to exotic and erotic places, I have had a few strange and awful liquids in my mouth. But that one beat all of them!

At the end of the month, I went back to see the Ayurveda doctor and he recommended that I have Phase Two of the treatment. Well, he would wouldn't he? Ha! It's like having your proctologist standing at the foot of your bed in their usual rectitudinal stance and saying that he would like to have one of his interns double check his findings from when he previously examined you. "You want to do what, again . . .???"

And now for something completely different.

Phase One was boiling oil. Phase Two was like oatmeal porridge. Well, if not exactly oatmeal porridge, it was something with a similar look and similar consistency. Whatever it was, they boiled it in a pan and then poured it all over me and rubbed it in with the synchronised swimming action again. But that stuff was rough! So, it was a bit like using grinding paste on the internal surfaces of a car engine to make them smooth and fit together. It actually felt like they were going to rub all my skin off!

Unless you happen to have some very unusual fetishes, I am not sure that most of you will be able to imagine what it's like being covered from head to toe – and all stops in between – in hot, thick oatmeal porridge. It's not really the sort of thing we do with our breakfast cereal normally. It's a very, very strange sensation.

But can you envision what it's like having the oatmeal scraped off your skin at the end of the session? If you think putting it on was bad, just try and visualise the scraping off!

I said earlier that the best bit of the treatment was having the oil wiped off with hot towels. Actually, that was not really the case. The best bit was the cup of really hot and incredibly sweet black tea they gave me in the waiting room at the end of each session. It was pure magic!

But, I am very glad to report, that the boiling oil and oatmeal porridge actually did work, believe it or not. My right hip, which had been very stiff and weak right from the beginning, could now swing forwards and backwards with relative ease so that I could walk with a much more even gait. (Not to be confused with the Wikkit Gate in *Life, the Universe and Everything)*).

So, overall, if you have a problem that the mainstream doctors cannot quite solve, you should consider giving it a try. These Ayurveda treatments have been around since 3000BC and something would not last that long if it did not work.

My new-found agility (ha!) meant that I was keen to show off my prowess at walking. It wasn't fast but at least I looked a lot less like my impersonation of Long John Silver when I first went to see Dr. Baroumi at SKMC in April 2013.

And now for something completely different (again).

Shortly after the end of my Ayurveda sessions I had an opportunity to revisit the Sharjah Rugby Club where I had my accident back in 2011. Last time I went there it was my "exorcism". This time, in 2014, it was different.

During the September 2013 – April 2014 rugby season I had been taking on the role of a Referee Coach. This meant I had to watch the referees belonging to the UAE Rugby Referees Society (UAERRS) as they officiated in league and tournament games. I couldn't run out on the pitch myself but I could certainly sit on the side-lines and (officially) bitch at the referees. There are always lots of "side-line referees" at every game, all over the world. "But Referee . . . !!!" is the most common phrase that you hear. Actually, it was more serious and structured than that as the Referee Coach has to go through their game plan with them before the game, take notes during the game, do a quick debrief afterwards and then later write a report and discuss things that need improving with the referee. But it did mean that I could stay involved and it "forced" me to get out there and do something in the rugby community.

When the 2014 Sharjah 10s rolled around again it needed a lot of referees to run it. As there were so many referees on duty, Stan Wright, Head Coach of the UAERRS, decided to hold a coaches meeting there. So, when that had finished I went out around the pitches talking to the referees, and lots of players from all the attending clubs.

Then, it turned out that it was time for the game between the Arabian Potbellies Vets and Sharjah Wanderers Vets. The exact same game that I had been playing in when I had my accident. But TINSTAAC surely!

I asked for a special favour of the organisers to allow us a few minutes to take some pictures of me with the two teams. There was no problem with this and they made an announcement so that everyone knew what was going on and why. Then the spectators and the other players gave me a standing ovation, which was really appreciated.

The Good, The Bad and the (Very) Ugly. Sharjah and the Arabian Potbellies

If you remember the pictures at the Sharjah Club back in August 2011 when I had my "exorcism", I was standing up – but with knee braces to stop me sagging and guys on each side of me really holding me up. I think you can see a definite improvement in the photo as I am really supporting my own weight and I'm standing without crutches.

That is three year's progress for you. Slow, yes. But inexorable, definitely!! At least it's significantly less than the seven and a half million years it took for DEEP THOUGHT to come up with the answer to "Life, the Universe and Everything"

49

I STILL ONLY HAVE ONE PENIS . . .

Yes, it's true. Things have not changed since Chapter 39. I still only have one penis but – courtesy of Urologist No. 4 – I also had a Supra Pubic Catheter (SPC) tube sticking out of my abdomen that I pee through. So, it's a bit like being a dog with two dicks . . . if you know what I mean. In the end, I had this tube for about eight months and it worked fine. But, of course, as it's only a parallel system, it did not make my real urinary system work any better.

As mentioned previously, while I was in the SKMC Rehabilitation Centre in April 2013 I met Urologist No. 5 and he had me record all the liquid input and output so that he had a baseline. He came in the room one day and looked at the SPC and shook his head. He was not a fan, obviously, and he said, "I'm going to take out the SPC."

"When will you do it?" I asked, expecting him to say, "In a couple of days." or something like that. But he just responded with, "Now".

That was a bit of a shock, but at least it didn't give me time to agonise over it and get worried. I was able to worry instantly instead!

"But what happens with the hole after you pull out the tube?" I asked. "Oh, we just put some tape over it and it heals up itself in a few days." he said casually. HMMmmmmmmm!

That word "just" again. Right!

So, almost as quick as a flash, he pulled it out and stuck some tape over the hole just as he had said he would.

Phew.............Easy Peasy..............(BTW – I am trying not to faint as I write this). I had sort of got used to the idea of a tube stuck through my abdomen and into my bladder, but now I had to come to terms with a hole in my abdomen instead. For some reason that is creepier than the tube. "Will it really heal and seal up?" I was thinking. I was very relieved by the nurse's daily reports, that the hole was gradually getting smaller each time they changed the dressings. I never dared look at it. I just believed the nurse!

I am glad to tell you that it did completely heal, but because the skin had been disturbed for such a long time it did not heal flat like a new piece of skin. It looks like I have a second belly-button (or navel) as there is a deep depression in my abdomen where the tube was. It's quite odd when you see yourself in a mirror as having two belly-buttons is a bit like looking up into the sky and seeing two moons instead of one.

But then – because I have what is called a Neurogenic Bladder - it was back to the diapers as I had to re-teach my bladder, urinary system, and brain how to function together again. And that is very far from easy – just ask any mother with a young toddler. Urologist No. 5 also prescribed some medication: one pill a day to relax my bladder and another one to help the valve function.

But when I left SKMC they recommended that I go to see yet another urinary specialist in the Al Noor Hospital. So, I dutifully made an appointment with Urologist No. 6 and turned up at the allotted time. Unfortunately, he was just about to go on vacation so, after I explained my condition and he realised that this was not just a one shot visit for someone with a UTI, he recommended that I go to see one of his colleagues.

I replayed the dutiful-appointment-making-sketch to see Urologist No. 7. When I got my consultation with No.7, he prescribed a whole bunch of tests - urine sample, blood test, flow test, bladder pressure test, ultrasound on bladder and kidneys etc. etc. Oooohh, I hated having all those tests but I put up with them in the hope that the results would tell the doctor how to make me better.

In fact, the results of all the tests fully supported the medication that had been prescribed to me by Urologist No. 5 at SKMC. So, I guess that was a good thing.

I was taking the pills daily and trying to get some functionality back into my fishing tackle. But it was not instant, nor was it always consistent. Sometimes I could hold and release on "command" and other times it would decide to let go all on its own. The phrase "Go with the flow" took on a whole new meaning. This meant that I still had to wear diapers in case I had "a little accident". It was a real work in progress.

Then one day in late 2013 I went for a consultation and a new prescription as my pills were running out. Urologist No. 7 was on leave so the receptionist asked if it was OK if I saw the "new" urologist. "Here we go with Urologist No. 8." I thought, "What the hell. Most people ask for a second opinion. I don't suppose an eighth opinion can hurt."

Actually, it couldn't have been better. It turned out that he was not just a "Doctor"; he was a "Professor Doctor" whose specialty was neurogenic bladders – so that was a bit lucky! TINSTAAC even! On top of that he was a very jolly German, always smiling and positive, and thereby the antithesis of my previous oxymoron. Plus, had the same name as a very famous F1 racing driver also from Germany and it's not Vettel - so it must be Schumacher – Professor Dr. Stefan Schumacher to be exact.

He knew and understood in great detail exactly what was happening with my urinary system; he did a basic flow test and then prescribed some different brands of medication to relax the bladder and control the valve.

YOU CAN CHECK ON THE INTERNET TO FIND HIM:
PROFESSOR DR. STEFAN SCHUMACHER

His diagnosis has really worked for me. It took about a year from when Urologist No. 5 took out the SPC to get the whole system working. It was a gradual shift from the full diaper to the pull-on pant type and then to having a "man-pad" in the underwear. I tried to go through this latter stage as quickly as possible as the "man-pad" is a bit like a women's sanitary napkin and that subconscious knowledge that you have a napkin stuffed in your underwear makes you feel somewhat less than manly.

Also, every time I put a "man-pad" into my underwear I thought of the Queen and David Bowie song "Under Pressure" written in 1981. What's the connection, you may well ask. Well, when I first went to the Philippines in October 1986 there was an advert on television that used the song and its very distinctive opening bars on the bass guitar - Duh Duh Duh Du Du Duuh Duh. The advert started with that riff and showed a long shot of a beautiful girl in a pair of white shorts riding a bicycle on a summer's day. Then it moved to a close up of her butt from the back – bouncing gently up and down on the saddle - as Freddie Mercury and Bowie sang the words.

CUE YOUTUBE VIDEO: UNDER PRESSURE
QUEEN AND DAVID BOWIE

Great advert, so far. Good piece of music and a girl's butt in a pair of really tight white shorts. What more can a guy ask for? But the advert was not aimed at guys. It was specifically for women as they were advertising sanitary napkins "Under pressure . . ."

Even now, when I hear that song on the radio, I get mental images of the sanitary napkin advert. So, you can see why I was mentally tortured every time I had to put a "man-pad" in my underwear. Fortunately, it didn't take too long to dispense with the "man-pads" for everyday situations and just be a normal guy wearing normal underwear.

By everyday situations I mean like going to work, to physiotherapy, or to the gym where I know the locations of the bathrooms and I can control when I use them. It's a bit harder if I am going somewhere new since I don't know where the bathrooms are or how long it will take to get there in the car. Then I feel a bit like the kid whose Mum always asks him if he has "been" to the bathroom before they leave on a trip. Or, as anyone who grew up in the 1950s will remember, the comedienne Hylda Baker would say to her stage friend all the time "Have you beeeeeeennnnnn?"

Then she would turn to the audience and say "She's been to the doctor and he says she is a little bit incontinental, you know."

Her act was full of malapropisms like that - a mix of "incontinent" and "continental". Unfortunately, I can't find any YouTube videos of her actually saying that as there is not much 1950s footage of her stage act. But this clip with her other famous saying "Be soooooooonnn I said. Be sooooonnn" will give you the idea.

CUE YOU TUBE VIDEO: HYLDA BAKER

Over the last two years, the pills do seem to be working as my retention is controlled and the volume stored is getting bigger all the time. That is just what you want. It's not perfect yet but it's a helluva lot better than catheters stuck in every orifice and big bags of cold, collected pee taped to your body. Believe me, my kids are thrilled too.

I had also been doing lots of physiotherapy and gym workouts. It's been non-stop. But, eventually, the neurological bits, the physical bits, the muscular bits, and the brain bits come together and it all works! So, now I am able to walk into a bathroom on my crutches, go in a cubicle, lean the crutches against the wall, stand up without assistance, extract Percy from his solitary confinement, point him at the porcelain and have a well-earned "man-pee".

And every man will tell you that it's a wonderful feeling – especially after several beers. AAAAAAaaaaaaaaaaaaaaahhhhhhh . . . !

There is one slight downside to this. I mentioned in a previous chapter about the hole in the end of my penis is somewhat distorted – like the mouth on Edvard Munch's painting *The Scream* – due to the constant pull from the taped-on plastic tube. Now that I am peeing regularly it sometimes causes me problems, particularly if the flow is slow. The distortions to the hole means that the flow can come out at funny angles so I have to keep watching it and adjust the direction in which I am pointing Percy. The worst situation is when it bifurcates and I get one main flow going roughly in the direction that I want it to and another going somewhere completely different. And I mean completely different.

This is a bit like when you are watering the garden and you stand there in the middle of the lawn for ten minutes with the faucet on at full bore squeezing the end of the hosepipe to make it go further and further in a big arc . . . then you look down at your shoes and you see that they are soaking wet because one bit of the spray went down instead of out!

So, it can be on my leg or on my shoes or – and this is the worst one – down the front of my pants. The problem with that one is that it looks like I am incontinent and have just peed in my pants. This is the ultimate insult when you have spent four years with eight urologists, lots of catheters, diapers, man-pads, and medications trying to correct that particular problem. When it happens to me, say at work, and I am walking back along the corridor to my office, I have started watching other co-worker's eyes. If everything is fine, they look at me in the face. But, if I have had a bifurcation, they always seem to look at the dark patches on my groin as they pass. It makes you want to say "Er. It was an accident. I didn't lose control. Honest Injun!"

The next worry that I have is when I "graduate" to using public urinals and I finish having my pee only to realize that I have also peed on the shoes of the guy standing at the next urinal. How do I explain that one away??? By the way – it generally squirts to the left. So, if you see me at a urinal sometime in the future, remember to stand on my right side!

So, there I was, gaining confidence with every pee that everything is working fine. But, in June 2015, it seemed to go bad again. There were some control issues that I could not work out why they happened and I started to get abdominal cramps when I stood up. It was like mini-spasms zapping me as I automatically squeezed my stomach muscles to help keep my balance as I was rising. Then one morning I went to the bathroom and looked down to check the direction of the flow – to make sure I wasn't wetting the front of my trousers or missing the bowl altogether – and I realized that there was blood in my urine. AAAaaaarrrrggghhhh!

That is a truly horrible feeling and I would never wish it on anyone. All sorts of thoughts go rushing through your mind. Have I got prostrate problems? Have I got some form of Sexually Transmitted Disease? Fortunately, I could write that one off completely as I have not found crutches to be a sure-fire turn-on for women you have just met in a downtown bar. Have I got some even worse problem? Wwwwwoooo that was the scary one!

Fortunately, the following morning I was able to self-diagnose the problem. During the night I have to have regular pees as my bladder will not hold for 8 hours. It's more like 2 hours per shot. But it's OK as this generally coincides with my need to turn over to a new position in bed so that my muscles don't seize up. Of course, I can't easily leap out of bed and go to the bathroom, so I use a white opaque plastic urinal. If you have never seen one this is basically a square bottle (or a round one with one flat side) which has a very large neck which is cranked up at about 20 degrees.

For a guy, it's easy to lie on your back, put the bottle between your thighs with the neck cranked upwards and "flip" your penis into the wide mouth of the bottle and have a pee. And guys, don't let your fertile, virile minds run away with you here. Having something between my thighs every two hours with its neck cranked up and being able to "flip" my penis into its wide open mouth is in no way a sexual bonus.

Also, if you are unlucky, when you are half asleep, you do a bad "flip", miss the mouth and pee all over yourself.

But, while all of this is not fun, it meant that when I saw the pink urine in the bottle next morning I could lift it up and hold it against the light to check it out. Yeah, I know, everyone likes holding their urine up the light and seeing a spectrum of colours. And that was when I saw the sediment in the bottom of the bottle! Straight away I realized that the sediment was from a disintegrated urinary system "stone". That was why I had been getting the cramps and peeing blood!

Naturally, I went to see my Urologist No. 8 for a second opinion, but I was correct. He prescribed some antibiotics and the blood cleared up quickly. But I had three more stones come out in the next couple of weeks and then the cramps stopped. Funnily enough, everything seemed to work better after that, probably because the stones had been irritating various parts of my system and causing wrong signals to be sent to my brain.

So, I still only have one penis – but now it works perfectly! Well, almost!

POST SCRIPT

All this talk of urination reminds me of an anecdote told by Mike Harding, another well-known northern comedian from the tough end of Manchester, who rose to fame in the early 70s. I heard him tell this one in a live show some time in 1973 or 1974:

One night young Jimmy had taken George's precious daughter Doris out for a few drinks just before Xmas. It was a cold and frosty night and there was lots of new snow on the ground. About 11:30 pm George heard some voices and giggling outside on the front lawn. So, he looked out of the bedroom window to see what it was. There was a bit of "steam" rising past the bedroom window so he could not see clearly at first and he couldn't figure out what was causing it. He soon found out!

He turned to his wife Gladys and said "Gladys! T' young Jimmy is widdling in't snow on our front lawn!"

"Oh, it's Okay" said Gladys "Never mind it's better than traipsing all that snow in't t' house"

"But Gladys" George said "He's writing 'is name in't snow with 'is widdle!!"

"Oh, don't fret pet. Boys will be boys" replied Gladys

"Yus, but 'is name is in our Doris's hand writin' . . . !!!!!

50

SPRING BREAK

Spring Break conjures up all sorts of images in people's minds. I think it depends where you are on the age scale and in which country you live as to what kind of image comes into your mind. But there is always an image.

If you are a kid it probably means that you get taken to the beach or for a picnic for the first time that year because the sun is (supposed to be) shining.

If you are a university student in California your mind is likely to be severely fogged by excesses of testosterone due to all the beautiful California girls that the Beach Boys have been singing about for years. In that case, what few brain cells are still working will be thinking of going across the border into Mexico to Cancun or Acapulco along with thousands of other similarly testosterone-fogged students. To them, Spring Break = Party Time. Yo!

If you are a retired pensioner in the North of England your thoughts will probably turn to being on the "prom" at Blackpool and watching thousands of holidaymakers on the beach sitting in deck chairs. It would be about 20 Degrees C (if you were lucky!), the sea will be a muddy brown and most people will be wearing woolly cardigans or sweaters and some of the men will have handkerchiefs tied on their head to protect their bald pates.

They all looked like the *Gumbys* in *Monty Python*. Compare this to Cancun with lots of beautiful young California girls in skimpy bikinis, the sun shining all day and azure blue sea. And not a cardigan or tied handkerchief in sight.

California Girls - Life's A Beach

Blackpool Gumbys - Life's A Bitch

When I was a kid, way, way, way back in the 50s, we would go to Blackpool and play on the beach and, for sure, there were guys with knotted handkerchiefs on their heads digging holes in the sand and eating Blackpool Rock. At the time there was a northern artist called George Formby, who even sang a song about Blackpool Rock. But it was actually full of double entendres and suggestive references, basically calling his penis a "Little Stick of Blackpool Rock". It was so suggestive that it was banned from being aired on the BBC. Of course, this was the 1950s. But listen to it and you will see what I mean.

CUE YOUTUBE VIDEO: LITTLE STICK OF BLACKPOOL ROCK
GEORGE FORMBY

Alas, for James and I in the spring of 2014, it was to be none of the above. Not even close.

James needed to blitz all his university applications as, due to other diversions, such as my daily physiotherapy, work and life in general, he was a bit late getting started. So, I took time off work, stayed at home with James for a week and we dedicated ourselves to churning through all his applications. But, silly me had offered to help without fully realising the enormity of the task. When I had done my university applications it was simple: name and address, what schools you had attended, what A-Levels you were taking, what universities you wanted to go to, and what course you wanted to take. If they were very advanced, the application form might ask if you had any hobbies. Choosing courses in those days was simple – as pointed out in Chapter 35 – on the Science side you could be one of about four types of Engineer or go onto the Arts side and take History, Geography, or Liberal Arts and become a teacher.

Back in the day, an application form took about ten minutes to fill in. But that was in the late 60s. Fast forward to 2014 and it's a whole different kettle of bananas. The university people now want to know everything, and I mean EVERYTHING! Of course, you had to fill in the Application Form for starters, but they were all way more complicated and detailed than anything I had ever seen before. Then the really hard bit was writing what many of them called a "Motivational Letter" or "Motivational Statement". This usually wasn't actually either of those things – if it had been, Jordan Belfort would have had acceptance letters from every university! They were usually in the form of a set of questions that you had to answer in open format, usually within a specified number of words.

They were not simple "yes" or "no" questions like the ones on, say a US Immigration Visa form. But, If you have ever filled in one of those, you will know there is a section of "trick" questions and you have to really dig deep and think about the answers, such as:

- Q. Have you ever been a drug dealer?
  A. No. (. . . but I took Panadol once).
- Q. Have you ever been a member of a terrorist organisation?
  A. No. (. . . but I am scared of my wife because she terrorises me if I come home late)

- Q. Have you ever committed any acts of terrorism?
  A. No. (. . . but I wore my wife's lipstick once and I am terrified she may find out)
- Q. Are you a sex offender?
  A. No. (. . . but I masturbated once when I was 15. But only once, honest).
- Q. Have you ever committed any war crimes?
  No. (. . . but I really enjoyed Quentin Tarantino's *Inglourious Basterds.* Is scalping considered a war crime?)

CUE YOUTUBE VIDEO: INGLOURIOUS BASTERDS
BRAD PITT

I mean, those questions are tricky, man! Do they really think that if you had been part of a terrorist organisation you would actually admit to it? Duuuuuuuuhhh! Yeah right!

Yes, that "motivational" bit of James' applications was really tough, as he had to write a mini-essay to answer each of their questions. Usually, the limit was something like 250 words and that does not sound too bad considering the average length of a chapters in this book is about 1800 words. But, actually, it is often harder to write something in a few words than it is to have it open ended. Though, some of the questions had the opposite effect and it was a struggle to get to 250 words.

Typical questions were:

- Q. Why do you want to study this subject?
  A. Because I want to earn lots of money when I graduate
- Q. What other universities did you apply to and why did you choose this one?
  A. Er, I forgot. (And I am not going to tell you even if I remember) But I like yours the best anyway.

- Q. What makes you so special that we should choose you?
  A. Aaahhh, because I am a really nice kid and want to go to university so my parents don't shout at me and make me take a job at McDonald's
- Q. Resilience. Please describe a time when you faced a difficult situation and how did you resolve it?
  A. Hmmmmm. I did not know how to answer this question, so I asked my Dad.
- Q. Results Focus. Please describe a task where you were working against fixed deadlines. What was the final outcome?
  A. Uuuummmmm. I handed homework in late. I got a "D".

Naturally, James did not say any of those things – or at least I hope he didn't! But every application was different. They all wanted some bit of information the others did not need and it took a whole chunk of time to do them all. So, we just hunkered down on the dining room table at home for the whole week and churned through them, James filling in the on-line questions and me checking and offering advice as he went along.

This enforced incarceration at home during the Spring Break turned out to have a positive by-product. To place this event on a timeline, all this university application activity was just about one year after I had the SPC removed from my abdomen in SKMC, and as described in the previous chapter, there had been a gradual improvement in my bladder functions and control month by month.

Because I was busy at home with James I was not going out anywhere. I was not going to and from the office. I was not going to meetings. I was not out in the hot sun and then back in the cool of an air-conditioned room. I was not getting in and out of the car. I was not walking up and down stairs. So, my personal environment was really consistent and controlled and I could have food and drinks just when I wanted them. But, more importantly, I could walk the twenty steps to the bathroom at exactly the moment in time that I needed to.

This latter point was very significant as, during the process of regaining bladder control, I was getting the signal that my bladder was ready to be emptied, but I had a very "short fuse". By this, I don't mean that my penis was short, but rather the time from first getting the mental signal that I needed to have a pee and the flow actually starting was not very long. My mind control to keep the valve closed once the bladder had signified its desire to be emptied was only effective for a fairly short duration. But being at home meant that I could get up and walk instantly – well, as "instantly" as my semi-functional legs would allow – and get to the bathroom within the time zone allowed by my brain/neurological system/bladder valve control parameters.

Amazingly, the end result of this perfectly managed urological environment was that my bladder control improved dramatically each day as – I guess – the system was operating under optimum conditions instead of sometimes having to wait too long before I could actually reach a bathroom.

This was so good for me that by the end of the week I was confident enough to ditch the safety factor of the "man-pad" and be a "bareback rider" with just my Marks & Spencer underwear between me and the major embarrassment of peeing in my pants and having to cover up the big wet patch on the front of my trousers. Yeeeeeeeehhhhaaaaahhhhh!!!

All the (8) Urologists had told me that it is really hard to regain bladder functions and control but, if I can do it, I am sure others can too.

I think I am going to form a new support group, a bit like Alcoholics Anonymous. I plan to call it Neurogenics Anonymous. Everyone can come to the meetings and sit around in a circle and tell the others about their incontinence problems. You get badges for how many days/weeks/months you have not peed in your pants or wet the bed, and you will get peer group praise and a little badge when you tell them "I've been dry for four months, three week, two days and ten hours."

So, Spring Break wasn't so bad after all. I didn't make it out on a picnic. I didn't get to Blackpool Promenade. I definitely didn't get to Cancun. But I did make it to the bathroom every time, on time and, as a result, my "Little Stick of Blackpool Rock" seemed to be working as it should. And I felt like I had made a huge leap forward in my neurological and urological recovery.

And for me, that was better than all the California girls you could throw my way. (Well, maybe just one? Please and pretty please?)

51

TINSTAAC

TINSTAAC – There Is No Such Thing As A Coincidence. I have said this many times in this book and I really believe it. Too many things have happened to me since I have had my accident to be called a coincidence. Maybe they were happening before but - for whatever reason - I did not really notice them. Perhaps, when you are lying in bed unable to move, as I was for a long time, you start to notice things that you didn't notice before. When you can't move, your brain starts to focus on different things. Sometimes it's a simple thing like "Can I reach the buzzer to call the nurse?" Sometimes it's more complex like a series of events that initially may seem to be unconnected but suddenly you start to join the dots, and the whole becomes much more than the sum of its parts and likewise, more than just a coincidence.

One particular series of events since my accident that has been very significant is the regular appearance of the song *Don't Stop Believin'*. This has been mentioned several times in the book already. In fact, the song itself has already been featured three times, first by Glee, second by Journey with Steve Perry on the Radio 2 compilation album, and third by Tom Cruise in *Rock of Ages*. But it's actually cropped up many, many more times for me and it has often been at moments when hearing it has meant something special.

One very specific example of this happened one Saturday afternoon in July, 2014 when Agnes and I saw the documentary about Arnel Pineda joining the band Journey. It's actually very unusual that Agnes and I were watching television together as she is definitely not a TV fan and usually prefers to be doing something on her Laptop/Big Mac/Little Mac/iPad/Samsung Tablet/iPhone or whatever. You can kind of guess from the preceding sentence that Agnes is more of a hands-on techno freak than a couch potato.

The documentary was shown on Sundance Channel. It was called "*The Arnel Pineda Story – Don't Stop Believin' – Everyman's Journey*". It was fantastic, heart-breaking and heart-warming all at the same time. The documentary tells how Arnel was a poor kid from the slums of Manila, sleeping in parks, literally singing for his supper. Then a friend posted a video on YouTube of him singing a Journey song in a Manila club and he was spotted by Neil Schon, lead guitarist of Journey, who was looking for a new singer as Steve Perry had left the band. Arnel is a small Filipino guy who happens to have a voice just like Steve Perry! Yo!

If you want to watch just the trailer for the documentary, click on the first link. If you want to watch the whole show click on the second link, and I recommend you do the latter.

CUE YOUTUBE VIDEO: ARNEL PINEDA STORY
DON'T STOP BELIEVIN' – EVERYMAN'S JOURNEY

LINK FOR TRAILER

LINK FOR FULL SHOW

Agnes and I sat through the documentary and soaked in the whole story. Naturally, I was very interested in the band but Agnes was glued to the screen because of the fact that the story was all about the well-deserved and amazing success of a fellow Filipino. I had already been writing this book since around mid-2014 and the *Don't Stop Believin'* song had cropped up many times and was already being featured in the book. Of course, by then I knew Arnel was the lead singer for Journey but I had no idea how he got there. So the documentary put a whole new perspective on it.

And talk about TINSTAAC. This was an absolutely massive TINSTAAC for sure!

That night I went to bed and I could hardly sleep, which is very unusual for me. I am normally a "hit the pillow and my eyes close" kind of guy. It's like a light switch. But that night my brain was working overtime and just would not shut down. I kept thinking about the documentary, Arnel, Journey, and *Don't Stop Believin'*...

I must have drifted off eventually, I guess, as I woke up with the blinding idea that – somehow – <u>I must persuade Arnel and Journey to do a live concert here in the UAE!</u>

How I was going to do that, I had no idea, but I knew that somehow I had to reach out and get in touch with Arnel and persuade him to come to the UAE. Easy Peasy, Lemon Squeezy! Ha! Of Course!

Where should I start? Well the obvious place was at home with Agnes – ask a Filipina to find a Filipino! She in turn asked her best friend, Agie Marelid, who used to work for the ABS-CBN TV Channel in Manila as – by good fortune – Arnel is contracted to ABS-CBN. So, Agie then put me in touch with William Penaredondo who also used to work for ABS-CBN. Luckily(!), William was working in Dubai at that time we were able to meet. He was really interested in the idea of a Journey concert as he had done a lot of work on big events in the past. So he promised to put me in touch with someone close to Arnel.

But then everything went quiet for quite a long while and I was beginning to think I had hit another dead end. But, like many things in my life, sometimes you just have to sit and wait for the "moment" to arrive as if you push too soon or too much it doesn't happen any faster anyway.

Everything comes to he who waits...

And, dear reader, you will have to wait too, as the story will unfold later. Well, at least before the end of the book!

52

LIGHTNING STRIKES TWICE AT THE YMCA

They say that lightning never strikes twice in the same place. But who are "they" and how can "they" be sure? It might be years between strikes and maybe no one was watching the second time around. Maybe "they" were watching but the watchers went for a tea break or a Kit-Kat or something just as it happened. Well, I have seen lightning strike twice in the same place. Not actual lightning, I have to admit, but metaphorical lightning. And that's good enough for me in the context of this book.

On 3 April 2013 I was watching the Abu Dhabi Harlequins first team game against Jebel Ali Dragons. Colby and Kyle had both been playing games earlier that day too, so I was there initially to watch them and we all stayed on for the big game as it was the First Division final for the cup. Suddenly, the game stopped and there was a man down! It was a young, fit, American player by the name of Mike Ballard. The tackle he made, on the opposition attacking player about ten metres out from the try line, looked fairly straight forward, but something was obviously wrong as Mike was lying prone on the pitch and not moving.

The medics went on the field and eventually they put Mike on a compression board – like the ones in Sharjah had done with me – and carried him off the field. I found out much later that they had a problem finding a doctor to see Mike as it was a Friday and everyone was off-duty – just the same problem that I had!

I wish someone would have had the presence of mind to ask me as I could have called my neurosurgeon, Dr. Salloum and I am sure he would have seen Mike immediately. Anyway, they eventually ended up at Mafraq hospital. Mike had some spinal damage but it was on Thoracic Vertebrae No. 12 (T12) which in the lower back just above the waist, whereas mine was on Cervical No. 5 (C5), which is in the neck.

So, as I said, lightning does strike twice. Two Abu Dhabi Harlequins members with serious spinal injuries. Is that metaphorical enough?

Mike had an operation here in Abu Dhabi and then, as he was working for an American company, he was flown back to the States for his rehabilitation. But Harlequins did a number of fund raising events to help Mike with the costs of his hospitalisation and physiotherapy – just as they and other UAE clubs did for me in 2011. One of the fundraisers in April 2014 was a 70s Retro Disco Party and Barbecue held in the Quins clubhouse at Zayed Sports City.

In order to help, I offered to do an after-dinner speech talking about Mike, the things I had been through and some of the things that he would have to endure. It was all arranged at fairly short notice so I did not have time to prepare a full-blown on-screen presentation and although I had a lot of photos and info it was scattered all over the place and not filed or tagged as I had not started writing this book at that time. So, I just made a list of some of the funny things that had happened to me and sat on a bar stool and told the stories.

I felt a bit like Dave Allen, an Irish comedian, who, in the early 70s, was the first comedian to do funny monologues about ordinary things that happened to him. He always sat or leaned on a bar stool and had a glass of whiskey in his hand and – prior to this particular clip – he always had a cigarette in his hand and smoked as he told the story.

CUE YOUTUBE VIDEO: SMOKING – DAVE ALLEN

It was a lovely sensation to talk about the experiences I had been through and hear people laughing as I tried to put a funny spin on some of the awful things that had happened to me. We recorded it and uploaded it onto YouTube so we could send it to Mike. Take a look for yourself.

CUE YOUTUBE VIDEO: TRIBUTE TO MIKE BALLARD
TSB - CONFESSIONS OF AN EX-HOOKER

Of course, it's not as polished as Dave Allen, but I had never done it before and I did not have a glass of whiskey in my hand. But the best bit about it – from my perspective – was that at the end when we played the Journey song, *Don't Stop Believin'*, most of the people in the room started singing it. They all knew the words! But even better was that lots of people came up afterwards and made positive comments about the speech and said that it was really inspirational.

Later, I was standing by the bar – note that I said I was <u>standing</u> by the bar – and Andy Cole, Chairman of Quins, came over and said "That was really great! And you <u>must</u> write that book!" He also offered to help in any way that he could – by some of his secretaries typing it up for me if I needed it. It did not work out that way – I typed every word with just my two finger (one on each hand) typing skills - but Andy's comment was the trigger that I needed and about a month later I actually did start getting organised to write this book.

And now you are probably wondering what the reference to YMCA is in the title of this chapter. What has it got to do with the story? Has he lost the thread or his marbles? Has he forgotten about it?

Well it's easy. YMCA = Young Men's Christian Association. And in the 70s the YMCA in San Francisco was an openly gay rendezvous point for those of mixed-gender genetics. A group called the "Village People" sang songs with gay themes while wearing wild fantasy stage costumes depicting typical macho male stereotypes. These included a biker, cowboy, construction worker, soldier, leather man and an Indian - an American "Red" Indian, not one from Bombay or Calcutta. Moustaches were also a very significant part of the attire for some reason.

Their biggest hit was - of course - Y.M.C.A. and it's always a great dance floor filler, especially at a 70s Retro Disco night. The Quins fundraiser was no exception. The song came on just after my conversation with Andy Cole and everyone was up on the floor doing the Y.M.C.A letters with their arms above their heads.

CUE YOUTUBE VIDEO: Y.M.C.A.
THE VILLAGE PEOPLE

It was a hugely popular song and the YouTube Video has had over 73 million hits! What made me really happy though was that I was also able to stand up, without my crutches, and give it plenty, doing the Y.M.C.A. letters with my arms above my head.

It's fun to stay at the Y.....M.....C.....A.....
It's fun to stay at the Y.....M.....C.....A.....

Yeeehahhh!

53

BIKING ON THE DARK SIDE OF THE MOON

On Tuesday, 19 June 2014 I had a really good day. Hamzah, my gym instructor at the Burjeel Hospital had been trying to persuade me for quite a while to walk from the main door up to the gym. It's actually quite a long way as you have to go through the lobby/reception area around to the elevator, up to the third floor, out of the elevator into the large third floor lobby and then down the corridor past the Physiotherapy Clinic and turn left into the long Gym corridor. All in all it was about 300 metres and took me about ten minutes to walk it in one go – no resting – that's cheating!

But I did it and Hamzah was so happy to see me walking in to the Gym. In fact, he was so happy that he put me straight onto the bicycle machine and set me a target of one kilometre in less than six minutes. (Thanks Hamzah!). So, there I was with my "tired little legs" swapping into a cycling motion. This particular bike was much more difficult than some bikes. It had a seat with a back on it and the pedals were out in front, under the screen. Therefore, my legs were sticking out forwards and not downwards as on a normal bike. This actually made it more difficult as gravity affects the leg action much more than on the normal upright bike.

Biking is not as easy as walking because the hip joint has to lift the knee up to make the cycling motion. At that time my right leg was still lagging behind the left, particularly in the lifting action. The hip joint muscles were just starting to have some action, but they still tired very easily. As I tried to cycle, sometimes the right leg would come around and then I had to lift it with my hand under the knee to flick it over the critical point at the top of the pedal circle. It usually got better as I went along. I guess it was warming up and getting into the action.

Mostly, when I was cycling, I kept my eyes closed. And no that's not because I was in any pain and, of course, the bike machine was not going anywhere so I wouldn't crash into something. But, to help me cycle, I had a picture in my mind of me cycling when I was about fifteen years old.

Yeah, yeah, yeah, I know that's a long, long time ago but I could still picture it perfectly in my mind. In 1964 I had a semi-racing bike which had a speedometer connected to a sensor on the front wheel. So, whenever I got the chance I would try and do a speed run and pedal as fast as I could in top gear to reach 50mph. See, I was always a speed-freak! My favourite place for doing this was a flat piece of smooth asphalt on a road called *Glen Way* in Brierfield, Lancashire.

Sooooo, looping back 50+ years from 1964 through a time warp to the present day and to me on the exercise cycle in the Burjeel Gym in Abu Dhabi. That bike sprint down *Glen Way* was what I always thought about when I was on their exercise bike. And it worked – amazingly! As I said earlier, I always started off slowly and sometimes had to flick my knee up with my hand to keep it going. Mostly the cycle speed was about 25 - 30 kph but Hamzah was always pushing me to keep it at 40 kph.

So, there was a lot of variation for the first few minutes. But then I would start looking at the time elapsed and the distance left to reach one kilometre and my brain would start computing average speeds and what speed I needed to do to make the full distance in less than six minutes. I was pretty good at this computation as I used to have to do average speed calculations a lot when I was a rally navigator in the 1980s – 1990s (but that's another story).

I also realised that, while I was pedalling, Meg the Filipina Gym Instructress, was playing lots of 70s music that I loved. Obviously, as evidenced everywhere in this book, music has a great effect on me so I am sure it was helping me pedal faster. One of the tracks she was playing was Pink Floyd, *Another Brick in the Wall – Part Two* from the album *Dark Side of the Moon.*

CUE YOUTUBE VIDEO: ANOTHER BRICK IN THE WALL – PART 2 – PINK FLOYD

With the combination of the music and knowing how fast I needed to go to make my target, the competitive bit in my brain would kick in and I would start pedalling faster and faster. And faster and faster. And all the time I was replaying the "video" in my head of me, aged fifteen, racing down *Glen Way* with my legs going round and round and round as fast as I could make them. And, because of this, my legs would "forget" that they didn't work too well right now and they would do what they were doing way back then. They just went faster and faster.

And I would be looking at the speedo on the screen as it crept up and up. 40 kph to 50 kph. Then a dip and then back up again and I would be gradually getting a higher and higher speed. 60 kph then 70 kph. And I would close my eyes and think of *Glen Way*. Then a quick squint at the speedo on the screen, just opening my eyes enough to see the numbers but not see the surrounding room – so I could stay in the "video replay". I would try and go faster and the speedometer would go up – 75 kph – and I would be looking at the clock too.

I was trying to balance whatever energy I had left in my muscles with the clock ticking down, the milometer getting nearer one kilometre and the speed I was pedalling. Then Hamzah would join in and he would be counting down the distance remaining as I was squinting at the clock.

I used to have no idea what my legs were doing as several minutes earlier I would have lost any real sense of feeling as they were just "moving". That's all I knew. But the pressure from Hamzah would mount as he counted down the distance and this would make me go faster till the speedo hit 80 kph, the clock flashed six minutes and the meter finally, finally flipped over from, 0.99 to 1.00 kilometres. Yeehaahhhhhhhh! I did it . . . !!

Of course, 80 kph was always the magic number as that I was trying to hit as 80 kph equals 50 miles per hour, my top speed when I was on my bike on *Glen Way*.

As I slowed down and eventually stopped, I would be breathing really heavily and my legs usually felt like they had turned to jelly. And then I would slowly start taking more notice of my surroundings again as I "returned" from *Glen Way* in 1964. On that particular night in June 2014, Meg and Hamzah and I started talking when we were doing the next exercises as there were hardly any clients training in the gym. It was a Thursday night, which is the start of the weekend in the Middle East!

I started telling them that I was twenty-five years old and "young, free and single" when Pink Floyd's mega album, *Dark Side of the Moon* came out. And that back in those days, I had a fancy house and a great stereo system and lots of girlfriends. Oh and a waterbed too – which came in very useful coupled with aforesaid music, fancy house and girlfriends! Of course they thought that all this was funny – as though maybe I was joking and it wasn't really true. They were looking at me on the basis that I was a crazy sixty-five year old guy who can't yet walk properly. The images didn't match, for them. But it doesn't matter. As long as they matched for me at the time! So, just shine on you crazy diamond . . .

CUE YOUTUBE VIDEO: SHINE ON YOU CRAZY DIAMOND
PINK FLOYD

Sometimes I don't know if I am writing this book or if it is writing itself. I had never actually thought about the lyrics of *Shine on You Crazy Diamond* till I wrote the last line to the paragraph above. There was just a subliminal link in my head between me being; (a) twenty-five years old again; (b) a crazy sixty-five year old, and; (c) Pink Floyd songs. Then, when I downloaded the words, I was amazed by their appropriateness.

Starting off with *remembering when I was young.* Then, hopefully, being a *target for faraway laughter* when people all over the world who read this book get a laugh out of it. And, if possible, will I become *a legend* in my own lunchtime? Who knows about the future?

54

A KNIGHT'S TALE

After all the biking and Pink Floyd reminiscences I moved on to the next exercise. This was standing up in various positions in front of a big frame and gripping a handle attached to weights via a cable and pulley system. I had to pull the weights this way and that while balancing and staying standing up in a vertical position. Sounds easy . . . Hmmmmnn! Not so when your core muscles are not at full strength (so your body wants to go floppy at the waist) and one ankle is weak (so it can't always keep up with correcting your balance). Oh, and lots of other body parts don't always cooperate and coordinate the way they should.

While I was doing this one Meg was playing various Queen songs – and I was trying to have more flashbacks to my old girlfriends and my waterbed, but it wasn't working. Then I realized why – it was because, for some unknown reason, I did not have any Queen albums back then even though I did love their music. But, I am certain the flashbacks would have kicked in if she had played the first track Eagles album, *One of These Nights* that I bought in 1975. Way back then was in 12" vinyl of course. It has the best guitar intro, ever, to the first track.

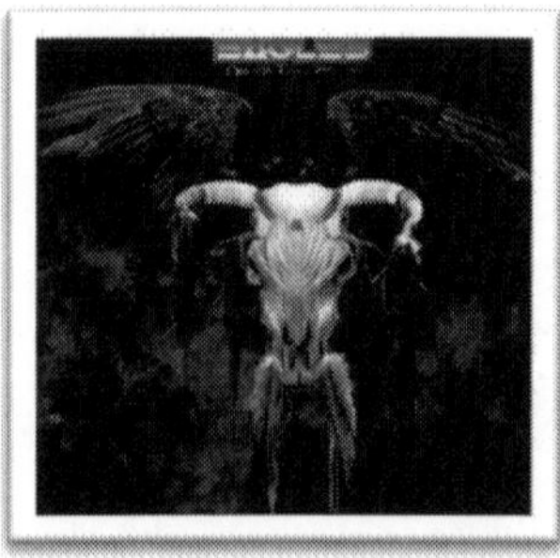

There Were Many of Those Nights!

Just listen to it – Duuh Dooop Dooo Waap, Duuh Dooop Dooo Waap and on and on. All the "Air Guitars" come out. Brilliant! Sorry if my written version does not quite live up to the actual sounds but click on the YouTube link and you will understand what I am talking about. And also listen to the lyrics . . .

CUE YOUTUBE VIDEO: ONE OF THESE NIGHTS
EAGLES

See what I mean? Any red-blooded male should be having orgasmic flashbacks thinking about those words. In 1975 it just had to be the first song of choice to be played when you got home with a new girlfriend!!

Anyway, back to the Burjeel Gym. Despite the lack of flashbacks each time Meg played a song we were talking about it. Hamzah was there too. He is a lovely guy and has an infectious laugh and a killer smile, but he knows absolutely, absolutely nothing about music. He is Jordanian and I think he grew up in a bubble capsule with earplugs, no radio, no CD player and no television. He did not know any major rock bands or music artists! Rattle off the big names like The Beatles, The Rolling Stones, Queen, Pink Floyd, The Eagles etc. and had never even heard of them. It was the same with new artists too, like Kelly Clarkson, Nickelback and even One Direction (perhaps a lucky fellow on that last one!). Actually, he was the same with movies and movie stars too.

One of the big Queen songs of the 70s era – and still very popular today – is *We Will Rock You* and when Meg played it I was reminded of a funny incident back in the Philippines in about 2004 when Kyle (now 15) was about two and a half or three years old. So, I just had to tell Hamzah and Meg. And, of course, the trick thing about telling stories to your physio or gym instructor is that you get a longer break before the onset of the next set of pain!

Before they could start me on the next exercise I kicked off with telling them about when we were living in Manila in 2003 and we were going up to Baguio for the weekend. The movie *A Knight's Tale* was out on Video CD and we had a copy. It was Kyle's favourite at the time and it was full of great rock music cleverly segued into the medieval theme. This was also Heath Ledger's breakout movie. So, as well as the film video we had the music soundtrack CD that we could play in the car. And the first track in the movie and on the album was *We Will Rock You* by Queen. In the movie, it starts with all the peasants banging on the guard rails and clapping their hands to the "Duh, Duh, Clap" intro to the song as they wait for the knights on horseback to start jousting.

CUE YOUTUBE VIDEO: A KNIGHT'S TALE
WE WILL ROCK YOU - QUEEN

And the lyrics are a perfect fit too as Heath Ledger plays a poor assistant to a knight but he has great aspirations to be a "big man" himself one day i.e. a knight of the realm.

Anyway, back to the Baguio story. The whole family jumped in the trusty Honda Sri at about 7:00 am and, before we could move out of the driveway of the house, Kyle said "Puck You, Daddy!" Kyle was only about two and a bit at this point in time so he could not speak perfectly. What he meant was that he wanted me to play *We Will Rock You.* Of course, "Puck You" = "Rock You". All parents know how to translate this stuff so I started playing it as we set off out of the gate. Baguio is a long way and it is high up in the mountains. But time and distance do not directly correlate for road travel in the Philippines. It all depends on how much "trappic" is between you and your destination! And no, that's not a spelling mistake. Filipinos have problems with "P's" and "F's" and usually transpose them when talking. So, "traffic" becomes "trappic".

Tricky this, especially when the name of your country begins with a letter that you can't say . . . And of course, using the Filipino transposition of "P's" and "F's" Kyle's innocent "Puck You, Daddy" could become something completely different.

Normally, Baguio is about a five-hour drive, but usually, there are far too many trucks, buses, jeepneys and "tricycles" in the way to keep up a high average speed. By the way, "tricycles" are not kids on three-wheeler bikes. They are 125cc Yamaha motorbikes with a sidecar and up to ten passengers. As you can imagine, these things are not actually breaking any speed limits.

On the first leg of the journey we were enjoying the soundtrack to *A Knight's Tale*. And as soon as it finished, Kyle said "Puck You, Daddy". So, we played it again. And then again! And again! And, each time it finished, this little voice piped up from the back seat saying "Puck You, Daddy". But then the journey went on and on and on. Instead of five hours it took us ten hours. Whoah! But, as we were getting towards the end of the trip I was getting tired and grumpy and Kyle said "Puck You, Daddy" one more time, I replied with "Yes, and Puck You too, Kyle!!!!"

Both Meg and Hamzah were very amused by this – especially Meg as she is a Filipina and knows Baguio – and I had achieved my goal of stretching my resting time from one minute to four minutes. Yes!!!!

The exercise they wanted me to do was on the big frame machine but it's like lifting free weights and your body has to resist the pull or the twist of your arms pulling the weight. When I started going to the Burjeel Gym in February 2014 I could only do this sitting in a wheelchair. Now in June, I was standing up without any support and doing the exercises on my own. To do this, first you have to stand up (and not crumple and fall), second you have to stay vertical (I hesitate to use the word erect – people may get the wrong idea), third your core muscles have to resist the twist (no Chubby Checker stuff here) and fourth you have to pull on the handle to open your arm out fully (this is actually the easy part of the whole thing).

But, but, but . . . that day I could do it! Yo! You really have to mark moments like this and then remember what it was like when you started doing that particular exercise. First, it was sitting in a wheelchair, next sitting on a box with Hamzah holding me, then it was standing with one crutch and Hamzah steadying me, graduating to holding onto the frame of the machine, but sitting down after each set. Next was doing the same but not sitting to rest, then I let go of the frame and Hamzah steadied me. And, finally, I could do it all by myself!

Sometimes you don't appreciate these small steps of incremental progress and you think you are not improving. So, you really do need to back-track every now and then to see what you have gained.

POST SCRIPT

Just after writing this chapter, when I was looking for the YouTube link for the *Knight's Tale* opening scene with *We Will Rock You* I saw this quote on Amazon's website advertising the movie Soundtrack CD:

> A KNIGHT'S TALE - SOUNDTRACK
> Performed by the original artists, the powerful music and lyrics are fun to sing along during workouts, parties, long drives or anywhere you can listen to your iPod

iPod's had not been invented – or even imagined in 2003 – but Brian Helgeland, the director of *A Knight's Tale*, must have somehow known my son Kyle and anticipated our "long drive" to Baguio and my need for workouts in 2014. Maybe he was prescient, had very strong Morphic Resonance or been a believer in TINSTAAC. Either way, it's a fun movie and a great soundtrack. Try it next time you go on a long drive!

55

TRAINS & BOATS & PLANES (PART 1) A.K.A BOMBER BRIGGS TOURS

I have just come back from a once-in-a-lifetime holiday! I tell you what, never again! (Boom-Boom)

Well, we hadn't had real family holiday since July 2010 and – as I write this its August 2014 – so that's four years ago. Of course, there has been a reason for the long gap. I don't think that we could have all enjoyed it any earlier as the logistics needed to enable me to move around and participate would just have been too much stress on everyone else. But the success of us going on the Rugby Tour to Sri Lanka in February 2014 with the Abu Dhabi Harlequins proved that it was possible. But of course, that was just one week and there were lots of people around to help. The summer 2014 holiday was a full-blown trip to Europe for a month – just the family - with plans to visit five different countries and about fifteen town, cities and places of interest while we were there. Bomber Briggs' Tours was back with a vengeance . . . !

The "Bomber Briggs' Tours" nickname came from my sister as a result of me organising minute-by-minute tour itineraries when my parents came out to visit me in Kenya in the 80s and the Philippines in the 90s. If it's Tuesday at 11:10am we must be on the Taal Volcano, Philippines!

For Summer 2014 we planned to go to The Netherlands, Germany, the Czech Republic, France and Switzerland plus lots of side trips in most of those places. So, it was going to be a real endurance test. Just so it wasn't all fun and frivolity, I also wanted to experience some physiotherapy from the experts in Germany while I was there. Agnes' sister, Cecille and her German husband Carsten and their kids, were living in Ludwigsburg near Stuttgart so that was "Base Camp Zero". Before departure I got a referral from Dr. Salloum and, fortunately, the top neurosurgeon in Stuttgart accepted my case. I was able to have a consultation and a local referral to RehaMed Centre Clinic. But more about that - and Vojta – later.

So, at the beginning of July we flew on KLM from Abu Dhabi to Schiphol Airport in Amsterdam. This was my first really long international flight in years. The trip to Sri Lanka was only about three and a half hours. Amsterdam was nine hours and overnight, so this was new territory in terms of experience for me. Anyone who has flown anywhere can tell you that sitting in an economy class seat for 9 hours is very far from ultra-comfortable even when you are a fully-functional human being. For me, it was potentially going to be a nightmare. Nowhere to move around in the seat, difficulty standing up and a narrow wobbly gangway to the teeny-weeny toilet at the back of the plane.

But I was not going to let Agnes know that I had any trepidations. My mantra was "I will be fine". I was a grown man, I had control of my bladder (ha!) and my legs moved back and forth on command. So, how difficult could that be? I found that the trick was to have an aisle seat so I could pull myself up using the back of the seat in front, sit on the arm of the seat, stand up and then "walk" back to the toilet by holding onto the tops of all the seat backs, pulling myself along. Forget the crutches; they are too difficult in a narrow gangway. James, of course, rode shotgun just behind me in case I fell over – but fortunately I never did.

The tricky bit was having a pee in the miniscule toilet with a curved wall/roof that comes towards your head because planes are rounded and not square. The only square plane I have ever been on was a 10 seater Irish-built twin propeller one that flew from Dhaka, Bangladesh to Thimpu, Bhutan. To be sure, only the Irish could come up with a square plane. But that's yet another story.

Anyway, it's not easy at the best of times for me to pee as I have to stand freely - without crutches - and lean forward over the bowl with one hand to steady myself and the other to hold my "fishing tackle". But the curved wall/roof meant that I could not lean forward enough as my forehead was pushed hard against the roof before I was at the correct leaning angle. This also meant that I could not look down to see where I was pointing Percy - so I had to try and curve my pelvis forwards, which it resists, and there was nothing really to hold onto with the free hand. And then, EVERY time I got into that position, the damn plane would hit an air pocket and drop what felt like about a 1000 feet – but was probably more like 10 - and I would go wobbly all over. OOOOoooooooohhhh whoooooosh no kidding!! My knees would start to buckle and I had to try to grip the shiny surfaces with my "bad" hand and try to control where I was peeing with the good hand. But, as I could not look down to see anything, I was judging my success by listening to the sound of the flow hitting the stainless steel bowl!! I can tell you, if you ever find yourself in this same situation, that if it goes silent you are probably peeing on your own trousers or your shoes . . .

But it was worth the turmoil. Once we got to Amsterdam we found that it was a really lovely city, incredibly laid back, full of picturesque canals and thousands upon thousands of people of all ages riding around on bicycles. But these are not cyclists wearing padded crotch, spandex shorts and plastic, pointy turban-style helmets on ultra-light bikes with tyres thinner than condoms. They are normal people of all ages, wearing normal clothes – which often means young girls in short skirts who have (unfortunately) mastered the ability to cycle with their knees together. They are all riding old, heavy bikes with "sit-up-and-beg" handlebars. For them, cycling is a social event and they trundle round in groups chatting away to each other or talking/texting on their cell phones.

The Birdman of Dam Square, Amsterdam

Of course, in line with its laid-back reputation, Amsterdam is full of bistros and coffee shops, sorry coffee houses. I have to correct myself there as, if you go to Amsterdam, don't ask for a COFFEE SHOP if you want a Coffee. You must ask for a COFFEE HOUSE. It's VERY important to understand the difference. In Amsterdam, COFFEE HOUSES sell, well, coffee. But there, COFFEE SHOPS sell . . . weed/marijuana/Mary Jane or 420, as it's apparently now called, according to my kids. My 19 year-old son, James, told me this when I, wrongly, kept asking for a coffee shop! Where he got that info from I don't know. And BTW, does anyone of my generation actually know where that 420 name came from? Answers on the back of a postcard please to PO Box 146110, Abu Dhabi, UAE.

Anyway, on the second night there, returning to the hotel from the city centre in a taxi after watching the Germany vs. France World Cup Quarter Final game, we were on a one lane bit of road and our taxi had to stop behind a car that had just pulled up outside a strip of shops. A guy ran out of the nearest one and handed something to the driver and took money for it. I wondered what was going on as the taxi driver was waiting very patiently. Then I looked over at the shop front and the window was full of plants and greenery. And the name above the window was, wait for it ....CHEECH & CHONG'S COFFEE SHOP! So the driver in front was buying a joint, ha! Hilarious!!!!!!!

Then I had to explain to my wife and the boys all about Cheech & Chong, their famous 1978 "cult" movie *Up in Smoke,* about a couple of stoners and the (then) counterculture of smoking cannabis. Of course, for many years now The Netherlands has allowed the legal sale of cannabis in its so-called coffee shops. Maybe Cheech and Chong should just move to Amsterdam and their lives would be perfect.

CUE YOUTUBE VIDEO: UP IN SMOKE (TRAILER)
CHEECH & CHONG

After three days in Amsterdam we took the train down to Stuttgart and we had to change at Dusseldorf. Unfortunately, we got off at the wrong stop – Duisburg instead of Dusseldorf – because they announced Duisburg over the crackly intercom. But the guy was saying it in a Dutch/German accent and I thought it was the German word for Dusseldorf. Like Koln is for Cologne and Munchen is for Munich.

So, we got off and had a harrowing time asking lots of people which of the platforms was Platform 16 – because that's what it said on our ticket. As you can imagine, it can be somewhat stressful when you have fifteen minutes to find Platform 16 in Dusseldorf and you are actually in Duisburg and that station only has thirteen platforms – but we didn't know we were in the wrong station. Strangely, everyone (who are all Germans of course) looks at you as though you are stupid when you ask for platform sixteen! Dumbkopf! Then you ask for a ticket office – to get information - and they point to an automatic ticket vending machine. It seems like you can't get info from a machine and you can't get it from a German!!!!! How do you tell the difference?? And in the middle of all this you think back to how the Dutch had all been incredibly helpful. Must be the weed . . . !!!!!!!!

Luckily, very luckily, the next train that came through the station was actually the Stuttgart train on its way to Dusseldorf! So, we actually got on ahead of all the crowds in Dusseldorf. But the getting on the train – which only stops for about a minute to keep up with it's perfect Germanic time schedule - was not easy when you have me with crutches and five of us in total with about ten bags of luggage, three laptop computers, a wheeled walker, a walking frame and all the rest of the holiday paraphernalia.

Amazingly, we actually made it to Stuttgart in one piece, were greeted there by Cecille and Carsten and taken to their apartment for a well-deserved beer. Sehr gut, ja!

One of the best trips that we did while we were there – but toughest on me - was the one to Prague in the Czech Republic. First of all it's about a six hour drive from Stuttgart which means I had to "pace" myself in terms of visits to the bathroom. In general, on German roads, rest halts and service stations are fairly plentiful. But, if you pass one and then realise you need a pee, it can feel like a long way to the next one.

Believe me! Generally, if you are cruising along at 120 kph its fine as you get to the next one in a reasonable time. But the problem comes when there are road works and the whole autobahn slows down to a crawl. It turns out the Germans are like the Brits when it comes to having many kilometres of lane closures for road resurfacing during the peak summer holiday traffic, and then having no one working on it at all . . .

The next morning after a good night's sleep, we caught a tram from near our hotel into the city centre where we could catch a "Hop-On-Hop-Off" bus sightseeing tour. Naturally, for me, it's not so much hop-on-hop-off as clamber-and-heave-on and wriggle-and-drop-off to get myself up and down the steps of the bus and then collapse on the first available seat.

Prague is wall-to-wall beautiful buildings but for me the most difficult thing was that every street and sidewalk was made out of rough cobblestones. For the uninitiated, that means lots and lots of stones about six inches square all over every surface. It was really butt-busting to ride in the walker/chair as it only had little wheels and a canvas seat, so I felt every stone. So, despite the distances, I ended up walking a lot which was actually good for me, although it didn't always feel so at the time!

A Church and One of Many Butt-Busting Cobbled Squares in Prague

In particular, I remember walking from one of the city squares to the river along a maze of narrow streets and everyone kept saying it was "not far" even though they had no idea where they were going.

Why we didn't just wait for the next "Hop on, Hop off" bus I will never know. Too easy maybe. Duuuuh . . .

Finally, we got to the river – we had to go there as the last thing on the city tour was a boat trip up and down the River Vlatava. This turned out to be a bit less cultural than the rest of the tour despite the tour guide telling us about this building and that bridge etc. This was because, running parallel to our boat, was another one that was hosting a huge stag party. Everyone was in fancy dress and singing at the tops of their voices and we were treated to a Czech party-goer "mooning" us. Really!

Mooning, Sorry, Cruising Down the River Vlatava, Prague.
Just Another Example of Daily Life in This Butt-Busting City

But, despite the mooning, Prague is a very beautiful city full of very beautiful women. It was just a pity that it was the men who were mooning and not the women. Sitting in one of the bistros on the main street near the Palladium Theatre, Carsten and I were taking serious note of the passers-by. And there were many to take note of!

In order not to alert our respective wives we were quietly making comments back and forth such as "It works for me" or, "I would give it a Ten" and other similar remarks.

I can fully recommend the experience.

The other great thing about Prague was that everything in the shops was incredibly cheap. At one point Colby came up to me and said "Oh, Mum bought me a jacket. Well, actually, she got me two. You know what Mum's like!" Er, yes I do Colby . . .

On the way back from Prague we managed to find another cultural edifice alongside the autobahn. It was easy to spot from miles away, even without a tour guide to help us, because it had a huge 'M' on a pole in the car park outside it. Of course, it was McDonalds. Have you ever tried doing a long road trip with kids in the car and been able to get to your destination without stopping at a McDonalds or some other mainstream fast food joint? If you have, please tell me the secret of how to do it . . .!!

So, when I had just about finished eating, I suddenly got all the warning signals that I needed to speedily go to the bathroom. This was not just a tiny tinkling feeling in the abdomen; this was the full-blown sirens, bells, whistles and flashing lights that were telling me that my once-a-week bowel movement was about to happen. NOW!

I talked earlier in the book about the re-learning curve for my bladder control. The bladder was a "work in progress" but my bowels were on the opposite modus operandi. In other words, instead of a regular daily "dump", my system stayed in shut down mode for about a week at a time and then gave me only a few minutes warning that the valve was going to open. So, I rushed to the McDo bathroom and plonked myself on the throne just in time. Just in time!! Fast food . . . fast poop.

Then, when I had finished, I looked around and, to my great dismay, there was no toilet tissue. Wonderful! Luckily, Kyle was waiting outside the door for me so I asked him to bring a pack of baby wipes out of the car. I was saved! When I got back to the table Ness said "Are you happy now?" And, quick as a flash, Kyle answered for me "Yes, I could smell the happiness . . . " That's my boy!

But I wasn't on holiday just for the fun of it – or so my wife kept reminding me. I was there for some genuine German-style physiotherapy. "Vee haf vays off making you valk, Britisher . . . !!!"

So, I was half expecting the Stormtrooper (Sturmtruppe in German) technique of standing behind you and firing bullets into the ground just behind your ankles. It surely makes you want to move forwards . . .

But, the Germans have gained a well-deserved reputation in the field of physiotherapy by using advanced but simple techniques – fortunately without resorting to Stormtroopers. My sessions with Rudi and Florian at REHAMED were primarily aimed at strengthening my core muscles – waist, abdominals, obliques and back – as they ascertained that this would enable my legs and body to work better. When you think about it, it makes sense as, for your bottom half, your legs hang off the massive hip bones and, for the top half, the spine originates there.

So, they started me with what were superficially very simple sitting exercises where I had to lean and tilt my hips in different directions. This sounds easy but when some of your muscles don't work the way they should, it is actually very hard and tiring. You just want to flop over at the waist like a rag doll. Then they had me doing other exercises where I was standing up holding on to the wall frame and stepping on and off half balls which were only partially inflated. Again, this sounds easy but, because the balls are only partially inflated, you have to do a lot of control and correction of your ankles and hips to stay balanced.

Either Agnes or James were always with me and they took lots of videos of me doing these exercises so we could bring them back to the UAE and show my physiotherapists there how to do these new exercises. It was a good idea and many of the REHAMED exercises were ultimately included in my routines in the UAE.

And then there was Vojta! Do any of you know what Vojta is? BTW it's pronounced V-O-Y-T-A not V-O-G-T-A. It's actually a person's name. The treatment was developed in the late 60s by Professor Vaclav Vojta, a Czechoslovakian-born doctor, who was working in Germany.

Basically, they are trying to induce a "reflex action" in your muscles to make them work. The medical/technical explanation of Vojta is in the Glossary at the back of the book but you won't be any wiser when you read it. What it means, in layman's terms, is that the Vojta Therapist puts you in a complicated pose either on your side or back with your arms and legs in sort of un-natural positions (i.e. read twisted and uncomfortable) and then pulls your shoulders one way while pushing your hips the other. Meanwhile, you, the patient, have to try and push your shoulders and hips in the opposite direction. And the therapist is pulling and pushing VERY hard, so it's not easy to oppose them.

Then comes the "pie'ce de re'sistance". You are lying on your side with your back to the therapist doing the "push-me-pull-you" routine and you suddenly feel a blunt object prodding you in the back. Of course, you immediately think "Oh no! What is he prodding me with? He has one hand on my shoulder and one hand on my hip. So, what is poking me in the back?" And you have quite a few nervous moments till you realise that – thankfully, it's not his penis - and he is actually standing on one leg and pushing the big toe of his other foot into the middle of your back. Yes, really! And do you get a reflex action? You are damn rigEht you do! Your leg or arm or both will jerk like crazy.

This always makes the therapist very happy. Yeah, right. And how does the patient feel? Abso-bloody-lutely exhausted! The interesting thing about it is that after the session, when you stand up, you feel incredibly light. This is a phenomenon of all Vojta treatments, but they have no idea why.

Look out, Sandra Bullock! Gravity can't hold me down. I'm going to float away into space in a minute. DON'T LET GO . . .

56

TRAINS & BOATS & PLANES (PART 2)
A.K.A JUKE BOX JURY

"Changing subjects". We have to say this in our family as my wife, Agnes – like many women – will instantly flip from one subject to another in the middle of a conversation without any warning or build up to it. She will suddenly be in the middle of something completely different and the rest of us are mentally scrambling to pick up the threads and hook into the new subject.

I thought it was a Filipina thing but apparently it crosses many borders, religions and cultures. I mentioned it one day to Nagy Abou Tar, my then boss at Orascom, who is Egyptian and he said that his wife does it too. And I asked Dr. Antoine Salloum, my Lebanese/Canadian neurosurgeon, and his wife also does it. So, it's universal. It's a woman thing.

Just writing that made me think of the fantastically funny, but totally accurate, sketch by Mark Gungor about the difference between men's and women's brains. And he is a lay preacher – so he wouldn't lie would he? Just watch how he tells one fact about the differences between the brains and all the men laugh and clap – and the women just stare. And then he talks about another difference and all the women laugh and the men nod sagely. It's brilliant.

CUE YOUTUBE VIDEO: MEN'S AND WOMEN'S BRAINS
MARK GUNGOR

So, "changing subjects". While we were in Germany we needed to hire a vehicle to achieve our planned sight-seeing trips. We needed something that had space for five people and a decent sized boot/trunk that would fit luggage, crutches and the rolling walker/wheelchair that I used for longer distances. We finally zeroed in on the Nissan Juke. It looks big – it also looks very stupid – but big and stupid. It was the biggest in its price bracket, but probably also the stupidest looking. It's got headlight/sidelight "pods" that for some reason are plonked in top of the front wings (fenders for the American readers). It has muscular looking wheel arches but they are ridiculously mismatched by tiny supermarket trolley-sized wheels. The boot and tailgate also look impressive but open up to a strange-shaped shoebox of a boot/trunk. I actually think there were some trick shape-shifting, moveable panels in the boot/trunk as every single time Agnes and James tried to put the rolling walker/wheelchair into it they had massive problems. They would turn the walker this way and that, then upside down and round and round before it finally went into the space.

Nissan Joke. Sorry, Juke

I am not kidding you. This happened every day and sometimes several times a day. It reminded me of the *Mr. Bean* episode *Do-it-yourself* where he bought a whole bunch of paint, shelves and an armchair but could not get the armchair into his Mini whatever he tried.

So, he tied the armchair on the roof and drove the car from up there by pulling ropes and pushing his broomstick onto the pedals. We never quite had to put the wheelchair on the roof, with me sat in it, but sometimes it was so exasperating trying to get it in the boot that I often thought about it . . .

CUE YOUTUBE VIDEO: MR. BEAN DRIVING ON THE ROOF OF THE CAR

How do cars like the Juke get through all the design exercises, 3-D computer generated images, part and full size model reviews, screening committees and board meetings? Why does no one stick up their hand and say "I think it looks crap"? It's like the fairy story "The Emperor's New Clothes" wherein no one tells the Emperor that he is stark naked - till a scruffy little kid in the crowd states the obvious that no one else dares to do. Anyway, it moved us from A to B and back again without fuss or any problems, so I guess that is why the vehicle exists.

Although the vehicle itself was happy to go from A to B the GPS had some different ideas about where exactly B was. Oh, we had lots of "fun" trying to set the GPS. Because it was a Japanese car, the GPS was obviously tuned to a Japanese mind-set.

We had decided on a bunch of daily side trips to places of interest within a few hours' drive of Stuttgart. But what we had not realised was that some German in the Middle Ages, whose job it was to name towns and cities, had either a very poor memory, couldn't spell very well, enjoyed a flagon or two of mead, was completely dyslexic or had a sense of humour. This last one being unlikely in medieval Germany as they mostly don't have one now and things are a lot better than they were back then.

What appears to have happened is that that guy went around naming towns and then probably got drunk on mead in the local hostelry that night and erased his memory banks. So that next day he gave some town close by more or less the same name as one he gave out the day before since any given area in Germany seems to have towns or cities with almost the same name. The difference may be in the spelling – Rothenberg and Rothenburg – or in some cases the suffix to the name – such as Guttenberg and Guttenberg am Rhein. The Germans all know this of course but kind of forget to mention it when they are giving you verbal directions. Then I guess they all have a little Germanic chuckle when the "dumbkopf Britisher" family drives off in the wrong direction.

This problem was exacerbated by the fact that no one had told the Japanese about this when they did the specifications and set up the Juke for export to Germany. So, as I said, the GPS had a Japanese mind-set. It also had a sort of predictive text but it only gave you one answer instead of a list of options. So, you typed in GUTEN… and it added BERG or maybe it added BURG. In either case, if someone has just told you verbally to go to Gutenberg (or Gutenburg or Guttenberg or Guttenburg) how do you know the spelling and that there may well be two of them within a 50 - 80km radius?

Even my German brother-in-law, who is very internationalised, didn't seem to be sympathetic when I complained about this to him. "Yes of course there are places with the same or similar spellings close by." (Duuuh viz a German accent). Suffice it to say we spent quite a bit of time motoring in the wrong direction along the autobahn towards the wrong town. And the only reason we realised that we were going in the wrong direction was that I had "cheated" and actually done it the "old fashioned" way and looked at a map – albeit on Google - so there was some modern technology involved. So, I sort of knew, for instance, that the Guttenberg/Guttenburg/Gutenberg/Gutenburg that we wanted was roughly to the north-east of Stuttgart and not to the north-west.

And then there is the name – Juke. Maybe it's another Japanese "in joke"? Maybe they spelt it wrong and it should have been Joke? Think how the Japanese speak "Engerish" – "It's a Jook! Ha ha ha. Ha so!" Or maybe it came from taking part of the 60's BBC music panel show name, *Juke Box Jury*. Good thing it wasn't the Nissan Box or the Nissan Jury.

Or maybe they think that we Westerners will somehow find the car more attractive if there is some mind-link to a Juke Box? Don't they know that Juke Boxes were a thing of the 60s and maybe early 70s? They were filled with Elvis Presley and *Love Me Tender*, the Beatles and early Motown songs. Of course, some of you reading this may not even know what a Juke Box is. Have a look at the picture if you have no idea what a Juke Box looks like. And the definitive record about Juke Boxes . . . ? Joan Jett and the Blackhearts, "*I Love Rock n' Roll (So, Put Another Dime in the Juke Box Baby)*".

Gimme Some of That Old Time Rock 'n Roll

CUE YOUTUBE VIDEO: I LOVE ROCK N' ROLL
JOAN JETT & THE BLACKHEARTS

Did you catch a glimpse of the Juke Box in the video? Nowadays they mostly reside in people's games rooms and "man-caves".

Mind you if we think the name Juke is dumb, what if it had been called after part of the ITV pop music show *Thank Your Lucky Stars?* Like the Nissan Lucky or Nissan Star?

There are a couple of instances of TINSTAAC related to the Juke. I wrote this in about August 2014 after our holiday in Germany. Then my wife bought me the Jeremy Clarkson book "*What Could Possibly Go Wrong . . . ?*" for Xmas 2014. I was so happy to read his chapter on the Juke which amazingly says a lot of the same things I have been saying. Maybe I am turning into a Grumpy Old Man . . . ??

All I need is a corduroy jacket and a pair of old jeans and I am set. Oh, and a Lamborghini Gallardo in the garage!

Then, I was watching Episode 4 of *The Grand Tour* with Clarkson, May and Hammond in December 2016 on the night that I was editing this chapter and, out of the blue, Hammond said that he absolutely hates the Juke. I was very happy to hear that as well.

And "changing subjects" again, back to the trips we took during our holiday. Exactly why did we want to go to Guttenburg or Guttenberg or Gutenberg or Gutenburg? We went to see the Eagles, of course. And, no, not the American country-rock band called the Eagles. These were real eagles, hawks and vultures flying on and off the parapets of a medieval castle. The handler was at great pains to tell us that the birds were not tame. But that they just did things for the handlers because they wanted too. Hmmm! It was a great experience especially when you get a full grown eagle or vulture with a two and a half metre wingspan flying within inches of your head.

And then there was the Rothenburg/Rothenberg trip on 15th July, 2014. We had the usual hiccups with the Juke's GPS trying to get the right Rothenburg/Rothenberg, but we eventually found it and it's one of the world's best-preserved medieval towns. It has everything. The wall round the outside, big gates with turrets to get through the wall, narrow streets, medieval housing, town hall with dungeons where they used to torture the serfs (and maybe still do) and a magnificent town square.

We had gone there, primarily, to see all the medieval stuff but we had a couple of very pleasant surprises that were not at all medieval – more like 30s, 40s and 80s. As we walked down the narrow street to the main town square we could hear strains of music. The nearer we got, the louder it became – of course, that's physics. Then we rounded the corner and walked into the square and in front of us was a whole orchestra – but there was yet another bizarre time warp phenomenon.

The musicians were all kids in their mid-teens playing music written in the 1930s and 40s – about fifty to sixty years before they were born. It turned out they were the Iowa State Youth Orchestra which had about 200 kids in it. Amazing! They were on a European tour visiting London, Paris, Amsterdam, Luxembourg and Rothenburg, which was their last stop on the tour. So, we were very lucky to catch that – by shear chance.

And, as if to prove a point, as we sat down, they played one of my all-time favourite tunes – *Summer Time* from the musical *Porgy and Bess* written by George Gershwin in 1935.

CUE YOUTUBE VIDEO: SUMMERTIME
GEORGE GERSHWIN

Hot on the heels of *Summertime* they played another huge favourite of mine, *Rhapsody in Blue*, also by Gershwin. But the story behind that will have to wait for another day – maybe even another book!

Then the orchestra leader made a great long speech to introduce the next piece of music which, according to him, was a rousing World War 2 marching tune written by John Philip Sousa. He did not actually say this but it was probably commissioned by the US Army to make the Yanks feel better when they got shipped out to Europe to have their heads blown off by the Germans. By a weird twist of fate, here we were about to listen to it in the middle of Germany in a medieval town that had somehow escaped being bombed to pieces in WW2 by B17 Flying Fortresses and Liberator Bombers – probably flown by some of the relatives of the kids playing the music. How can this happen? TINSTAAC? Ironically, the piece is called the Liberty Bell, which, in itself, was an iconic American historical mind-link.

This was all very impressive and a huge build up for the piece – at least until they started playing! As soon as the orchestra played the first few bars I burst out laughing – definitely LOL. It wasn't a big dramatic marching song - well it was – but it was really the opening theme to Monty Python's Flying Circus. For any Python lovers reading this, you know exactly what I mean! Even my eldest son, who is 35 years younger than me, can recite, verbatim, whole sketches from Python. So, the legacy was carried forward to other generations.

So the Liberty Bell March probably gained more fame in post-war years as the theme tune to the Python opening credits which consisted of a mass of cartoon images and collages of funny pictures done by Terry Gilliam, a crazy Canuck. The main feature was that it ended with a huge cartoon foot coming down from the sky and squashing the mini-cartoon figures to the accompaniment of a big "squelch" which actually sounded like a wet fart. Then it cut to the rear view of a naked guy sitting at an upright piano, who turned to the camera and said "And now for something completely different!" Just watch this YouTube clip and you will see what I mean.

CUE YOUTUBE VIDEO: LIBERTY BELL MARCH
JOHN PHILIP SOUSA – MONTY PYTHON THEME

When the orchestra's show ended – fortunately without any huge foot (or B52) appearing from the sky – we sat at a bistro café on the edge of the main square. Were just tucking into our Sauerkraut (Ja!) and Schnitzel (Ja!) when I saw one! It was just creeping around the far edge of the square. No, it wasn't a B52 bomber or a huge foot, it was a Mark 1 Toyota Previa, Metallic Maroon with Grey lower sills and alloy wheels – just exactly like the one we used to have in Manila. In a few seconds it disappeared behind some buildings so I could not see it anymore . . .

What was that 24 year old vehicle doing there? Germany is like UAE, no old cars. Was it just a coincidence? But TINSTAAC surely? Maybe it had come to check on me to make sure I was OK. Who knows? I certainly don't! After the "Close Encounter of the Third Kind" on Reem Island, Abu Dhabi I had not seen a Previa for about three months. But, interestingly, after the European holiday I started to see Mk 1 Toyota Previas regularly in the UAE again.

After all the side trips in Germany, which alternated with days of having physiotherapy or Vojta, Agnes finally "agreed" that we should do the Switzerland trip. Up to that point she had been saying "I've been to Switzerland before. I don't need to go again . . . !" The fact that we had only been to the city of Basel the last time – four years previously – did not seem to matter. She had "done" Switzerland. Tick the box! Anyway, I wanted to go to Bern, Lucerne, and Zurich as James had submitted university applications there. Plus I wanted to see the SMC University Campus in Zug (near Zurich for the geographically challenged readers) as it had a great-sounding Motorsport Management Course.

One day, when I was checking the location of SMC in Zug on Google, Kyle asked what I was doing – while laughing and giggling all over his face. When he eventually stopped giggling enough to speak to me, it turned out that "SMC" is a texting/SMS acronym like "LOL", which we all know (right?) means "Laugh Out Loud". Unfortunately, "SMC" is not as innocuous as it means "Suck My Cock" . . . What can I say? You learn something every day, but it kind of surprised me to learn this fact from my 13 year old son!

Basel was our "base camp" in Switzerland as we were able to stay at the beautiful house of our friends Esther and Daniel Vogel, high up on the hill overlooking the city. Unfortunately, they were not there so we had the place almost to ourselves. I say "almost" as a huge Rhodesian Ridgeback called Cuba (as in Cuba Gooding Jr) was also there.

Our youngest son, Colby, was nine at the time and absolutely loves animals, but we had only been there about ten minutes when he was bitten on his upper cheekbone by the dog! Colby was sitting on the edge of the dog's rug and hugging it around the shoulders. I think the dog thought Colby trying to get him off the rug so he could steal it. Then Agnes took a photo with a flash and I think the flash un-nerved the dog. It was no big deal. It bled a bit, but no swelling. Strangely, Colby still has a slightly pink scar on his cheek. I told him he can say he got it fighting a duel at dawn, over a beautiful maiden, with rapiers as the chosen weapon. Unfortunately, he has not seen as many Errol Flynn or Zorro movies as I have so the idea was a bit lost on him.

The next morning we were having breakfast in the garden and he was stung by a bee!!!! He screamed and screamed and screamed . . . and then he screamed some more!!! "Get me to a Doctor! Get me to a Doctor!!!" He had never screamed like that before. Luckily there was a clinic in the village and the Doc pronounced him OK. No allergic reactions, just the intense pain from the sting. He was fine, but the interesting thing was that the night before, when the Rhodesian Ridgeback bit him on the cheek, he never cried or screamed at all. Kids?????

The house itself created a bit of daily – and often several times a day – physiotherapy for me, much to the happiness of Agnes. Of course, Switzerland is full of mountains and Basel is no exception. Like most houses there, it was built on a very steep incline and you entered from the back on the high side of the hill so that the front of the house had all the views. So, I had to navigate four flights of steps up and down from the road to the house. It was really tough. Good for me, but tough . . .

We managed to do our mini-tour of Switzerland by doing a circuit - Basel, Lucerne, Zug, Zurich and back to Basel and see some sights on the way. Lucerne is the biggest tourist attraction in summer as it is at the head of the very beautiful Lake Lucerne (der *Vierwaldstättersee),* where the River Reuss flows into it from the mountains.

Like all good tourists, we had to take a walk – or in my case a hobble - across the famous Kapellbruke, the cranked, covered footbridge across the Reuss. It even has with a guy wearing Lederhosen blowing a genuine Flugelhorn.

The Japanese tourists loved it! There were massive flocks of them on the bridge and everywhere in Lucerne, all wearing very silly hats and the most outlandish, unmatched ensembles of clothes imaginable. Bright colours, baggy pants, striped long socks – you name it they wore it. But, whatever the outfit, it was obviously decreed in the handbook "*How to be a Japanese Tourist. 101*"that they absolutely must wear a silly hat at all times whatever the location they were in and whatever the weather was like.

Many of them also pull their suitcases along with them when sightseeing. I think it's so they can do a complete change of outfit and hat for every location they visit . . . !

The S-Bs At The Kapellbruke, Lucerne – Not Wearing Any Silly Hats

Naturally, when you go to Lucerne you have to take a boat ride on the lake – it's obligatory – and also mandated in the Japanese Tourist Handbook. So, we did.

The gangplank was an interesting exercise with crutches and keeping balance while standing on the moving boat is also tricky. Unfortunately, I was not allowed to perform my impression of Leonardo di Caprio on the front of the Titanic. But I thought about it, at least. Swiss boat crews on lake ferries don't have a sense of humour – or a sense of adventure for that matter. If they did they would be out on the open sea being attacked by Somali pirates like Captain Phillips in the movie of the same name that Kyle and I had watched just before going on holiday.

CUE YOUTUBE VIDEO: CAPTAIN PHILLIPS
TOM HANKS

Agnes & Kyle – Look Out! The Boat Behind You May Be Somali Pirates. Prepare to Repel Boarders!

Well, surprise, surprise, we did not get attacked by Somali pirates on Lake Lucerne but we did find out that the mountains on each side allegedly used to have dragons in them. This really, really impressed Colby as he was in his dragon phase as a result of watching "*How to Train Your Dragon 1 and 2*"

Also, we did manage to find Zog on the loop back from Lucerne and we did see the SMC building but could never get quite to it due to a trick cyclical one way street system that kept making us go in the opposite direction to the one we wanted. So, we said "SMC" and drove off into the sunset . . .

Our fifth country visit was to Strasbourg in the Alsace region of France. This is just a hop skip and a jump over the border from Germany. Note the spelling! It's got B-O-U-R-G rather than BERG or BURG. So, you can be sure it's in France. Though from all appearances it could still be Germany and the food is a mixture of German and French and funnily enough the McDo hamburgers taste just the same as they do in Germany – and anywhere else for that matter. But our Japanese GPS still managed to screw it up as it deposited us about a kilometre from the car park in the centre of the city even though we had programmed it with the same location as Carsten punched into the GPS in his Mercedes Benz. What more can I say?

All too soon our month in Europe came to an end. But we had seen a lot of things and taken in a lot of interesting sights that will always be remembered.

Also, I proved to myself that I could manage international travel and sightseeing, plus I had some German Physiotherapy and learnt a bunch of new techniques. Not bad really!

So, during the course of the holiday we managed to travel on all forms of transport - Planes, Trains, Trams, Buses, Taxis, Boats, Cars, Wheelchair and Crutches. You name it we did it. It reminds me of the movie "*Planes, Trains and Automobiles*" with John Candy and Steve Martin where they use every form of transport to try get home for Thanksgiving Dinner. One of the funniest scenes is Steve Martin's rant at the car rental counter after many misadventures with John Candy. Caution, its XXX rated! It has more expletives than normal words. I counted twenty "F" words in 2.11 minutes. That's one every six and a half seconds. Way more than Jordan Belfort. But in this case Steve Martin is angry and not at all motivational. They probably just told him that the only vehicle available was a Nissan Juke . . .

CUE YOUTUBE VIDEO: PLANES, TRAINS & AUTOMOBILES
CAR RENTAL RANT – STEVE MARTIN

But if you want something more heart-warming from the same movie, watch the final scenes when Steve Martin finally gets home for Thanksgiving – albeit two days late due to his co-star John Candy.

CUE YOUTUBE VIDEO: PLANES, TRAINS & AUTOMOBILES
LAST SCENE – STEVE MARTIN & JOHN CANDY

And the song to go with it for the European Holiday? It has to be *Trains & Boats & Planes*, sung by many artists, including Dionne Warwick, The Box Tops, Sandy Shaw and Billy J. Kramer & the Dakotas - separately of course as this was many years before the current era of having someone "Featured" (i.e. Ft.) on your single. All of them are good but I have a bit of a leaning towards the Billy J. Kramer version because they were one of the first bands I ever saw live back in 1963 when they were part of the Merseybeat Roadshow with the Beatles.

CUE YOUTUBE VIDEO: TRAINS AND BOATS AND PLANES
BILLY J. KRAMER & THE DAKOTAS

We did have a great holiday and I even managed to avoid having any Steve Martin type rants at anyone to do with transport – which was pretty good I thought – given that we were driving a Nissan Juke, all the different modes we used and the many thousands of kilometres travelled in Europe, plus getting there and back from Abu Dhabi.

As it was four years since the last one, I had almost forgotten how important it is to have a real break from your normal working life. And especially if, like me, one of the family members has some form of disablement – or temporary un-ablement. This puts an additional and sometimes huge stress on the rest of the family. So, it's even more crucial to have that holiday. And, believe me, the money is not wasted or "blown" away on a short burst of pleasure. You all end up with memories that can last a lifetime and you experience some wonderful times together as a family. Go for it!

57

STRICTLY COME DANCING A.K.A THE EAGLES HAVE LANDED

I said at the very beginning of this story that I always had a great pair of running legs – till the accident. But, conversely, I have never had a good pair of dancing legs, at least not for waltzes, sambas, cha-chas and the like. I grew up in the era when discos were being invented – when I was about sixteen, way back in 1965 – so I could usually manage a blast on the floor to whatever was the current hot dance tune. But the dark disco atmosphere, strobe lights and even the disco balls helped disguise the fact that dancing was not my forte.

But real dancing – the Bruce Forsythe, *Strictly Come Dancing* stuff – I could never manage. Far too many left feet . . . !!!

However, one day not so long after the accident – in a fit of bravado, (read – stupidity) or in that "happy place" under the influence of many pain-killers – I promised Agnes that when I recovered I would learn to dance.

Well, on 01 August 2014, I had my first lesson and it turned out to be much better than expected.

Actually, it started off as a home PT session. As usual, Agnes was pushing me to do some home PT, this time using some of the new techniques that we had just learnt from Florian and Rudi at Rehamed, while on vacation in Germany.

At the same time I happened to be playing a new CD of an old Eagles album, *When Hell Freezes Over*. I had just bought it again in Germany as the last version of it that I had was on cassette tape when it came out in 1994.

The Eagles split up in 1980 and got back together in 1994 and (twenty years later, ha!) Agnes and I went to see their live concert at The 7s rugby ground in Dubai in April 2014. Brilliant! The harmonies were perfect and Joe Walsh, the lead guitarist, is still something else! The weird thing was that for the first 20-30 minutes he did not seem to play any of the solos or the "licks". He was just on stage. I thought that maybe his past excesses (which were many) had caught up with him. Or, being kinder, that he had arthritis or something. And then, all of a sudden, he took over the lead guitar role and the stage just lit up, for me at least. He was phenomenal and, I believe, what differentiated the Eagles from being just another country-rock band. He just has that hard edge to his guitar licks. And, of course, he played his anthem, *Rocky Mountain Way*. (Go back to Chapter 26 and listen to that one again. It's that good!)

So, going back to the home PT Session, I sat down on a wooden bench and the album was playing on the Harmann Kardon next to me. The track was the über classic *Hotel California* with the extended acoustic Spanish guitar intro and, as I listened, I launched into my exercises. First rocking back and forth pushing hard on the core muscles in the stomach and abdomen. Then it was the alternate side-to-side buttock lifting exercise. This seems relatively easy at first. It is easy as I was doing the "cheating" version in which I just lift alternate buttocks. The harder bit comes when you also lift and stretch out the arm on the same side as you are lifting your buttock.

But even that is easy compared to when you twist over your hand so the palm is upright. Heavy breathing starting now.

Then Agnes "kindly" pointed out that I was supposed to stretch my arm diagonally upwards across my chest – not just stick it out in front. Now that really hurts as it pulls on your oblique muscles as your torso twists and your butt lifts. For symmetrical exercising, you then switch sides and do it with the other buttock and the other arm.

Lots of fun! OOOuuuccchhh!!!

I am going at this as *Hotel California* is playing. Listening to the all the clever lyrics in that song. But it's a long track, made even longer as it was recorded live. In fact, its 7 minutes and 12 seconds long to be exact. That's long for any song. And Agnes was insisting that I keep going through the whole track . . .

CUE YOUTUBE VIDEO: HOTEL CALIFORNIA
EAGLES

Note that some versions of this have 49 million hits!

So, it's – Right butt lift, right arm out, twist hand, swing arm across body, twist torso, drop arm to my side and then left butt lift, left arm out, twist hand, swing arm across body, twist torso, drop arm back to my side and then do it all over again.

And again and again and again! It's a bit like *"Come on, come on. Do the Locomotion with me!"*

"Just keep going!" said Agnes.

And the Eagles played on . . . *"You can check-out any time you like, but you can never leave . . . !!"* And that's how I felt!

Finally, finally, the track ended and I could stop the buttock lifting. Wphhheeewww!!

Then Joe Walsh's *Pretty Maids All in a Row* came on and I started my stand up – sit down exercise that Florian had pushed me to do in Germany. It's one of those things that is hard to do at first as the natural tendency is to want to push yourself up slowly with your arms and then gradually get your legs to take over the action to stop you crumpling in a heap on the floor in front of the chair.

And all the time you are hoping that you don't overbalance and fall forward on your face. Wooooooo!

Of course, the best way is to "just" stand up in one fluid motion without pushing off with your arms and using the upward momentum of your body to get past the fulcrum point where your leg muscles have enough strength and leverage to keep it all going. Easy Peasy!

Ha! Typically all of the above complex movements are done on autopilot by the subconscious part of your brain. People with nerve damage have to relearn all of these complex coordinated movements and we start off by having to "tell" all our muscles what to do individually. In reality it is actually a choreographed dance for muscles, tendons, and joints.

I did a couple of warm-up stands using my arms too. Agnes was taking a video so – as always when you think the world may eventually be watching you on Facebook or YouTube – you push just that bit harder. And, "lo and behold", I could do it. I was thinking: swing my arms forward, push up, stick my butt out backwards for balance, let the gluteus maximus muscles contract and pull on the back of my thighs, straighten my legs, squeeze my stomach and abdomen and, finally, altogether, push my chest out, squeeze my butt tight and push the pelvis forwards. And, there I was, standing upright and balancing.

Of course, there was a bit of grunting too, but that, in fact, really helps to focus the mind and push you to do it. I have no idea why, but it really seems to work – for me and for many tennis champions at Wimbledon when they let out a grunt as they serve or return a shot.

Just think of Maria Sharapova doing those grunts – and of course we would all like to be the guy making her grunt, but somewhere far, far away from the centre court . . . But I digress!

CUE YOUTUBE VIDEOS:

TSB RECOVERY
1 AUGUST 2014

PRETTY MAIDS ALL IN A ROW
EAGLES - JOE WALSH

I actually didn't realize till much later that there was also some significance in the lyrics of the *Pretty Maids all in a Row* song because it talks about "*coming a long way*" and that we "*learn so slow*". In my world of physiotherapy and rehabilitation, we have indeed come a long way. And it is true, we do learn so slowly. The first time I stood up out of my bed was on 26 August 2011, exactly six months after the accident. But that time it took three male nurses to get me upright. My arms around the shoulders of one on each side of me and another one to push my knees back to lock them so I did not crumple to the floor. And here I was, three years later, able to do it myself. We *have* come a long way, and we do *learn so slowly*. But it's way better than not being able to move forward at all and not being able to learn at all. Believe me on this!

And then the next track started. It's *I Can't Tell You Why* sung by Timothy B. Schmidt - he is the long-haired bass player, if you didn't know.

Agnes immediately said "Come on you have to dance with me to this song".

"Yeah right!" I thought (silently, so as not to upset the apple cart).

But up I jumped. Er, not really jumped but more like got to my feet with as much haste as possible - remember I had just been practicing this move - and we started dancing together. Strangely, it was actually really good fun and Colby, my youngest son, started taking a video on Agnes' Samsung Android Phone.

Now, Agnes is a naturally good dancer. And, as I said at the beginning, I am totally not. But the rhythm seemed perfect. The song is very melodic, Timothy Schmidt has a very "soft-sweet" voice, and the lyrics have a certain poignancy and, undoubtedly, some significance for Agnes and I. Just watch the video and listen to them – and sing along too.

So, we danced through the track and both of us were singing along to the song. It was like a Karaoke duet. The amazing thing about this is that Agnes has never been known as a singer at all. That title usually falls to Colby and myself - even if its cheesy songs like Abba's *Gimme, Gimme, Gimme (a man after midnight)*. The song played on and it was like there was little "bubble" surrounding us.

I am usually overly conscious about my lack of dancing abilities, so much so that I stiffen up even more. But this time I got caught up in the moment and was able to relax into some rhythmical motions. Hey, this was not any huge ballroom dancing moves, or Rock n' Roll bebop, swinging your partner between your legs stuff. But (for me at least) it was a slow smoochy sway. The good thing about it was that Agnes was not really supporting me as I was able to stand up, move, and wave my arms around without the crutches and without putting lots of pressure on her. Yo! Almost human!

Colby continued to take the video the whole way through our dance and he even moved slowly up the stairs near the end to get a different angle as we bowed at the end of the track to the clapping and cheers of the live audience just as the Eagles had at their concert. It actually felt as though the audience was clapping for us . . .

CUE YOUTUBE VIDEOS:

TSB & AGNES DANCING

I CAN'T TELL YOU WHY - EAGLES

Sorry: In some cases the sound is not available on our dancing video so you need the other one to get the music that goes with the dance.

As I mentioned, the lyrics of I *Can't Tell You Why* have a certain significance for Agnes and I. Why was it **that** song that she had chosen for the dance with me? I don't know, but as I have said many times – TINSTAAC – There Is No Such Thing As A Coincidence. To be honest, I had never truly listened and noted what the lyrics of that song were all about before. I was just hearing the words without really comprehending their meaning.

And the significance of that particular song? Anyone who knows Agnes and I can testify that we have had some huge "rip-your-heart-out" arguments over the years, including many about my accident and its effect on our family.

But, despite all of those arguments, and the tough times that we have had going through the slow, slow process of my rehabilitation, we are still together. The song is all about walking away, but something makes you stay and *"I can't tell you why"*

I know my accident and subsequent ongoing recovery has been very hard on the family, and especially on Agnes. But, together, we have managed to come a long way in improving what I can do with my body.

And she never walked away . . .

POST SCRIPT

Eagles – Near the Beginning
Walsh, Schmidt, Frey & Henley

Eagles – Near the End
Walsh, Schmidt, Frey & Henley

RIP Glen Frey: 1948 – 2016. Founder Member of the Eagles

The Bad News: When Glen Frey passed away in 2016 the remaining three said that was the end of the Eagles. The Good News: In early 2017 they changed their minds and decided to re-form the band again.

2015

58

HOW MANY FINGERS AM I HOLDING UP?

"How many fingers am I holding up?" This is the classic question from any rugby team paramedic when they run on to a rugby pitch to administer to someone who potentially has concussion. This is often as a result of receiving a "Hospital Pass" from his team mate who threw him the ball so late that he could not avoid the impending tackle.

If your eyes are rolling around in their sockets, or you look totally confused and spaced out while insisting that you are OK and can keep on playing, it's very likely that you are concussed. So, the paramedic will do the "How many fingers am I holding up?" test to see if you have double vision.

When our coach/physio, Bill Middleton, ran onto the field after my scrum collapsed he did that test on me. Very surprisingly considering what had happened, I passed that test. But then immediately failed the being able to move my hands and toes tests. Well, you can't win 'em all!

So, as you have been reading on your way through this book, you will be aware that I have had to spend a LOT of time with physiotherapists trying to make my legs work again. Not to mention the time spent with a myriad of urologists trying to make my peeing parts function normally too.

But, as I said above, not only did I fail the toe wiggling test, I also failed the hand waving test. My fists were clenched tight like I was about to hit someone - and they wanted to stay that way. Maybe I did subconsciously want to hit someone! Like the guys in the Sharjah front row.

In order to uncurl my hands and make the fingers work again I have had to have regular Occupational Therapy (OT). Unfortunately – in my opinion anyway – this is a very bad choice of name for what is basically physiotherapy on your hands. A lot of people, apparently including hospital administrations and insurance providers the world over, have the mistaken concept that Occupational Therapy is something related to getting dressed in the morning by yourself or fitting back into your work at the office while using crutches or being in a wheelchair. Or maybe it's an American terminology used to describe the treatment prescribed when an employee has a mental breakdown at the office because the coffee machine does not work. Or perhaps they think it's something that is highly esoteric and of no use whatsoever to the patient and therefore he does not need it. Well, whatever people think, it appears that they focus mostly on the assumption that Occupational Therapy is *"......highly theoretical and without obvious practical application......."* as per the Wiktionary definition of esoteric. The Wiktionary also says *"....often with mystical or religious connotations......"*

This is actually very, very far from reality, of course. Basically, if your hands don't work, how do you do anything, anything at all? You can't pick things up. You can't feed yourself. You can't write or type. You can't drive. And you cannot even do basic functions like having a pee – because you can't undo your trousers, or scratch your balls – because clenched fists are not good at scratching. Or even wipe your own butt – because you can't hold the toilet tissue at the correct angle. Actually, you probably cannot hold the toilet tissue at all and even if you can, the desired micro-motor actions in your fingers will probably be so uncontrollably major that you will end up sticking your finger through the tissue. Which is not fun at all – believe me!

I don't actually think that there is anything mystical or religious about any of those things.

What exactly was wrong with my hands – or should I say – what is still wrong with my hands? Well, initially, the fingers on both hands were curled up and did not work at all. Then, suddenly one morning after about 6 weeks, the left hand was partially working. Yo! I could move the fingers up and down a bit.

But the fingers on the right hand hardly moved and I had no grip at all. The problem was that the right thumb would not move in and out, the first finger wanted to stay straight and would not bend or curl on command, the second finger was just a bit droopy and did not really do anything, and the third and fourth fingers were the opposite as they wanted to stay curled up and did not want to open.

This is actually a somewhat risky combination in the UAE. Just imagine trying to hold up your hand and wave at someone with the fingers in the positions described above. What you actually appear to be doing is giving someone "The Finger" sign! Basically, if you don't already know, it means "Up Yours". Now, we have all seen "The Finger" on TV and in movies – and undoubtedly in real life too. In some countries it may be acceptable – or at least part of the cultural "lingua franca" – so that people just shrug it off. For example, New York is well known as a tough city where people are in a rush and have none of the down-home charm of, say, a small town in South Carolina. If you do something that even mildly upsets another driver in New York – especially a taxi driver – you are very likely to get "The Finger". Well, in the Arabic regions, it's regarded as much, much worse. There have been instances reported on the news where one driver has given another driver "The Finger" and the recipient has reported it to the police, resulting in a severe legal punishment for the giver. No joke!

I have to admit that there have been a few occasions when I have been driving and just wanted to wave my hand at someone – perhaps to let them out of a side road into the main road – and I have inadvertently used my right hand. And, to the other driver, it undoubtedly could have looked like I was giving him "The Finger". OOOoooopppss! Not a good idea! But, I have been lucky so far and at least I can show my crutches and explain that my hand does not work too well . . .

"And how many fingers were you holding up?" asked the Judge. "Well, er, one your honour."

So, I think you can appreciate that I have needed a lot of OT sessions and therefore my OT story is a bit similar to the Urologist saga, but with a twist. Like the myriad of options that the Urologists had on catheters, Occupational Therapists (OTs) seem to have widely differing opinions on what constitutes the perfect finger splint. Luckily though, there is much more consistency in what OTs do to your hands in their sessions.

But the main problem with OTs is that they are in extremely short supply in the UAE. Plus, it seemed to me that I acted as some sort of unintentional career catalyst for virtually every OT with whom I had sessions. I would just get settled in with one particular OT and the sessions would be going well. Then they would find a new job in another hospital – usually in a different town or even a different country – which meant that I could not follow them to continue with their OT treatment. This was very frustrating as it usually meant that I then had a six-month gap in my OT treatment till the next therapist came along. So, whatever progress had been made was virtually blown away. Does this happen in other countries or is it just a UAE phenomenon?

As a result, I have actually had ten OTs in four years! Perhaps this was one for each of my fingers and thumbs. This also happened with my Physiotherapists but, as there are a lot more of them than there are OTs, there was usually an immediate replacement available. Some of the OTs actually joked that it was great having me as a patient as I was a guaranteed stepping-stone to a better job!

This phenomenon actually peaked (well I hope it was a peak!) in about May/June 2015 when I had six therapist changes in two different clinics within the space of four weeks . . .

Shalini – an Indian lady - at the Rochester Wellness Centre was my first OT back in May 2011. One of the things that sticks in my mind was the metal frame she used for my therapy. It was like a wire sculpture in a shape resembling a rollercoaster. She would hand me a wand with a metal ring attached to it and the idea was for me to move the ring along the roller coaster sculpture without the ring touching the wire along the way.

Fortunately, there was no buzzer sounding and no nasty electric shock if you did touch the wire with the ring as that happened very often in the beginning.

It was a bit like the things Bruce Forsythe had people do on the TV game *Beat the Clock.* One of the games was the roller coaster wire and hoop which buzzed when the two made contact – and that meant the contestant lost. It sounds easy, but you have to twist and turn your hand and wrist to negotiate the twists, turns, inclines, and declines of the sculpture.

Strangely, doing this, the pain inflicted on my shoulders was worse than the wrists. You tell me why!

I did this exercise so often for so many days that I half expected Shalini to greet me with Brucie's "Nice to see you, to see you nice!" when I was wheeled into the OT room.

Then Shalini gradually became pregnant. That sounds like another oxymoron of course, but I say "gradually" as the onset of her bump was incredibly slow and she looked normal (i.e. un-pregnant) from the back. Unfortunately, she decided to leave and go back to India to have the baby. So, I moved on to my second OT, Prithvi, who was a very beautiful Indian girl and it was very enjoyable having her hold my hands . . .

She alternated with the third OT, another young Indian girl called Kriti, so the sessions were double the pleasure at that point in time.

I am not going to go through the OTs one by one - like I did with the Urologists - describing the type of treatments they each gave me as the exercises they did were relatively consistent. Some preferred hot towel relaxation followed by manipulation; others had me screwing nuts and bolts together. Some had me picking up shiny pebbles and manipulating them in my fingers, others gave me ultra-sound treatment.

This latter is not to see if I was pregnant or what sex my baby was going to be (Duuuh), but research has shown (apparently, allegedly) that ultra-sound waves stimulate blood flow and muscle healing.

Maybe someone should try using it to counteract Erectile Dysfunction (ED). Then ultra-sound could be useful for the full spectrum of the baby making and baby growing cycle.

However, there was a huge difference between all the OTs as regards the type of splint they each thought I should have to straighten up my fingers.

My first splints were described earlier in Chapter 12 and I needed those specifically so that I could start typing on my computer. But those were very cumbersome and really only of use for typing. I think I could manage about 100 wph (words per hour) rather than a skilled touch-typing secretary's speed of 100 wpm (words per minute). All the action was on the forearms not the wrists and fingers. And I really felt a bit like *Edward Scissorhands* . . .

But the next splint iteration went the other way. These were like perforated, hard plastic condoms on my fingers. And you can all figure out how much use a perforated condom is! They were moulded from some sort of heat sensitive material – just dip it in warm water and it becomes totally mouldable to any shape. Have a look at the pic. This idea seems simple enough but the problem is that you cannot do anything at all with hardened finger ends. I could not grip objects at all.

Oxymoron - Perforated Condoms

I struggled along with this combo of Scissorhands and perforated condoms for a while till I went into SKMC hospital for my Blitzkreig on PT and OT when we moved back to Abu Dhabi.

There, the four resident OTs - who I saw on different days depending on my schedule - brought in a specialist splint maker to do me a couple of splints. One for when I was sleeping and the other for daytime use. However, this specialist splint maker probably got paid by the pound or by the number of straps, loops, elastics, outriggers and complexity of his splints. I have certainly never seen anything like them.

The one for night time was another Scissorhands type of creation. It was a long u-shaped splint that was strapped up my forearm with heavy, padded, Velcro straps. The first and second fingers were free as they generally wanted to stick out straight. But the third and fourth fingers were on a flat platform to stop them curling up. Then there was an alloy "outrigger" on the left side which had an elastic strap with a loop on the end of it. That was there to pull my thumb out and away from my palm.

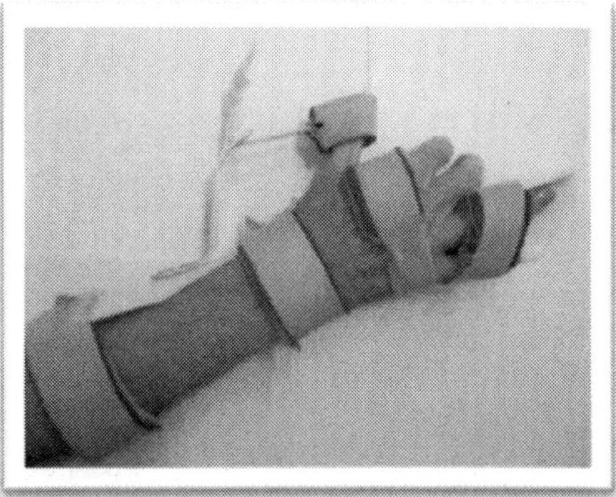

And How Do You Scratch Your Balls in the Middle of the Night?

Just have a look at the picture. Fortunately, I only had one of these contraptions as by that time (April 2013) it was mainly my right hand that was still a problem. But this splint was big and heavy and sleeping with it on was not at all easy. The biggest problem came as a result of my bladder functions improving. When I first got the all-singing-all-dancing night splint I was still in the diapers-and-pads phase of night time bladder activities. But this gradually changed to using small plastic urinal bottle about every two hours through the night.

Now, can you imagine trying to manipulate a penis into the neck of a urinal bottle under the bedsheets in the dark at 4:00 am while wearing the Scissorhands Mark 2 contraption? It's not difficult. It's absolutely impossible. I can tell you that with absolute authority.

I don't think the splint maker had figured on this when he made the splint. This is a recurring problem with many people who are trying to help someone like me to recover. The person proposing the remedy or solution to the problem has never experienced it. So, while they may solve part of the problem they often create another in the process.

This, basically, meant that I had to take off the splint each time I turned over in the night and had a pee. Which meant ripping open the multitude of Velcro straps holding the contraption on my arm. And you know that it's really noisy as you pull the bits of Velcro apart.

The weird thing is that, like Pavlov's Dog, my brain became attuned to the sound of ripping open Velcro. For Pavlov's Dog the ringing of the bell meant food. For me that Velcro sound meant that I was about to have a pee. So even now I have to be very careful as the sound of Velcro may trigger a chain of events in my brain that might not be appropriate when, say, you are trying on a pair of gloves with a Velcro fastener in a department store!!

Eddie Izzard, who has much to say about many things, and who seems to make the most mundane things very funny, has a theory about Pavlov's Dog and also the lesser known experiments with his Cat ...

CUE YOUTUBE VIDEO: PAVLOV'S DOG AND CAT
EDDIE IZZARD

Ha! But getting back to the splints, the night splint had absolutely nothing on the day splint that the guy made me. That thing had so many outriggers and extensions hanging off the main body that it looked more like a model space station than anything else. Just take a peek at the picture! Pull this finger that way, these two another way, this one in that direction and the thumb over there. The major problem with it was when I wore it I was virtually completely immobile as I could not do anything with my right hand ...

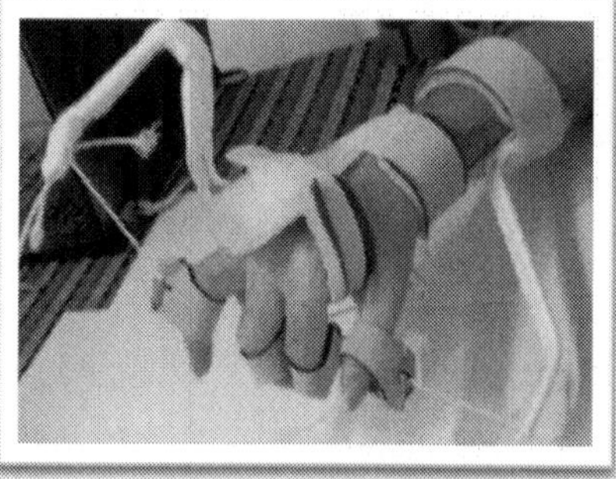

Is it Space Station Deep Space 9 or a Finger Splint?

Just imagine writing, typing, driving, getting dressed, and getting undressed or even trying to get your hand inside your trousers when you want to have a pee! You could end up with a do-it-yourself circumcision or, worse still, a self-inflicted vasectomy. Just think about trying to do anything at all while wearing this monster. Needless to say, I really never wore it.

Meanwhile, I was busy going through the career improvement process for my next two OT's. Blair Agero, a Filipino OT at Al Noor, left to move to a specialist hand rehabilitation clinic in Dubai. Then, his replacement, Deepak Paul, an Indian from Kerala (where else?), moved on to the German Clinic in Abu Dhabi after about a year with me. The annoying thing about that one was that my insurance provider would approve payment for my sessions with Deepak Paul while he was at Al Noor but would not do the same when he moved to the German Clinic. Talk about continuity of treatment or determining what is best for the patient. These things are not a consideration.

Then – after a 6-month gap - along came Praveen. He was another Indian, from Blankety-Blank of course, but he obviously graduated from the Indian-School-of-Doing-Things-as-Simply-as-Possible. I don't know exactly where it is located in India but it's probably somewhere near *The Best Exotic Marigold Hotel* where the manager explains away problems by saying "Everything will be alright in the end. If it's not alright, it's not the end" which gives a positive tone to solving problems.

He started me with lots of finger exercises. The absolute hardest exercise was curling my right hand forefinger to pull a one inch wide strip of Velcro, attached to a little block of wood, off the Velcro board. Just take a look at the picture. You can see the strain on my face and the tension in my muscles. Normally, you would do this by just using the tiny muscles in your fingers to curl it. I have to enlist the help of all the bigger muscles in my arms and have them pull on the tendons to curl the finger. Look at my biceps. To me this was harder than bench pressing 200 pounds.

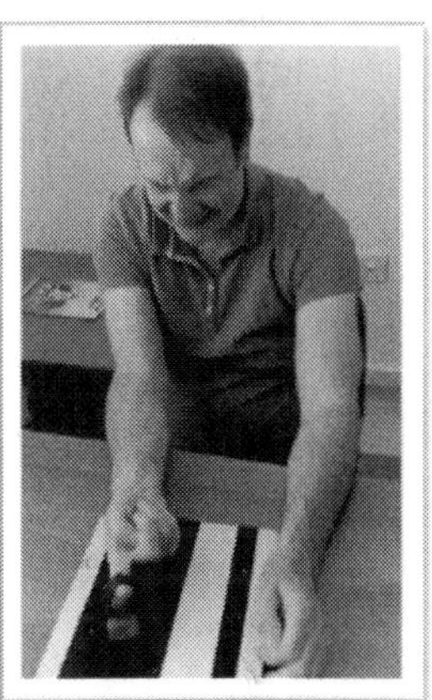

It's Just a One Inch Square of Velcro!

During my session I told him about my Scissorhands Mark 2 and my Space Station and he just laughed and offered to make me some splints of his own design that would do the same thing. "Go for it." I said. I mean what could be worse than the two splints I already had?

A couple of days later he turned up with a sample splint that he had made using his own hand as a mould. It was not a perfect fit for me, of course, but it worked in principle.

It was basically a sort of three dimensional infinity sign wrapped around two sections of my finger with my joint in the gap between the loops.

I was amused by the infinity shape and had a hard time repressing a shout of "To infinity, and beyond!" the very famous catch phrase of Buzz Lightyear the toy spaceman in the animated movie, *Toy Story*. Watch him fly!

CUE YOUTUBE VIDEO: TOY STORY- BUZZ LIGHTYEAR STARRING TOM HANKS AND TIM ALLEN

So, at the next OT session he made two infinity splints to fit my hand in order to straighten the third and fourth fingers from their permanent curl. Then, once he had got them fitting OK, he let them set and put them on my fingers.

As soon as they were on he got a permanent marker and put an "R" on the third finger and an "L" on the fourth finger. So, I looked and said "Ah! That's for Right and Left. Yes? But it's the wrong way around as the "R" is on the finger to the left side and the "L" is on the finger to the right side". But he said "No. It's "R" for Ring and "L" for Little finger!"

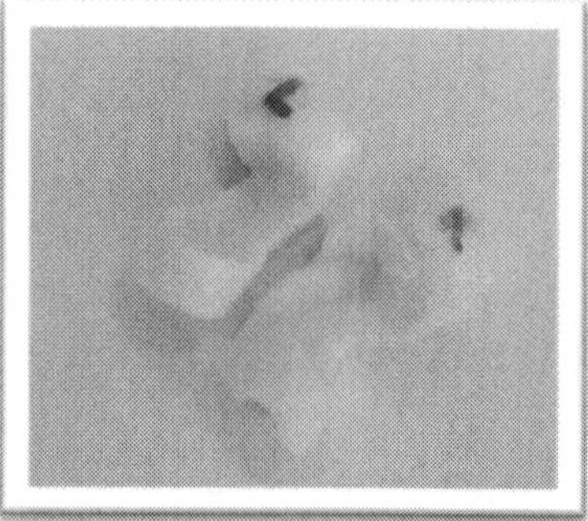

L for Left and R for Right. Right?

I burst out laughing as I thought it was so very funny. We both had different interpretations of exactly the same thing. And the world is full of situations like that. Our brains are getting information from what our eyes see and our ears hear. But each person's brain will be processing that information and painting a different virtual picture inside our heads with it. It's a bit like the difference between the reaction of Pavlov's Dog and his Cat!

One of the reasons I laughed so much was that the "R" and the "L" reminded me of a story I was told many years ago when I lived in Kenya. Brian Haworth was a guy I worked with on the construction of a water pipeline from Lake Naivasha around an extinct (!) volcano crater to the Kedong Ranch cattle farm on the other side of the crater. Brian was what was then known as a "White Kenyan". You probably cannot say that anymore because it will be politically incorrect – very non-PC. But back then, in the late 70s, it was just a straightforward description of people who generally had western genetic lineage but had been born and bred in Kenya. Brian was a keen rally driver and that was where I also got the bug for my subsequent racing and rallying exploits in South East Asia.

One day Brian had instructed his chief mechanic, a Kenyan, but this time an indigenous one, to refurbish the front suspension on his rally car. He wanted the suspension on each side of the car to be stripped down, cleaned, all the bushings etc replaced, and then the suspension reinstalled in the car. But he was very specific in his instructions to the mechanic, saying that he should mark each part with an "R" or an "L" so that it could be assembled properly on the right or left side of the car.

But when he got back to the workshop at the end of the day he looked at the car and all the parts on the left side of the car had an "R" on them and all the ones on the right side of the car had an "L" on them. Brian exploded at the mechanic and asked why he had put them all back on the wrong sides of the car. But the mechanic was sure that it was correct.

"Look sir," he said. "It is correct. Everything with an "R" on it is on the Reft side of the car and everything with an "L" on it is on the Light side of the car."

The Kenyans' English pronunciation was not perfect and he mixed up his "R's" and "L's" – a bit like the Chinese and Japanese. He had marked everything on the left side of the car with an "R" for "Reft", and everything on the right side of the car with an "L" for "Light".

So, it's just like my "R" and "L" splints – we just have to appreciate, as we go through life, that there are many perspectives to the same picture! Are you a glass half full person or a glass half empty? Do you see having a major spinal trauma as the end of your life as you knew it or the opportunity to write a book about your experiences? I know which side of that equation I find myself!

But I bet that when Brian Haworth was walking out of the workshop, his Kenyan mechanic was behind him doing a personal "How many fingers am I holding up test?" And I am sure it was only one!

59

A-TISHOO! A-TISHOO! WE ALL FALL DOWN

The title of this chapter is actually a line from a very old British children's nursery rhyme *Ring-a-Ring o' Roses.* I say it's specifically British as it allegedly originates from the time of the Great Plague in 1665.

Ring-a-ring o' roses,
A pocket full of posies,
A-tishoo! A-tishoo!
We all fall down.

The first line of the rhyme comes from the rosy rash, which was a symptom of the plague. The second line refers to the posies of herbs which were carried as protection and to ward off the smell of the disease and the rotting corpses. Sneezing and coughing was a final fatal symptom, and "We all fall down" was exactly what happened in the end when people died.

Just have a look at the *Bring Out Your Dead* sketch set in the time of the Great Plague in the movie *Monty Python and the Holy Grail.* It's hilarious.

And the moral of the story is, if you ever fall down, don't let anyone clunk you on the head before you have chance to get up again!!!!

CUE YOUTUBE VIDEO: BRING OUT YOUR DEAD
MONTY PYTHON AND THE HOLY GRAIL

And what has this kid's somewhat macabre nursery rhyme got to do with my recovery you might well ask? And anyway, even if you don't ask I am going to tell you.

Well, as you have read through the preceding pages, I was gradually getting better at walking. However, progress was slow and sometimes measured in millimetres rather than metres. But at least there was a continuum of progress. But, every now and then there were setbacks.

One of the amusing parallels to the nursery rhyme came as I became more and more confident when going to the bathroom for a pee. It was OK when the weather was warm, but when the winter came along I found a new quirk in my neurological system. What happened was this. I would stand to have a pee in front of a toilet bowl. But to do this I couldn't just unbutton/unzip my fly as my right hand was still not fully functional. I had to pull down my pants below my butt so that access to my gentleman's sausage was easier. So, now my butt would be sticking out in the cold air and that would make me sneeze. And, like most men having a pee, this also has the tendency to make you fart. I guess it's some sort of mutual relaxation of the bladder and sphincter muscles.

Earlier in the book I argued that men can multi-task – well at least boys can. But multi-tasking for men is probably limited to doing two things at once. Like walking and chewing gum. So, doing three things at once is pushing the envelope. And, if you have any kind of neurological impairment (or five beers inside you), I can categorically state that it is not easy to pee, sneeze, and fart at the same time. It had the effect of making little electrical shocks run up and down my legs and when the muscles relaxed I felt like I was going to collapse. "A-tishoo. A-tishoo. We all fall down"

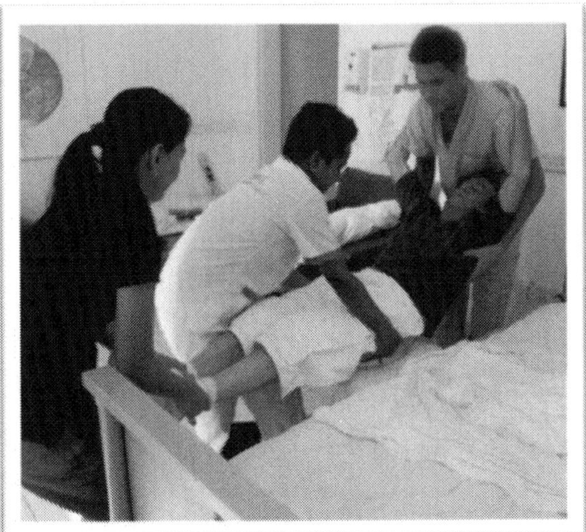

No, it is Not my Birthday and We are Not Doing "The Bumps". It Used to Take Three People to Get Me Out of Bed to Go to the Bathroom!

I am writing this in late February, 2015, exactly four years after my accident and I have managed to progress a long way. Initially, to go to the bathroom at the Rochester, I would have to have three people lift me out of bed and lay me flat on the seat of the commode with the back removed. They would then tilt me up and slot the back into place so I was in a sitting position. Just have look at the photo to see what I mean. Once I was on the commode I had to be wheeled into the bathroom by the nurse and assisted to have a shower and do my other bodily functions. None of the above falls into the category of "much fun" so it now feels wonderful to be able to mobilize myself and do those "normal" functions without help.

So, whenever I feel like I have not progressed, I have only to think back to situations that I described above and it makes me appreciate where I am right now and what I have achieved so far.

At this point I can now walk a little bit without any supporting aids such as crutches, Zimmer frames, walking sticks, ankle foot orthoses (AFOs) etc. But so far I can only do that in controlled conditions by which I mean having parallel bars (like ballerina bars) to walk between and grab if I need any support or if I feel like I am going to fall. They have parallel bars in the physiotherapy clinics and I now have a set at home too.

By the way – just in case you are wondering – I do NOT wear a tutu when I am doing that stuff!

My walking style is still very wobbly and it requires a lot of rocking from side to side to lift each leg in turn. I also wave my arms around in the air to help me balance. Just think of a toddler starting to walk across the room and you have the picture. Ritzel, my Filipina physiotherapist at Al Noor Hospital, started me walking sort distances with one crutch only.

And after Ritzel left Al Noor - remember I am always a stepping stone to a new job for my PT's and OT's - Amina and Hemath have continued to push hard on me to do more. The strange thing is that sometimes I can walk better with no crutches than I can with one. Sometimes I seem to get all out of sync with the arms and the legs and the crutch when I only have one. It's a bit like my lack of synchronicity when I am dancing.

A good example of what I mean is the song *I Can't Dance* by Genesis. In the video there are several scenes where the three band members walk across the screen one behind the other – but very close. The funny thing about it is that they are swinging their arms out of sequence with their legs. Normally, when you walk, the right arm swings forwards as the left leg does the same. And then the left arm swings forwards as the right leg does. And it's like that when you walk with crutches. But in the Genesis video they swing the right arm and the right leg forwards at the same time. And the same with the two left appendages and it looks really strange and funny at the same time. Just watch the video.

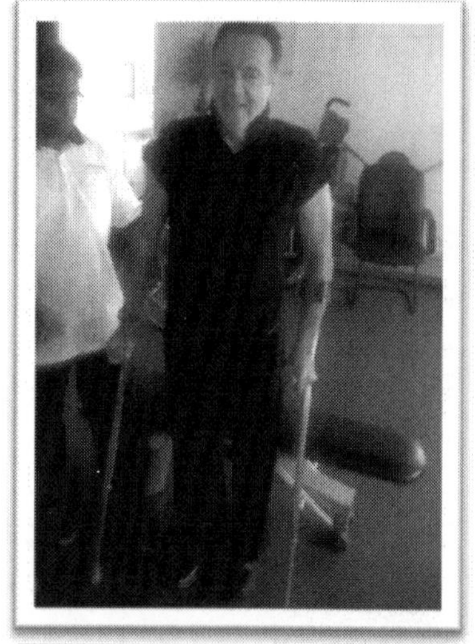

Standing Up with Crutches was the Easy Bit

As the lyrics of the song say, "Only thing about me is the way I walk". Never mind that my walking may be funny. Eventually it will improve, even though sometimes the gains are almost imperceptible. But there are gains if you keep working at it.

CUE YOUTUBE VIDEO: I CAN'T DANCE
GENESIS

There were also some setbacks too and those could be very frustrating. I had a number of trips, slips, falls and "crumples". For me, the crumples can be described as a slow sinking to the ground when somehow the fall has been slowed down by either me holding on to something or by propping myself up with one of the crutches.

The first of these was when I tripped on the wooden ramp in my "Grunge Patient" bedroom-garage in the Garden View Villas in Dubai during October 2012. The welt of my shoe caught on a nail. I sprained my ankle and pulled my Achilles tendon with that one.

Then I was thrown out of my wheelchair at the Dubai 7s in December 2013. This was sort of funny and almost slapstick comedy. I had driven on my own to the 7s ground in the BMW as I knew that there would be lots of guys inside from the team that would help me. So, the guards let me park in the VIP/Disabled parking nearest to the entrance, but there was a concrete ramp up to the actual entrance gate. As I was getting out of the car an Indian parking attendant came along so I asked for his help. He got the walker/chair out of the boot and set it up so I could sit in it without any problem. Then he started pushing me across the sandy car park towards the ramp. Suddenly, without warning, as we neared the ramp he started running so that he would have momentum to get me up the steep slope. The problem was that there was a significant edge to the bottom of the concrete ramp where it interfaced with the sand. The small front wheels of the chair hit that and the chair stopped dead. Unfortunately, my body still had forward momentum; I carried on travelling through the air and was unceremoniously dumped onto the bottom of the concrete ramp. It was just like watching clowns at a circus!!

Luckily, that day I was wearing football goalkeeper's pants that Agnes had bought me and they had pads sewn into the hips and the knees. So I was OK, and after lying there a couple of minutes to check the function of my body parts, a "Man Mountain" bouncer helped me up, settled me back into the chair and then pushed me all the way up the ramp and to the pitch to meet with my friends.

In May 2014 Agnes and I went to the Abu Dhabi Harlequins End of Season Summer Ball at the Jumeirah Etihad Tower Hotel. During the pre-dinner cocktails Agnes and I were standing by the bar – or rather I was using the bar as a leaning post. The call came to move into the ballroom. I set off and did not realise that a waiter had spilt a gin and tonic on the highly polished tiled floor and not mopped it up. I walked straight into this "booby trap" and my crutches slowly slipped forwards and I sank to the floor. I ended up on all fours – doggie style – but my knees had hit the floor with a real bang. Lots of people were around to pull me up and I went into the ballroom. But by the end of the night, my knees had locked up solid with the "shock factor" and I could hardly stand up from the table. It was one of those situations that, had I been a litigious American in the US, I would probably have sued the hotel for negligence. Fortunately, next morning, my knees seemed to have recovered reasonably so I just got on with life.

The next fall was in October 2014 when I had a slow crumple at "Jones the Grocer's" doors at the Al Mamoura Building in Abu Dhabi. In this one, we had eaten a meal outside in the bistro area and I was going inside to use the bathroom. Jones has automatic, double sliding glass doors but there is a step up from the sidewalk and that slowed me down. I got caught in between the outside opening sensor and the inside closing sensor as they are programmed on the basis that people walk through at a certain speed. I am much slower than the average walker so I had passed the outside sensor but had not reached the inside one. Therefore, the system assumed there was no one there. Actually, I was on the outside of the doors and my crutches were ahead of me on the inside and the doors just closed on them, trapping and squeezing the crutches together. Consequently, I had no support and I just crumpled slowly to the pavement. Again, I lay there for a few minutes and then James helped me up. No damage done!

One of the biggest fears I have while using crutches is slipping on bathroom floors. I am sure anyone who has to use crutches will tell you the same. In the UAE most public bathrooms have tiled floors – but not non-slip tiles – they are highly-polished, slippy ones. These tiles are dangerous enough on their own but when you add water to them they are lethal. Unfortunately, as in any Muslim country, the use of the high-pressure water sprays in toilet cubicles in the UAE means that, virtually all the time, the floors are very wet and really slippery. The stress and tension of holding myself carefully upright and taking small steps when walking on wet bathroom floors is incredibly exhausting.

Ironically, the worst fall that I had in a bathroom was in my own house and that was due to water on the floor just outside the bathroom door. I did not see it and my crutch slid across the floor till it hit the wall opposite the door. Again this was a slow crumple and the hardest bit was finding a way to get myself back up on my feet again.

Fast-forward to 26 February 2015. It was four years and one day since I had had the original accident. It was my son Kyle's birthday and we had planned to go to The Meat Co. for a steak dinner. But before that I needed to have my gym session at Fitness First with Gilbert, one of the personal trainers. It was aerobics day so I went on the cross-trainer but the cyclical walking action means that you never actually have either leg straight below the body and your knees are always cranked. This is where the problem began for me as I usually have one leg straight below my body as all my muscles – even now - are not fully functional. One set was OK, but when I started the second set, my legs turned to jelly and I could not walk/pedal at all. But when the pedals stopped, one leg was stretched fully forward and the other was stretched fully back. Disaster!

My legs would not support me and I crumpled down onto my haunches. The problem was that my legs were all akimbo and my knees were squashed up on my chest – a position that they were not really designed to be in – even prior to my accident. This really stretched my muscles and ligaments way beyond the norm, so when Gilbert lifted me up, my muscles were having spasms like crazy. That night I had to be carried down the steps outside my house to go out for Kyle's birthday dinner! That was the second time something happened to me just before Kyle's birthday . . .

For most of the following week the biggest problem was going down steps or stepping off kerbs as, when my right leg was hanging in free air before it touched the next step below, I would get high intensity spasms that would make the left leg want to collapse. Since that was the leg supporting me it was not a pleasant sensation . . . ! Not at all!!

By the following Saturday, as result of having acupuncture, stretches, physiotherapy, ultrasound deep muscle treatment, plus a LOT of Ibuprofen, I was just about OK and back to walking on crutches. Then – you know the phrase "Shit Happens" – well, "Shit Happened".

I had been sitting at the desk writing Chapter 24 – DREAMS and I stood up to go to the bathroom. I had probably been sitting too long and my leg muscles – or what pass for leg muscles – were a bit dead. Anyway, I started to walk away from the desk and suddenly the right leg gave way and I started to crumple. There was a "Lazee Boy" type recliner chair just behind me so I thrust on the crutches to push myself back towards the chair as I fell. I landed just on the edge and thought I had made a soft landing. But, unfortunately, it was a rocking Lazee Boy so it tilted down at the front. Also, to compound matters, Colby had left his shiny Dracula cape on the chair, so my butt had zero grip on a sloping surface. Baaadumpfff! I fell on the tiled floor hitting my right buttock with a big thump when I landed.

"Shit" wasn't the only expletive that went through my mind as you can well imagine. But the hard bit was getting back up again. The only person in the house with me was Kyle who had just turned fourteen. Kyle is not a big-built fourteen-year old so he could not pull me up. The only thing I could do was crawl on all fours over to the big sofa and drag myself face down onto it and then turn over and sit up. Phhheeeew!

As I write this - it's Monday and I fell last Saturday night - I can still feel the stiffness in the right buttock and it's going to take the best part of a week to get it back to where it was before . . .

But what can I say? As you can see from the above, I have fallen over, in one way or another, six or seven times at least. The ones I have described have been the major ones and there have also been a few minor ones. But I work on the principle that if you don't fall over every now and then, you are not trying hard enough. Have you ever seen a baby learn to walk without ever falling over? It is not possible.

And then there is the old adage "If you fall off the horse, the best thing you can do is to get straight back on it".

The best song that describes this situation is the 1998 hit, *Tubthumping (I Get Knocked Down)* by Chumbawamba. This is always played between games at the big international rugby tournaments such as The Hong Kong 7s and the Dubai 7s. It sort of encapsulates the rugby ethos which is that as soon as you are tackled or knocked down on the ground for any reason, you get up and carry on with the game.

CUE YOUTUBE VIDEO: TUBTHUMPING
(I GET KNOCKED DOWN) – CHUMBAWAMBA

I think that's the only way to be. So, as the kid's nursery rhyme says "*A-Tishoo. A-Tishoo. We all fall down*".

Then, as Chumbawamba says, "*But I get up again. You're never gonna keep me down!!!!*"

60

DON'T STOP BELIEVIN'

In the chapters of this book I probably haven't included enough accolades for the people closest to me – my wife Agnes and my boys. But, in a way, I have been saving that up for the end.

There is no doubt that a major part of my recovery is attributable to my wife and family and I cannot thank them enough for all the large and small things that they have done, and continue to do, for me. However strong-willed we are, we all need some help and some motivation at different times.

Agnes often thinks I don't realize the enormity of all these tasks and she complains that I don't appreciate her. But I do know how much she takes on, and how much she always achieves. So, a HUGE, HUGE "Thank you", my darling, for everything you have done to get me this far and to keep me moving forward all the time. I could not have done it without you.

And then there are the boys. They too have played a huge part in my recovery. All four of them have always been there whenever I asked for something or needed help. James, now 21, has lifted me, stretched me, dressed me, undressed me, changed my diapers, emptied countless litres of pee from urine bags and plastic urinals, driven me here, there, and everywhere when I could not drive myself and he has always responded to my requests.

But in September 2015 he went off to university in UK and that left a big hole in my support system. But the other boys stepped up to the mark. Kyle, now 16, always comes to see me every morning when he wakes up and is always checking to make sure I am OK. He has put on my socks and shoes hundreds of times. He has pushed me in a wheelchair all over the place, through malls, to cinemas, restaurants and rugby games. Colby, now 12, and generally regarded as the family "pest", has suddenly grown into a useful human being in recent months. He leaps up without asking when I start to move, bringing me the crutches that I need to get around. And he has just learnt how to make a perfect cup of tea. What more can you ask from a small mestizo British kid? And, of course, there's Elliott, now 32 and working far, far away in Australia. Even though he hasn't been close enough to actually do things for me, he has been there at the end of a phone line or on an email to help and also as an excellent role model for the other boys. I have always been able to quote his achievements as a yardstick for the other three.

What more could I ask from all the five of them? Nothing really, they have all been brilliant.

But, before I wrap-up this opus, there is one last song that needs slotting in here. It's a reprise, it's the finale and just one more encore!

Earlier in the book I have talked several times about the song "*Don't Stop Believin'*" by Journey and now sung by their Filipino lead singer Arnel Pineda. As I previously wrote, that song has appeared and re-appeared so many times in different guises through the last six years as I slowly recovered and rehabilitated from my accident. So, I had been trying to find a way to somehow get a link to Arnel Pineda.

Everything had been very quiet on this for several months and then suddenly in early 2015 thing started to happen. William Penaredondo called me "out-of-the-blue" one Saturday in about March 2015 told me that a Lay Pastor called Fred Monasterio wanted to meet me later that afternoon. When we met, Pastor Fred listened to my story and told me that he knew Arnel Pineda's mentor and spiritual manager, whose name is Coach Leo Arnaiz. Up to that point, lots of other people had said that they could put me in touch with Arnel but none had come up with the goods. But somehow Pastor Fred's promise sounded believable.

He told me he would talk with Coach Leo and let me know if anything could be done. But then I had to wait for a while again.

Fast forward to the morning of 1st June 2015. I had been feeling somewhat "down" for the preceding month and that was unusual for me. I had not even written a single word of this book for a month as I was just not in the mood. The reason for it was that I was being "retired" from Orascom and it was depressing me a bit. It's an unusual feeling for me but it was hard to shake off, mainly because I did not feel like I was ready to be a retired person yet. My legs may not yet be in the Usain Bolt sprinting category but my brain and my mouth definitely work fine. Plus, I still have a young family and need to get three boys through school and university so I need to keep working and earning. Anyway, 31st May 2015 was my last day at work so I went home at the end of the day and had a quiet night with the family.

But, when I woke up, for some unknown reason my head was buzzing – in a good way! I was thinking about finishing writing this book, especially now that I had more time. And a whole bunch of ideas were bouncing around in my head about somehow promoting a concert featuring Arnel/Journey so I could raise money for the TSB Fund for Injured Rugby Players and Arnel Pineda's Street Children Charity . . . !!

I was having my breakfast with all these ideas rattling around in my head and James, came in after dropping the two younger boys at school. I started telling him about some of my ideas and said that I felt so much happier that morning and it was no use being miserable about being a new retiree. In fact, I was going to be really, really busy and I said to him "So, this is the first day of the rest of my life!"

He laughed and walked out of the room and just then *Don't Stop Believin'* started playing on the radio! I couldn't believe it! Yet again, Kenny Jones on the Radio 2 Breakfast Show somehow managed to be psychic and choose exactly the right song at the right moment . . .

It has to be more than a coincidence – it has to be TINSTAAC. But I can tell you it gave me a monumental psychological boost. I suddenly "knew" that everything would work out fine and I felt instantly much happier than I had done for a few weeks.

AND THEN THINGS REALLY STARTED HAPPENING………..!!!

A couple of days after my "First day of the rest of my life" epiphany moment, I had yet another "out-of-the-blue" phone call from Pastor Fred Monasterio. He said that Coach Leo was coming to Dubai and wanted to meet me. Wow! Great! I felt one step closer already.

And sure enough, Coach Leo came and we met for the first time on Friday 19 June 2015. It was a fantastic meeting and we talked and talked for about four and a half hours. Coach Leo told me he had met with Arnel back in Manila just before he flew to the UAE and that Arnel was interested in coming to Dubai for a concert. Whhoooo! Big breaths!

During the following week Coach Leo and Pastor Fred came down to Abu Dhabi and spent the afternoon at my house and met Agnes and the rest of my family. At one point Agnes and I were discussing something with Pastor Fred and Coach Leo was messing with his phone. Then suddenly he handed it to me and said "Arnel is on the line and he wants to talk to you"

Yo!!! There I was, sitting on my own sofa, talking with Arnel Pineda, the guy who sings *Don't Stop Believin'* for a living. And he is telling me he is really looking forward to coming to Dubai and let's make the concert happen. It doesn't get any better than that, believe me . . . !!!

Coach Leo went back to Manila and a few days later had lunch with Arnel to tell him all about our meetings. Then he sent me an email with the photo below of himself with Arnel and a special message for me.

A Message from Arnel Pineda
Lead Singer of Journey
With Coach Leo Arnaiz

Then Agnes went to Manila in August 2015 and had lunch with Arnel, his wife and Coach Leo, which was a wonderful opportunity to let Arnel get a feel of what I am trying to do with this book and talk about doing a concert. I doesn't matter how long it takes, somehow I want to find a way to do it.

Filipino Mafia - Agnes and Arnel

You can see why *Don't Stop Believin'* has become an "anthem" for me. And, through this book, I really, really hope that it can also somehow inspire other people who have injuries, temporary inabilities and disabilities to believe in themselves - and the human brain and the human body that they possess – so that they will recover and regain what they thought they had lost.

So, please, right now if you can, fire up your iPod, iPhone, Android device, CD player, stereo system or whatever you have to play music on. Okay, even a Sony Walkman from a past distant technology era will do! Get the *Don't Stop Believin'* track and turn up the volume. I guarantee it will catch you at the back of the throat, send shivers up your spine or somehow move your spirit.

I have included all the lyrics so you can sing along and really feel what it's all about. Plus, here is the You Tube link to the Oprah Winfrey Show when she featured Arnel Pineda, Journey and *Don't Stop Believin'*.

Just listen to Oprah's introduction on the video. She said . . .

"Don't you just love it when a song raises you up and makes you believe you can do anything! When all you have to do is hear it and you are motivated, you're inspired! *Don't Stop Believin'* is one of those songs and the legendary rock band Journey gave us that one. Journey have had some ups and downs over the years but they never stopped believing"

What more can I say?

CUE YOUTUBE VIDEO: DON'T STOP BELIEVIN'
ARNEL PINEDA WITH JOURNEY ON OPRAH

Just a small town girl
Livin' in a lonely world
She took the midnight train
Goin' anywhere

Just a city boy
Born and raised in South Detroit
He took the midnight train
Goin' anywhere

A singer in a smokey room
The smell of wine and cheap perfume
For a smile they can share the night
It goes on and on and on and on

Strangers waiting
Up and down the boulevard
Their shadows searching
In the night

Streetlight people
Livin' just to find emotion
Hidin' somewhere in the night

Workin' hard to get my fill
Everybody wants a thrill
Payin' anything to roll the dice
Just one more time
Some will win
Some will lose
Some were born to sing the blues
Oh, the movie never ends
It goes on and on and on and on

Strangers waiting
Up and down the boulevard
Their shadows searching in the night
Streetlight people
Livin' just to find emotion
Hidin' somewhere in the night

Don't stop believin'
Hold on to that feelin'
Streetlight people
Don't stop believin'
Hold on
Streetlight people
Don't stop believin'
Hold on to that feelin'
Streetlight people!

As I write this last chapter I am not yet at the end of my personal journey but I can see the light at the end of the tunnel. It's still a fairly long tunnel, to be sure, but I am certain that one day I will burst out into the sunlight and will be able to walk, run and do most, if not all the things I could do before.

But you don't have to have suffered a major accident or life-changing illness to believe in yourself. My wife Agnes was that small town girl, living in a lonely world. For her it was a little place called Mapandan in Pangasinan, Philippines surrounded by rice fields. And there was no midnight train to take, so she had to get on an aircon bus to Manila.

For me, I wasn't exactly a city boy, and a Lancashire mill town called Nelson was a long way from Detroit. But I knew I didn't want to be there for the rest of my life. Likewise, there was no midnight train going anywhere – British Rail stopped operating about 10:00pm due to union rules! So, I jumped in a Land Rover with some friends and I drove across Africa then, after 6 years in Kenya, moved to the Philippines, where Agnes and I met.

And here we both are in Abu Dhabi, which looks nothing like Mapandan or Nelson, enjoying a life and a lifestyle that neither of us could ever have imagined when we were kids. But, somehow, inside both of us, there must have been a belief that somewhere out in the world there was something better than where we started from.

So, whether it's getting through a tough recovery from an accident, fighting your way through a debilitating illness or taking the plunge to do something you are not quite sure will be successful, you can do it too. Just as long as you Don't Stop Believin'...............................

TSB
April 2017

The End

(Well, except for the Glossary and a few other bits and bobs)

GLOSSARY

This Glossary has definitions, explanations and all sorts of bits of info that readers of various ages may need to help them understand some of the things I have written about in this book. Especially younger ones (i.e. anyone below the age of 25), who can't imagine life before Computers, the Internet, Facebook, Twitter, Instagram, Cell Phones, PS4s, Flat Screen TVs and all those things that we now take for granted. This information may also be especially useful to non-Brits, prop forwards and anyone with "cauliflower ears".

AC COBRA - A British-American sports car. Was often called the "Widow Maker" as the lightweight body, poor brakes, and cart spring suspension coupled to a powerful V8 engine made the Cobra lethally fast and lethally dangerous. It was great at accelerating in straight lines but not quite so good at decelerating or going round corners.

ADULT DIAPER - See chapter 39 for a sneak peek at the sartorially elegant TSB wearing the latest in garbage bin liners.

AFFLATUS - Divine Inspiration. As sometimes issued from the mouth of the Religious Advisor of the MH3.

ANKLE FOOT ORTHOSIS – An AFO is a lightweight moulded polymer brace strapped to your calf. There is also a piece that goes under the foot and the two sections are joined by rubber/elastic hinges. These hinges help to lift your foot up when the ankle muscles don't work properly. Without the AFO you get "foot drop" and it's hard to walk.

AND NOW FOR SOMETHING COMPLETELY DIFFERENT – The very well-known catch-phrase uttered by a naked piano player at the end of the opening credits of Monty Python's Flying Circus.

ANOTHER BRICK IN THE WALL – Pink Floyd anthem. See Chapter 42 for more on this and a YouTube video link.

ARGY-BARGY – English slang for argument or quarrel. Also sometimes used as the jokey title of the Falklands war between Argentina and Britain.

BERNIE THE BOLT - Was one of Bruce Forsythe's catch phrases on Beat the Clock, which was a segment on the hit TV show Sunday Night at the London Palladium. It had contestants from the audience trying to win prizes and one of the games had them shooting a real crossbow at a target. And, of course, so that the contestant did not inadvertently fire the crossbow too soon – or into the audience - they waited till he was facing away, looking at the target at the back of the stage, before they loaded the bolt into the crossbow. The guy who did that was called Bernie – hence the catch phrase "Bernie, the Bolt". So anyone in that era called Bernie must have really suffered! Because I could not drive for the first year of my physiotherapy, we needed a family driver. He was unlucky enough to be called Bernie. See also Chapters 57 and 58.

BEVERAGES – The generally acceptable euphemism in a Muslim country to describe drinks that are not "soft".

BLACKPOOL ROCK – Rock is a hard, stick-shaped, boiled sugar confectionery about an inch in diameter, usually flavoured with peppermint or spearmint. It is commonly sold at seaside resorts in the UK such as Blackpool or Brighton.

BLACKPOOL TOWER – A smaller "replica" of the Eiffel Tower on the "prom" (a.k.a promenade) at a Lancashire seaside resort in UK. Possible location for final scene of the remake of *Sleepless in Salford* movie or *King Kong*.

BLITZKRIEG - The word, of German origin, means "lightning war". In its strategic sense it describes a series of quick and decisive short battles to deliver a knockout blow to an enemy state before it could fully mobilize. In my case, I was to have a series of quick and decisive physiotherapy sessions, within a period of one month, to deliver a positive knockout blow to the parts of my metabolism and body systems that continuously wanted to degrade my muscle and nervous system capabilities if I did not fully mobilize them on a regular basis. A derivative of the word has also been given a new lease of life as the South African Rugby 7's team is nicknamed the "Blitzbokke".

BORACAY – A tiny island in the Philippines archipelago of 7007 islands. It's about 7km long and a maximum of 1km wide and has a beautiful 5km long white sand beach on one side with very calm aquamarine blue sea and palm trees fringing the back of the beach. Another tough day in Paradise! Agnes and I were married on that beach.

BOWL CUT – Many kids in the 1950's had this hairstyle – if you could call it a hairstyle. It looked like the barber (they were still called barbers for men in those days – hairdressers were for women) had cut the hair on top of the head to about an inch or two in length and then put a bowl on your head and trimmed everything below it with a pair of sheep shearers. The overall effect looked like you had a mop-head a bit like Moe Howard of the Three Stooges. Google it if you have no idea what I am talking about!

BRAZILIAN – The complete opposite of a bowl cut. Nothing to do with the 2016 Olympics or football players. If you are male and you don't know what a Brazilian is, ask your wife, girlfriend, mistress or S.O. Alternatively, consult the centrefold of Playboy or Penthouse magazines. If you are female and you don't know, ask your husband, boyfriend, lover or S.O. And if he knows and you don't, then slap his face and ask him "How come?

BRIDGING – You lay on your back with feet flat on the bed and your knees cranked up at forty-five degrees and your hands and arms above your head, so you can't push with your hands. Then you have to thrust your hips off the bed and push them up in the air. And you keep checking between your legs in case the baby's head has popped out yet!

BRISTOL CITIES – Cockney rhyming slang. In case you can't work it out for yourself, Bristol Cities = Titties.

BROMIDE – Allegedly, Bromide was added to the tea in HM Prisons and in the Armed Forces as it was reputed to dull and/or reduce the pent up sexual desires in men who were separated from their WAGS.

CAKE OR DEATH – Remember what I told you about Eddie Izzard in Chapter 26 and did you watch the You Tube video link?

CHICKEN ADOBO – A Filipino recipe. Large chunks of chicken marinated overnight in soy sauce with lots of garlic, pepper and bay leaves. Then it's boiled slowly till the chicken is very tender and dark brown from the marination. Most Westerners instantly love this dish.

CHICKEN TINOLA – Large chunks of chicken in a light, watery soup flavoured with ginger and garlic with unripe green papaya as the main vegetable. It's the proverbial "Chicken Soup for the Filipino Soul".

CLIFF RICHARD – The British equivalent to Elvis Presley. Started in the late 1950's and still performs – now aged 75. Was the first British rock 'n roll singer with "Move It". Now Sir Cliff Richard

COJONES – The Merriam-Webster Dictionary has two definitions. (1) Boldness or courage needed to do something. Like "Boy you need real cojones to pull that stunt off" or (2) A man's testicles (Er, are there any women with testicles? Oh sorry, I forgot about the sweet transvestites from Transylvania, a few of those from Thailand and the father of all those Kardashians)

COMMODE – A bedpan/potty/toilet/chamber pot with wheels on. So you can shit and move from place to place at the same time. It's a good way of saving time for people living in the "fast lane".

CORONATION STREET – The mother of all "soaps". Been running since December 1960 – yes that's 55 years! Simple plot. A street of terraced houses with a pub at one end and a corner shop at the other set in Salford, Lancashire. Straight forward people with straightforward accents who don't generally go in for murders, betrayals and Machiavellian business deals. But they do have a few affairs. Home from home!

CREPUSCULAR – Active around dusk and in the twilight zone. An adjective often applied to Hashers.

DEEP THOUGHT - Spoiler Alert! In the third novel by Douglas Adams, Deep Thought is a computer created by the pan-dimensional, hyper-intelligent species of beings (whose three-dimensional protrusions into our universe are ordinary white mice) to come up with the answer to the Ultimate Question of Life, the Universe, and Everything. Deep Thought is the size of a small city but it took it seven and a half million years to come up with the answer.

DÉJÀ VU ALL OVER AGAIN – Attributed to Yogi Berra, former New York Yankees coach. Berra was well known for his pithy comments and witticisms, known as Yogiisms. These very often took the form of either an apparently obvious tautology or a paradoxical contradiction.

DESPERATE HOUSWIVES – Popular American soap. The show followed the lives of a group of women, living in the picket-fence-pretty Wisteria Lane, as seen through the eyes of a dead neighbour who committed suicide in the very first episode. Maybe she committed suicide as she did not like the storyline which was one part comedy, one part drama, one part mystery and ten parts unbelievable. It seems that ordinary America housewives regularly kill their neighbours and then tell all their friends about it.

DESPERATE SCOUSEWIVES – And yes, there really was a TV show with his awful title. It tried (and failed) to convince the audience that scouse men and women are all about having a boss night out on the town but also that looking good is a 24/7 job. Apparently, if you went up the bleached bottom end of the Mersey Tunnel you would find the most depressing bunch of faked-up, vacuous wannabes you were ever likely to meet. BTW - Scouser is slang for a Liverpudlian i.e. someone who came from Liverpool. Scouse was the name of a common stew in Liverpool.

DON'T PANIC - Is a phrase on the back cover of The Hitchhiker's Guide to the Galaxy (HHGTTG). The novel explained that this was partly because the device "looked insanely complicated" to operate, and partly to keep intergalactic travellers from panicking when something went wrong – which it often did. It is said that despite its many glaring (and occasionally fatal) inaccuracies, the HHGTTG itself has outsold the Encyclopaedia Galactica because it is slightly cheaper, and because it has the words 'DON'T PANIC' in large, friendly letters on the cover.

DOUGLAS ADAMS – Had a mind even more convoluted than mine. I say "had" as he unfortunately died in 2001 at the age of only 49. He wrote the best seller "The Hitch Hiker's Guide to the Galaxy" (HHGTTG), a trilogy in five parts, (sic!) of which "Life, the Universe and Everything" was the third. All the books are brilliant. I recommend you go out and buy them, but not until you have finished this one!

DYSLEXIC – A word that is so hard to spell that even people who don't have dyslexia have difficluty gettnig the lettres in the rihgt ordre. Example: "A dyslexic man walks into a bra."

DYSTOPIA – The opposite of UTOPIA. In other words a Dysfunctional Utopia. These are portrayed as huge mega-cities that are not at all nice places to live in for the majority of the residents. In the 1927 movie, Metropolis, it was fine for the rich elite but the labour force, which was required to make it all function, were marched in and out of their work places and lived in poverty and very spartan conditions. In 1927, cities like Metropolis did not actually exist. Now they do. So Fritz Lang was way ahead of his time. DYSTOPIA is also an underlying theme of the books and movies in *The Hunger Games* series, which were written in 2008. Great movies. Go and see them if you haven't already!

ESOTERIC – The Wiktionary definition is: *"Having to do with concepts that are highly theoretical and without obvious practical application; often with mystical or religious connotations".* Any wiser?

EXACERBATED – A nice way of saying you are exhausted after you masturbated.

FAX MACHINE – If you are a younger reader – like less than 25 – you may never have seen or used a fax machine. You have to roll back thirty years to 1985 when the height of technology at the time was a fax machine. This machine had a little bright white light inside it and it scanned a page of writing or pictures or whatever was on the paper and then transmitted it over a telephone line and then the fax machine at the other end reversed the procedure to print it out It was like time travel or teleportation for words & pictures. Magic stuff! The internet had not yet been invented – or at least it was not available to the general public. Communication between most corporations in different countries was then by telegram. Amazing really how far we have come.

FIFTH AMENDMENT - Americans will understand this immediately. It's the Fifth Amendment to the Constitution which states that you don't have to answer any question or make any statement in a Court of Law that will incriminate you. Claiming the "Fifth" means that the answer to the question is one to which you do not want to admit.

FLUGELHORN - the long curved horn, gradually increasing in diameter and upturned near the end, which rests on the ground so the trumpet mouth points to the sky. I think it was used by guys wearing lederhosen to attract cows, milkmaids or Julie Andrews before cell phones were invented. It is the European equivalent of the Vuvuzela - the South African one-note horn that rose to international popularity during the 2010 Football World Cup. It's a good thing the Swiss have not taken up the idea of using Flugelhorns at football matches.

FRACTALS - A natural phenomenon or a mathematical set that repeats. In geometry it's a repeating shape, gradually getting smaller but the combination of all the same shapes makes the whole picture. In this book, it's something that happens which forms a connection with something else that may not have seemed connected in the first place. But those two then form another level of connection to a third thing - which probably happened at a different time or place to the first two. And so on. Complex and convoluted, ha! A bit like Leonardo di Caprio's movie, Inception. Read the damn book and you will get what I mean.

GANGBUSTERS - The radio show (1935-1957) began with a barrage of loud sound effects - a shrill police whistle, convicts marching in formation, police sirens wailing, machine guns firing, and tires squealing. In other words, a whole lotta noise. This noisy introduction led to the popular catchphrase "He came on like Gang Busters"

GET OUT OF DODGE - Leave the place you are in as quickly as possible. The phrase came from getting out of Dodge City - notorious for gunfights during the Wild West era - before the shooting began.

GET OUT OF JAIL CARD - From the kid's board game Monopoly. The game was all about buying and selling property and occasionally you would end up on the "Jail" square. Probably based on the real life stories of unscrupulous developers selling unbuilt property units "off-plan" and then running off with the money. So you need a "Get Out of Jail" card to move again.

GRAVITY – Probably Sandra Bullock's best ever movie. The movie tag line - Don't Let Go! George Clooney has a cameo but drifts off into space with a fading battery pack. He let go. Duuuuh!

GOVERNMENT HEALTH WARNING – You should only have Greggy's Gimmick/Valsalva Manoeuvre performed by male nurses who have beautiful girlfriends or nurses who are female themselves.

GRUNGE – Grunge music was invented by "garage bands" from Seattle. Grunge is generally characterized by a sludgy guitar sound that uses a high level of distortion, fuzz, and feedback effects. Grunge fuses elements of hard-core punk and heavy metal. Actually, I reckon the distortion and fuzziness came from the reverberation of the sound on the back of the metal up-and-over door, the hard floor and the walls of the garage, coupled with the incessant hammering of the Washington State rain on the roof.

HAPPY BIDET – Just in case you are wondering, the Happy Bidet came about as a slow, step-by-step corruption of Happy Birthday over many years. It went from Happy Birthday to Happy B-Day to Happy B-D to Happy Bidet. It sounds the same as B-Day, but of course the underlying meaning of the word is different.

HASH NAME – Every Hasher has one (except for Virgin Hashers). This name is somehow bizarrely related to their persona or something they foolishly did on a run before they were named and sometimes there are derivatives of the name. I was called Briggs & Stratton, the B&S Twins and the Hyphenated Taxidermist.

HASHTAG – This is a Twitter rip-off. I think the Hash House Harriers should sue Twitter for stealing their idea.

HASH TRASH – The weekly (or weakly) story of what 'may' have happened on the Hash trail and afterwards! The Hash Trash never lets the truth get in the way of a good story.

HMP ROCHESTER – In this case, HMP stands for Having My Physiotherapy at the Rochester.

HMP SLADE – HMP stands for Her Majesty's Prison. All prisons have endearing names like Slade, Wandsworth, Wormwood Scrubs and Strangeways, this latter one being in Manchester. I think the names say it all. I wonder why there is no HMP Bali Hai, for instance?

HOSPITAL PASS – It's not a fake pass to skip school or work and pretend to visit a sick friend in hospital. It's Rugby terminology for when you receive the ball just a Nano-second before one of the opposition's 200 pound, front row forwards slams into your body at full speed. You don't see it coming as you are usually looking sideways watching the ball glide through the air towards you. You might get some forewarning from the sudden "Oh shit" expression on the face of the player who passed you the ball as he realises what an asshole he was for passing at that precise moment. And for American Football fans – in Rugby you can only be tackled if you are in possession of the ball, unlike in AFL, where anyone can tackle anyone else, whether they have the ball or not.

HOT FOOTING IT – English slang for moving quickly. Usually running away from something. Possibly something to do with running over hot coals.

HOW I MET YOUR MOTHER – Sounds like a good title for a TV series. Funny that. In my case, I met the boy's mother Agnes in Dunkin' Donuts on Roxas Blvd in Baclaren. But that's another story for another day and another book.

HYLDA BAKER – A classic, northern comedienne in the 1950s – 1960s. She had many "Spend a penny" jokes. This was a euphemism for going for a pee as, in UK at that time, you needed one penny in the slot of the door lock on a public toilet cubicle to open it. Her stage friend was a "stooge" who never said anything through the entire comedy sketch. According to Hilda she suffered from being "incontinental". Hence, the constant question of "Have you beeeeeeennnn?"

INCREMENTAL – Progressing in such small steps that it drives you crazy

IKEA SLOPING COMPUTER PLATFORM – The best thing in the whole damn store. Only $5.00. It puts the keyboard on a 15 degree slope and makes the screen at eye level. It stops carpal tunnel syndrome and neck ache in one go. Listen to Dr. TSB, he knows these things.

INOCULATTE (v): To take coffee intravenously when you are running late.

IN'T SHOE BOX IN'T MIDDLE OF ROAD – Did you watch the Monty Python sketch "You Were Lucky" in Chapter 8? If not, do not pass go, return to Chapter 8 and watch it now. You naughty person, you!

IRREVERENT QUOTATIONS AND SAYINGS – In India there is a saying – "Everything will be alright in the end. So if it is not alright, it is not yet the end" This was a line by Dev Patel in the movie *"The Best Exotic Marigold Hotel"*. And it was also attributed to John Lennon. But maybe he heard it from the Maharishi Mahesh Yogi in India when the Beatles were into their transcendental meditation and naughty substance abuse phase in the late 1960s.

JOUSTING - For anyone who has not seen jousting – two knights in armour on horses would charge at each other holding very long poles and try and knock their opponent of the horse. Silly idea, yes?

JUKE BOXES – Every coffee bar had one in 1963. Now extinct except in billiard table rooms and "man-caves" of people over the age of 55 with big houses. Or go to a Hard Rock Café to see one. Basically, it was a big cabinet with maybe 50 or so "single" 45 rpm records in a circular stack. They were all listed inside the glass cover and you put coins in the slot and pressed buttons to select a song. The stack rotated, dropped the disc onto the turntable and the stylus moved into place to play it. Nowadays people have iPods which are much smaller and fit into your pocket easier than a Juke Box.

JUKE BOX JURY – British TV show in the early 60s. A panel of guest stars made banal comments on the latest record releases. They rarely told the truth if the record was bad – except for panellist Johnny Rotten, lead singer of the Sex Pistols, one of the most influential British punk rock bands of the era.

KERALA – India has a population of 1.27 billion. But every Indian nurse, physiotherapist, accountant and engineer that you talk to in the UAE comes from Kerala. So, I have a theory that there is actually no one left in Kerala and it's a completely deserted state.

KERAPUDLIANS – People from Liverpool are called Liverpudlians. The most famous being John, George, Paul and Ringo who formed the rock band, The Beatles. So why not Kerapudlians for people from Kerala?

KING OF 'D ROAD – A favourite bit of signage on Philippine Jeepneys. The 'D is common replacement for "the" in Filipino catch phrases. Also, see Chapter 46 for the Sri Lankan version of King of 'D Road. And it's nothing like a Jeepney.

KNOTTED HANDKERCHIEFS - The stereotype of the English, working-class holidaymaker in the 1950's wore high-waisted trousers, braces (suspenders for Americans), Fair Isle sweaters or cardigans (vests for Americans), round wire-rimmed glasses, had toothbrush moustaches and wore knotted handkerchiefs on their heads to protect their balding pates from the sun. This stereotype was personified by The Gumby's sketches in Monty Python. The Gumby's would come out with statements such as "I like peace and smashing bricks together"

KRIKKIT – In the HHGTTG books by Douglas Adams the people of the planet Krikkit – Krikkiters of course – want to destroy the Universe. Arthur Dent, in his dressing gown, his "girlfriend" Trillian, alien friend Ford Prefect, Zaphod Beeblebrox - the Galactic President, and Slartibartfast, who is a designer of planets, somehow manage to re-assemble the Wikkit Gate and save the Universe. Oh, and don't forget the depressed robot, Marvin the Paranoid Android. The intergalactic pan-dimensional mind-links between cricket and krikkit have to be read to be believed. You just have to buy the books to appreciate them . . .

LEDERHOSEN – the short leather pants with braces worn by kinky adult Swiss guys who, despite growing up, have not yet reached puberty.

LEFTOVERS – This is by far the most favourite Filipino dish due to their inability to cook for a specific head count. The amount cooked is usually at least twice whatever is required for that meal.

LIFE, THE UNIVERSE AND EVERYTHING – Spoiler Alert! Another hilarious book by Douglas Adams. The answer to "Life the Universe & Everything", according to DEEP THOUGHT, is 42. When everyone is unhappy with this, DEEP THOUGHT concludes that they had never actually known what the question was.

LOOSIDITY – It's when your verbal lucidity has diminished to the point where you start "wurring your slurds" and your legs get floppy and uncontrollable.

MASSAGE PARLOURS IN ASIA – I have absolutely no personal knowledge of any of the facts contained in Chapter 48 about massage parlours in Asia. All such information was passed on to me by a friend of a friend of a friend. And, if it was one of my close friends of a friend of a friend, married to a friend of a friend of a friend of my wife, he had never been there either and will also definitely "claim the Fifth".

MAMA MIA! – A musical set in Greece – like Summer Holiday starring Cliff Richard - but this time with the music of Abba sung by Pierce Brosnan and Meryl Streep. A couple of good rock and rollers for sure! (Not).

MANILA HASH HOUSE HARRIERS (MH3) – A drinking club with a running problem. Motto "We don't give one, but we know where to find one". The Hash House Harriers are a huge non-organisation to be found in most major cities in virtually every country in the world. Wherever you are, if you can find the Hash on a Monday night, you know they will be a bunch of like-minded souls to have fun, run and a drink with.

MEDICATION – A technical name that doctors use for the drugs they give you to ameliorate pain. But they do have other mind bending, crazy-making side effects too!

MODIFIED WORDS – The Washington Post Annual Style Invitational has a simple rule. Take any word from the dictionary, alter it by adding, subtracting, or changing one letter, and supply a new definition. Example "Ignoranus (n): A person who is both stupid and an asshole".

MOLOTOV COCKTAIL – A generic term for a bottle-based incendiary bomb or petrol bomb. Basically, put petrol in a bottle, stick a cloth fuse into the neck to seal it, light the fuse and throw it at something. The bottle smashes on impact and explodes with flames engulfing the target. The name "Molotov Cocktail" was coined by the Finns during the Winter War in 1939 as an insulting reference to Soviet foreign minister Vyacheslav Molotov. In my case, the Molotov Cocktail of cod liver oil and laxatives was going to make me explode on (or more likely before) impact with the toilet seat.

MONGO – Mong/Mung Beans, which are bean sprouts before they have sprouted, steeped and boiled slowly seasoned with lots of garlic, onions, ginger and, sometimes, small pieces of chicken, pork or shrimp. Without the meat it's like a Filipino version of "Mushy Peas" and tastes pretty much the same if you eat it with a meat pie and put salt & vinegar on it. Nothing to do with Mungo Jerry and the hit song *In the Summertime.*

MONTY PYTHON'S FLYING CIRCUS – There are several references to Monty Python running through the book because I loved it. Most of world knows about Monty Python. But, if since the early 70s, you happened to be living in a bunker, wearing sound cancelling headphones, or in living under a rock in the boondocks of America and you know nothing about Monty Python, I will explain. Python was on British television in the early 70s. It was a ground-breaking, irreverent comedy series full of short sketches which challenged many things and poked fun at the British public, the Government, the church and anything else it could lay its hands on – including all Australians called Bruce - which are most of them.

MOODY BLUES - An English rock band, formed in 1964 and still active in 2016. Among their innovations was a fusion of rock with classical music, as heard in their 1967 album *Days of Future Passed.* The Moody Blues have sold 90 million albums, becoming known internationally with hit singles including *Go Now*, *Nights in White Satin*, *Tuesday Afternoon* and *Question.* They have been awarded 18 platinum and gold discs.

MR. TRAVIS – Hamza at the Burjeel Hospital Gym could not quite get my name right as "Mr. Trevor". So it was easier to accept "Mr. Travis" than keep correcting him!

MULBERRY BUSH – This bush appeared to be a favourite of nursery rhyme writers back in the day. The mulberry bush was popular in the 18th Century, when England tried to copy the silk trade in China. They used them as the habitat for the silkworms. But our winters were too cold and hence the last line of the verse being a sarcastic reference to the failure of the concept "On a cold and frosty morning". One is also in the first two lines of *Pop Goes the Weasel.* "All around the mulberry bush, the monkey chased the weasel". Then the monkey stops to pull up his sock or pull on his cock – depending on if you are singing the kids version or the rugby club one. The last line is "Pop! Goes the Weasel". So make your own judgement.

MURPHY'S LAW – It's the Irish theory that something will happen just the way you didn't want it to happen or just at the moment you least wanted it to happen so that it screws up your carefully laid plans. "To be sure, to be sure", as the Irish would say.

NEOLOGISMS – Alternative meanings to common words. Example: "Lymph (v.). To walk with a lisp". I know that feeling well!

NILAGA – It's a bit like British boiled beef and cabbage, but with "attitude". Chunks of beef and bones boiled slowly with onions and lots of black peppercorn. Potatoes and veggies are added just before serving so that they don't go soggy and brown like they do in the Brit version.

NODDY CAR – This term came from the world-famous Noddy books by Enid Blyton. Noddy had a little red and yellow car that he drove around in with his friend Big Ears, usually getting into trouble with Mr. Plod the Policeman. The first book, Noddy Goes to Toyland, was published in 1949. Every British kid for generations read Noddy books. Then some Inspector of Political Correctness decided that Noddy must be gay as he did not have a girlfriend and hung around with Big Ears all the time. Happily, they sorted these PC issues out and I heard that a Noddy movie may be under production.

OAP – It's a British thing. The letters stand for Old Age Pensioner. It's probably not politically correct any more and definitely would not be if it was an American terminology. In Britain when you reach the age of 65 for men and 63 for women you are entitled to a government pension which is supposed to be just about enough on which to live a simple life. As a recipient of one I can tell you it's not, no matter how simple the life

OLD PEOPLE'S HOME – Probably another totally politically uncorrect name. Maybe it should be a nursing home, convalescent home, skilled nursing facility (SNF), care home, rest home or intermediate care facility. Whatever the name it's a place which provides a type of residential care for older or disabled people. Most OAPs hate them.

OMPHALOSKEPSIS – More commonly known as navel-gazing. Supposed to be an aid to meditation. From Greek omphalos (navel) + skepsis (act of looking, examination). Some consider the navel to be "a powerful chakra of the body". The use of omphaloskepsis as an aid to contemplation of basic principles of the cosmos and human nature is found in the practice of yoga. Perhaps that is how DEEP THOUGHT came up with the answer to "Life, the Universe and Everything". See Chapters 41 and 48 for more on that topic. Phrases such as "contemplating one's navel" or "navel-gazing" are frequently used, usually in jocular fashion, to refer to self-absorbed pursuits.

ORASCOM – At the time of my accident I worked as the Business Development Manager for Orascom, an Egyptian company and the largest construction contractor based in the MENA region.

OXYMORON (1) – Two words or ideas put together in a name or a phrase which, at first glance, seem to be contradictory to one another. Such as "A little pregnant", "American culture", "Pretty ugly", "Act naturally", "A German sense of humour", "British cuisine" or the mother of all oxymorons "Happily married"

OXYMORON (2) – Dr. Schumacher, my Urologist No. 8 disproved my earlier example of oxymoronesque phrases such as "A German sense of humour" as he smiles and laughs a lot. Who knows?

PACIFIC COAST HIGHWAY – It's the name of US Highway 1 where I taught my eldest son, Elliott, to drive fast on a road trip for his fifteenth birthday. You can have a Student Driving Permit at fifteen in California. Most kids there have cars. So any High School Student car park is huge in comparison to the Teacher's car park.

PANCIT – a.k.a. PANCEEEEET! It's vermicelli noodles cooked in soy sauce and garlic with lots of bits of vegetables, tiny bits of meat and small shrimps.

PAN-GLACTIC GARGLE BLASTER - The HHGTTG states that the effect of one of these drinks "Is like having your brain smashed out by a slice of lemon wrapped round a large gold brick".

PARAPROSDOKIANS - Figures of speech in which the latter part of a sentence or phrase is surprising or unexpected and frequently humorous. Apparently, Winston Churchill loved them. Example: "To be sure of hitting the target, shoot first and call whatever you hit the target".

PARROT ON THE SHOULDER – The Long John Silver parrot was famous for saying "Pieces of Eight", which were gold coins. According to Eddie Izzard, that's a bit like having a parrot on your shoulder today saying "Twelve Pounds Forty Two Pence". Doesn't translate very well, does it? I guess that is why Johnny Depp, a.k.a Captain Jack Sparrow, does not have one on his shoulder in *Pirates of the Caribbean.*

PAVLOV'S DOGS – Ivan Pavlov showed that a dog's brain can be conditioned to expect something positive to happen – and respond accordingly – even when stimulated with a neutral stimulus. Like a ringing bell meant food was available. It works for humans too.

PENIS – Wikisaurus lists 214 different names for the male organ for copulation and urination. Did you know all these? Anaconda, baloney pony, choad, choda, chode, chopper, cock, crank, dick, diddly (sometimes childish), dingaling, ding-a-ling (as in the Chuck Berry song), ding-dong, dinger (Canada, US), dingle, dingus, dingy (childish), dink (Canada), disco stick, dong, donger (Australia, Britain), Donkey Kong, doodle (sometimes childish), dork, fuckpole, jimmy (US), johnson, John Thomas, joystick, kielbasa, knob (Britain), lad (Ireland), langer (Ireland), love muscle, love truncheon, Master John Goodfellow, male member, manhood, meat, meatstick, meat stick, member, membrum virile, nob (Britain), one-eyed trouser snake, organ, package, pecker, peen, pee-pee (childish), pee-wee (childish), pego (archaic, slang), penis, peter, phallus, piece, pink cigar, pintle, pizzle (Australia, Britain), pork sword, prick, pud, putz (Yiddish), rod, sausage, schlong, shaft, shlong (Yiddish), shmekl, skin flute, snake, sausage, spitstick, swipe (archaic, slang), tadger (Australia, Britain), tallywacker, tarse, third leg, todger (Australia, Britain), tool, trouser snake, unit, virile member, wang, weapon, wee-wee (childish), weenie, weeny, whang, wick, wiener (childish), willie, willy, winky, yard (obsolete). Amazingly, after that lot, I do know two more – plonker and fishing tackle. So that's 216 and counting.

PEYTON PLACE – Is it a coincidence that this one comes directly after PENIS? This TV show was apparently, allegedly (according to Wikipedia, anyway), an American copy version of Coronation Street – except with more sex, fights and murders but less of those than in the book of the same name. (Hmmm!) Oh, and no terraced houses. It ran from 1964 – 1969. Needs another 50 years to match Coronation Street.

PORRIDGE - "Doing porridge" is British slang for serving a prison sentence, porridge once being the traditional breakfast in UK prisons.

RECTITUDINAL - Rectitude (n.), the formal, dignified bearing adopted by proctologists. (The Washington Post)

PROPRIOCEPTION – The human body's capability to recall the exact position of all your joints and limbs when you want to touch something in the same place again and again. It's an important capability when you need to locate your penis at 4:00 am in the middle of the night and you are still asleep but have to have a pee in a plastic urinal.

RADIO CAROLINE - In the mid-60s, Radio Caroline was illegally broadcasting rock/pop music to young listeners who preferred it's fun image and up-to-date music playlist to the stodgy and dowdy, parent-oriented music played by the BBC. It was based on a boat, anchored in international waters in the North Sea, just off the coast of UK. Being in my mid-teens, I was an avid, impressionable, listener. Baby Bob Stewart was the first American DJ that anyone had heard in UK and he brought a whole new style to radio. "It's your Bobby Baby that loves you so crazy!"

RAM - Acronym for Random Access Memory. Usually used to describe the hard drive of a computer. It's basically a spinning disc about three inches in diameter with a flat tin arm pivoted so it runs in an arc over the top of the spinning disc. There is a thin wire bent down from the end of the arm to touch the surface of the disc in order to collect information from it. But how does it move back and forth so fast? It looks like the inventor of this amazing bit of technology (that I still don't believe really works) grew up in the 1960's when record players were all the rage as the RAM Hard drive looks like an updated, high-tech version.

RECORD PLAYER - Every home had one in the 1960s. Then they became totally extinct for many years due to digital technology. In the 60's a record player was a box about 13 inches x 13 inches x 5 inches high covered in plastic fake leatherette. It had a lid and inside was a record turntable and an arm that could swing across a vinyl record with a tiny diamond "needle" on the end of it. The arm and needle was dropped onto the surface of the record by a mechanism and the diamond point fitted in the groove in the record. The groove had little serrations on it and the vibrations created in the needle - the other end of which was inside an electromagnet - made electricity which was amplified by valves and transistors into sound. There was usually a white plastic knob on the front of the box - often with a bit of gold trim on it - and you turned it to the right to make the noise louder. The single tiny, tinny speaker was hidden behind a bit of coloured gauze on the front of the box. Nowadays music is stored digitally on micro-chips housed in slim, cell-phone like packaging which can produce high quality music without any moving parts. My kids - and probably yours - have never seen a record player. But vinyl record albums and record players are now back in favour because the sound is better than digitally processed sound.

REX HARRISON – Famous for his role as Professor Higgins in My Fair Lady with Audrey Hepburn. See Chapter 47 for more on this.

REX THE WONDER DOG - Was initially featured in DC Comics in the 1950's and the kept re-appearing many years later in comics, TV, movies and in other super-hero series such as The Green Lantern.

ROCHESTER WELLNESS CENTRE – My physiotherapy clinic. It's now in Abu Hail, Deira. See http://www.rochesterwellness.com/

RUGBY ETHOS – When someone tries to tackle you or knock you over, any and every rugby player will try to stay on his (or her) feet. If they are tripped or they stumble and fall on the ground, they will try to get up again and carry on running. Conversely, in football, if another player so much as touches the player who has the ball, that player will immediately fall to the ground and hold his leg, knee, ankle, foot or some body part. You never see any rugby player holding on to his leg or other body parts when he goes down – even if he is injured - as his first reaction is to try and hold onto the ball to stop the other team stealing it.

SALFORD – A very tough, industrialised, working-class city, next to Manchester. The only similarity to Seattle is that it rains all the time.

SATED – Absolutely, totally and completely satisfied. If it was food, your stomach is full to bursting. If it was sex you are drained but happy. It's way better than being exacerbated.

SEX CHANGE – The lead actress in Summer Holiday starts off as a boy. Maybe they did sex change operations in Greece back in the 60's. Nowadays, if you want a "chop and change", most people go to Thailand. It's a well-known fact that the most beautiful girls in Thailand used to be men.

SHURRUP LAD! – Used with kind permission of Pauline Marsden (nee Lenton), one of my sister's friends, who I teased relentlessly when she was a teenager. She always retorted with "Shurrup lad!"

SIGNIFICANT OTHER (S.O.) – S.O. is a PC (Politically Correct) American acronym for Significant Other. It seems to be a noun missing to me. Like Significant Other . . . what? Significant Other Bitch? Significant Other Woman? It is used as a term to describe a person who is not actually your wife, or girlfriend, or fiancée but for some reason cannot be described in any nicer way than Significant Other (Nothing). Pretty horrible if you are the S.O., yeah?

SMS – One of the stupidest names in the world. Everyone in the Philippines used to "text" each other as it was much cheaper than a call. So much so that the Philippines had the highest text count of any country in the world. Then the rest of the world caught up and started using the name Short Message System – which, even with the acronym SMS – is longer to say than the word it replaced.

STRICTLY COME DANCING – It's on British TV. Similar to Dancing With The Stars. But used to have the advantage - or disadvantage depending on your preference – of having (Sir) Bruce Forsythe as the host for many years. Brucie was famous for his catch phrase "Naice ter see you. Ter see you, naice!" See also Chapters 25 & 58

STRANGE AND AWFUL LIQUIDS – On a rugby tour you are usually required to drink – along with everyone else – whatever the Drinks Master chooses in that particular bar. It's even worse if you are fined – and everyone gets fined – for whatever transgressions of rugby team protocol the Fine Master and his Snitches catch you doing. The worst drink to be forced to drink is undoubtedly a "Come Shot" or "Cum Shot". Its Baileys Irish Cream and Lime Juice, which makes the cream in the Baileys curdle in a few seconds. So when you down it, it has gone all sour and lumpy and it makes you want to throw up!

SUMMER HOLIDAY – A 1963 movie. Spoiler Alert! Don (Cliff Richard) and his friends are bus mechanics at the London Transport bus workshop. During a (typically) miserable, wet British summer lunch break, Don tells his friends that he has persuaded London Transport to lend him an AEC Regent III RT double-decker bus. They convert into a holiday caravan and drive across continental Europe, intending to reach the South of France but end up in Greece. Of course, there was no such thing as GPS in 1963. And they were 40 years too soon for Mama Mia!

SUPPORT – Verb: To assist someone in need. Noun: Elastic "Jock Strap" worn by rugby players to keep their testicles safe from harm.

TEN BOB - British slang for ten shillings back in the 60s and before the metric system was forced upon us by the EU. Maybe we can go back to the original British system now that the BREXIT vote was to leave the EU. Twenty shillings = £1 = One Pound Sterling. So it was half of one pound to see the Beatles. That equals approx. Dhs 2.80 = approx. US 60 cents in today's money. WOW!

THANK YOUR LUCKY STARS – One of the first pop/rock 'n roll TV programs on British television in the early 1960s. All acts mimed to their songs and I recorded them so I could play them back later in my room or at parties with me acting as the DJ. Yeah right!

THE BARFINE - The by-line was "The Official Organ of the Manila Nomads Rugby Club". No prizes for guessing which organ was being referred to. I actually kept a copy of all the issues and had them bound in a hard cover. So if this book is successful maybe I will "re-publish" that compendium. There are some good rugby club stories in there!

THE BOLD AND THE BEAUTIFUL – World-renowned American soap opera. All about wealthy families having love affairs, scandals, Machiavellian business deals and betrayals – just like they do in real life! A ridiculously good looking cast – there should be some ugly throwback in there. Started in 1987 and still going strong.

THE BRIDGE ON THE RIVER KWAI – A movie about building a bridge during WWII for the notorious Burma-Siam railway by prisoners of war. The Japanese needed it to support their large army in Burma. During its construction, about 13,000 POWs died and were buried along the railway. Conditions in the POW camps were horrendous. It is widely considered to be one of the greatest films in history.

THE HITCH HIKERS GUIDE TO THE GALAXY - the first book by Douglas Adams and subsequently made into a movie starring Martin Freeman of *Lord of the Rings*, *The Hobbit* and *Sherlock* fame. In the movie he plays Arthur Dent, a very, very ordinary person, who spends the entire movie in his dressing gown. He also insists on taking his towel everywhere he goes on his inter-galactic adventures.

THE ROCKY HORROR PICTURE SHOW – One of the greatest cult musicals of all time. Starting as a West End stage show, then a movie in 1975 starring Tim Curry as Dr. Frank N. Furter, it was a parody and a tribute to all the classic horror B-movies from the 30s to the 70s. It soon became known as a "Midnight Movie" with audiences dressing as the characters, participating with the film, talking back to the screen and lip-synching to the lines. Still in limited release four decades after its premiere, it has the longest-running theatrical release in film history. Be sure to watch it if you get the chance!

TIN LIZZIE – Ford Model T, produced from 1908 to 1927. Still in the Top Ten of cars sold of all time at 16.5 million. You could have any colour you liked as long as it was black.

TOYOTA PREVIA – There is a long story about these vans in Chapter 27. The difference between the Invacar and the Toyota Previa was that the Invacar had sliding doors on both sides. So, if they had a death wish, Invacar owners could choose to get out on the "outside" of the car (on the road side, not the sidewalk side) to assemble their wheelchair in the road. This would pretty much ensure that they would shortly be pasted onto the front of the next double decker bus that passed by. But at least they had a choice. My Toyota Previa in the Philippines only had one sliding door and it was already on the outside so you stepped out into the Manila "trappic". Remember – Filipinos have problems saying "f" so they replace it with a "p".

TOY STORY – In the movie, the toys are all "alive" but pretend to be lifeless when humans are around. Woody a cowboy, played by Tom Hanks, is jealous of the new astronaut toy, Buzz Lightyear, played by Tim Allen. But they become friends when disaster strikes the group.

TRAUMA PSYCHOLOGY SYNDROME - When an accident happens which causes a significant trauma or disability for the patient, there are several stages that the human brain goes through as it attempts to deal with the situation. These are Shock, Denial, Anger, and Acceptance. Relatives and loved ones can also go through these phases and often take longer to get to the Acceptance phase than the patient does. Usually, the Anger phase lasts longer for them than for the patient.

TSB BIRTHDAY – Please mark the 5th January in your calendars for the future. I am always happy to receive presents of a liquid nature.

TSISMUS – The Filipino version of "tittle-tattle". Basically it's spreading negative rumours about someone which may or may not be true. And they get embellished the more they are told.

TWERK – Originally a combination of the words "twitch" and "jerk". But circa 2000 the word twerk was popularised by being featured in hip-hop video dancing. It's now used to describe moving the body in a sexually suggestive twisting or gyrating fashion. It features regularly on the Ellen De Generis TV show where she, her guests and audience twerk all over the place.

UTI – Urinary Tract Infection. When you get a bladder infection you know urine trouble (!) Boom-Boom.

VENERY – The pursuit of pleasure. Usually under the influence of alcohol. It's just possible that this word has some linkages to Venereal Disease.

VOJTA – The medical description is as follows: The therapeutic use of reflex locomotion enables elementary patterns of movement in patients with impaired central nervous systems and locomotor systems to be restored once more — at least in part. Through therapeutic use of reflex locomotion, the – involuntary – muscle functions necessary for spontaneous movements in everyday life are activated in the patient, particularly in the spine, but also in the arms and legs, the hands and feet, as well as in the face. Got it? Complicated stuff!

WAGS – Acronym for WIVES AND GIRLFRIENDS of players in teams. Tennis players don't have WAGS. Whereas, Rugby and football players do.

WATER SPRAY – It's the traditional Arabic/Muslim way of cleaning oneself after using the toilet. The French and Thais also do the same whereas Westerners/Non-Muslims generally use toilet tissue.

WHEN HELL FREEZES OVER – This Eagles album is part studio tracks and part live from their first concert in 1994 when they got back together. The album title comes from Don Henley, who, when they broke up, was quoted as saying "The Eagles would only get back together when Hell freezes over". But on the album Glenn Frey comments, "For the record. We never split up. We just had a 14 year vacation . . . "

WHEN THE GOING GETS TOUGH, THE TOUGH GET GOING - The origin of the phrase has been attributed Joseph P. Kennedy (1888–1969) father of former U.S. President John F. Kennedy. Nowadays, most people think of the song by Billy Ocean.

WILLY-NILLY - An adjective meaning impotent. (Washington Post Annual Style Invitational)

ZAPHOD BEEBLEBROX - In HHGTTG, Zaphod was briefly the President of the Galaxy - a role that involves no power whatsoever, and merely requires the incumbent to attract attention so that no one wonders who's really in charge. It's a role for which Zaphod was perfectly suited.

ZIMMER FRAME – A 'U' shaped frame with four legs and two handles. I don't know who Mr. Zimmer was but he must have been a very slow walker! It's impossible to move at much more than 1 mile per hour with a Zimmer as you have to continuously lift up the frame and move it forward about six inches at a time. The "hot" version of the Zimmer Frame has two small wheels on the front legs and rubber stoppers on the back legs. With this model you can have optional "boy racer" go–faster racing stripes, alloy wheels, low profile tires, leather bound hand grips and other modifications to make you feel like you are going faster. But, believe me, you are not. I couldn't wait to ditch the Zimmer and get some high-speed crutches.

APPENDIX A: LIST OF MUSIC

A. SONGS IN THE BOOK – with Text Box and QR Code or URL

1. *A Hard Day's Night* – Beatles – Ch. 29 – Kenny & Accalia . . .
2. *Another Brick in the Wall (Pt. 2)* – Pink Floyd – Ch. 53 – Biking . . .
3. *Bright Lights, Bigger City* – CeeLo Green – Ch. 34 – GGG&GG
4. *Called Out in the Dark* – Snow Patrol – Ch. 27 – Transformers . . .
5. *Cloud Number Nine* – Bryan Adams – Ch. 31 – Cloud Nine – H&J
6. *Come As You Are* – Nirvana – Ch. 34 – Glitz, Glamour, Grunge . . .
7. *Come On Eileen* – Dexy's Midnight Runners – Ch. 37 – Grumpy Eileen
8. *Coronation St.* – Eric Spear - Ch. 16 – Nostalgia Isn't What it Used to Be
9. *Dem Bones* – Delta Rhythm Boys – Ch. 44 – Dem Bones
10. *Die Another Day* – Madonna – Ch. 23 – Die Another Day
11. *Don't Stop Believin'* - Tom Cruise – Ch. 38 – Rock of Ages to 7 Dwarfs
12. *Don't Stop Believin'* - Glee - Ch. 15 - Glee on the Gogglebox
13. *Don't Stop Believin'* - Journey+Steve Perry - Ch. 29 – Kenny & Accalia
14. *Don't Stop Believin'*– Journey+Arnel Pineda- Ch. 60 – Don't Stop Believin'
15. *Drive* - The Cars – Ch. 40 – The Fastest Invalid Carriage in the World
16. *Feelin' Good* – Michael Buble' – Ch. 12 – How to Conquer the World
17. *Fun, Fun, Fun* – Beach Boys – Ch. 35 – Fun, Fun, Fun
18. *Get The Party Started* – Pink – Ch. 28 - While You're Down There.
19. *Gimme Some Lovin'* – Spencer Davies Group – Ch. 6 - Thunder Road
20. *Gimme, Gimme, Gimme* – Abba - Ch. 45 – Happy Bidet
21. *Hotel California* – Eagles – Ch. 57 – Strictly Come Dancing . . .
22. *I Can't Dance* – Genesis – Ch. 59 – A-tishoo, A-tishoo, We All Fall Down
23. *I Can't Tell You Why* – Eagles – Ch. 57 – Strictly Come Dancing . . .
24. *I Love Rock n' Roll* – Joan Jett & the Blackhearts - Ch. 56 – T&B&P (Pt. 2)
25. *I Will Make You a Man* – Tim Curry – TRHPS – Ch. 20 - WTGGT . . .

26. *In Dreams* – Roy Orbison – Ch. 24 – In Your Dreams!
27. *Jingle Bells* – James Lord Pierpont - Ch. 33 – Jingle What? Jingle Where?
28. *Liberty Bell March* – John Philip Sousa – Ch. 56 – T&B&P (Pt. 2)
29. *Life in the Fast Lane* – Eagles – Ch. 31 – Cloud Nine - Hammad and Joyz
30. *Little Stick of Blackpool Rock* – George Formby – Ch. 50 - Spring Break
31. *Little Wonders* - Rob Thomas – Ch. 36 – Reiki and High Spirits
32. *Live & Let Die* – Paul McCartney – Ch. 32 – Macca, The Boss and Me
33. *Long Road Out of Eden* – Eagles – Ch. 26 – Rocky Mountain Exorcism
34. *Love's Theme* – Barry White – Ch. 19 - Radio Ga-Ga
35. *One of These Nights* – Eagles – Ch. 54 – A Knight's Tale
36. *Philadelphia* – Bruce Springsteen – Ch. 17 – Well, Goodness Gracious Me!
37. *Pink* – Aerosmith – Ch. 41 – On The First Day of Xmas . . .
38. *Please, Please Me* – Beatles – Ch. 29 – Kenny & Accalia . . .
39. *Pretty Maids all in a Row* – Eagles – Ch. 57 – Strictly Come Dancing . . .
40. *Pump up the Volume* – M.A.R.S – Ch. 27 – Transformers . . .
41. *Radio Ga-Ga* – Queen – Ch. 19 – Radio Ga-Ga
42. *Rock Star* – Nickelback – Ch. 41 – On the First Day of Xmas . . .
43. *Rocky Mountain Way* – Joe Walsh – Ch. 26 – Rocky Mountain Exorcism
44. *Sexual Healing* – Marvin Gaye – Ch. 27 – Transformers . . .
45. *Shine On You Crazy Diamond* – Pink Floyd – Ch. 53 – Biking . . .
46. *Show and Prove (OAP Mix)* – Zimma Frame – Ch. 44 – Dem Bones . . .
47. *Stronger (What Doesn't Kill You)* – Kelly Clarkson - Ch. 30 – HWGRTMB
48. *Summertime* – G. Gershwin – Ch. 56 – Trains & Boats & Planes (Pt 2)
49. *Sweet Transvestite* - Tim Curry – TRHPS – Ch. 43 - Blitzkrieg
50. *Thunder* – Jessie J – Ch. 23 – Die Another Day
51. *Too Busy Being Fabulous* – Eagles – Ch. 13 – Too Busy Being Fabulous
52. *Trains & Boats & Planes* – Billy J. Kramer – Ch. 56 – T & B & P (Part 2)
53. *Tubthumping* - Chumbawamba - Ch. 59 – At-ishoo, At-ishoo . . .
54. *Twelve Days of Rochester* – TSB – Ch. 41 – On the First Day of Xmas . . .
55. *Under Pressure* – Queen + Bowie – Ch. 49 – I Still Only Have One Penis
56. *Up* – James Morrison and Jessie J – Ch. 19 – Radio Ga-Ga
57. *Walking On The Moon* – Police – Ch. 43 - Blitzkrieg
58. *Wanna Marry You* – Bruno Mars – Ch. 30 – HWGRTMB
59. *We Will Rock You* – Queen – Ch. 54 – A Knight's Tale
60. *Well, Goodness Gracious Me* – P. Sellars + S. Loren – Ch. 17 - WGGM
61. *When I'm 64* – Beatles – Ch. 42 – When I'm 64
62. *When the Going Gets Tough* – Billy Ocean – Ch. 20 – WTGGT . . .
63. *YMCA* – The Village People – Ch. 52 – Lightning Strikes Twice . . .
64. *Your My First, Last, My Everything* – Barry White – Ch. 19 – Radio Ga-Ga

APPENDIX B: LIST OF MOVIES, TV SHOWS ETC

A. MOVIES IN THE BOOK – with Text Box and QR Code or URL Link

1. *A Hard Day's Night* – The Beatles – Ch. 29 – Kenny & Accalia and the Kid
2. *A Knights Tale* – Heath Ledger – Ch. 54 – A Night's Tale
3. *Apollo 13* – Tom Hanks – Ch. 22 – I Didn't Know whether to Laugh or Cry
4. *Back to the Future* – Michael J. Fox – Ch. 39 – I Only Have One Penis
5. *Captain Phillips* - Tom Hanks – Ch. 56 – Trains & Boats & Planes (Pt. 2)
6. *Cast Away* – Tom Hanks – Ch. 25 – The Cast Away
7. *Days of Thunder* – Tom Cruise – Ch. 6 – Thunder Road
8. *Die Another Day* – Pierce Brosnan – Ch. 23 – Die Another Day
9. *Dr. Strangelove* – Peter Sellers – Ch. 12 – How to Conquer The World
10. *Edward Scissorhands* – Johnny Depp – Ch. 58 – How Many Fingers?
11. *Forrest Gump* – Tom Hanks – Ch. 3 – The Game
12. *Inglourious Basterds* – Brad Pitt – Ch. 50 – Spring Break
13. *Karate Kid* – Pat Morita – Ch. 20 - When the Going Gets Tough
14. *Larry Crowne* – Tom Hanks – Ch. 22 – I Didn't Know Whether to Laugh
15. *Mamma Mia!* –Meryl Streep/Pierce Brosnan – Ch. 45 – Happy Bidet
16. *Monty Python and the Holy Grail* – Ch. 59 – A-tishoo, A-tishoo . . .
17. *My Fair Lady* – Rex Harrison – Ch. 47 – Motivation is a Four Letter Word
18. *Planes, Trains & Automobiles* – Steve Martin – Ch. 56 - T & B & P (Pt 2)
19. *Reach for the Sky* – Kenneth More – Ch. 40 – The Fastest Invalid Carriage
20. *Rock of Ages* – Tom Cruise – Ch. 38 – From Rock of Ages to Seven Dwarfs
21. *Rocky* – Sylvester Stallone – Ch. 20 – When the Going Gets Tough
22. *Sleepless in Seattle* – Ch. 34 – Glitz, Glamour, Garages, Grunge & G's G
23. *Snow White & the Seven Dwarfs* – Ch. 38 – From Rock of Ages to 7 Dwarfs
24. *Star Trek*– Chris Pine/Leonard Nimoy – Ch. 18 – How To Choose A Nurse
25. *Summer Holiday* – Cliff Richard – Ch. 46 - Going On A Summer Holiday
26. *The Boat That Rocked* – Philip Seymour Hoffman - Ch. 19 – Radio Ga-Ga
27. *The Bridge on the River Kwai* – Alec Guinness – Ch. 46 – Summer Holiday
28. *The Exorcist* – Linda Blair – Ch. 26 - Rocky Mountain Exorcism
29. *The Green Hornet* – Trailer – Seth Rogan – Ch. 9 – Boys Will Be Boys

30. *The HHGTTG (Trailer)* – Martin Freeman – Ch. 45 – Happy Bidet
31. *The HHGTTG* – Life, Universe & Everything – Ch. 41 – First Day of Xmas
32. *The Millionairess* – Peter Sellars – Ch. 17 – Well Goodness Gracious Me
33. *The Railway Man* – Colin Firth – Ch. 46 – Summer Holiday
34. *The Wolf of Wall Street* – Leonardo Di Caprio – Ch. 47 – Motivation . . .
35. *Toy Story* –Tom Hanks/Tim Allen – Ch. 58 – How Many Fingers . . . ?
36. *Transformers* – Shia LaBeouf - Ch. 27 – Transformers – Truth is Out There
37. *Treasure Island (Trailer)* – Robert Newton – Ch. 43 – Blitzkrieg
38. *Up in Smoke* – Cheech & Chong – Ch. 55 – Trains, Boats & Planes (Part 1)
39. *You've Got Mail* – Tom Hanks – Ch. 30 – Round the Mulberry Bush

B. MOVIES - With Mentions in Text but no QR Code or URL

1. *Cast Away* – Tom Hanks – Ch. 22 – I Didn't Know Whether to Laugh . . .
2. *Close Encounters of the 3rd Kind* – Ch. 27 – Transformers – The Truth . . .
3. *Dr. Doolittle* – Ch. 17 – Well, Goodness Gracious Me
4. *Edward Scissorhands* – Johnny Depp – Ch. 12 – Conquer the World
5. *Fifty Shades of Grey* – Ch. 48 – Ayurveda – Boiling Oil & Oatmeal
6. *Fire in the Sky* – Ch. 27 – Transformers – The Truth is Out There
7. *Gravity* – Sandra Bullock – Ch. 55 – Trains & Boats & Planes (Part 1)
8. *How to Train Your Dragon* – Ch. 56 – Trains & Boats & Planes (Pt. 2)
9. *Jewel of the Nile* – Kirk Douglas – Ch. 20 – When the Going Gets Tough
10. *Karate Kid (2010)* – Jackie Chan/Jaden Smith – Ch. 20 - WTGGT
11. *Lion King* – Circle of Life – Ch. 20 – When the Going Gets Tough
12. *Lord of the Rings* – Ch. 25 – The Cast Away
13. *Mama Mia!* – Meryl Streep – Ch. 46 – Going On A Summer Holiday
14. *Men in Black* – Will Smith – Ch. 27 – Transformers – Truth is Out There
15. *Metropolis* – Fritz Lang (1927) – Ch. 19 – Radio Ga-Ga
16. *Oblivion* – Tom Cruise – Ch. 27 – Transformers – The Truth is Out There
17. *Pirates of the Caribbean* – Johnny Depp – Ch. 43 - Blitzkrieg
18. *Rhapsody in Blue* – George Gershwin – Ch. 56 – T & B & Ps (Pt. 2)
19. *Scream* – Ch. 39 – I Only Have One Penis
20. *The Best Exotic Marigold Hotel* – Dev Patel – Ch. 58 – How Many Fingers?
21. *The Edge of Tomorrow* – Tom Cruise – Ch. 27 – Transformers – Truth . . .
22. *The Fourth Kind* – Ch. 27 – Transformers – The Truth is Out There
23. *The Hobbit* – Martin Freeman – Glossary
24. *The Hunger Games* – Jennifer Lawrence – Glossary
25. *Top Gun* – Tom Cruise – Ch. 40 – Fastest Invalid Carriage in the World

C. TV/Radio Shows, Videos, Books – With Text Box, QR Code or URL

1. *A Hard Day's Night/Richard III* - Peter Sellars – Dedication
2. *Arnel Pineda Story* – Don't Stop Believin' (Trailer) – Ch. 51 - TINSTAAC
3. *Arnel Pineda Story* – Don't Stop Believin' (Show) – Ch. 51 - TINSTAAC
4. *Awakened Soul* - Rachel Beavan - Ch. 36 – Reiki and High Spirits
5. *Breaking Bad* – Bryan Cranston – Ch. 4 - SNAFU
6. *Cake or Death* – Eddie Izzard - Ch. 24 – In Your Dreams!
7. *Coronation Street* - Ch. 16 – Nostalgia Isn't What It Used To Be
8. *Smoking* - Dave Allen – Ch. 52 – Lightning Strikes Twice At The YMCA
9. *Heimlich Manoeuvre* – Eddie Izzard – Ch. 34 - GGG G & GG
10. *Be Soooon* - Hylda Baker – Ch. 49 – I Still Only Have One Penis
11. *Illustrado* – 100 Influential Filipinos in Gulf – Ch. 13 – Busy Being Fab
12. *Jeff Dunham* – Achmed the Dead Terrorist – Ch. 7 – Dr. Mohammed
13. *Manila Hash (MH3)* – Ch. 33 – Xmas 2011 – Jingle What? Jingle Where?
14. *Men & Women Brains* – M. Gungor – Ch. 56 – Trains, Boats, Planes (Pt. 2)
15. *MPFC* – 4 Yorkshiremen – Ch. 7 – Nurses, Bed Baths, Choc Cake & LBMs
16. *Monty Python* – Spanish Inquisition – Ch.2 – Earlier That Day
17. *Mr. Bean* – Do it Yourself – Ch. 56 – Trains & Boats & Planes (Pt. 2)
18. *Old Man "Rushing" to Bus Stop* – Eye of the Tiger – Ch. 44 – Dem Bones
19. *Oprah* – Arnel Pineda & Journey – Ch. 60 – Don't Stop Believin'
20. *Oprah* – Tom Hanks Confession – Ch. 22 – Whether to Laugh or Cry
21. *Pavlov's Dog & Cat* – Eddie Izzard – Ch. 58 – How Many Fingers . . . ?
22. *Porridge* – Ronnie Barker – Ch. 17 – Well, Goodness Gracious Me
23. *Prof. Dr.Schumacher* – Urologist – Ch. 49 – I Still Only Have One Penis
24. *PWIN* – Facebook Page – Ch. 13 – Too Busy Being Fabulous
25. *Sherlock* – Martin Freeman - Glossary
26. *The National* – Vet Rugby Player – Ch. 22 – Whether to Laugh or Cry
27. *The National* – TSB & Paul McCartney – Ch. 32 – Macca, The Boss & Me
28. *The National* – Exiles Cheque – Ch. 38 – Rock of Ages to Seven Dwarfs
29. *Reliant Robin* – Top Gear – Clarkson – Ch. 40 – Fastest Invalid Carriage . .
30. *TSB – Confessions of an Ex-Hooker* – Ch. 52 –Lightning Strikes Twice . . .
31. *TSB/Illustrado* – Woman of Substance – Ch. 13 – Too Busy Being Fab

D. TV/Radio Shows, Videos, Books etc. – With Mentions in Text

1. *Deal or No Deal* – Ch. 40 – The Fastest Invalid Carriage in the World
2. *Desperate Housewives* – Ch. 16 – Nostalgia Isn't What It Used To Be
3. *Desperate Scousewives* – Ch. 16 – Nostalgia Isn't What It Used To Be

4. *Gangbusters* – Ch. 48 – Ayurveda – Boiling Oil & Oatmeal
5. *I'm A Celebrity - Get Me Out Of Here* – Ch. 5 – Nightmare Ward
6. *Juke Box Jury* – Ch. 56 – Trains & Boats & Planes (Pt.2)
7. *Life, the Universe & Everything* – Ch. 48 – Ayurveda – Boiling Oil, Oatmeal
8. *Widdle Int' Snow* – Mike Harding – Ch. 49 – I Still Only Have One Penis
9. *Monty Python* – The Gumby's – Ch. 50 – Spring Break
10. *Peyton Place* – Ch. 16 – Nostalgia Isn't What It Used To Be
11. *Strictly Come Dancing* – Bruce Forsythe – Ch. 57 – Eagles Have Landed
12. *Bernie the Bolt* - Sunday Night at London Palladium – Ch. 25 – Cast Away
13. *Beat the Clock* - Sunday Night at London Palladium – Ch. 58 –How Many?
14. *Survivor* - Ch. 3 – The Game
15. *Survivor* – Ch. 47 – Motivation is a Four Letter Word
16. *Thank Your Lucky Stars* – Ch. 56 – Trains & Boats & Planes (Pt.2)
17. *THHGTTG* – Don't Panic – Ch. 48 – Ayurveda – Boiling Oil & Oatmeal
18. *THHGTTG* – Pan-Galactic Gargle Blaster – Ch. 45 – Happy Bidet
19. *The Bold and The Beautiful* – Ch. 16 – Nostalgia Isn't What It Used To Be
20. *TSB-Trevor Stott-Briggs Rugby* - FB – Ch. 12 - How to Conquer the World
21. *The Grand Tour* – Clarkson etc – Ch. 56 – Trains & Boats & Planes (Pt.2)
22. *What Could Possibly Go Wrong*? – Clarkson – Ch.56 – Ts & Bs & Ps (Pt.2)

COPYRIGHT

The End

(This really is The End)

Printed in Great Britain
by Amazon